ADVANCES IN LIBRARY ADMINISTRATION AND ORGANIZATION

Volume 17

Advances in Library Administration and Organization

Delmus E. Williams and Edward D. Garten, *Series Editors*

Volumes 1-14, 1982–1996,
  edited by Gerard B. McCabe and Bernard Kreissman

Volumes 15-17, 1997–2000
  edited by Delmus E. Williams and Edward D. Garten

ADVANCES IN LIBRARY ADMINISTRATION AND ORGANIZATION

Editors: ## DELMUS E. WILLIAMS
Dean, University Libararies
University of Akron

EDWARD D. GARTEN
Dean of Libararies and Information Technologies
University of Dayton

VOLUME 17

JAI PRESS INC.
Stamford, Connecticut

ISBN: 0-7623-0647-5
ISSN: 0732-0671

Manufactured in the United States of America

CONTENTS

INTRODUCTION

As in past years, this seventeenth volume of *Advances in Library Administration and Organization* brings together a number of articles relating to issues that impact on the lives of library managers. As always, we have tried to bring together scholarship that is both timely and timeless, presenting both research-based articles and more descriptive ones that may provide a faster read for the practitioner.

The lead article is a piece by W. Bede Mitchell on the publication requirements for academic librarians. This issue has been one of constant confusion throughout my career as a librarian. Those who work in libraries try constantly to determine how the standards placed on them as faculty relate to those of classroom faculty on their campuses and to gauge their appropriateness. I believe that you will find Mitchell's article a clear statement of what we now know about publication requirements matter and provides a starting point for further discussion.

Carol Ritzen Kem follows this discussion of writing requirements with a study of the community that is academic librarianship. Kem is interested in looking at management theories relating to how we motivate people in the workplace and applying them to librarians. She approached our community with two different tools designed to look both at work behavior types and job satisfaction, and produced a very useful analysis of who we are and how we gain satisfaction from our work. It is reasonable to expect that this study can provide insights into how we recruit for our profession, how we develop our staff, where we place our people, how we manage them, and what has to be done to build effective teams within our organizations.

Distance learning is the subject of the next three pieces. Students learning at distance presents a very special challenge to libraries as we enter the new century. The idea that libraries must support students studying remotely from the campus is not new. But, as the mechanisms for delivery extend from the sending of individual faculty to remote locations to the use of video that can be delivered to more places and to the Internet where classes can be offered without reference to place or time, the challenge has grown exponentially. Carol Hammond and her colleagues at Thunderbird, the American Graduate School of International Business, describe how they have addressed the problem of library support for students studying in Latin America and elsewhere through the development of *My Thunderbird*, a set of electronic resources that it makes available through the online web.

This is followed by an article by Kim Dority and Martin Garnar on Jones International University's approach to library services. As the first University offering courses only through the web, Jones International has broken ground for those who are developing distance learning programs, and I think you will agree that their approach to library support is worth noting.

Mary Lynn Rice-Lively comes at the subject from a different angle. Dr. Rice-Lively is a faculty member at the University of Texas, and her study looks at how students studying synchronously in a video classroom at distance make sense of the subject matter being offered to them. While this discussion of student learning might seem a little bit removed from pure discussions of management, it provides an insight into how students react in this environment and provides information about how libraries like mine that are charged with managing these kinds of networks need to address their clients.

The next article is a piece written by Jon O'Donnell and Izzie Newman on the role of Chief Information Officers. Much has been written in this area, but O'Donnell and Newman have added a good summary of where we stand in the literature as more campuses look at this way of organizing information services. The survey they conducted in the course of their study, when compared with earlier ones, provide a benchmark as to how this movement is going.

David Bunnell then adds an article about efforts to assess the effectiveness of GALILEO, the Georgia cooperative information project. As those of us in networks know, it is easy to talk about what we hope to get from cooperation or even to describe its impact. However, few seem to have developed the kind of assessment tools that Georgia has to determine how they are doing in the eyes of their patrons. A system of this sort that is both informative and easy to use would be of use in most places.

John Painter then offers a view of how a faculty library advisory committee can be established on a community college campus, along with an overview of the literature relating to these bodies, their purpose, and their value. This piece should be instructive to any institution that does not have such a body and a good reminder of how they might work for those of us who do.

Finally, Wonsik Shim's study uses a tool called DEA to study the technical efficiency of libraries within the Association of Research Libraries. The study identifies a group of "best performing" libraries that can serve as models for other libraries that wish to improve their program and provides information that can tell parent organizations how these libraries are doing. These kinds of studies are critical to those of us who are being asked to provide performance measures for the work we do in support of the academic enterprise.

As is past volumes, what we offer you here is an eclectic group of articles covering a number of areas of concern to library managers. We hope that you will find them as interesting and as informative as we do.

Delmus E. Williams
Co-editor

PROMOTION AND TENURE
FOR ACADEMIC LIBRARIANS
CURRENT PRACTICES AT
SELECTED INSTITUTIONS

W. Bede Mitchell

INTRODUCTION

In the summer and fall of 1998, a colleague and I conducted a survey of academic libraries at institutions that are classified by the Carnegie Foundation as Research I or II, Doctoral I or II, or Master's (formerly Comprehensive) I or II. The purpose was to seek the most recent success rates of librarians in earning tenure, in order to determine whether a persistent concern was justified: that librarians with faculty status who are expected to conduct scholarly research may be substantially less likely to meet tenure requirements than other faculty. The results of that study were published in *College & Research Libraries* (Mitchell and Reichel 1999) and are summarized briefly below. In addition to the tenure approval data, 201 of the respondents forwarded information that provides an interesting picture of the current state of librarian promotion and tenure requirements in U.S. postsecondary

Advances in Library Administration and Organization, Volume 17, pages 1-21.
Copyright © 2000 by JAI Press Inc.
All rights of reproduction in any form reserved.
ISBN: 0-7623-0647-5

1

institutions. In examining the responses, I attempted to answer the following questions.

1. Are the librarians held to the same tenure criteria as all other campus faculty, or are they expected to meet criteria that are designed with librarians in mind? If the latter, have the "special" criteria for librarians been intended to accommodate the nature of librarianship as a discipline? Or to accommodate librarians' typical 12-month contracts and 40-hour work weeks?

2. Is scholarship just one of a number of equally acceptable professional activities such as professional service, or is it a separate category as in the classic formulation of teaching, research, and service? What activities are accepted to meet scholarship expectations?

3. Do the scholarship criteria employ the Eugene Rice/Ernest Boyer expanded definition of scholarship?

4. Are there specific weights assigned to each performance category, for example, "80 percent library duties, 15 percent scholarship, 5 percent service"? Are there quantitative productivity requirements?

5. Does a librarian's scholarship have to be within the broadly defined field of librarianship and information studies in order to count toward tenure?

6. Where it is explicitly stated, what kind of documentation is the tenure candidate expected to provide? If external reviewers are required, who selects them?

7. "Weak candidates are usually weeded out via nonreappointment prior to final tenure review." How many respondents reported this?

8. Where librarians have ranks, can one be tenured in the entry level rank? Is promotion to the next level automatic if the candidate is granted tenure?

9. Is there a campus-wide promotion and tenure committee? Do the respondents report any issues or problems related specifically to such a body?

10. Under what circumstances, if any, are advanced degrees required in addition to the M.L.S.?

The answers to these questions are addressed in this paper. In order to establish the proper context, a summary of the overall study is offered first.

BACKGROUND

According to the latest Carnegie classification report (Carnegie 1994) there are 768 Research, Doctoral, and Master's institutions. All were sent questionnaires except for nine Master's II universities for which current information was not readily obtainable. After several follow-up mailings, a return rate of 90.9 percent (690 of 759 institutions) was achieved. Of the 690 responding institutions, 374

(54.3%) reported having tenure-track librarians, and of these 60.9 percent required librarians to show some evidence of scholarship in order to earn tenure, while 34.6 percent encouraged it and 4.6 percent gave it little or no weight. The respondents indicated that in the three academic years of 1995–96, 1996–97, and 1997–98, 92.2 percent of all librarians reviewed for tenure were ultimately approved, with most being approved at all levels where there is more than one review level, that is, library-level review, university promotion and tenure committee (if any), and provost-level review. Of the 66 librarians who were not granted tenure, 32 (48.5%) were thought by the library directors to have been turned down primarily due to inadequate scholarly records. Of those 32, 31 were rejected out of 509 librarians reviewed at institutions where scholarship is required (6.1%), while only one was rejected out of 319 librarians reviewed at universities where scholarship is encouraged.

In short, of the 7.8 percent of the librarians reviewed for tenure who were rejected, fewer than one-half were thought to be unsuccessful due to inadequate scholarly records. Of course, it must be remembered that reasons for tenure application rejections are not typically public knowledge, and library directors themselves might not always know the exact reasons for rejection depending on the tenure review procedures under which they are working. Yet even if all of the unsuccessful candidates had failed to achieve tenure due to inadequate records of scholarship, a 7.8 percent failure rate is not very high.

It was further reported that 88 librarians were thought to have resigned to avoid tenure reviews. We do not know for certain that it was the scholarship aspect of the tenure review that caused the resignations. Some of the 88 may have thought their service records, daily job performances, or other factors were not going to be acceptable to the tenure review committees. But even if we treat the 88 as if they all resigned due to scholarly expectations, the overall impact on the tenure approval data is not large. If we add the 88 to the total of 844 librarians who *were* reviewed for tenure, 778 approvals out of 932 is 83.5 percent, which still appears to be an impressive approval rate.

Our research, along with several related studies (Smith and DeVinney 1984; Mitchell and Swieszkowski 1985; Mitchell 1989; Henry et al. 1994), showed that tenure-track librarians are achieving tenure at very high rates, both overall and at individual universities. In spite of often expressed fears that librarians with faculty status and publication requirements would fail disproportionately to meet tenure standards (if not at the library-level review then at some higher, university-level review), or choose to resign prior to final tenure review at higher rates than other faculty, there is a notable lack of empirical support for these concerns. The vast majority of responding institutions had very high librarian tenure approval rates during the three years surveyed, while only a very few universities reported high librarian tenure rejection rates. There is no other empirical evidence that would lead us to conclude that unusual tenure approval problems exist for librarians beyond these few institutions. Interested readers are referred to our study for further information.

It is also worth noting as an aside that there are academic libraries where the librarians are not tenure-track and yet which still require or encourage evidence of scholarly accomplishment. Examples may be found in the following comments from two survey respondents.

> Although we have neither tenure nor continuous employment status for librarians, we do require some scholarship/professional development for performance review process and reappointment process (Research I).

> Scholarly activity is only one of 4 areas of evaluation, which also include teaching, college service and community service. Exceptional performance in other areas of evaluation may compensate for minimal scholarly activity (Master's I).

Even the lack of tenure-track status does not necessarily ensure that librarians will not be expected to make scholarly contributions to the profession.

In short, the fears that tenure-track librarians would be unable to meet scholarly expectations are largely groundless. One Master's I library director put the issue into perspective this way:

> Fear drives people on this. The fear completely distorts the reality. If one person in a thousand was denied tenure the fear level would be equally high. It is a disgrace, a protection mechanism and a serious problem constraining our profession.

Part of the explanation for librarians' success in achieving tenure may lie with the tenure criteria they are expected to meet. Rather than be held to criteria which are more appropriate for faculty who work primarily in the classroom or in laboratories, librarians may be aiming to meet expectations that take into account their job responsibilities, work schedules and conditions, and so forth. Another possible explanation is the hypothesis that library administrators tend to be effective at mentoring tenure-track librarians to amass records of accomplishments that will meet tenure requirements. Some support for these theories is found in the documentation and comments provided by 201 of our survey respondents, and it is to a discussion of their tenure requirements that we will now turn.

EXPECTATIONS FOR LIBRARIANS SEEKING TENURE

The 201 institutions which sent copies of their formal tenure criteria statements, or sent summaries or brief comments, constitute a subset of the 374 tenure-track institutions which is distributed in a roughly similar pattern as the 374 with regard to whether they required, encouraged, or gave little weight to scholarship in tenure reviews (see Table 1). However, it is important to bear in mind during the fol-

Table 1.   Weight of Scholarship in Tenure Reviews

	Required	Encouraged	Little/No Weight
Res I and II respondents	39	28	0
(sent comments/criteria)	(25)	(15)	(0)
Doc I and II respondents	25	19	3
(sent comments/criteria)	(15)	(7)	(2)
MA I and II respondents	163	82	14
(sent comments/criteria)	(98)	(34)	(5)
Totals	227	129	17 = 373
			(One data point is missing)
	(138)	(56)	(7) = 201

lowing discussion that many of the complete tenure documents did not provide information that addressed all of the questions below. Therefore, it is only possible to identify patterns in tenure criteria, as opposed to drawing statistically valid inferences.

Are the librarians held to the same tenure criteria as all other campus faculty, or are they expected to meet criteria that are designed with librarians in mind? If the latter, have the "special" criteria for librarians been intended to accommodate the nature of librarianship as a discipline? To accommodate librarians' typical 12-month contracts and 40-hour work weeks?

Eighty-four respondents forwarded tenure criteria that were designed specifically for library faculty members: 14 Research I's, 8 Research II's, 4 Doctoral I's, 5 Doctoral II's, 47 Master's I's, and 6 Master's II's. About half a dozen institutions sent criteria statements that were taken from university policies and were intended to apply to all faculty, with no specific mention of subgroups like library faculty. Thus, there were more than 100 who sent short summaries or brief comments of their criteria from which it was not possible to conclude confidently that the criteria were for librarians and not for all faculty. Nevertheless, it is clearly not unusual for academic libraries to have tenure criteria intended to accommodate the nature of librarianship and/or the demands of librarians' 12-month contracts and 40-hour work weeks. Furthermore, this finding is consistent with what Vesper and Kelley discovered in their recent CLIP Note on promotion and tenure criteria in small academic libraries: 41 percent of the 114 which granted tenure and/ or offered promotion had separate promotion and tenure criteria for librarians (Vesper and Kelley 1997).

In most cases there is no means of determining whether the creation of tenure criteria documents for librarians was done out of the perceived need to address the uniqueness of the discipline or to accommodate librarians' work schedules. However, seven tenure criteria statements assert that the nature of librarianship and librarians' assignments necessitate an adaptation of performance requirements.

Such an explicit position has been avoided by many librarians out of concern that calling attention to the difference between librarians and other faculty might lead to questions about whether librarians should have faculty status. The various statements addressing the uniqueness of the library profession are revealing and worth citing:

> The diversity of academic enterprise in the library profession is to be taken into account when promotions are considered. Administrative functions, committee service...and the like are some examples of professorial roles worthy of appropriate recognition...Many other equivalents exist and have to be recognized by members of the successive committees on promotions (Research I).

> The wide range of librarians' assignments...and the demands of year-round professional duties lead to much variation in the kind and amount of scholarly or creative activities in which they engage (Research I).

> The criteria used for academic faculty have been especially adapted to relate to the annual assignments made to librarians (Research I).

> The factors used to evaluate faculty must be tailored to meet the characteristics of the library profession (Research I).

> This category [scholarly ability] is not emphasized because librarians work under a calendar year obligation and do not have the opportunity to pursue in-depth research or to publish on a regular basis (Master's I).

> The nature and emphasis of librarians' contributions differ from those of teaching faculty, and so should the criteria used to evaluate library faculty. Librarians have a twelve-month contractual obligation to provide day and evening library service. Library service, rather than classroom instruction, research, or publications must be the primary factor in evaluating a librarian's contribution to the College's and College Libraries' missions (Master's I).

> Time for research and scholarship is limited for library faculty by hours of departmental service and a twelve-month schedule (Master's I).

These statements send a strong message that librarians should not be held to exactly the same standards that exist in other disciplines. Asserting the uniqueness of one's discipline, or at least the important differences, is what lies behind the *Redefining Scholarship* movement that grew out of the perspective advanced in Ernest Boyer's (1990) *Scholarship Reconsidered*. Boyer, drawing upon the work of Eugene Rice, posited four types of scholarship instead of one: discovery, integration, application, and pedagogy or teaching. Since then more than two dozen professional associations, including the Association of College and Research Libraries, have written formal statements applying Rice's and Boyer's four-fold definition of scholarship to their disciplines and demonstrating that certain forms of scholarship are more appropriate and common in some disciplines than in others (Mitchell et al. 1998; Diamond and Adam 1995). The statements are intended, among other aims, to serve as guides for establishing campus scholarly expectations which do not attempt to treat all disciplines as if their scholarly procedures and means of communicating scholarly findings are identical. Thus there may be much less risk today in designing tenure criteria for academic librarians which reflect the spirit of campus expectations but accommodate the nature of the academic library field. With this in mind, we will examine the actual use of the Boyer/Rice definition of scholarship in tenure criteria.

Do the scholarship criteria employ the Eugene Rice/Ernest Boyer expanded definition of scholarship?

The influence of Ernest Boyer's (1990) *Scholarship Reconsidered* and the expanded definition of scholarship that he and Eugene Rice promulgated are reflected explicitly in the tenure criteria statements of five Master's I institutions and one Research I. One Master's I director wrote "Scholarship is defined broadly, including Ernest Boyer's ideas on scholarship redefined. Librarians fit well in these categories." Another Master's I library director stated

> We subscribe to Ernest Boyer's broadened definition of scholarship and have submitted a several page document articulating scholarship for library faculty to our Appointment, Rank, and Contract faculty council who reviews all applications for promotion and extended contracts.

Perhaps there is such a small number of institutions explicitly employing the Boyer/Rice definition because that conception is, in the terms of academe, relatively recent and novel. But if in fact the use of Boyer/Rice is taking hold slowly, then it is even more striking that at least 84 of the 201 institutions are already recognizing tenure criteria specifically intended for librarians. It could be that in spite of the critics of Boyer/Rice there is a greater recognition that one model of tenure criteria is not sufficient, but such recognition does not necessarily imply acceptance of the Boyer/Rice model as the best alternative. With regard to academic librarians in particular, it will be interesting to see whether in the next several years more library faculty adopt the Boyer/Rice expanded definition of scholarship.

The Research I university which bases its tenure expectations on the Boyer/Rice model does so for all faculty, not just for its librarians. That university has expanded the four-fold definition to include a fifth type of scholarship, namely artistic creativity, and it has developed overviews for each kind of scholarship which describe the nature of the scholarship, the primary audiences, the primary means of communicating the scholarship, and the primary criteria for evaluating the scholarship. This document is remarkable because of its sophisticated elaboration of the principles behind the Redefining Scholarship movement. It states, in part:

The several forms of scholarship have in common one vital element—each form creates something that did not exist before: new understanding in the minds of students, new knowledge about ourselves and our universe, new beauty that stimulates the senses, new insights, and new technologies and applications of knowledge that can benefit humankind. To be of lasting benefit to society, scholarship must be communicated to others.

Teaching and Learning: Develops and communicates understanding and skills to individuals, develops and refines new teaching methods, fosters lifelong learning behavior; aimed primarily at learners, peers and counterparts, lay publics, postgraduate professionals; communicated through classes, curricula, teaching materials and methods, teaching portfolios, publications and presentations to peers/lay publics and educators broadly; evaluated for depth and duration of understanding, lifelong benefits to past and present learners, and benefits to broader communities.

Discovery: Generates and communicates new knowledge and understanding, develops and refines new methods; aimed at professional peers, educators, students, supporters/patrons/users of information; communicated through peer-reviewed publications and presentations, public reports and presentations; evaluated for originality, scope, and significance of new knowledge, applicability and benefits to society.

Artistic Creativity: Interprets the human spirit, creates and communicates new insights and beauty, develops and refines new methods; aimed at various publics, peers and patrons; communicated through shows and distribution of products/performances/reviews/news reports, peer publications, juries; evaluated for originality, beauty, impact, duration of public value, scope and persistence of such influence and public appreciation.

Integration: Synthesizes and communicates a new or different understanding of information and its relevance, develops and refines new methods; aimed at users, educators, public, peers; communicated through presentations, publications, demonstrations, and role-modeling for users, educators, and peers; evaluated for originality and usefulness of integration to understanding and application of new insights.

Application: Develops and communicates new technologies and applications, fosters inquisitiveness, develops and refines new methods; aimed at users, public, peers; communicated through demonstrations, role-modeling, presentations to audiences, publications for users, news and reports, peer talks and publications; evaluated for breadth, value, and persistence of usefulness and impact.

The Boyer/Rice model of scholarship offers great potential for the development of and justification for tenure criteria most appropriate for librarians. Interested readers are referred to ACRL's statement on redefining scholarship for further information.

Is scholarship just one of a number of equally acceptable professional activities such as professional service, or is it a separate category as in the classic formu-

lation of teaching, research, and service? What activities are accepted to meet scholarship expectations?

In musing about the commonly used faculty performance categories of Teaching, Scholarship, and Service, a Research I academic library director wrote on the back of his/her survey response:

> My own preference is to place importance on professional development which includes professional activities, membership on and contributions to committee work, conferences, etc....Publications are *just another* piece of evidence of professional activity.

The tenure criteria of 25 responding universities (4 Research I's, 2 Research II's, 3 Doctoral I's, 1 Doctoral II, 11 Master's I's, and 4 Master's II's) take this approach, placing scholarly activities within a larger category which included other possible activities. These categories are variously labeled:

Academic Achievement
Contributions to the Profession
Professional Achievement and Growth
Professional Activity
Professional Activity and Scholarship/Professional Development
Professional Competence
Professional Development
Professional Growth
Professional Growth and Achievement
Professional Growth and Development
Research/Creative and Professional Activities
Scholarly Activity and Professional Development
Scholarship and Professional Activity
Scholarship and Professional Service

On the other hand, the majority of institutions employ some version of the classic Teaching (Librarianship), Scholarship, and Service model, which frequently includes professional activities in the Service category and reserves for the Scholarship category the publication or presentation of research results. However, closer inspection of all the documents reveals that the difference in the two approaches is largely cosmetic. In fact, even the institutions with Librarianship, Scholarship, and Service as their performance categories usually accept as scholarship a wide range of professional activities.

All of the institutions accepted as scholarship books, articles in refereed journals, presentations at professional conferences, editorial work, articles in encyclopedias and other reference tools, and published bibliographies. The following other work is accepted as scholarship at various universities, listed in descending order of frequency:

- fellowships and grants (5 Research I's, 3 Research II's, 1 Doctoral I, 1 Doctoral II, 27 Master's I's, 2 Master's II's),
- in-house publications, for example, pathfinders, brochures, annotated bibliographies (2 Research I's, 2 Research II's, 1 Doctoral I, 1 Doctoral II, 16 Master's I, 1 Master's II),
- book or other literature reviews (3 Research I's, 1 Research II, 1 Doctoral I, 1 Doctoral II, 11 Master's I's, 1 Master's II).
- consulting in area of library expertise (3 Research I's, 2 Doctoral I's, 11 Master's I, 2 Master's II's),
- managing web sites, electronic publications (4 Research I's, 1 Research II, 1 Doctoral II, 9 Master's I's),
- professional committees, attendance/participation at professional meetings (2 Research I's, 1 Doctoral I, 12 Master's I's),
- additional formal degrees beyond the M.L.S. (2 Research I's, 1 Research II, 9 Master's I's, 1 Master's II),
- continued development of library skills (2 Research I's, 1 Research II, 1 Doctoral I, 7 Master's I's, one Master's II),
- creative endeavors in literature, music, art, media (1 Doctoral I, 7 Master's I's, 1 Master's II),
- use of research in developing curricula, library services and programs (1 Research I, 1 Research II, 1 Doctoral I, 6 Master's I's),
- articles in non-refereed journals (2 Research I's, 6 Master's I's),
- development of pedagogic skills, techniques, innovations (2 Research I's, 1 Research II, 3 Master's I's, 1 Master's II),
- development or creative application of computer software (1 Research I, 1 Research II, 4 Master's I's),
- significant unpublished research reports (1 Research I, 5 Master's I's),
- internal reports, departmental manuals, major policy documents (1 Doctoral II, 4 Master's I's),
- contributions to scholarly growth of faculty, students, peers (3 Master's I's, 1 Master's II), and
- reviewing for grant applications/research funding (1 Research I, 2 Master's I's).

Virtually all of the tenure documents listed activities such as these as examples, and even the most lengthy lists were not portrayed as being exhaustive. Therefore, many of the above are in all likelihood acceptable at more institutions than indicated, but simply were not listed among the examples. In any event, it is clear that many universities recognize many different activities to be evidence of scholarship. Once again, these findings are similar to those of Vesper and Kelley. The majority of their promotion and/or tenure-granting respondents defined scholarship as a continued commitment to professional growth and service.

Are there specific weights assigned to each performance category, for example, "80 percent library duties, 15 percent scholarship, 5 percent service"? Are there quantitative productivity requirements?

Thirteen universities reported that they assigned specific weights to each of their performance categories:

- "Teaching" 80%, Scholarship 15%, Service 5% (Research I)
- Librarianship 40%, Research 40%, Service 20% (Research I)
- Professional Performance 80%, Scholarship and Professional Service 10%, Institutional and Community Service 10% (Research II)
- Librarianship 70%, Professional Growth 20%, University/Community Service 10% (Doctoral II)
- Primary Job Responsibilities 70%, Scholarship 15%, Service 15% (Doctoral II)
- Scholarship 15%, other category weights not reported (Doctoral II)
- Librarianship 70%, Scholarship 20%, Service 10% (Master's I)
- Library Responsibilities 65-80%, Research 10-25%, Service 10-15%. "Each faculty member is responsible for allotting appropriate weights in order to create an appropriate body of research for permanent tenure and/ or promotion" (Master's I)
- Librarianship 75%, Scholarship 15%, Service 10%. But "requirements are specific for each librarian, depending on the mix of responsibilities assigned" (Master's I)
- Effectiveness in Performance 50%, Professional Ability 20%, Continuing Professional Growth 10%, Contributions to Profession 10%, Effectiveness in University and Community Service 10% (Master's I)
- Professional Responsibilities 40%, Scholarly Activities 40%, Service 20% (Master's I)
- One-third scholarship, one-third job performance, one-third college service/ professional organizations (Master's I)
- Librarianship 70%, Research, Scholarship, & Creative Work 15%, Service 15% (Master's I)

Thus, based on this very small sample and with a few notable exceptions, it appears that effectiveness in assigned library duties carries the greatest weight in the assessment of most academic librarians' performance.

A few institutions did comment on quantitative scholarly requirements for librarians:

One should average more than 1 article a year by time of promotion and tenure evaluation to ensure tenure (Research I).

A minimum of 2 articles published in a refereed journal (Research II).

There are no specific quantitative criteria for scholarship, but it is generally understood that at least 1 refereed journal article is required. Few candidates feel comfortable putting forward an application with fewer than 3 (Doctoral II).

Evidence of refereed journal articles (2 would be considered as a minimum), book chapter or book in lieu of articles, 3-5 papers in conference proceedings would be accorded substantial weight (Master's I).

Teaching is an absolute requirement as well as collegiality/plays well with others spirit-appropriate because we are a small, regional university; scholarship/publications (5-10) and some national presentations expected (Master's I).

In practice, requirements are very minimal in my experience. For example, a poster session or an article in a non-refereed professional journal would be enough to get tenure if other requirements were strong (Master's I).

The specific requirements are general; however, the current interpretation requires at *least* 1 scholarly, refereed publication during a 5-year period; at *least* 1 conference presentation every year (Master's I).

If an instructor, one scholarly article or multiple non-scholarly articles/reviews have become the norm as *evidence* that the person can maintain a record of scholarship expected of tenured faculty at the assistant professor level and beyond. For an assistant prof seeking tenure (rare), a scholarly article in a refereed journal or a similar contribution is the expectation (mine) (Master's I).

Collaboration on a book; 2-3 articles in professional journals, local library guides; studies or presentations at professional meetings (Master's I).

Definitive evidence of the ability to contribute to the base of scholarly literature in the field. Such as, at least 2 papers of which one is sole authored and published in a peer reviewed journal (Master's I).

Either a book or several journal articles in professional publication required (Master's II).

Each candidate must have published a *minimum* of *one refereed article* prior to tenure review and have presented *at least three* papers and/or workshops at professional conferences (Master's II).

At least some required for any promotion/tenure; at least 3 research/peer-review articles required for *full* professor status (Master's II).

To reiterate, it would be a mistake to draw inferences from such a small sample. Yet it is interesting that there do not appear to be substantially greater demands at the reporting Research and Doctoral level institutions than there are at the Master's universities. The expectations may be related more to the discipline than to the institutional classification.

Does a librarian's scholarship have to be within the broadly defined field of librarianship and information studies in order to count toward tenure?

The following universities answered in the affirmative:

Scholarship requirement: any evidence whatsoever of intellectual contributions in librarianship beyond basic job requirements, for example, a presentation (Master's I).

Definitive evidence of the ability to contribute to the base of scholarly literature in the field (Master's I).

[Master's I institution describes publication patterns in librarianship, lists sample library periodical titles, and does not mention the possibility of publishing in another field.]

Have demonstrated continuing effort to maintain a current base of knowledge in the discipline taught and maintain recognition by peers beyond the limits of the campus and local region (Master's I).

[Should] publish in a refereed journal in library science or subject-related discipline (Master's I).

Faculty members...are expected to provide evidence of research and scholarly accomplishments that are consistent with the unit's mission and goals. The discipline of the faculty of the University Libraries is librarianship/information science (Research I and Master's II campus as well).

...a librarian should pursue active participation in professionally-relevant associations, scholarly associations, research, publishing, additional education, and/or other professionally relevant, creative or service activities (Research I).

The following universities accept scholarship in other fields in addition to librarianship:

Emphasis will be placed on contributions to the profession of librarianship. Publications in other disciplines will be considered on their individual value (Master's I).

Performs creative endeavors in areas such as literature, music, art, and media (Master's I).

Publications and presentations in any format may be in either the discipline of librarianship or an area of subject expertise (Master's I).

Since the fields of librarianship, information science, and media represent research disciplines, most publications offered for consideration in the promotion and tenure process should be discipline-related. At the same time what constitutes the discipline itself should be interpreted broadly...Publications in other scholarly fields are also acceptable, but may not be given primary consideration (Research I).

The following statements seem to indicate that only research in librarianship would be acceptable, but could be interpreted to accept research in the subject specialty of, for example, a bibliographer:

Creative activities must be related to the individual's directed service responsibilities (Research II).

Only those creative works focused on professional assignment will be considered for rank advancement and continuing status review (Research II).

Where it is explicitly stated, what kind of documentation is the tenure candidate expected to provide? If external reviewers are required, who selects them?
Only six respondents included information which related to these questions which are reproduced here in full.

A minimum of five external confidential letters of evaluation from qualified persons shall be solicited by the candidate's unit director and/or by the University Librarian. External referees should be selected on the basis of their standing in the field and the institutions with which they are associated...The candidate may suggest potential outside evaluators and may discuss with his/her unit director qualified persons from whom letters may be solicited. The candidate, in addition, may prepare a list of persons in his/her field from whom he/she prefers letters of evaluation *not* be solicited (Research I).

A minimum of three—but no more than five—letters of recommendation, in addition to the supervisor's letter, from those inside or outside the operational area who can best provide evidence of the quality of the work performance of the candidate and who can evaluate qualifications for a backup position if there is one. A candidate may suggest to the supervisor the names of persons who could write these letters, but the supervisor should select the writers and request the letters. Required: cover letter, letter of recommendation from head of staff member's operational area, letter from supervisor if different, resume, 1-2 page statement providing highlights of his/her past accomplishments and professional goals (Research I).

Promotion to highest rank requires evaluation from three external disinterested referees. Selected jointly by candidate and review committee: candidate suggests five people, committee selects three (Doctoral I).

Tenure dossier should include appropriate request forms, summary of accomplishments since last review, annual reports/reviews for the evaluation period, current vita, representative samples of scholarly and service accomplishments and products for the evaluation period, librarianship materials deemed appropriate by the faculty member, any additional materials the faculty member deems relevant (Doctoral I).

Evaluation Portfolio should include, to document accomplishments in Librarianship, a Cumulated Faculty Report of Professional Activities, current position description, reports of activities, documents developed, published documents, letters of support/appreciation from librarians, teaching faculty, etc. To document Research/Creative Activity, include copies of research activity, reviews or work cited. To document Service, include statements summarizing membership and performances (Doctoral II).

Current vita, description of job responsibilities, summary of job-related accomplishments, samples of written reports, samples of various library publications, list of professional memberships and association activities, list of library and campus community memberships/offices/activities, list of professional meetings/workshops/ conferences/training sessions attended, details of scholarly activity (lists of publications, papers presented, workshop sessions moderated), letters of thanks or commendations from library users or colleagues, evaluation forms from BI or workshop presentations, description of major projects or publications in progress, honors or distinctions received, community service activities (Master's I).

"Weak candidates are usually weeded out via nonreappointment prior to final tenure review."

Five respondents reported that they make it a practice to avoid mandatory tenure reviews of librarians who have not shown adequate progress toward tenure during their probationary periods. The purpose of the probationary period is to give a candidate the opportunity to prove that s/he has the potential to be a productive and effective faculty member. Typically, the institution has the right to not reappoint a probationary faculty member for reasons that would be insufficient to terminate a tenured faculty member. Furthermore, it is the policy of many institutions that such reasons are not provided to the terminated probationary faculty member and there is no course for appealing or grieving such a termination decision. So while a tenured faculty member can usually be terminated only for cause (e.g., incompetence, moral turpitude), a probationary faculty member might not be reappointed to the remainder of his/her probationary period if s/he is judged after a few years to have the potential to be only a marginal (albeit not incompetent) faculty member. Termination of a marginal faculty member before tenure is considered (and possibly conferred, perhaps after a grievance) gives an institution another opportunity to recruit a faculty member with the potential for excellence.

It is worth quoting these five respondents' comments in full:

Most people who are unable to achieve tenure are counseled to leave before voting takes place (Research I).

Generally, librarians do not get reappointed if record is not sufficient. Therefore, when a tenure review is done, they have already survived six years of reappointment decisions (Research I).

We do a good job of mentoring at early stages. If someone is not making adequate progress, we do not renew their term appointment. Hence, our cases are strong when they go to the university-wide review committee and none have been rejected during my ten years as Dean (Research II).

[Two librarians recently] left because they were told they were not making adequate progress toward tenure. One left voluntarily, and one was terminated. These actions should take place long before the final tenure review (Master's I).

We do not allow inadequate performance to continue to the tenure decision year. We do
not reappoint in a year before the tenure decision is required (Master's I).

One of the intriguing questions that arises from considering these comments is
whether the high rate of tenure-approval for librarians is due, at least in part, to a
tendency to weed out the weak candidates before formal, final tenure review is to
take place. In the summary of the full study given earlier, it was reported that 88
librarians were thought to have resigned to avoid tenure reviews. We do not know
how many may have resigned at the suggestion of the institution, and due to the
lack of reported research we also do not know how the figure of 88 librarian resignations prior to tenure review compares with similar resignations in other disciplines. While the comments from the five institutions above are suggestive, they
are not sufficient to do more than encourage further investigation into this theory.
Because librarians have tended to be defensive about faculty status, it is certainly
possible that they have been more reluctant than other faculty to have marginal
candidates reviewed formally for tenure, out of a concern that the weakness of
such candidacies would lead administrators and other faculty to question the
appropriateness of tenure-track status for librarians. Unfortunately, it would be
exceedingly difficult to reliably measure the extent to which given disciplines/
departments forward marginal candidates for tenure review.

It would be similarly difficult to test the theory that librarians may be more
effective in mentoring their probationary faculty's efforts to achieve tenure. In
addition to the Research II institution above, several respondents indicated that
they worked diligently to lead their librarians through the tenure process, and
were gratified at the extent to which they had succeeded in helping their recruits
earn tenure. They regard such mentoring programs, both formal and informal, as
sound investments. But by what methodology could we reliably establish whether
academic librarians mentor their probationary faculty's efforts to achieve tenure
more effectively than do faculty in other disciplines?

To conclude this section, let us consider that the desire to avoid final tenure
reviews in the cases of marginal candidates may not be solely to keep weak performance records from coming to the attention of university administrators and
other faculty. No reason usually needs to be given for not reappointing a probationary faculty member, and the procedure for reviewing a probationary faculty
member's application for reappointment may not be as time consuming as the
final tenure review. The decision to not reappoint may, therefore, require less time
and effort to make, and not be as susceptible to challenge as a decision to reject
tenure. What complicates the decision to terminate before the end of the full probationary period is the need to judge whether it would be impossible for the candidate to establish a record worthy of tenure in the time remaining before the
mandatory tenure review. While the faculty member may not be entitled by right
to the full probationary period, it is obviously only just that the institution avoid a
premature decision to not reappoint. But if the library feels confident, on the basis

of performance during the preceding years and the faculty member's expected accomplishments in the future, that a probationary librarian cannot hope to achieve a record worthy of tenure, then much time and anguish (to the institution, anyway) may be saved by avoiding the final, mandatory tenure review. This may be as likely to lie behind terminations prior to tenure review as the fear of weak candidacies being considered by administrators and faculty review bodies outside the library.

Where librarians have ranks, can one be tenured in the entry level rank? Is promotion to the next level automatic if the candidate is granted tenure?

Although our study involved tenure reviews and did not solicit information regarding promotions, there were 14 documents sent to us which did refer to the relationship between tenure and ranks. One Master's I institution indicated it is possible to be tenured at the entry-level rank, but the other 13 (4 Master's I's, 1 Master's II, 6 Research I's, and 2 Research II's) made it clear that librarians could be tenured at the entry rank only under unusual circumstances. The general position was expressed by a Research I library director:

> The Assistant Librarian rank is the basic entry level for professional librarians. An appointee may remain in this rank for a maximum of six years, a period which is considered sufficient for an appointee to demonstrate professional competence and a potential for further professional growth.

In other words, the entry-level rank tends to be synonymous with probationary status.

Is there a campus-wide promotion and tenure committee? Do the respondents report any issues or problems related specifically to such a body?

In their 1997 study of tenure and promotion practices at small colleges and universities, Vesper and Kelley found that there were campus-wide review committees at 56 percent of the 114 responding institutions which have tenure or promotion for librarians. Our questionnaire did not ask respondents to indicate whether their campuses had such committees, but 5 Master's I universities and 1 Research I institution stated explicitly that they had university-wide promotion and tenure committees. For what it is worth, none of the respondents indicated any qualms or concerns regarding this. It should be further noted that of the 66 librarians in the tenure-approval study who were turned down when they applied for tenure, only 26 were rejected by a review outside of the library after receiving endorsement in the library level review. We do not know how many of those rejections were done by a university-wide tenure review committee or, in the absence of such a committee, how many were done by some administrator to whom the library director would forward tenure recommendations. However, 26 rejections out of 844 applications is only 3.1 percent, and, given that there were no complaints from the library directors who responded to the survey regarding reviews beyond the library, it seems safe to conclude that there is at most a marginal disadvantage for academic librarians at institutions where there are university-wide tenure review committees.

Under what circumstances, if any, are advanced degrees required in addition to the M.L.S.?

In most of the tenure documents that we received, the ALA-accredited M.L.S. (or equivalent master's in library/information science degree) was accepted as the terminal degree for librarians. Similarly, Vesper and Kelley found that the majority of their responding institutions where librarians had ranks accepted the M.L.S. as the only degree required even at the highest rank. However, there were a number of institutions in the Vesper/Kelley study and in our research where librarians with the M.L.S. alone would have been handicapped in seeking promotion or tenure, and at other universities they would not have been tenurable or promotable.

Vesper and Kelley found that at the rank of Assistant Professor or equivalent, 90 percent of the respondents required only the M.L.S., while 4 percent also required at least a second master's degree. At the rank of Associate Professor or the equivalent, 74 percent required only the M.L.S. while 15 percent also required at least a second master's and 4 percent also required a doctorate. To achieve the rank of Professor or the equivalent, 60 percent required only the M.L.S., 14 percent also required at least a second master's, and 19 percent also required a doctorate.

We did not ask our respondents specifically about educational requirements, but among the tenure and promotion criteria statements that were sent to us there were several which stated such requirements. One Master's II university indicated to us that "[librarians] are eligible for tenure and promotion...IF they obtain (or bring with them upon appointment) a doctoral degree," while a Master's I required a doctorate for promotion to associate professor. More common were the institutions where at least "a second master's is required [for promotion or tenure]" (Master's I). This included 1 Research I, 1 Doctoral I, 9 Master's I, and 2 Master's II universities. One of the Master's I universities required a doctorate if the candidate wished to be promoted to the highest rank, while another such institution's highest rank required "a second advanced degree." A third had constructed an ascending educational scale to match each rank:

> To qualify for assistant professor an individual must have the M.L.S. and 30 credits. To qualify for associate the individual must have a second master's. In order to become a full professor, the individual must have a Ph.D. (Master's I).

Despite the fact that most institutions still seem to accept the M.L.S. as the terminal degree for librarians, the information above adds fuel to Phillip Jones's (1998) recent assertion that additional advanced degrees are now preferred or required for a great many academic library positions, as his perusal of librarian recruitment ads suggested. Jones inquires why ACRL continues to uphold its official statement that the M.L.S. is our terminal degree in spite of such evidence to the contrary, and in light of the fact that many influential library leaders throughout the twentieth century have argued academic librarians should have educational qualifications beyond a library science degree. One answer is that the M.L.S. is, as the ACRL statement reads, the terminal *professional* degree, meaning that a doctorate or specialist degree in librarianship is optional. The M.L.S. is the degree one must earn before one is qualified to be a professional librarian. The doctorate and the advanced certificate serve a different purpose, that is, to further educate librarians. This is all the ACRL statement is intended to communicate.

However, this does not fully address Jones's concern. There does seem to be a growing need for academic librarians to be further educated in subjects *outside* of librarianship. Is this because of the need for specialization in just a few librarian positions (e.g., in the case of subject bibliographers), or is there in fact a general and growing feeling that the M.L.S. alone is no longer adequate scholarly preparation for members of the profession? If the latter is the case, then do we need to take up Jones's challenge to the profession and reexamine what should be the requisite academic preparation for librarians?

One obvious difficulty is that not all academic library positions will require the same educational background. Will a community college reference librarian, who presumably will need to be a generalist, require the same education as a large research university's reference librarian who is expected to be a social sciences specialist? Will the educational needs for a Liberal Arts college's cataloger and a research institution's library director be the same? Even within the same Carnegie Classification, positions as diverse as access services librarian, cataloger, and subject bibliographer may have different educational needs. Such distinctions can be identified and accommodated, but it would be a time-consuming and complex process.

Perhaps this work could tie in with some new ALA initiatives. After the ALA Executive Board and Council discussions about the recommendations of the 1999 Education Congress, ALA President Sarah Ann Long announced her intention to appoint task forces to develop a core values draft statement, to draft a statement of core competencies, to develop detailed recommendations regarding the formation of an independent accrediting association, and to investigate the need and possibility for different levels of trained personnel working in libraries, including but not limited to library technicians/technical assistant programs and bachelor of library and information studies programs.

The charges to President Long's task forces, while intended to address the library profession as a whole and not just academic librarianship, could be extended to include consideration of educational requirements for different kinds of academic library positions. But in the end, is such a project really necessary? Do library directors need a set of educational requirements specific to each kind of librarian position? Do library school faculty need such requirements for the purpose of counseling library school students about other educational qualifications they will need to achieve their career goals? Additionally, if the library school faculty do not think they need this information, do the students feel they need it? Apart from Jones's article, there has been little if any discussion in the professional literature since the adoption of the ACRL statement which indicates these needs exist. Until we see research that shows otherwise, I suspect that there is little enthusiasm for investing considerable time and energy on a set of educational expectations for various positions within each Carnegie Classification, which in all likelihood would be out of date before the task force completed its work.

CONCLUSION

In answering the questions posed at the outset about the tenure documents, some tendencies and possible avenues for future investigation emerged.

1. In both our study and in Vesper and Kelley's, there is evidence that almost one-half of the institutions where librarians are tenure-track employ tenure criteria designed for librarians. Also, given librarians' high tenure approval rate, it appears that most librarians, even those at universities where separate tenure criteria do not exist, are aiming to meet expectations that take into account their job responsibilities, work schedules and conditions, and so forth.
2. Boyer's and Rice's expanded definition of scholarship is not being cited in many library tenure documents, but the theory behind it is widely accepted. That is, many institutions acknowledge the wisdom of not applying one set of tenure criteria to all disciplines.
3. Scholarly expectations are frequently met through achievements beyond publications and presentations. Work in professional associations, consulting, and continuing development of professional skills and knowledge are examples of accomplishments that are also often counted as scholarship.
4. The most important criterion for achieving tenure appears to be performance of one's daily library responsibilities.
5. Where tenure-track librarians are also assigned ranks, achieving tenure tends to be associated with promotion beyond the entry-level rank.
6. The little evidence we have does not support the theory that tenure-track librarians are more likely to be rejected for tenure if they are reviewed by university-level tenure committees.
7. It has become common for librarians to be expected to hold advanced degrees in addition to the M.L.S. before they can be promoted or tenured.

More research should be done into these and related promotion and tenure issues. It is essential to not only learn from the good practices of peers, but to also refute incorrect assumptions and preconceptions. We must get beyond the fears which, in the words of the Master's I library director quoted earlier, have driven our professional discussions about faculty status. We must understand the reality and the potentialities inherent in our situation before we can make informed decisions and take action.

REFERENCES

Boyer, E.L. 1990. *Scholarship Reconsidered: Priorities of the Professoriate.* Princeton, NJ: Carnegie Foundation for Advancement of Teaching.

_____. 1994. "Carnegie Foundation's Classification of 3,600 Institutions of Higher Education." *Chronicle of Higher Education* 6(April): A18-A26.

Diamond, R.M. and B.E. Adam, eds. 1995. *The Disciplines Speak: Rewarding the Scholarly, Professional, and Creative Work of Faculty.* Washington, DC: American Association for Higher Education.

Henry, E.C., D.M. Caudle and P. Sullenger. 1994. "Tenure and Turnover in Academic Libraries." *College & Research Libraries* 55: 429-435.

Jones, P.J. 1998. "Academic Graduate Work in Academic Librarianship: Historicizing ACRL's Terminal Degree Statement." *Journal of Academic Librarianship* 24: 437-443.

Mitchell, W.B. 1989. *Faculty Status for Academic Librarians: Compliance with Standards, Opinions of University Administrators, and a Comparison of Tenure-Success Records of Librarians and Instructional Faculty.* Ann Arbor, MI: University Microfilms No. DA 892 5784.

Mitchell, W.B. et al. 1998. *Academic Librarianship and the Redefining Scholarship Project: A Report from the Association of College and Research Libraries Task Force on Institutional Priorities and Faculty Rewards.* Chicago: Association of College and Research Libraries (www.ala.org/acrl/ipfr.html)

Mitchell, W.B. and M. Reichel. 1999. "Publish or Perish: A Dilemma for Academic Librarians?" *College and Research Libraries* 60: 232-243.

Mitchell, W.B. and L.S. Swieszkowski. 1985. "Publication Requirements and Tenure Approval Rates: An Issue for Academic Librarians." *College and Research Libraries* 46: 249-255.

Smith, K.F. and G. DeVinney. 1984. "Peer Review for Academic Librarians." *Journal of Academic Librarianship* 10(May): 87-91

Vesper, V. and G. Kelley, eds. 1997. *Criteria for Promotion and Tenure for Academic Librarians.* Chicago: American Library Association.

THE RELATIONSHIP BETWEEN WORK BEHAVIOR TYPE AND ELEMENTS OF JOB SATISFACTION OF A SELECTED GROUP OF ACADEMIC LIBRARIANS

Carol Ritzen Kem

INTRODUCTION

Purpose of Study

For the majority of adults in the United States today, work is a central factor and defining characteristic of life. More than at any other period in our history, paid employment fills a large portion of time for both women and men. Accordingly, it is even more important to realize that "In order that people may be happy in their work, these three things are needed: They must be fit for it. They must not do too much of it. And they must have a sense of success in it" (Ruskin 1851, p. 7). Two of the three things Ruskin set forth as necessary for happiness in one's work are major elements in this study—namely, work behavior type, or "fit,"—and job satisfaction, or "sense of success."

Advances in Library Administration and Organization, Volume 17, pages 23-66.
Copyright © 2000 by JAI Press Inc.
All rights of reproduction in any form reserved.
ISBN: 0-7623-0647-5

This study was designed to relate the Herzberg theory that job satisfaction and job dissatisfaction are affected by motivators and hygienes to the theory derived from Nickens and Bauch that motivators and hygienes are perceived differently by different work behavior types. The following questions guided the study.

1. What are the work behavior types of academic librarians in Florida as measured by the Marcus Paul Placement Profile (MPPP)?
2. What are the motivators and hygienes perceived by academic librarians in Florida as reported on the Minnesota Satisfaction Questionnaire (MSQ)?
3. Do factors derived from a factor analysis of the MSQ show characteristics of motivators and hygienes?
4. Do the different work behavior type scores of academic librarians in Florida, as measured by the MPPP, relate differently to the motivator and hygiene scores derived from the MSQ?

BACKGROUND AND REVIEW OF RELATED LITERATURE

Job Satisfaction

Definition

There is no universally accepted definition of job satisfaction (Locke 1976). However, a particularly relevant definition for this study is that of Davis (1977) because he related the degree of job satisfaction to the fit between an employee and a particular job. Davis stated that:

> job satisfaction is the favorableness or unfavorableness with which employees view their work. It results when there is a fit between job characteristics and the wants of employees. It expresses the amount of congruence between one's expectation of the job and the rewards that the job provides (p. 74).

Historical Overview

If the activities of employers are to contribute to the realization of organizational goals, successful management, including direction and motivation, is important. Thus, research on employees in a variety of work situations has been conducted for almost a century. A particularly significant topic of personnel research involves the job satisfaction of employees. According to Chwe (1976), more than 5,000 articles, books, and dissertations were written on the subject of job satisfaction from the 1930s to the mid-1970s. As the effective management of human resources is one of the most important tasks for any organization, it is not surprising to find such a large and varied volume of research focused on this subject.

Research into work behavior and job satisfaction has been conducted since the early years of the twentieth century when industrial psychologists such as Frederick Taylor (1911) began to show an interest in job satisfaction studies. Although Taylor's major research interest was in using time and motion studies to increase productivity, while simplifying and compartmentalizing work tasks to increase efficiency and productivity, he also called attention to the importance of the human element as a factor in job success. According to Nauratil (1989, p. 44), "Taylorism" was widely accepted in libraries in the early years of the twentieth century, and the philosophy was advocated by Melvil Dewey who urged librarians to "keep a watch or clock hanging before you."

In 1927, Elton Mayo began a series of experiments which stimulated the development of the Human Relations School in organizational psychology and occupational sociology. His studies, which involved the manipulation of various physical conditions, demonstrated that productivity increased in unexpected ways. Mayo observed that positive human relationships, which were important to workers, could lead to greater job satisfaction and, ultimately, to increased productivity (Mayo 1933). Another early study of job satisfaction involved 500 teachers who were questioned about different aspects of their jobs. Hoppock (1935) analyzed the 100 most and the 100 least satisfied responses and concluded that job satisfaction consisted of many factors, whose presence in a work situation led to satisfaction and whose absence led to job dissatisfaction. Based on his research, he formulated a theory suggesting that satisfaction and dissatisfaction form a continuum.

A.H. Maslow (1943) investigated elements of job satisfaction and developed a theory based on an ascending hierarchy of human needs, beginning with the lowest order, basic physiological need, and extending through the highest level, self-actualization. He concluded that, although lower-order needs had to be satisfied before higher-order needs began to assume any importance, when a need was met, it no longer served to motivate people.

Maslow's work was a foundation for Herzberg (1966; Herzberg, Mausner and Snyderman 1959) who developed a two-factor theory of job satisfaction (Glenn 1982; Wellstood 1984). In 1957, Herzberg and his associates published an important review of job satisfaction research in which they challenged Hoppock's view that job satisfaction is a continuous variable (Herzberg, Mausner, Peterson and Capwell 1957). In their book *The Motivation to Work*, Herzberg, Mausner and Snyderman (1959) developed the concept that certain factors are more frequently associated with feelings of satisfaction while other factors are associated with feelings of dissatisfaction. Herzberg and his associates, employing the critical incident method developed by Flanagan (1954), tested the concept on 203 male engineers and accountants in Pittsburgh, Pennsylvania. From these data, they developed the theory of job attitudes called the Two-Factor Theory or the Motivator-Hygiene Theory. They concluded that motivation does not exist on a continuum, as postulated by Hoppock, but consists of two continua, job satisfiers or

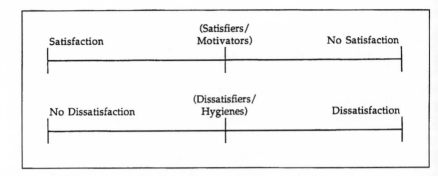

Figure 1.   Herzberg's Two-Factor Attitude Model

motivators, and job dissatisfiers, or hygienes, as displayed in Figure 1. This emphasis on the contribution of psychological growth to job satisfaction and the recognition that opportunities for psychological growth can be found within work itself are of particular importance in the development of general job satisfaction theory.

Motivators, which included achievement, recognition, advancement, responsibility, possibility of growth and interest in the work itself were intrinsic factors which, when present in a job, acted as satisfiers with a positive effect on employee productivity (Herzberg 1966, pp.193-198). Of the motivators, achievement was the strongest, followed by recognition. The motivators corresponded to the higher-order needs in Maslow's ascending hierarchy of needs.

Analogous to Maslow's lower-order needs, hygiene factors included pay, security, supervision, interpersonal relations, company policy and administration, status, personal life and physical working conditions (Herzberg 1966, pp.193-198). They were extrinsic to the job and, when absent, linked to dissatisfaction. It is critical to recognize that Herzberg et al. (1959) emphasized that the presence of a particular hygiene factor did not necessarily lead to job satisfaction and that the lack of a motivator did not automatically create job dissatisfaction. That is, "the opposite of job satisfaction is not job dissatisfaction, it is an absence of job satisfaction. Conversely, the opposite of job dissatisfaction is not job satisfaction, it is an absence of job dissatisfaction" (Olson 1988, p. 32).

Since the first publication of Herzberg's theory, hundreds of studies based upon it have been conducted. These include studying virtually every kind of worker. More than 65 dissertations have been written since 1964 that relied, at least in part, upon Herzberg for a theoretical base. Previous studies (e.g., Thomas 1977; Kozal 1979; Burr 1980) have investigated aspects of Herzberg's theory among various groups, including academic administrators. Additional studies (Glenn 1982; Wellstood 1984; Olson 1988; Poston 1988; Barber 1989) added the application of the Marcus Paul Placement Profile (MPPP) in their studies of medical technologists, vocational educational administrators, college placement officers, faculty and deans in colleges of nursing and cooperative-extension service mid-level managers. Three studies applied aspects of the theory to professional librarians. Plate and Stone (1974) used the Herzberg "critical incidence technique" (Herzberg 1966) in an analysis of job incidents among American and Canadian librarians attending motivational workshops held in conjunction with professional meetings. They concluded that the theory applied with as much force to librarianship as to other occupations. Hamshari (1985) compared the job satisfaction of professional librarians in the technical and public service departments in 20 academic libraries in Jordan. Dahlstrom (1982) investigated the motivation for participating in continuing education. He administered a questionnaire to a random sample of 550 librarians throughout the southwestern United States and identified 20 factors that were classed as motivators for participating in continuing education. The seven items that were shown to be most significant were identified as Herzberg motivators.

Measuring Job Satisfaction

Typically, job satisfaction has been measured by an objective, a descriptive or a projective survey. Objective surveys generally contain questions with pre-determined responses while descriptive surveys are more subjective, allowing for unstructured replies through open-ended questions. Projective surveys are devised by psychologists or psychiatrists to assess mental health and are used less often in a work setting (Glenn 1982; Wellstood 1984). The critical incident technique used by Herzberg was a form of descriptive survey. Thomas (1977), Kozal (1979), and Burr (1980) used modified versions of the technique in their studies of community college, college, and university administrators and staff members. Glenn (1982) and Wellstood (1984) both reported the lack of many standardized measures of job satisfaction and selected the Job Descriptive Index (JDI) to measure job satisfaction and dissatisfaction for their studies of vocational education administrators and medical technologists, respectively. Olson (1988) used the Minnesota Satisfaction Questionnaire (MSQ) in his study of college placement officers.

D'Elia (1975, 1979) was the first investigator to use the MSQ to measure job satisfaction among librarians. The MSQ is one of several measures developed in conjunction with the Minnesota Studies in Vocational Rehabilitation or, as they are better known, the Work Adjustment Project. It is designed to measure an employee's satisfaction with his or her job. The MSQ provides more specific information on the aspects of job satisfaction than do more general measures. Chwe (1976, 1978) and Rockman (1984, 1985) also used it, with D'Elia and Rockman selecting the short form while Chwe used the long form. Based on his experience, Chwe argued strongly that, because of the repetitive format of the long form, the short form was more appropriate for subjects, like academic librarians, with high levels of education (Chwe 1978, p. 50). The MSQ is appropriate for use with individuals who can read at the fifth grade level or higher. The 100-item long form MSQ is quite repetitious. The short form MSQ uses the same response categories as the 1977 long form and provides satisfactory data. The MSQ short form was selected for this study. Robert Guion (1978, p. 1679), in evaluating the MSQ, wrote that it "gives reasonably reliable, valid, well-normed indications of general satisfaction at work and of 20 aspects of that satisfaction, collapsible into intrinsic and extrinsic components."

Work Behavior Type

Definition

Neff (1969, p. 72) describes adult work behavior as "the complex product of a long series of learned and habitual styles of perceiving and coping with demands of the environment." That is, an individual's coping behaviors consolidate to form a particular work style.

Evolution of Work Behavior Type

The theory of work behavior types suggests that basic differences in personality traits may have an impact on work behaviors. The study of work behavior traits and types as they are understood today began with the work of William Moulton Marston, a psychologist and scientist who published *Emotions of Normal People* in 1928. Marston built his early theories on the work of the German psychologist Wilhem Wundt, the founder of experimental psychology, who established the first official psychology laboratory in 1879. Wundt departed from the view, then current, that pleasantness and unpleasantness are the only two emotions and proposed in addition four other emotions: excitement, depression, tension and relaxation (Marston 1928). Marston spent many years building on these original ideas and, through scientific research, began to perfect his own theories.

Marston also reviewed the work of C.G. Jung (1923) who, in his work, *Psychological Types*, wrote about the clusters of characteristics and the "collective unconscious" that helps to mold the personality and behavior of an individual. Jung emphasized that people choose a dominant attitude toward life: introversion, which is an orientation toward inner processes, or extroversion, which is an orientation toward the external world of people and events. He also viewed the human personality in terms of polarities: conscious values and unconscious values, sublimation and repression, rational and irrational functions, and the previously mentioned introversion and extroversion. Finally, Jung (1923) wrote that each person has only four ways in which to orient toward the world: two "rational" functions of thinking (recognizing meaning) and feeling (experiencing pleasure or pain) and

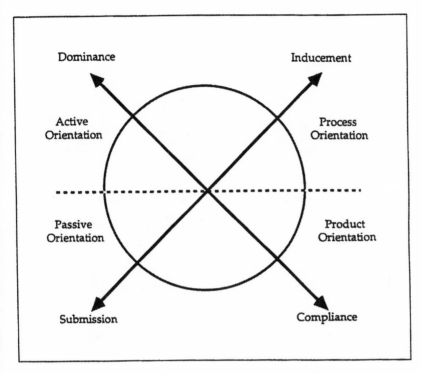

Figure 2. Marston's Two-Axis Model (Nickens 1984)

two "irrational" functions of sensation or perceiving by means of unconscious and sub-liminal processes.

Through his review of the work of Wundt and Jung and based on research into motation (emotions as measured by motor consciousness, nerve, and muscle response), Marston (1927, 1928) identified four primary emotions which he termed dominance, compliance, inducement, and submission. He defined a primary emotion as "an emotion which contained the maximal amount of alliance, antagonism, [and] superiority of strength of the motor self in respect to the motor stimulus" (Marston 1928, p. 106). Marston illustrated the four emotions as forming a two-axis model with dominance and compliance constituting one axis and inducement and submission constituting the second axis. Individuals attempt to maintain a balance between the extremes of each axis and the point of balance varies, explaining differences in behavioral tendencies.

In Marston's model, as seen in Figure 2, dominance and compliance form one axis; inducement and submission form the second axis. The two emotions of each pair are located at opposite ends of a continuum and are separated by the degree of response, which may be active or passive, as well as an outward or inward orientation. The two axes

Dominance	Inducement	Submission	Compliance
aggressiveness	alluring	accommodating	adapting
boldness	appealing	admiration	awe
courage	attraction	"a good child"	caution
dare-deviltry	"attractive	altruism	candor
determination	personality"	benevolence	conforming
egocentricity	captivation	considerate	well disciplined
ego-emotion	charming	docility	empathy
fighting instinct	convincing	"being an easy mark"	fear
force of character	converting	generosity	"getting down to brass tacks"
fury	"inducing a person"	gentleness	harmony
high spirit	leading	good nature	humility
inferiority feeling	"making an impression"	"being manageable"	"oneness with nature"
initiative	"personal magnetism"	meekness	open mindedness
persistency	persuasion	obedience	peace
rage	seduction	obliging	being a realist
self-assertion	"selling an idea"	slavishness	resignation
self-seeking	"selling oneself"	sweetness	respect
stick-to-itiveness	"winning a person's confidence"	tender heartedness	"swimming with the stream"
stubbornness	"winning a person's friendship"	"being tractable"	timidity
superiority complex		unselfishness	tolerance
unconquerableness		willing service	weak will
will		willingness	yielding to

Figure 3.   Marston's (1928) Behavioral
Description of the Four Primary Emotions

are divided horizontally. The active component and outward orientation are seen in the upper dimensions of dominance and inducement while the lower dimension includes the inward orientation and the passive component made up of submission and compliance.

Geier (1979) updated and clarified some of Marston's terminology. He defined the four emotions as follows: (1) *Dominance* is an active positive movement in an antagonistic environment; (2) *Compliance* is a cautious tentative response designed to reduce antagonistic factors in an unfavorable environment; (3) *Submission* is passive aggressiveness in a favorable environment; (4) *Inducement* is active positive movement in a favorable environment (p. 2). He also added the idea that persons whose traits cluster predominantly in the upper dimension of the model have a process orientation. These individuals "want to shape the environment according to their particular view. These are individuals who continually test and push the limits" (Geier 1979, p. 3). Those people whose traits cluster in the lower dimension are more product-oriented and "focus on the how and why" (p. 3). The dimensions in Marston's Two-Axis Model indicate behavioral tendencies. The behavior traits of an individual tend to cluster around one dimension more than the others, but each individual exhibits some or all of the types of behavior to at least some degree.

Clustered Traits

Marston also identified clusters of traits associated with each of the four primary emotions. These clusters, shown in Figure 3, helped shape Marston's data

Dominance	Influencing (Inducement)*	Steadiness (Submission)*	Compliance
adventurous	admirable	accommodating	accurate
aggressive	affectionate	attentive	adaptable
argumentative	animated	cheerful	adherent
arrogant	attractive	companionable	agreeable
assertive	boastful	confidential	calculating
bold	charming	considerate	calm
brave	companionable	contented	cautious
competitive	confident	controlled	conformist
daring	convincing	deliberate	consistent
decisive	cordial	earnest	contemplative
defiant	energetic	easy mark	cultured
determined	expressive	even-tempered	devout
direct	fervent	friendly	diplomatic
eager	flexible	generous	easily-led
fearless	fluent	gentle	exacting
firm	good mixer	good-natured	fearful
force of character	high-spirited	gracious	fussy
forceful	inspiring	hospitable	God-fearing
inquisitive	jovial	kind	harmonious
inventive	joyful	lenient	humble
irritable	life of the party	loyal	logical
nervy	light-hearted	mild	objective
original	open-minded	moderate	obliging
outspoken	optimistic	modest	peaceful
persistent	persuasive	neighborly	precise
pioneering	playful	nonchalant	receptive
positive	polished	obedient	resigned
rebellious	popular	patient	respectful
restless	prideful	peaceful	soft-spoken
rigorous	proud	possessive	strict
self-reliant	responsive	reliable	systematic
stubborn	self-assured	sentimental	tactful
unconquerable	spirited	sympathetic	timid
vigorous	talkative	trustful	tolerant
will power	trusting	willing	well-disciplined

Note: *Marston's (1928) origingal terms.

Figure 4. Geier's (1980) Revised List of Traits
Which Correspond to the Four Primary Emotions

and theories into a model which could be used in understanding normal behavior (Wellstood 1984). Factor analysis by subsequent researchers (Allport and Odbert 1936; Cattell 1946; Geier 1967, 1979, 1980) substantiated these trait clusters, with Geier (1980, p. 14) reporting that "many of Marston's suggested adjectives for each of his four emotions had correlated together at least R = .60." Marston's model has a non-pathological orientation with four categories supported by cluster traits. This is in contrast to other theories which are pathologically oriented and contain multiple clusters (Wellstood 1984; Nickens 1984). Marston's non-pathological orientation makes the model particularly appropriate for work behavior analysis as work is a normal activity for adults.

Geier (1980, p. 12) stated that "one must consider semantic change, or change of meaning. Then, too, some words acquire negative connotations over time, or with much repetition have lost their original vividness and become worn and faded." Accordingly, he built on the work of Marston (1927, 1928) and Alpert and Odbert (1936) in developing an updated list of traits. On the whole, most traits were listed as adjectives which made them easier to review and use in additional research. Geier's list of clustered traits is presented in Figure 4.

Marcus Paul Placement Profile

Building theoretically on Marston's model and Geier's research, Bauch (1981) and Nickens (1984) developed the Marcus Paul Placement Profile (MPPP). The instrument was designed to measure work behavior type for the purpose of matching individuals and jobs. Counseling, career development, job recruitment and placement, training, team building, job enhancement, and selection were all possible uses for the MPPP (Bauch 1981). The MPPP system incorporates theories of management, career counseling and placement into "a tool" designed to determine work behavior type in order to facilitate correct job placement. The MPPP is based on the premise that different personality types excel at different types of work (Holland 1959). It is intended for use in both educational and business environments. If this construct is accepted, then a successful matching of jobs and personnel can be expected to increase satisfaction in the worker, lead to greater productivity, and more adequately fill the needs of both the organization and the individual (Nickens 1984). A particular strength of the instrument is its recognition that individuals possess a variety of qualities and patterns of behavior in any work situation (Glenn 1982, p. 94).

Bauch (1981) did not view work behavior traits and types as judgments of work behaviors but rather as terms that could be used to increase the understanding of work behavior to the benefit of both the organization and the individual. He advocated positive or neutral terminology with specific terms reflective of work behaviors. In particular, he replaced some of Marston's and Geier's terms which had negative connotations with positive or neutral terms applicable to a work environment. For example, Geier changed Marston's original categories of dominance, inducement, submission and compliance to dominance, influence, steadiness and compliance while Bauch and Nickens designated the four work behavior types as energizer, inducer, concentrator and producer.

Energizer (Dominance)* (Dominance)ø	Inducer (Inducement)* (Influencing)ø	Concentrator (Submission)* (Steadiness)ø	Producer (Compliance)* (Compliance)ø
aggressive	attracts people	accepting	accurate
bold	change agent	attentive	agreeable
certain	convincing	caring	careful
competitive	enthusiastic	committed	cautious
decisive	expressive	contented	compliant
demanding	friendly	considerate	conforming
determined	happy	diplomatic	contented
direct	hopeful	disciplined	devoted
dominant	inspiring	easy going	exacting
eager	playful	exacting	follows orders
forceful	personable	loyal	follows procedures
independent	persuader	orderly	governed
leader	popular	patient	logical
new ideas	respected	peaceful	precise
original	seeks new ideas	reasonable	resigned
outspoken	sociable	respectful	respectful
sure	talkative	satisfied	responsible
takes charge	team leader	sharing	systematic thinker
venturesome		steady	
vigorous		tolerant	
		trusting	
		understanding	

Note: *Marston's (1928) original terms; a Geier's (1980) revised list of traits.

Figure 5.   Marcus Paul Placement Profile List of Traits (Bauch 1981)

Definition of Work Behavior Type and the Four Types

Work behavior type means a description and categorizing of an individual's general qualities and predisposing behavior traits as they relate to the work situation and are defined by the Marcus Paul Placement Profile. The Energizer type (result-oriented) describes an individual who is typically assertive, direct, impatient with detail, interested in getting results and quite creative in the work situation. The Inducer type (people-oriented) indicates an individual who is sensitive and optimistic and who places more emphasis on interpersonal relations and getting things accomplished within the group rather than on the organization itself. The Concentrator type (technically oriented) describes an individual who is a loyal, steady worker and who tends to be patient, systematic, and effective. The Producer type (quality-oriented) indicates an individual who strives for quality, follows guidelines carefully, and supports his/her work and decisions with documentation.

The MPPP work behavior traits are listed under each type in Figure 5. The semantic development from Marston's descriptions of primary emotions through Geier's list of traits to the MPPP list can be reviewed through a comparison of Figures 3, 4, and 5.

The behaviors that cluster on the dominance dimension are placed under the energizer work behavior type. The term energizer is more positive and also more descriptive of the type as found in a work environment. Marston's inducement and Geier's influence became inducer, a positive and descriptive term for the second work behavior type. The Marcus Paul Placement Profile (MPPP) type, concentrator, is a more positive representation than Marston's submission dimension and a broader description of the type than Geier's term, steadiness, which is only one aspect of the trait. Finally, the more descriptive and more positive term producer replaced compliance. In all four instances, the MPPP labels were changed from adjectives to nouns to indicate a type as opposed to a trait (Bauch 1981).

The theoretical basis of the MPPP is similar to Herzberg's motivator-hygiene model for job satisfaction. That is, Herzberg recognized that the factors which enhance job satisfaction (the motivators) do not automatically produce dissatisfaction when absent and the factors that induce dissatisfaction (hygienes) do not necessarily produce satisfaction when absent. Nickens (1984) viewed the primary behaviors of dominance, submission, compliance and inducement as independent pairs. This does not mean that Nickens denied the existence of strong inverse relationships between the "opposite pairs" in statistical models. The recognition of trait independence provided a more powerful tool for explaining complex behaviors on an individual basis (Nickens 1984, p. 13).

The MPPP also has been shown to have predictive validity when used for career planning. Glenn (1982), Wellstood (1984), Olson (1988), and Barber (1989) studied work behavior types as they relate to job satisfaction, attrition, specific vocations, perception of individuals in leadership positions and occupational stressors. According to Glenn (1982, p. ix), "significant relationships were found between (MPPP) work behavior types and areas of job satisfactions. Additionally, specific areas of job effectiveness were found to be significantly related to work behavior type. These findings were consistent with expectations." Glenn (1982, p. 135) concluded that,

> in order to maintain maximum effectiveness and worker satisfaction, employees need to be placed in jobs which meet their needs for degree of structure, autonomy, supervision, feedback, and contact with co-workers. One way to understand these various needs is to have knowledge of individual work behavior types and personality functions.

Wellstood (1984, p. vi) further reported "results indicate that work behavior type relates to overall and to specific aspects of job satisfaction" on the MPPP. "Supervisors and managers could make valuable use of knowledge about work behavior types as well as the types of their subordinates when assigning tasks or projects…teaching and training techniques should also differ for the various work behavior types" (pp. 113-114). The results of these and other studies have shown that information on work behavior types can be useful in a variety of work-related areas, including job satisfaction and career planning.

Academic Librarians

Personality Studies

A considerable literature exists on the personality of the librarian. Bryan (1952), Douglas (1957) and Rainwater (1962) studied various populations of librarians between 1948 and 1962. All three studies showed the average librarian to be more submissive or deferential than the general population and to possess a set of qualities summarized by the term "endurance." They also showed the librarian to be less affiliative, less dominant, less heterosexual in interests and less aggressive than the normative population. All the studies agreed that the same characteristics applied to both males and females within the total population of librarians.

In the decade of the 1960s, Baillie (1961) studied a small sample of 65 librarians and found that although they conformed to "normal" personality patterns, they were aloof, suspicious and wary. McMahon (1967, p. 2) reported on librarians' lack of leadership potential and noted that "people with certain personality traits are drawn towards librarianship as a career." Morrison (1961), Clayton (1968), and Magrill (1969) produced three doctoral studies related to the personality of librarians. Morrison (1961) used the Ghiselli Self-Description Inventory to study academic librarians. He concluded that librarians with dynamic personality traits were needed and that the personality profile of academic librarians was not especially suited to the needs of the modern library. Clayton (1968) administered the California Personality Inventory to entrants to the profession who showed an orientation to academic librarianship and found the subjects to be disinterested in decision making and lacking in initiative and assertiveness.

During the 1970s studies reporting the docile nature and passivity of library students were published. The works of Segal (1970), Goodwin (1972), and Plate and Stone (1974) are representative of this research, with Segal, in particular, reporting male librarians to be practical, somewhat unfeeling, and generally suspicious. Presthaus (1970) and Hamilton (1976) found the librarians they studied to be bureaucratic and resistant to change, both sociological and technological change. In a study of 160 full-time librarians, Clift (1976) investigated the personality characteristics of the group and the accuracy of library patrons' stereotype of librarians. Results revealed high needs for achievement, endurance, and order, and low needs for exhibition, aggression and change. Males (but not females) had high needs for nurturance and deference and a low need for autonomy. Both sexes scored high on measures of self-control and personal adjustment. Lee and Hall (1973) employed the Sixteen Personality Questionnaire (16PF) to determine mean differences in selected personality characteristics between a female college norm group and a group of female prospective librarians. In contrast to the occupational stereotype of librarians as rigid, conventional, tense and less stable, the library science students were not found to exhibit these characteristics to any greater degree than the norm group. In addition, the three scales with significant differences (more intelligent, experimenting, and self-sufficient) were favorable to the prospective librarians.

Personality studies of librarians and prospective librarians continued throughout the 1980s. Two of these examined the difference between the behavioral styles of university technical service librarians and public service librarians (Frankie 1980) and among first, second or alternative career academic librarians (Moore 1981). Frankie (1980, p. 163) concluded that "university librarianship constitutes an occupational sub-culture characterized by very distinctive and potentially very dysfunctional values, attitudes and work preferences." She found that the academic librarians studied lacked self-confidence, avoided aggression, were resistant to job challenges, were primarily motivated by extrinsic rewards and showed little inclination toward leadership, assertiveness, social interaction and change. Moore (1981) reported no differences in personality characteristics as related to managerial talent for those who selected librarianship as a first career, those who worked in another field which required graduate training prior to entering librarianship, and those who chose it as an alternative career. "Regardless of the route by which a person comes to academic librarianship, it appears that the same type does ultimately come" (Moore 1981, p. 146). Moore did find librarians closer to the norm on general personality characteristics than earlier studies had reported. Webreck's findings (1985) suggested that librarians exhibit introverted and judging personality types. This was consistent with Agada's (1984, 1987) assertion studies.

In one of the most recent studies available David (1990) concentrated on librarians working in technological environments. She reported that "all librarians, independent of their sub-specialties, were dominant on Holland's Artistic Type" (p. 164). She also found that none of the groups tested were dominant on Holland's Conventional Type nor were they conservative, as both earlier studies and stereotypical representations of the profession would imply.

Fisher (1988) analyzed measures used in early studies of librarians' personality, including the California Psychological Index (CPI) and, in the case of the CPI, found questions designed to reveal feminine traits to be "ideological and not a little farcical" (p. 41). For example, replying "true" to the question "I think I would like the work of a librarian" indicates a feminine orientation. In other words, the very job of librarian is considered a feminine activity. Fisher argued strongly that there is doubt in the utility of the entire psychological approach to librarianship. He reviewed several studies and concluded that each attempted to generalize from samples which were frequently very small and used personality tests shown to be largely inappropriate. "No real attempts have been made to link the individual and the social, personality traits are mostly viewed as absolute, existing across all situations" (Fisher 1988, p. 45). Agada (1984b), who has written extensively on the librarian's personality, especially on the aspect of assertiveness, also criticized earlier studies for using questionable control groups, limited and/or nonrandom sampling, other career professionals as "norms" and for a lack of replication.

> Most important, most of the studies used dated multitrait global personality inventories which do not meet current high standards of reliability and validity, failing especially to show a high degree of convergent and discriminant validity. Most of these instruments have a psychopathological basis which is usually inappropriate and inadequate for the understanding of normal behavior (pp. 38-39).

Fisher (1988) advocated a more sociological approach to this area of study, one which acknowledges the interaction between the individual and the social, and which uses techniques or instruments suitable for varied and normal individuals. "The conflicting results...would lead one to believe that libraries like other organizations are populated by staff with varied interests and attributes" (Fisher 1988, p. 46). Agada (1984b, p. 49) wrote "there is a need for personality studies in librarianship to focus on the behavior-reactions of the personality types in the context of their particular job experiences." Van House (1988, p. 173), in her study of library science students' choice of career, stated that "more research is needed in career choice generally, on environmental and personal influencing factors, and on the process of people's decisions to enter librarianship." One additional factor which should be considered is the "strikingly homogeneous demographic characteristics" (Heim and Moen 1992, p. 95) displayed by library and information science students over the last 30 years. A 1988 study of students in the (then) 54 American Library Association accredited library and information science programs in the United States revealed survey respondents to be overwhelmingly white (93.7%) and female (80.9%).

Job Satisfaction of Academic Librarians

As previously stated, interest in job satisfaction can be seen in the number of studies related to it. Locke (1969) estimated that more than 4,000 articles on the subject had been published while Chwe (1976) increased that number to 5,000. But, of those 5,000, Chwe was able to identify only about 10 in the field of librarianship in the United States (pp. 23-27).

Additional studies were completed after 1976, including at least eight relevant dissertations. Frankie (1980) studied university catalog and reference librarians using worker analysis techniques. Lindstrom (1980) compared community college and college/university librarians and found different levels of satisfaction for each area. Swe (1981) compared bibliographers and nonbibliographers in academic research libraries, while Hook (1981) concluded that library administrators in academic libraries were significantly more satisfied with higher-level intrinsic aspects of their work than non-administrators. Glasgow (1982) found academic librarians' perceptions of their work, position in the library organization, salary, and perceptions of their promotion opportunities to be the variables most useful in predicting job satisfaction. Green (1982) studied library personnel employed in the University of North Carolina system and investigated the relationship between communication satisfaction and job satisfaction. Hegg (1982) and Rockman (1985) used the MSQ in studies designed to reconcile inconsistent findings regarding job satisfaction and to produce a demographic profile of academic librarians.

A number of additional studies related to the job satisfaction of librarians have appeared in the past 25 years. Vaughn (1972) found the concept of multidimensional job satisfaction to be an important research concept useful in exploring environmental and behavioral features of the work setting of one university library with work, pay, promotion and supervision emerging as key parameters in the analysis of data. A second study (Vaughn and Dunn 1974) expanded the concept to six university libraries and emphasized again the multidimensional nature of job satisfaction, in addition to the causal influence of managerial performance upon employee productivity and satisfaction. Miniter (1975) found women to be generally more satisfied in their work than men, Scammel and Stead (1980) reported relatively constant levels of job satisfaction across different age and tenure categories, and Limpiyasrisakul (1980) identified involving librarians in decision-making processes as a factor in improving job satisfaction. Lindstrom (1980) determined that the work itself and pay were the most critical areas related to low job satisfaction with independence, challenging work and service opportunities related to higher satisfaction. Smith and Reinow (1984) reported that a perception of low professional status and lack of professional development and advancement opportunities related to dissatisfaction. Of particular interest to this study is the finding reported by Lynch and Verdin (1983, p. 445) that "new entrants…into the profession report some of the lowest levels of [job] satisfaction." They find this troublesome and suggest several possible explanations for the finding, including problems of accommodation to working within an organizational context, difficulty with work-flow demands, and the nature of the "entry-level work for professionals in large research libraries [which] may be more routine and nonprofessional than librarians expect" (p. 446). Reporting on a study of librarians 10 years after their graduation, White (1990, p. 61) wrote: "The graduates…report that…they thought they knew what their preference for both type of library and type of work was before they enrolled in library school. By the time they graduated, a significant percentage had changed their minds." More importantly, White continues "almost half...end up doing something different from what they originally thought they would do." Given the ever increasing costs of recruitment and training, it would seem to be in the best interest of academic libraries to attempt to determine what aspects of work will provide satisfaction for librarians or, at a minimum, to avoid those aspects that cause dissatisfaction.

Additional research (Hook 1981; Glasgow 1982; Chopra 1984; Bernstein and Leach 1985; Bengston and Shields 1985; Sherrer 1985; Allison and Sartori 1988; Washington 1988; Mirfakharai 1991; Horenstein 1993) revealed library administrators to be more satisfied with intrinsic aspects of their work than non-administrators, management style to be the best predictor of librarian satisfaction in an academic setting, and faculty status or rank to be a predictor of overall job satisfaction. Intellectually challenging work, advancement opportunities, independence and autonomy, support for professional travel and research and salary continued to appear as factors in job satisfaction/job dissatisfaction.

Studies Related to Maslow and Herzberg

Maslow's theory of the hierarchy of needs and Herzberg's dual-factor theory were also specifically considered in a series of studies. One of the earliest (Wahba 1973) provided an empirical test of the applicability of the theories to librarians. Promotional opportunities, pay levels and security were sources of strong dissatisfaction with women reporting greater dissatisfaction with the factors in addition to that of supervision. Women also expressed greater need deficiencies than men in esteem, autonomy, and self-actualization. Library administrators expressed higher satisfaction in these areas with technical services librarians expressing the lowest levels. Wahba (1985) also explored the differences in job satisfaction for men and women in a later study which concentrated on their perceived degree of need fulfillment and need deficiencies. Similar levels of fulfillment were reported in lower-order needs, such as social or security needs, with women reporting significantly lower levels of fulfillment than men in esteem and autonomy needs. In the area of need deficiency, women indicated larger degrees of need than men in all areas except for the social need.

A particularly relevant study involving 237 American and Canadian librarians investigated job satisfaction in relation to Herzberg's theory (Plate and Stone 1974). These authors reported findings corresponding to those of Herzberg, most notably that the factors involved in producing job satisfaction (and motivation) are distinct and different from the factors that lead to job dissatisfaction and the factors producing job satisfaction (and motivation) are concerned primarily with the actual job content (or work-process factors): the reasons for dissatisfaction (or hygiene factors) deal primarily with factors relating to the context in which the job is done—the job environment. Both sets of factors are closely interrelated (p. 97).

Additional studies of librarians which drew upon Maslow's or Herzberg's theories investigated the role of work space in productivity and satisfaction (Isacco 1985), decision making and staff morale (Nitecki 1984), expectations of administrators (Price 1987; Fink 1987) expectations by administrators (Alley 1987), work-related stress (Bunge 1987), and job satisfaction of ethnic minority librarians (Squire 1991). Baker and Sandore (1991) considered Maslow's hierarchy in relation to the rapid pace of institutional and technological change in libraries. Building on their earlier work, they concluded that the introduction of automation, in particular, led many librarians to feel threatened concerning job security, professional knowledge and professional competency. "Professionals who are already at ease with many of the levels on Maslow's needs hierarchy are suddenly faced with starting all over, possibly to satisfy beginning or basic job security needs" (Baker and Sandore 1991, p. 43). They concluded, however, that it is the uncertainty and turbulence of change rather than specific individual events, such as the introduction of new technologies into libraries, which have caused ambivalence and insecurity and lowered the reported job satisfaction of librarians.

Studies Using the Minnesota Satisfaction Questionnaire

The Minnesota Satisfaction Questionnaire has been used in several studies related to librarians. One of the first studies to use the instrument was a short longitudinal investigation in which data pertaining to vocational needs and job expectations were collected prior to subject entry into work environments with data on vocational need, environmental reinforcers and job satisfaction collected after subjects had been working at least six months (D'Elia 1975). Job satisfaction was determined to be a function of both need gratification and expectation fulfillment. A later study (D'Elia 1979) found two job factors related to supervision (human relations and ability utilization) to be most closely related to satisfaction. The level of general job satisfaction showed no significant difference for university catalogers or reference librarians in a study that used the long form MSQ, although some specific areas, such as "variety," "compensation," or "working conditions" did show substantial differences (Chwe 1976, 1978).

Additional studies using the MSQ concluded bibliographers were more satisfied than nonbibliographers on intrinsic satisfaction (Swe 1981), age was associated with job satisfaction while participation in continuing education was not, and job satisfaction as a single variable was not related to faculty status (Hegg 1982, 1985, 1986). Women librarians in Nigeria derive greater satisfaction from their work than men, in contrast to studies of librarians in the United States where men were either more satisfied or where no difference was determined (Nzotta 1985). Autonomy and decision-making opportunities were more important in predicting job satisfaction than gender (Rockman 1984, 1985), and factors related to superior-subordinate relations (supervision) were significantly related to general job satisfaction (Swasdison 1989).

PROCEDURES

Sample Population

The sample population in this study comprised 350 individuals selected from the membership of the Association of College and Research Libraries, a division of the American Library Association, and the Academic Caucus of the Florida Library Association. A limited number were members of other divisions of the American Library Association. All prospective participants were members of one or more of these Associations. The criteria for the use of data received from respondents included current employment in an academic library in Florida and holding a Master in Library Science (MLS) degree or an appropriate other degree (for example, Master in Librarianship, Master in Media or Master in Information Science.)

An academic library was defined as a library in a postbaccalaureate institution, including community or junior college, college or university, as well as special libraries connected with postbaccalaureate institutions. Thus, respondents worked at all levels of higher education and in both large and small schools. Correspondingly, the libraries in which they are employed ranged from those with a staff of five or fewer to those employing 100 or more. However, the commonality of employment as an academic librarian was viewed as more basic to the selection of the study sample than individual differences in institution or specific professional responsibilities. All subjects for whom data were used were currently employed academic librarians in Florida who showed an orientation and commitment to the profession through active participation in one or more major professional organizations.

Data Collection

Data relating to work behavior type (WBT) were collected using the Marcus Paul Placement Profile (MPPP). Job satisfaction data were collected using the Minnesota Satisfaction Questionnaire (MSQ). Both measures are self-reporting forms, described as appropriate for distribution through the mail. A supplementary demographic data form was also distributed. Instrument packets were numerically coded to eliminate personal identification but to permit correlation of responses. Study participants who wished to receive a printed profile reporting their work behavior type were instructed to put their names on the MPPP form. Following the distribution of the MPPP reports and before the analysis of data, responses were recorded with a second numbering scheme to ensure confidentiality.

```
┌─────────────────────────────────────────┐
│              Sample Box                   │
│     Most                      Least       │
│                                           │
│      1         careful         1          │
│                                           │
│      2          fast           2          │
│                                           │
│      3         alert           3          │
│                                           │
│      4          nice           4          │
│                                           │
└─────────────────────────────────────────┘
```

Figure 6.   Illustration of a Marcus Paul Placement Profile "Box"

Marcus Paul Placement Profile

The MPPP was designed to describe the individual work behavior patterns of people for the purpose of matching individuals and jobs. The work of Argyris (1964), Blake and Mouton (1964), and McGregor (1960), who were instrumental in integrating humanistic principles into the workplace, were incorporated into the design of the MPPP with the intent of developing an instrument that would increase the understanding of work behavior for employer and employee alike. The terminology used in the MPPP is positive or neutral. This reflects the philosophy of Bauch (1981) who believed that work behavior traits and types are terms that can be used to increase understanding of work behaviors rather than as judgments of work behaviors. Finally, the terms used in the profile reflect work rather than social behavior (Nickens 1984). The MPPP can be completed in less than 10 minutes. Test–retest reliability is about 98 percent, as reported by Wellstood (1984).

The MPPP consists of 24 sets or "boxes," each containing four forced-choice terms from which an individual selects the one that is most descriptive of his or her self-perceived work behavior. The individual then selects the word in each box that is least descriptive of his or her work behavior. Each word choice in a box is numbered one, two, three, or four in both the "most" and "least" category. The number of one word is circled in the "most" category and the number of another word is circled in the "least" category. An example of an MPPP "box" is illustrated in Figure 6. Only one "most" and one "least" choice is made in each of the 24 boxes. By entering these numbers into a computer program that associates them with a MPPP behavior type score, a profile is developed.

```
                          PLACEMENT PROFILE
                                OF
                             JANE DOE

Energizer .  .  .  .  .  .  .  .  .  .  .  .  .  .  .  x  .  .  .  .  .  .  .  .  .  .  .  .  .  .  .
Inducer .  .  .  .  .  .  .  .  .  .  .  .  .  .  .  x  .  .  .  .  .  .  .  .  .  .  .  .  .  .
Concentrator .  .  .  .  .  .  .  .  .  .  .  .  .  .  .  .  x  .  .  .  .  .  .  .  .  .  .  .  .  .
Producer .  .  .  .  .  .  .  .  .  .  .  .  .  .  .  .  .  .  .  .  .  .  x  .  .  .  .  .  .  .  .  .
           - 15 14 13 12 11 10 9  8  7  6  5  4  3  2  1  0  1  2  3  4  5  6  7  8  9  10 11 12 13 14 15 +

Interpretation:

Jane Doe is a producer type. Producers strive for quality as they carefully follow procedures. . . .
Jane Doe is of the worker group noted for high levels of . . .
```

Figure 7. Sample MPPP Profile

Four independent scores are reported on the profile derived from the MPPP. The scores relate to the four work behavior types: energizer, inducer, concentrator and producer. The four independent scores are plotted on a scale that extends from −15 to +15. At the center of the scale is the norm score, zero. This allows for easy observation of the relationship of each individual score to the norm as well as to each other score. The scores are scaled, a graph with the scores plotted on it is produced and, following the graph, a narrative description of the behavior associated with the score of best fit is provided. In addition, an interpretation of the behavior associated with the relative scaled scores is included in the MPPP report (Nickens 1984). Figure 7 illustrates an abbreviated sample MPPP profile.

The four terms listed in the profile represent the four primary work behavior types. The highest score of these four is the individual's "primary type of best fit" (Nickens 1984, p. 11). The description of the four primary types, as they would be included in a report of a profile, are found in Figure 8.

With its reliance on a sound theoretical basis, the MPPP reflects what is called face validity. The statistical procedures that were employed to obtain the 96 MPPP "most/least" adjectives and to associate them with work behavior type, also provide evidence of reliability and validity.

Minnesota Satisfaction Questionnaire

The Minnesota Studies in Vocational Rehabilitation, or the Work Adjustment Project, are a series of research studies which began in 1957 and which have led to the development of a variety of instruments to measure indicators of work adjustment. The Minnesota Satisfaction Questionnaire (MSQ) is a measure for one of the primary indicators of work adjustment. It allows for the attainment of a more individualized assessment of worker

Energizer (E) type worker: These workers are actively engaged in getting results. They are assertive, choosing a direct approach as they pursue goals. High 'E' type workers are impatient with detail, desiring a direct answer and action from associates. They are creative and have many ideas for improving the work processes.

Concentrator (C) type worker: Normally, the 'C' types apply their skills in orderly ways, resisting distractions. They are steady workers and are loyal to the organization, showing great patience. They are systematic, effective, and help to maintain moderation in tense situations.

Inducer (I) type worker: These people involve others as they pursue their objectives. They are sensitive to needs of their associates, and share optimistic outlooks as they influence others. They are good at using group processes to accomplish goals, being able to clarify ideas for themselves and others. They place more emphasis on people and interpersonal relations than on their organization.

Producer (P) type worker: Producers strive for quality as they carefully follow procedures, guidelines, or standards. They can support their decisions and actions with irrefutable documentation. Producers expect clear directions but they can be relied on to meet their deadlines, follow orders, and carry out their assignments with precision.

Figure 8. The Four Primary Types

satisfaction, that is, two individuals may express similar amounts of general satisfaction with their work but the reasons for this satisfaction may be very different.

Scale	Items
Intrinsic	1 2 3 4 7 8 9 10 11 15 16 20
Extrinsic	5 6 12 13 14 19
General Satisfactions	1-20

Figure 9. Minnesota Satisfaction Questionnaire Scales

The MSQ is available in long form and in short form. Some previous studies of the job satisfaction of librarians used one of the two MSQ forms (D'Elia 1975; Chwe 1976; Rockman 1985; Nzotta 1987). The short form MSQ, selected for this study, is considered more appropriate for distribution though the mail as it can be completed in about 10 minutes, thus making it more likely that potential subjects will participate in a study. The MSQ is self-administering with directions on the first page. Although no time limit is imposed, respondents are encouraged to complete responses quickly.

The short form MSQ consists of 20 questions that measure 21 dimensions of job satisfaction (ability utilization, achievement, activity, advancement, authority, compensation, coworkers, creativity, independence, moral values, policies and practices, recognition, responsibility, security, social service, social status, supervision-human relations, supervision-technical, variety, working conditions, and general job satisfaction). Each item refers to a possible motivator or hygiene. The first 20 items are measured by a Likert-type scale which asks respondents to indicate their degree of agreement with a statement related to that dimension of job satisfaction. Five response possibilities (strongly agree, agree, undecided, disagree, or strongly disagree) are provided for each item. The responses are weighted from five to one in descending order so that strongly agree is assigned a maximum of five points while strongly disagree is assigned a minimum of one point. The 21st dimension, general job satisfaction, is interpreted as an aggregate of scores in the 20 dimensions measured separately. The three scales of the short form MSQ consist of the items illustrated in Figure 9 (Weiss et al. 1967, p. 4).

The most meaningful way to interpret the MSQ is to use the most appropriate norm group for the individual and then to use percentile scores for each scale obtained for the norm group. The most appropriate norm group would be one that corresponds exactly to the individual's job. As norm groups are not available for all occupational areas, a similar norm group which shares characteristics such as tasks performed, type of supervision, physical working conditions, and so on, may be used. If no appropriate norm group has yet been developed, the MSQ raw scores can be converted to percentile scores using Employed Disabled or Employed Nondisabled norms. Finally, MSQ raw scores for all scales can be interpreted by ranking them. This will indicate areas of relatively greater or lesser job satisfaction (Weiss et al., pp. 4-5). When used with an individual subject, percentile scores of 75 or greater generally represent a high level of job satisfaction, scores in the 26 to 74 percentile range indicate average satisfaction, and a percentile score of 25 or lower indicates a low level of satisfaction.

The short form MSQ was developed by choosing 20 items, each representative of one of the 20 scales on the long form MSQ. Those items correlating most frequently with a respective scale were selected. A group of 1,460 employed individuals completed the measure. A factor analysis of the resulting data yielded two factors: intrinsic satisfaction and extrinsic satisfaction. The 12 items that loaded high on one factor constitute the intrinsic scale. Six factors constitute the extrinsic scale and all 20 items constitute the general satisfaction scale. This allows for scores on all three scales.

The stability of scores obtained from the short form MSQ is currently being studied but no data have, as yet, been reported. However, data on the General Satisfaction Score for the long form MSQ show correlations of .89 for a one-week test-retest period and .70 for a one-year test–retest interval. Stability for the General Satisfaction Score of the short form MSQ may be inferred from these data.

Research on both forms of the MSQ continues, focusing on improving the psychometric characteristics of the scales and expanding the range of dimensions which may be measured by the MSQ. A 30-scale form has been developed and is being tested. Finally, researchers using the MSQ agree to report results to be used in the development of new norm tables.

Statistical Procedures

The Marcus Paul Placement Profile was analyzed using the MPPP software. The procedures for the analysis are well-validated. Scaled scores were calculated, and scores were plotted on a graph. The scores for all 202 subjects were then analyzed by computer to determine the number of subjects in each type, with these numbers further divided into male and female subgroups. The percentile of type by total and by sex was calculated.

The responses to the Minnesota Satisfaction Questionnaire were analyzed using the FACTOR procedure which provides several types of common factor and component analysis. Preliminary factor procedures were done which resulted in loadings on three, four, and five factors. The three-factor loading was selected. The Promax rotation was used to report the results. The purpose of the factor analysis was to allow responses to be characterized as motivators or hygienes. The mean score and standard deviation for each of the 20 items on the MSQ, the mean score and standard deviation for the Intrinsic Scale, the Extrinsic Scale and General Sat-

Table 1.   Response to Survey

Type of Response	N	Percent
Usable Responses	202	57.7
No Response	92	26.3
Other	18	5.1
Retired	16	4.6
Blank Forms Returned	15	4.3
Invalid Responses	7	3.0
Total	350	100.0

isfaction Scale, and the mean score and standard deviation for each item and the three scales by type were calculated.

The CANCORR Procedure was used to produce canonical correlations. This is a technique used for analyzing the relationship between two sets of variables, each of which can contain several individual variables. The canonical correlation procedure was used to determine the relationship of work behavior type scores revealed by the MPPP to the motivators and hygienes identified through the factor analysis of the MSQ.

RESULTS AND ANALYSIS OF DATA

Description of the Sample Population

Of the 350 subjects contacted, 258 or 73.7 percent responded. One response option requested subjects to return blank forms if they did not wish to be included in the study. A group of 15 people, or 4.3 percent of the subject pool, selected this option. Another 16 individuals, or 4.6 percent, responded that they were retired. An additional 18 people, 5.1 percent, responded that they were not eligible because they had left the profession, left Florida for employment in another state, returned to graduate school or were not presently employed in an academic library. Finally, seven respondents, or 2.0 percent, returned incomplete or invalid sets of measures and were eliminated from the data analysis, and 92 individuals, or 26.3 percent, did not respond in any way. The data analysis thus involved complete responses from 202 individuals, or 57.7 percent, of the initial sample of 350 (see Table 1).

The data on the academic librarians obtained from the demographic sections of the measures are summarized in Table 2. Female subjects accounted for 71.78 percent of the usable responses, or 145 of 202 subjects, while the 57 male respondents constituted 28.22 percent of the usable responses. The largest percentage, 39.6 percent or 80 subjects, had been in their current position for 2 to 5 years while 22.28 percent, or 45 subjects had been in their current position for 6 to 10

Table 2.   Characteristics of the Participating Academic Librarians

Characteristic	N	Percent
A. Gender		
Male	57	28.22
Female	145	71.78
B. Age		
<30	5	2.48
30-39	28	13.86
40-49	94	46.53
50-59	46	22.77
>59	18	8.91
No response	11	5.45
C. Education Level		
Master in Library Science or appropriate equivalent	202	100.00
Additional Master's degree	55	27.23
Doctoral degree		
Ph.D.	19	9.40
Ed.D.	6	3.00
Other advanced degree or certification	8	3.96
D. Years in Current Position		
<2	32	15.84
2-5	80	39.60
6-10	45	22.28
11-20	29	14.36
21-30	12	5.94
>30	2	.99
No response	2	.99
E. Total Years in Profession		
<2	3	1.49
2-5	26	12.87
6-10	29	14.36
11-20	74	36.63
21-30	55	27.23
>30	12	5.94
No response	3	1.49
F. Current Employment by Type of Institution		
Community/Junior College	31	15.35
College	20	9.90
University	142	70.30
Other	9	4.45

years. Over 84 percent of the subjects had been in the profession for 6 years or more, a sufficient time to evaluate their employment, attain promotions, or change specific jobs one or more times. This corresponds with the fact that over 78 percent of the subjects were aged 40 and over. Thus, the individuals whose responses were included in the data analysis were, for the most part, mature, experienced academic librarians. They fit into Black's (1981) group of mid-career librarians

Table 3. Work Behavior Type by Gender

Row variable: work behavior type as percentage of same sex respondents

Column variable: work behavior type as percentage of same type respondents

Cell format: frequency/ percent: total/percent: row/ percent: column

Gender	Concentrator	Energizer	Inducer	Producer	Total
Female	65	9	11	60	145
	32.18	4.46	5.45	29.70	71.78
	44.83	6.21	7.59	41.38	
	70.65	64.29	57.89	77.92	
Male	27	5	8	17	57
	13.37	2.48	3.96	8.42	28.22
	47.37	8.77	14.04	29.82	
	29.35	35.71	42.11	22.08	
Total	92	14	19	77	202
	45.54	6.93	9.41	38.12	100.00

who showed evidence of job frustration and a fissure between their work behaviors and position demands.

The largest number (142 or 70.3%) reported that they were currently employed in a university library. Another 31, or 15.35 percent, were employed in a community college, while 20, or 9.0 percent, were employed at a 4-year college. All subjects held an appropriate master's degree for their particular position with 55, or 27.23 percent, holding one or more additional master's degrees and 25, or 12.38 percent, holding a Ph.D. or Ed.D. degree with the Ph.D. predominant in this latter group.

Work Behavior Type

The frequency distribution of work behavior types found among academic librarians in Florida is shown in Table 3. Overall, 45.54 percent, or 92 individuals were concentrators. Of these, 65 were female (44.83% of the 145 female subjects) while 27, or 47.37 percent, of the 57 male subjects showed concentrator as their dominant work behavior type.

The second largest group were producers with 77 individuals or 38.12 percent of the total sample fitting here. Sixty females, or 41.38 percent of their total, and 17 males, or 29.82 percent of their total, constituted this group. Together, those individuals with either concentrator or producer as their dominant work behavior type totaled 169 or 83.66 percent of the total sample of 202.

By comparison, previous studies of members of a variety of professions showed quite different results. Glenn (1982) sampled vocational educational administrators. She found 47 percent concentrators, 25 percent producers, 21 percent inducers and 7 percent energizers. Poston (1988) sampled nursing faculty and found that 39.13 percent were concentrators, 36.96 percent producers, 17.39 percent inducers and 6.52 percent energizers. Olson (1988) studied college placement officers. In this group he found 15 percent to be concentrators, 11 percent producers, 67 percent inducers, and 7 percent energizers. Barber (1989) examined the work behavior types of Cooperative Extension Service mid-managers and found them to be more evenly divided among the four categories, with concentrators making up 31.8 percent, producers 28.2 percent, inducers 24.5 percent and energizers 15.5 percent.

The distribution of work behavior types of academic librarians is skewed toward concentrators and producers, as can be observed in Table 3. According to the MPPP user manual, approximately 60 percent of the general population are either concentrators or producers, with producers dominating. In this study it was found that academic librarians are almost 84 percent concentrators and producers, but concentrators are predominant. Female academic librarians are even more predominantly producers or concentrators (86%), again with concentrators, about 45 percent, dominating. By contrast, the male academic librarians are 77 percent concentrators or producers, although concentrator is still the largest group, accounting for 47 percent of the male subjects. When compared to other studies on work behavior type, the distribution of academic librarians by type was closest to that reported by Wellstood (1984). Her study of medical technologists reported 52.3 percent producers, 33.3 percent concentrators, 7.2 percent inducers, and 7.2 percent energizers. The only significant difference concerned the distribution of concentrators and producers; the totals were almost identical but the individual numbers of the two types were reversed. This indicates some similarity in the type of person attracted to these two different professions.

Those who are categorized as concentrators and producers are most likely to work to maintain their organization in its present form. They tend to follow the rules and regulations of the organization and can be relied upon to do the job assigned to them. Although this may be appropriate for laboratory technicians, who must be precise and follow careful procedures and who may need to work uninterrupted, it does not necessarily fit the dynamic and rapidly changing environment of an academic library. In contrast, energizers and inducers, who represent about 20 percent each of the general population, tend to seek to alter the system and to effect change in their organization (Bauch 1981). Energizers are represented in this study by 6.93 percent of the subjects (6.21% of the females and 8.77% of the males) while inducers account for 9.41 percent of the subjects or 7.59 percent of the females and 14.04 percent of the males. Thus, energizers, who embrace challenges, welcome change, and exhibit bold behavior, along with the charming and convincing inducers, would appear to be both sorely underrepresented among academic librarians and needed by the profession.

Table 4. Mean Score and Standard Deviation by Item (Minnesota Satisfaction Questionnaire, short form)

MSQ Item and Job Characteristic	Concentrator Mean	Concentrator Std. Dev.	Energizer Mean	Energizer Std. Dev.	Inducer Mean	Inducer Std. Dev.	Producer Mean	Producer Std. Dev.	Total Mean	Total Std. Dev.
1. Ability to keep busy*	4.34	0.84	4.50	0.52	4.37	1.01	4.25‡	0.93	4.32	0.87
2. Chance to work alone*	4.12	0.84	4.36	0.74	4.11‡	0.74	4.13	0.89	4.14	0.84
3. Opportunity to do something different from time to time*	4.35	0.79	4.57	0.51	4.47	0.51	4.22‡	0.82	4.33	0.77
4. Chance to be "somebody" in the community*	3.77	0.93	3.93	0.92	4.00	0.82	3.13‡	0.99	3.56	1.00
5. How the boss handles his/her workers**	3.45	1.19	3.21	1.25	2.95‡	1.27	3.07	1.24	3.24	1.23
6. Supervisor's decision-making ability**	3.50	1.18	3.57	1.09	3.21‡	1.44	3.40	1.08	3.44	1.16
7. Being able to do things that don't go against my conscience*	4.22	0.80	4.07	1.07	3.74‡	0.99	3.94	1.00	4.05	0.93
8. Job provides steady employment*	4.40	0.84	4.36	0.84	4.21‡	0.98	4.23	0.77	4.32	0.83
9. Opportunity to do things for others*	4.39	0.74	4.50	0.85	4.53	0.84	4.14‡	0.76	4.32	0.77
10. Opportunity to tell people what to do*	3.51	0.78	3.50	1.09	3.26‡	0.87	3.44	0.70	3.46	0.78
11. Chance to do something that makes use of my abilities*	4.24	0.93	4.29	0.91	3.95	0.91	3.83‡	1.06	4.06	0.99
12. How company policies are put into practice**	3.08	1.02	3.00	1.24	1.89‡‡	0.81	2.56‡	1.14	2.76	1.12
13. My pay and the amount of work I do***	2.88†	1.20	2.64	1.34	2.47‡	1.26	2.61	1.28	2.72	1.25
14. Chances for advancement**	2.90	1.24	2.57‡	1.16	2.42‡	1.12	2.66	1.14	2.74	1.19
15. Freedom to use my own judgment*	4.13	0.89	4.07	1.20	3.84‡	0.76	3.84‡	1.02	3.99	0.96
16. Opportunity to try my own methods*	4.11	0.80	4.29	0.91	4.00	0.67	3.86‡	1.06	4.01	0.91
17. Working conditions	3.80	0.99	3.86	1.17	3.16‡	1.21	3.30	1.16	3.55	1.11
18. Relationships of coworkers with each other	3.58	1.05	2.93‡	1.07	3.53	1.22	3.44	1.08	3.48	1.08
19. Praise I get for doing a good job**	3.37	1.21	3.43	1.28	2.95‡	0.91	3.08	1.16	3.22	1.17
20. Feeling of accomplishment I get*	4.11	0.90	4.21	0.97	4.00	1.00	3.64‡	1.14	3.93	1.03
	(n = 92)		(n = 14)		(n = 19)		(n = 77)		(n = 202)	

Notes: *Intrinsic items; 12 with score range 12-60.
  **Extrinsic items; 6 with score range 6-30.
  †Lowest mean score for each type.
  ‡Lowest mean score for each item.   Total score: 20 items with score range 20-100

51

In comparison to the general population which includes 60 percent concentrators and producers with producers predominant, 20 percent energizers and 20 percent inducers, this study showed academic librarians to be almost 84 percent concentrators and producers with concentrators predominant, about 7 percent energizers and about 9.5 percent inducers. Chi-square analysis showed strong evidence that these results are significantly different from those of the general population, supporting the theory that different work behavior types are attracted to different professions.

Job Satisfaction

The MSQ has 20 items which are divided into Intrinsic, or job content items, and Extrinsic, or job context items. These are closely analogous to Herzberg's classic motivators and hygienes. The short form MSQ used in this study generates three scores; that is, an Intrinsic score, an Extrinsic score, and a General Satisfaction or Total score. Higher scores by area or a higher total score imply a greater degree of job satisfaction either with job content or job context or in general. Furthermore, scores for individual items are presented allowing for more specific analysis. Table 4 presents the mean score and standard deviation for each item. The scores are presented for each work behavior type along with the score for the total sample population.

As shown on Table 4, inducers had the lowest mean score on 11 of the 20 items, producers had the lowest mean score on 7 of the items, while energizers had the lowest mean score on one item. Inducers and producers had identical mean scores on one item. On 19 of 20 items, concentrator mean scores were above the total mean; producer mean scores were below the total mean on all 20 items. The lowest individual mean score per type was item 13 for concentrators (pay and amount of work), item 14 for energizers (chances for advancement), and item 12 (how company policies are put into place) for inducers and producers.

Although the mean score differences are not particularly large, they reveal a pattern. Concentrators, the largest number of subjects, are consistently more satisfied with all aspects of their position, followed closely by energizers, the smallest numbers of subjects. Inducers and producers consistently show the lowest mean scores per item with the exception of item 18 (relationship of coworkers with each other), the only item on which one of these two types did not show the lowest mean score.

Producers are comfortable following procedures and guidelines. They prefer clear directions, will follow orders, meet deadlines, and produce precise, thoroughly documented results. Given the changing dynamics in procedures and activities associated with the current academic library environment, the somewhat lower degree of satisfaction of producers with job content factors could be anticipated. On the other hand, energizers, who are assertive, creative, impatient with detail and direct in their approach to the pursuit of goals, score highest of the four

Table 5.   Mean Score and Standard Deviation for Intrinsic, Extrinsic, and
Total Scores on the Minnesota Satisfaction Questionnarie (short form)

	Intrinsic Items		Extrinsic Items		Total by Type	
Work Behavior Type	Mean	Std. Dev.	Mean	Std. Dev.	Mean	Std. Dev.
Concentrator	49.68	6.54	19.16	5.1	76.23	11.94
Energizer	50.64	7.04	18.43	5.49	75.86	13.24
Inducer	48.47	6.21	15.89	4.05	71.05	9.03
Producer	46.65	7.24	17.39	4.97	70.78	12.55
Total: All Groups	48.48	6.94	18.13	5.07	73.64	12.25

Note: Intrinsic score range 12-60 for 12 items; Extrinsic score range 6-20 for 6 items; Total score range 20-100
for 20 items.

types on Intrinsic or job content items. The dynamic and changing responsibilities associated with the modern academic library would be challenging to these individuals and would allow them to exercise their skill in planning and their interest in the improvement of work processes.

Inducers like to use group processes to accomplish goals, place more emphasis on people and interpersonal relations than on organizations, and are sensitive to the needs of associates. They had the lowest mean score on Extrinsic (hygiene) or job context items such as the amount of praise given for work well done, advancement opportunities, company policies, supervisor abilities and administrative decisions. Concentrators, who are orderly and steady in their approach to work, loyal to their organization, and systematic in productivity had the highest mean score on the Extrinsic, or job context items. These results may indicate that inducers find their work satisfying but the way in which changes occur are less satisfying to them.

As indicated on Table 4, the intrinsic items on the MSQ are numbers 1, 2, 3, 4, 7, 8, 9, 10, 11, 15, 16 and 20. With the exception of 2 (freedom to work alone) and 8 (opportunity for steady employment), two of Herzberg's hygienes, these items all correspond to Herzberg motivators. The extrinsic, or job context items, on the MSQ are numbers 5, 6, 12, 13, 14 and 19. The first 4 and 19 correspond to Herzberg hygienes. The exception is 14 (advancement on current job). Numbers 17 (working conditions) and 18 (relationships of coworkers) correspond to Herzberg hygienes. In the MSQ, they contribute to an overall general score.

Table 5 presents means and standard deviations for the Intrinsic score, the Extrinsic score and the Total score by type and for the entire sample. The means for concentrators and energizers are both above the total mean while the means for inducers and producers are below the total mean. This is consistent for both Intrinsic and Extrinsic scores. The lowest mean score for intrinsic items, or those related to job content, is that of the producers while the lowest mean score for extrinsic, or job context, items is that of the inducers. Overall, concentrators had

Table 6.   Factor Loading on Job Satisfaction Items from
the Minnesota Satisfaction Questionnaire (short term)

MSQ Item Number	Factor I	Factor II	Factor III
5	0.70157	−0.13713	0.11158
6	0.69630	−0.22041	0.11110
12	0.59752	0.09730	−0.03583
19	0.57007	0.21418	−0.13415
18	0.47441	0.11522	−0.08747
17	0.45858	0.16487	0.18808
13	0.38671	0.29018	−0.12743
8	0.30778	0.10257	0.06334
9	−0.00164	0.63928	−0.10148
11	−0.04466	0.55972	0.29152
10	−0.02269	0.52428	−0.02346
20	0.16444	0.47476	0.20258
4	0.10487	0.47332	0.15867
14	0.31146	0.44883	−0.13036
3	−0.11126	0.42545	0.37365
2	0.00205	−0.22953	0.71932
1	−0.15959	0.16746	0.53505
7	0.29114	0.16151	0.44019
15	0.12019	0.26234	0.41843
16	0.16303	0.26466	0.40113

N = 202

Note: Factor I (items 5, 6, 12, 19, 18, 17, 13, 8); Factor II (items 9, 11, 10, 20, 4, 14, 3); Factor III (items 2, 1,
7, 15, 16). Variance explained by: Factor I, 2.639930; Factor II, 2.306518; Factor III, 1.759460.

the highest total mean score, 2.59 above the all group total, while producers had
the lowest total mean score, 2.86 below the group total.

Table 6 shows factor loadings on the MSQ. Factor I includes items 5, 6, 12, 19,
18, 17, 13 and 8. These all correspond to Herzberg hygienes, or job context items,
with the exception of the last item, number 8 (steady employment), which has the
lowest factor loading for Factor I, 0.308. In MSQ scoring, number 8 is characterized as an Intrinsic item. The other items in Factor I are part of the Extrinsic score.

Factor II includes items 9, 11, 20, 4, 10, 14 and 3 which are all Herzberg motivators, or job content items. They are all part of the MSQ Intrinsic score, except
number 14 (opportunity for advancement). This item shows a loading of 0.449 in
Factor II and a loading of 0.311 in Factor I. Factor III includes items 2, 1, 7, 15,
and 16. They all form part of the MSQ Intrinsic score and, except for item 2
(opportunity to work alone) are all Herzberg motivators.

Factor analysis of responses to the MSQ do show characteristics of motivators
and hygienes. With the exception of "freedom to work alone" and "opportunity
for steady employment" the 12 items on the Intrinsic (job content) scale of the
MSQ all correspond to a Herzberg motivator. Five of the six items on the Extrin-

sic (job context) scale of the MSQ correspond to Herzberg hygienes along with two items the MSQ uses to determine the General Satisfaction score ("working conditions" and "relationship with coworkers"). The exception is "advancement on current job," a Herzberg motivator.

In order to analyze the relationship between MSQ scores and work behavior types, data were analyzed by canonical correlation. Given two or more sets of variables, this analysis leads to the canonical variable of each set and maximizes the correlation between the variables. The simple correlations between the four work behavior types and individual MSQ items were weak. In addition, correlations between work behavior type and the three factors derived from the factor analysis of the MSQ were also weak. However, the largest correlations in absolute value were 0.1952 for concentrator to Factor I (MSQ extrinsic items; Herzberg hygienes or job context items) and a negative correlation of −0.1944 for producer to Factor II (MSQ Intrinsic items; Herzberg motivators; job content items). Factor III is also made up of MSQ Intrinsic items (Herzberg motivators or job content items) and producers had both the strongest correlation, in absolute value, and the only negative correlation (−0.1167).

The general interpretation of the first canonical correlation is that the strongest relationship is between Factor II (Herzberg motivators or job content items) and concentrators. The first canonical correlation is significantly different from zero at the .05 level and is even significant at the .01 level.

A second set of canonical correlations was established between the 4 work behavior types and the 20 individual MSQ items. As with the canonical correlations for work behavior type to the three factors, the correlations are weak. Eight of the 12 items whose weighted differences make up the first canonical variable for the MSQ item variables are motivator, or intrinsic, items. The canonical variables for work behavior type indicate greater emphasis on producer (−0.7171). There is some evidence that the correlation is different from zero at the .05 level. There is a weak to moderate relationship between work behavior type and "social status," "social service," and "achievement." Finally, there is a weak to moderate relationship between producer and intrinsic, or job content, items on the MSQ. A detailed representation of the canonical correlation data will be found in chapter four of *The Relationship between Herzberg's Motivator/Hygiene Theory and Work Behavior Types of Academic Librarians in Florida* (Kem 1994).

CONCLUSIONS AND IMPLICATIONS

The literature of academic librarianship frequently includes discussion concerning the changing nature of the profession. Lauer (1989) stressed that librarianship is a social, rather than solitary, profession. Those who do not have the ability to communicate effectively, who have little interest in management and planning, who avoid controversy to the extent that their occupational creativity is stifled and who lack leadership qualities may find that academic librarianship is an inappropriate career choice. Black (1981) reported evidence of a frustration level for mid-career librarians which may indicate disharmony between personality traits or work behavior and career demands. According to Slater (1979, p. 18), we should "screen and warn entrants to the profession, tell them what it is really all about, and encourage the painfully shy and the anti-social to seek other occupations (in which they will be happier)." Agada (1984b) advocated a focus in studies on behavior reactions of personality types in the context of specific job experiences. Furthermore, after discussing the self-effacing and nonassertive stereotype of librarians, as reported in the studies he reviewed, Agada suggested that an evaluation of library education and training programs along with revised position design and adjustments in work environments could remedy the presence of inappropriate traits and attitudes among library professionals.

Although individuals leave jobs for a variety of reasons, including many positive ones, a certain number of positions are vacated because of a mismatch between employee and job. Recruiting and training personnel are expensive as is the loss of time and productivity when an employee leaves a position. Remaining employees experience stress when established working relationships are disrupted and they may experience an increased workload, another factor in stress (Allison and Sartori 1988). When a job–employee mismatch occurs, both administrator and employee feel a loss as each has experienced failure (Nickens 1984).

A good match between organization and individual contributes to the health of both and is mutually beneficial. Matching an individual's work behavior type with characteristics of the work environment could promote job satisfaction, increase productivity, and lead to a dynamic symbiosis.

According to Geier (1979), people in working situations will exhibit specific qualities and patterns of behaviors. If individuals are provided with information about their particular work behavior styles and are placed into jobs that require and encourage those styles, the opportunity for job satisfaction and success in employment will be increased. In addition, the possibility that an employee may become frustrated and leave a specific job or even a profession may be less if the correct "fit" between employee and employment is made.

Job dissatisfaction is costly to individuals and organizations. High turnover rates, low employee morale and a feeling of failure on the part of both administrator and worker can be the result of a mismatch between a job and an employee. The work behavior type of an individual may be a factor in his or her adaptation to a particular work environment or specific job. If an employee were placed in a work situation consistent with his need for structure, supervision, autonomy, recognition and contact with other people, satisfaction might increase and attrition be reduced.

There are several implications of the findings of this study for personnel management in academic librarianship. Specific areas to which these findings could make a contribution include recruitment and education for the profession, job placement, professional development and training, administrator management style and team building.

Work Behavior Type

Determining the work behavior type of students enrolled in graduate library science programs could be useful in allowing inappropriate traits or outmoded behaviors to be recognized and curriculum to be developed to help students strengthen those qualities identified as important to employment as academic librarians. The method of instruction should differ for the various work behavior types. For example, producers prefer structure, step-by-step instructions and organization, while inducers prefer group interaction as part of an instruction method. Although quotas by type are not advocated, the predominance of concentrators and producers in the sample studies would indicate some recruitment of inducers and energizers could be useful to the profession as a whole. According to Woodsworth and Lester (1991), the profession needs to both recruit and nurture self-confident change agents and potential leaders. "There must be recognition among current research librarians and library educators of the need for more staff who are both entrepreneurial and intrapreneurial, and fewer who just do as they are told" (p. 208).

In the area of job matching, the component of work behavior type, when added to the professional qualifications of the prospective employee and the technical requirements of the job, could be a useful factor in placement decisions. If employees are placed in positions which meet their needs for degree of structure or autonomy, individual or group work and supervision or recognition, worker effectiveness and satisfaction could be maximized.

Professional development and training could be more effective if work behavior type was considered. This is an area which can lead to increased employee satisfaction and, from management's point of view, is an investment made to increase employee skills, effectiveness and productivity. Knowledge of work behavior type could be used to select specific participants for particular training programs and in designing programs that use varied learning and training methods. Based on research into work behavior type, it can be assumed that different work behavior types would respond to different training methods. For example, producers might prefer training that is organized, with clearly defined course objectives, precise and predetermined methods of evaluation, written materials and logical step-by-step instruction. A self-paced learning method would be a possible choice for this group, in contrast to inducers, who would react favorably to a less-structured format with opportunities for involvement with other people. They would respond well to an innovative training approach. Energizers could thrive in a competitive atmosphere, responding well to role-playing, "games" and other methods that would allow them to take charge and make use of their forcefulness and independence. Concentrators would probably prefer an orderly and comfortable training approach but their easy-going, accepting and reasonable nature would make them willing to try a variety of methods suggested by administrators. As they are generally attentive, disciplined and exacting, they could benefit from several different instructional methods.

If administrators understand that the needs of individuals within a job environment differ, both initial hiring decisions and future task assignment will be more effective. Some individuals are process-oriented and are predisposed to active, external orientations (energizers and inducers) while others are product-oriented, are more passive and internal (producers and concentrators). The different needs of individuals are not related to skill, intelligence or competence but are simply modes in which they feel comfortable. Thus, different management styles will be more effective with different work behavior types. For example, energizers and inducers would react favorably to participatory management while producers, who want everything spelled out clearly, might find it frustrating.

Some of the work in academic libraries is done by teams or task forces. Selecting team members with different work behavior types could allow members to focus on those areas of the assignment which they find most satisfying, thus maximizing the productivity of the entire team. However, it is not clear what particular mix of types would be most effective or whether some tasks would be better performed by more homogeneous groups.

Consistent with a review of the literature on work behavior type, the theory was supported by this study. Almost 84 percent of academic librarians had two work behavior types as their primary orientation. These two types were consistent in description with personality traits reported in earlier research studies of librarians. In addition, possible relationships between MPPP scores and Myers-Briggs Type Indicator (MBTI) scores of librarians (Webb 1990) appear to be consistent with relationships reported by Glenn (1982), in particular the significant relationship between MPPP energizer scores and MBTI intuitive and perceptive scores, and MPPP producer scores and MBTI introvert, sensing and judging scores. According to the Center for the Application of Psychological Type (CAPT), the 267 people in CAPT's 250,000-person database who listed their occupation as "librarian" showed the following preferences: Introverted (61%), Sensing (54%), Feeling (67%), and Judging (64%). The ISFJ type accounts for approximately 6 percent of the population of the United States.

It should be noted that the sample group's ISFJ preference is not particularly strong (Webb 1990). However, the characteristics associated with the ISFJ type (quiet, friendly, responsible, conscientious, thorough, painstaking, accurate, loyal, considerate, patient with details, willing to work devotedly to meet their obligations and concerned with others feelings; Webb 1990) are consistent with Marcus Paul Placement Profile trait lists for concentrators (e.g., caring, committed, considerate, disciplined, exacting, loyal, orderly, patient, respectful, steady, and trusting) and producers (e.g., accurate, careful, cautious, compliant, conforming, devoted, exacting, follows orders, follows procedures, precise, respectful, responsible and systematic; Nickens 1984).

As part of a 1992 Association of College and Research Libraries (ACRL) study, a random sample of American Library Association (ALA) and Special Libraries Association (SLA) members were asked to complete the Expanded Analysis Report (EAR) version of the MBTI. The sample group used for analysis numbered 1,600. The data from the ACRL study showed the following preferences by individual type indicator: Introverted (63%), Intuitive (59%), Thinking (61%), and Judging (66%; Scherdin 1994, pp. 128, 131). However, the greatest frequency for a four-letter type, 16.5 percent or 265 subjects, was Introverted, Sensing, Thinking, Judging (or ISTJ) which is represented in about 6 percent of the general population (Scherdin 1994, p. 133).

The second MBTI type most often found in the ACRL study was Introverted, Intuitive, Thinking, Judging (or INTJ) with a frequency of 184 subjects or 11.5 percent of the sample (Scherdin 1994, p. 134). The INTJ type is found in about 3 percent of the general population. As there are significant differences in these two types, as well as with the ISFJ type from the CAPT database, additional study of other subject groups would seem to be of interest to the profession.

Just as it is important to remember that human beings are complex and multi-faceted entities and that the tendency toward one of four work behavior types is just one aspect of an individual, so is it important to keep in mind the accepted context for applying any theory of type. Isabel Briggs Myers wrote in *Gifts Differing* (Myers and Myers 1980) that all individuals have some development on both sides of each pair of functions and attitudes; each type has advantages and pitfalls; accepting and understanding one's type helps an individual to be more effective; and understanding the full range of types helps an individual to communicate and work effectively with others (Segal 1997, p. 99). In *Type Talk at Work*, Kroeger and Thuesen (1992) wrote that applications of type theory in an organizational or work setting could include matching an individual's potential with position requirements through an understanding and appreciation of strengths and weaknesses; allowing employees to work according to their own style, thus breaking down work-flow bottlenecks; recognizing a wider range of employee perspectives, needs and ideas as a way in which to set more realistic and accepted organizational goals; and reducing stress levels through an understanding that the same events or activities which energize one individual in the organization can cause stress in another.

Job Satisfaction/Dissatisfaction

Factor loadings from MSQ scores showed strong evidence of Herzberg motivators and hygienes and were almost perfectly divided between intrinsic and extrinsic items. Taken in conjunction with the mean score by type for Extrinsic,

Intrinsic, and total, or General Satisfaction, MSQ scores, some implications can be seen.

Concentrators were most satisfied with both dimensions of their jobs. Given the loyalty and adaptability of individuals with a preference for this work behavior type, the changing dynamics of the academic library at the end of the twentieth century would be accepted and although they might not produce the ideas and new practices needed to cope with change, they appear to be well satisfied with their jobs and quite able to continue to contribute substantially to the profession.

Energizers were particularly satisfied with the intrinsic (motivator or job content) aspects of their positions, a finding consistent with their willingness to try new things, generate solutions and act decisively.

The implication for academic libraries is to meld the strengths of these two types, while continuing to provide an environment conducive to their job satisfaction. The lowest score on the MSQ was "my pay and the amount of work I do" for concentrators and "chances for advancement" for energizers. Pay is a constant area of concern in libraries in general. The results of this study show that all subjects were concerned with low salaries. However, only concentrators showed this as their least satisfied work item. Advancement opportunities were also sources of dissatisfaction for all types, but particularly for energizers who show leadership characteristics but may find few opportunities to use them. Dissatisfaction with pay and advancement opportunities has long been reported in the literature. This is the first study to tie these items to work behavior type.

Producers and inducers were less satisfied on both Intrinsic and Extrinsic MSQ scores as well as on the General Satisfaction or total score. Inducers were reasonably satisfied with job content items. This is consistent with their work behavior traits and the changing role of the academic library. However, they had the lowest mean score of all types on five of six extrinsic (job context or hygiene) items. Their lowest individual score related to "company policies," the lowest score for any type on any item. Producers had the lowest total score of all types and the lowest intrinsic, or job content, score. Along with the inducers, "company policies" drew producer's lowest score. However, they also showed the least satisfaction of any type on 8 of 12 job content items. As producers are a significant group in academic libraries (38.12% of the sample), the effect of institutional change and position alteration on this type should be carefully assessed.

Additional research in the area of work behavior type and job satisfaction is suggested, in particular a study using a large national sample of academic librarians. Sufficient subjects would allow work behavior type and job satisfaction to be broken out by position in an academic library as well as by administrator/non-administrator designation. Studies focusing on a particular type of postsecondary institution, such as community colleges or research universities, could provide interesting and useful comparative data. Finally, the work behavior types of students enrolled in graduate programs and academic librarians with less than 10 years in the profession could be sampled to determine their work behavior type.

This might show whether any change has or is occurring in the type mix of prospective or newer members of the profession and would allow comparison with the mature and experienced group represented in this study.

REFERENCES

Agada, J. 1984a. "The Impact of Library Education on Student Assertion: A Comparison of Nigerian Beginning and Graduating Students with Their Counterparts in Other Undergraduate Programs." Unpublished doctoral dissertation, University of Pittsburgh. (Abstracted in *Dissertation Abstracts International* 45: 1900A, 1985.)

_____. 1984b. "Studies of the Personality of Librarians." *Drexel Library Quarterly* 20(2): 24-45.

_____. 1987. "Assertion and the Librarian Personality." Pp. 128-144 in *Encyclopedia of Library and Information Science*, Vol. 42, Suppl. 7, edited by A. Kent. New York: Marcel Dekker.

Alley, B. 1987. "What Professional Librarians Expect from Administrators: An Administrator's Response." *College & Research Libraries* 48: 418-421.

Allison, D.A. and E. Sartori. 1988. "Professional Staff Turnover in Academic Libraries: A Case Study." *College & Research Libraries* 49: 141-148.

Allport, G. and H. Odbert. 1936. *Trait-names: A Psycho-lexical Study*. (Psychological Monographs No. 211). Princeton, NJ: Amercian Psychological Association.

Allport, G. and H. Odbert. 1936. "Trait-names: A Psychological Study." *Psychological Monographs* 211.

Argyris, C. 1964. *Integrating the Individual and the Organization*. New York: Wiley and Sons.

Baillie, S. 1961. "An Investigation of Objective Admission Variables as They Relate to Academic and Job Success in One Graduate School Library Education Program." Unpublished doctoral dissertation, Washington University. (Abstracted in *Dissertation Abstracts International* 22: 2804, 1962.)

Baker, B. and B. Sandore. 1991. "Motivation in Turbulent Times: In Search of the Epicurean Work Ethic." *Journal of Library Administration* 14: 37-50.

Barber, P.S. 1989. "Occupational Stressors and Work Behavior Types of Cooperative Extension Service Mid-managers." Unpublished doctoral dissertation, University of Florida. (Abstracted in *Dissertation Abstracts International* 51: 689A, 1990.)

Bauch, J. 1981. *Marcus Paul Placement Profile User Manual*. Nashville, TN: Marcus Paul Computer Systems.

Bengston, D.S. and D. Shields. 1985. "A Test of Marchant's Predictive Formulas Involving Job Satisfaction." *Journal of Academic Librarianship* 11: 88-92.

Bernstein, E. and J. Leach. 1985. "ALA/OLPR Sponsored Survey: Plateau: In Career Development Attitude Sampling, Librarians See Advancement as Problem." *American Libraries* 16: 178-180.

Black, S.M. 1981. "Personality: Librarians as Communicators." *Canadian Library Journal* 38: 65-71.

Blake, R.R. and J.S. Mouton. 1964. *The Managerial Grid*. Houston, TX: Gulf Publishing.

Bryan, A.I. 1952. *The Public Librarian*. New York: Columbia University Press.

Bunge, C. 1987. "Stress in the Library." *Library Journal* 112(15): 47-51.

Burr, R.K. 1980. "Job Satisfaction Determinants for Selected Administrators in Florida's Community Colleges and Universities: An Application of Herzberg's Motivator-hygiene Theory." Unpublished doctoral dissertation, University of Florida. (Abstracted in *Dissertation Abstracts International* 41: 3794A, 1981.)

Cattell, R.B. 1946. *Description and Measurement of Personality*. New York: World Book.

Chopra, K. 1984. "Job Satisfaction among the Librarians of Lucknow City." *Herald of Library Science* 23: 151-161.

Chwe, S.S. 1976. "A Comparative Study of Librarians' Job Satisfaction: Catalogers and Reference Librarians in University Libraries." Unpublished doctoral dissertation, University of Pittsburgh. (Abstracted in *Dissertation Abstracts International* 37: 1854A, 1976.)

_____. 1978. "A Comparative Study of Job Satisfaction: Catalogers and Reference Librarians in University Libraries." *Journal of Academic Librarianship* 4: 139-143.

Clayton, H. 1968. *An Investigation of Personality Characteristics among Library School Students at One Mid-western University*. Washington, DC: U.S. Department of Health, Education, and Welfare.

Clift, R.B. 1976. "The Personality and Occupational Stereotype of Public Librarians." Unpublished doctoral dissertation, University of Minnesota. (Abstracted in *Dissertation Abstracts International* 37: 3145B, 1976.)

Dahlstrom, J.F. 1982. "Motivation for Participation in Continuing Library Education." Unpublished doctoral dissertation, Texas A&M University. (Abstracted in *Dissertation Abstracts International* 43: 625-626A, 1982.)

David, I.M. 1990. "A Study of the Occupational Interests and Personality Types of Librarians." Unpublished doctoral dissertation, Wayne State University. (Abstracted in *Dissertation Abstracts International* 51: 2555A, 1991.)

Davis, K. 1977. *Human Behavior at Work*. New York: McGraw-Hill.

D'Elia, G.P.M. 1975. "The Adjustment of Library School Graduates to the Job Environments of Librarianship: A Test of the Need Gratification and Expectation Fulfillment Theories of Job Satisfaction." Unpublished doctoral dissertation, Rutgers University. (Abstracted in *Dissertation Abstracts International* 36: 585A, 1975.)

_____. 1979. "The Determinants of Job Satisfaction among Beginning Librarians." *Library Quarterly* 49: 283-302.

Douglass, R.R. 1957. "The Personality of the Librarian." Unpublished doctoral dissertation, University of Chicago, Chicago.

Fink, D. 1987. "What Professional Librarians Expect from Administrators: Another Librarian's View." *College & Research Libraries* 48: 413-417.

Fisher, D.P. 1988. "Is the Librarian a Distinct Personality Type?" *Journal of Librarianship* 20(1): 36-47.

Flanagan, J.C. 1954. "The Critical Incident Technique." *Psychological Bulletin* 51: 327-358.

Frankie, S.O. 1980. "The Behavioral Styles, Work Preferences and Values of an Occupational Group: A Study of University Catalog and Reference Librarians." Unpublished doctoral dissertation, The George Washington University. (Abstracted in *Dissertation Abstracts International* 41: 3307A, 1981.)

Geier, J.G. 1967. "A Trait Approach to the Study of Personalities." *The Journal of Communications* 17: 316-323.

_____. 1979. *Personal Profile System*. Minneapolis, MN: Performax Systems International.

_____. 1980. *Introduction to Emotions of Normal People*. Minneapolis, MN: Performax Systems International.

Glasgow, B.J.L. 1982. "Job Satisfaction among Academic Librarians." Unpublished doctoral dissertation, University of North Texas. (Abstracted in *Dissertation Abstracts International* 43: 575A, 1982.)

Glenn, M.A. 1982. "Relationships among Work Behavior Type, Personality Function, Job Satisfaction, and Effectiveness Ratings of Vocational Education Administrators." Unpublished doctoral dissertation, University of Florida. (Abstracted in *Dissertation Abstracts International* 43: 2843A, 1983.)

Goodwin, M. 1972. "Correlates of Career Choice: A Comparative Study of Recruits to Health Professions and Other Professional Fields." Unpublished manuscript, Vancouver, B.C.

Goodwin, M. 1972. "Correlates of Career Choice: A Comparative Study of Recruits to Health Professions and Other Professional Fields." Unpublished manuscript, University of British Columbia, Vancouver, B.C.

Green, C.W. 1982. "An Investigation of the Relationship Between Communication Satisfaction and Job Satisfaction among Librarians in Higher Education." Unpublished doctoral dissertation, George Peabody College for Teachers of Vanderbilt University. (Abstracted in *Dissertation Abstracts International* 43: 03A, 1982.)

Guion, R.M. 1978. "Minnesota Satisfaction Questionnaire." Pp. 1677-1680 in *The Eighth Mental Measurements Yearbook*, Vol. 2, edited by O.A. Buros. Highland Park, NJ: The Gryphon Press.

Hamilton, S.S. 1976. "Work Motivation of Alabama librarians: A Challenge for Change." *The Alabama Librarian* 27: 4-7.

Hamshari, O.A.M. 1985. "Job Satisfaction of Professional Librarians: A Comparative Study of Technical and Public Service Departments in Academic Libraries in Jordan." Unpublished doctoral dissertation, University of Michigan. (Abstracted in *Dissertation Abstracts International* 46: 3179-3180, 1986.)

Hegg, J.L. 1982. "Relationship of Continuing Education to Job Satisfaction of Academic Librarians in Four Midwestern States." Unpublished doctoral dissertation, University of Missouri, Columbia. (Abstracted in *Dissertation Abstracts International* 44: 1961A, 1984.)

_____. 1985. "Continuing Education: A Profile of the Academic Librarian Participant." *Journal of Library Administration* 6(1): 45-63.

_____. 1986. "Faculty Status: Some Expected and Some Not-So-Expected Findings." *Journal of Library Administration* 6(4): 67-79.

Heim, K.M. and W.E. Moen. 1992. "Diversification of the Library and Information Science Entry Pool: Issues from the LISSADA Survey Report. *Journal of Library Administration* 16(1/2): 96-107.

Herzberg, F. 1966. *Work and the Nature of Man*. Cleveland, OH: The World Publishing Company.

Herzberg, F., B. Mausner, R.O. Peterson and D.F. Capwell. 1957. *Job Attitudes: Review of Research and Opinion*. Pittsburgh, PA: Psychological Service of Pittsburgh.

Herzberg, F., B. Mausner, and B. Snyderman. 1959. *The Motivation to Work*. New York: John Wiley & Sons.

Holland, J. 1959. "A Theory of Vocational Choice." *Journal of Counseling Psychology* 6: 35-44.

Hook, C.A. 1981. "Intrinsic Job Satisfaction of Library Managers at Selected Academic Libraries." Unpublished doctoral dissertation, University of Southern California. (Abstracted in *Dissertation Abstracts International* 41: 4871-4872A, 1981.)

Hoppock, R. 1935. *Job Satisfaction*. New York: Harper and Company.

Horenstein, B. 1993. "Job Satisfaction of Academic Librarians: An Examination of the Relationships Between Satisfaction, Faculty Status, and Participation. *College & Research Libraries* 54: 255-269.

Isacco, J.M. 1985. "Work Spaces, Satisfaction, and Productivity in Libraries." *Library Journal* 110(8): 27-30.

Jung, C.G. 1923. *Psychological Types*. New York: Harcourt, Brace, and World.

Kem, C.R. 1994. "The Relationship Between Herzberg's Motivator/Hygiene Theory and Work Behavior Types of Academic Librarians in Florida." Unpublished doctoral dissertation, University of Florida. (Abstracted in *Dissertation Abstracts International* 56: 4293A, 1996.)

Kozal, A.P. 1979. "An Application of the Reformulated (Herzberg) Theory of Job Satisfaction to Selected Administrative Affairs Staff in the Florida State University System." Unpublished dctoral dissertation, University of Florida. (Abstracted in *Dissertation Abstracts International* 40: 1788A, 1979.)

Kroeger, O. and J.M. Theusen. 1992. *Type Talk at Work*. New York: Delacorte Press.

Lauer, J.D. 1989. "Recruiting for the Library Profession: 1970 to the Present." Pp. 277-283 in *Encyclopedia of Library and Information Science*, Vol. 44, Suppl. 9, edited by A. Kent. New York: Marcel Dekker.

Lee, D.L. and J.E. Hall. 1973. "Female Library Science Students and the Occupational Stereotype: Fact or Fiction?" *College & Research Libraries* 34: 265-267.

Limpiyasrisakul, K. 1980. "A Study of the Presence or the Absence of Participative Management as Related to Library Performance Characteristics in Selected Public Universities in Thailand." Unpublished doctoral dissertation, University of Kansas. (Abstracted in *Dissertation Abstracts International* 41: 4997A, 1981.)

Lindstrom, W.E. 1980. "Job Satisfaction: A Study of Community College Librarians as Measured Against College/University Librarians." Unpublished doctoral dissertation, University of Southern California. (Abstracted in *Dissertation Abstracts International* 40: 6051A, 1980.)

Locke, E.A. 1969. "What Is Job Satisfaction?" *Organizational Behavior and Human Performance* 4: 309-336.

_____. 1976. "The Nature and Causes of Job Satisfaction." Pp. 1297-1349 in *Handbook of Industrial and Organizational Psychology*, edited by M.D. Dunnette. Chicago: Rand McNally.

Lynch, B.P. and J.A. Verdin. 1983. "Job Satisfaction in Libraries: Relationships of the Work Itself, Age, Sex, Occupational Group, Tenure, Supervisory Level, Career Commitment and Library Department." *Library Quarterly* 53: 434-447.

Magrill, R.M. 1969. "Occupational Image and the Choice of Librarianship as a Career." Unpublished doctoral dissertation, University of Illinois. (Abstracted in *Dissertation Abstracts International* 31: 776A, 1970.)

Marston, W.M. 1927. "Primary Emotions." *Psychological Review* 34: 336-363.

_____. 1928. *Emotions of Normal People*. New York: Harcourt, Brace.

Maslow, A.H. 1943. "A Theory of Human Motivation." *Psychological Review* 50: 370-396.

Mayo, E. 1933. *The Human Problems of an Industrial Civilization*. Cambridge, MA: Harvard University Press.

McGregor, D. 1960. *The Human Side of Enterprise*. New York: McGraw-Hill.

McMahon, A. 1967. *The Personality of the Librarian: Prevalent Social Values and Attitudes Towards the Profession*. Adelaide, Australia: Libraries Board of South Australia.

Miniter, J.J. 1975. "An Analysis of Job Satisfaction among Public, College or University and Special Librarians." Unpublished doctoral dissertation, University of North Texas. (Abstracted in *Dissertation Abstracts International* 36: 5090-5091, 1976.)

Mirfakhrai, M.H. 1991. "Correlates of Job Satisfaction among Academic Librarians in the United States." *Journal of Library Administration* 14(1): 117-131.

Moore, M.M. 1981. "First Career, Second Career, and Alternative Career Academic Librarians: A Study in Personality and Leadership Differentials as Related to Managerial Talent." Unpublished doctoral dissertation, Florida State University. (Abstracted in *Dissertation Abstracts International* 42: 7A, 1981.)

Morrison, P.D. 1961. *The Career of the Academic Librarian: A Study of the Social Origins, Educational Attainments, Vocational Experience, and Personality Characteristics of a Group of American Academic Librarians*. Chicago: American Library Association.

Myers, J.B. and P.B. Myers. 1980. *Gifts Differing*. Palo Alto, CA: Consulting Psychologists Press.

Nauratil, M.J. 1989. *The Alienated Librarian*. Westport, CT: Greenwood Press.

Neff, W. 1969. *Work and Human Behavior*. New York: Atherton Press.

Nickens, J.M. 1984. *The Marcus Paul Placement Profile and Work Behavior Analysis*. Gainesville, FL: University Laboratories.

Nitecki, J.Z. 1984. "Decision-making and Library Staff Morale: Three Dimensions of a Two-sided Issue. *Journal of Library Administration* 5(2): 59-77.

Nzotta, B.C. 1985. "Factors Associated with the Job Satisfaction of Male and Female Librarians in Nigeria." *Library & Information Science Research* 7: 75-84.

_____. 1987. "A Comparative Study of the Job Satisfaction of Nigerian librarians." *International Library Review* 19: 161-173.

Olson, J.E. 1988. "Relationships among Work Behavior Types and Job Satisfaction/dissatisfaction Factors of College Placement Service Officers." Unpublished doctoral dissertation, University of Florida. (Abstracted in *Dissertation Abstracts International* 50: 1881A, 1990.)

Plate, K.H. and E.W. Stone. 1974. "Factors Affecting Librarians' Job Satisfaction: A Report of Two Studies." *Library Quarterly* 44: 97-110.

Poston, L.I. 1988. "Relationship of Work Behavior Types and Situational Leadership Within Colleges of Nursing." Unpublished doctoral dissertation, University of Florida. (Abstracted in *Dissertation Abstracts International* 50: 1327B, 1989.)

Presthaus, R. 1970. *Technological Change and Occupational Responses: A Study of Librarians.* Washington, DC: Office of Education.

Price, C. (1987). "What Professional Librarians Expect from Administrators: One Librarian's View." *College & Research Libraries* 48: 408-412.

Rainwater, N.J. 1962. "A Study of Personality Traits of Ninety-four Library School Students as Shown by the Edwards Personal Preference Schedule." Unpublished master's thesis, University of Texas, Austin.

Rockman, I.F. 1984. "Job Satisfaction among Faculty and Librarians: A Study of Gender, Autonomy and Decision Making Opportunities." *Journal of Library Administration* 5(3): 43-56.

_____. 1985. "The Influence of Gender, Occupation, Ecological Status, Autonomy, and Decision Making Opportunity on Job Satisfaction." Unpublished doctoral dissertation, University of California, Santa Barbara. (Abstracted in *Dissertation Abstracts International* 47: 376A, 1986.)

Ruskin, J. 1851. *Pre-Raphaelitism: By the Author of Modern Painters.* London: Smith, Elder.

Scamell, R.W. and B.A. Stead. 1980. "A Study of Age and Tenure as it Pertains to Job Satisfaction." *Journal of Library Administration* 1(1): 3-18.

Scherdin, M.J. 1994. *Discovering Librarians: Profiles of a Profession.* Chicago: ACRL/ALA.

Segal, M. 1997. *Points of Influence: A Guide to Using Personality Theory at Work.* San Francisco: Jossey-Bass.

Segal, S.J. 1970. *Personality and Ability Patterns of Librarians.* Washington, DC: Office of Education.

Sherrer, J. 1985. "Job Satisfaction among Colorado Library Workers." *Colorado Libraries* 11: 17-21.

Slater, M. 1979. *Career Patterns and the Occupational Image: A Study of the Library/information Field.* London: Aslib (Occasional Publications, No. 23).

Smith, H.L. and F. Reinow. 1984. "Librarian's Quality of Working Life: An Exploration." *Journal of Library Administration* 5(1): 63-76.

Squire, J.S. 1991. "Job Satisfaction and the Ethnic Minority Librarian." *Library Administration & Management* 5: 194-203.

Swasdison, N. 1989. "Job Satisfaction of University Librarians in Thailand: An Analysis of Selected Factors with a Focus on Superior-subordinate Relations." Unpublished doctoral dissertation, Ohio University. (Abstracted in *Dissertation Abstracts International* 50: 3401A, 1990.)

Swe, T. 1981. "Job Satisfaction in Academic Libraries: Differences Between Bibliographers and Other Librarians." Unpublished doctoral dissertation, University of Michigan. (Abstracted in *Dissertation Abstracts International* 42: 3798-3799A, 1982.)

Taylor, F.W. 1911. *The Principles of Scientific Management.* New York: Harper and Brothers.

Thomas, S.C. 1977. "An Application of Herzberg's Two-factor Theory of Job Attitudes to Selected Community College Administrative Roles." Unpublished doctoral dissertation, University of Florida. (Abstracted in *Dissertation Abstracts International* 38: 3326A, 1977.)

Van House, N. 1988. "MLS Students Choice of a Library Career." *Library and Information Science Research* 10: 157-175.

Vaughn, W.J. 1972. "Predictors, Correlates and Consequences of Job Satisfaction in University Libraries." Unpublished doctoral dissertation, North Texas State University. (Abstracted in *Dissertation Abstracts International* 33: 5357-5358A, 1973.)

Vaughn, W.J. and J.D. Dunn. 1974. "A Study of Job Satisfaction in Six University Libraries." *College & Research Libraries* 35: 163-177.

Wahba, S.P. 1973. "Librarian Job Satisfaction, Motivation and Performance: An Empirical Test to Two Alternative Theories." Unpublished doctoral dissertation, Columbia University. (Abstracted in *Dissertation Abstracts International* 33: 6376A, 1973.)

_____. 1985. "Job Satisfaction of Librarians: A Comparison Between Men and Women." *College & Research Libraries* 36: 45-51.

Washington, N. 1988. "Focus on the Academic Librarian: Job Satisfaction and Continuing Education Needs." *The Southeastern Librarian* 39: 103-105.

Webb, B. 1990. "Type Casting: Life with Myers-Briggs." *Library Journal* 115(11): 32-37.

Webreck, S.J. 1985. "The Effects of Personality Type and Organizational Climate on the Acquisition and Utilization of Information: A Case Study Approach Involving the Professional Staff of Four Academic Libraries." Unpublished doctoral dissertation, University of Pittsburgh. (Abstracted in *Dissertation Abstracts International* 46: 3180A, 1986.)

Weiss, D.J. R.V. Davis, G.W. England and L.H. Lofquist. 1967. *Manual for the Minnesota Satisfaction Questionnaire*. Minneapolis, MN: University of Minnesota Press.

Wellstood, S.A. 1984. "Work Behavior Types, Job Satisfaction, and Attrition in Medical Technology." Unpublished doctoral dissertation, University of Florida. (Abstracted in *Dissertation Abstracts International* 45: 2092-2093B, 1985.)

White, H.S. 1990. "White Papers (The Education and Selection Librarians: A Sequence of Happenstances). *Library Journal* 115(17): 61-62.

Woodsworth, A. and J. Lester. 1991. "Educational Imperatives of the Future Research Library: A Symposium." *Journal of Academic Librarianship* 17: 204-209.

AN INTERNATIONAL
INFORMATION GATEWAY
THUNDERBIRD'S INTRANET FOR
TEACHING, LEARNING, AND RESEARCH

Carol Hammond, Wes Edens,
Ann Tolzman, and Catharine Cebrowski

INTRODUCTION

An international graduate program operating from a single campus but with programs worldwide requires a unique solution to provide library services. The creation of an instructional intranet to accommodate the many dispersed users of an international business school, whether they are on campus or elsewhere, is the solution used at Thunderbird, The American Graduate School of International Management. Development of a virtual library through the intranet, *My Thunderbird*, with paperless services and remote access to resources, uses technology to overcome the problems of distance and national boundaries. Using web pages for specific courses, departments, and individual profiles, *My Thun-*

Advances in Library Administration and Organization, Volume 17, pages 67-92.

derbird offers a system for sharing and exchanging various types of informa tion, including that which is typically found in a library.

BACKGROUND AND DESCRIPTION OF THUNDERBIRD

Educating high potential individuals for roles in the global economy is the mis sion of Thunderbird, The American Graduate School of International Manage ment. As globalization becomes a major trend in business and the multinational corporation grows in significance, training for managers with expertise to operate in an international environment becomes more relevant, important, and valued Long a leader in developing individuals for management in international enter prises, Thunderbird is the world's oldest and largest school of international man agement. In March of 1999, *U.S. News and World Report* ranked Thunderbird as the number one school in the United States in the specialty of international busi ness for the fourth year in a row. Using its strengths in teaching, a unique curric ulum, an international mix of students, and a new technology infrastructure Thunderbird (the School) and its library have evolved to meet new challenges in global education.

Located in Glendale, Arizona, a suburb of Phoenix, the School offers a single degree—a Master of International Management (MIM). Thunderbird originated the MIM degree, which is now offered by a handful of other institutions as well. Founded at the close of World War II, the School was established on the principle that business on a global scale requires managers who can speak different lan guages, understand the customs and cultures of different peoples, and have inter national business skills. Developing a program based on this concept has created an institution that is highly attractive to those who seek international careers. Thunderbird recruits globally for its students, and is well known for its interna tional mix of business scholars. Some 75 nations are represented in those who are enrolled, and over 50 percent of the students are foreign. This ratio is higher than that at all similarly ranked institutions. The faculty is equally diverse; a large majority is bilingual and 45 percent are from countries outside of the United States.

Proficiency in a foreign language, business training and overseas experi ence are some of the features that distinguish graduates of the program. The exposure to the rich mix of cultures and languages represented in the students themselves is just one way Thunderbirds gain an international background. Many courses require students to work in cross-cultural teams, and learning from one another in small groups as well as in the classroom in this international blend is an important benefit of the program. The abil ity to apply technology in business practices is essential, and students are expected to be proficient users of various software, hardware, networks, and systems. So that students are familiar with and skilled in using electronic systems, technology is infused in the classroom, in teaching and assignments, and in many other programs and activities at Thunderbird.

The experience and education that students gain from the formal part of the MIM is achieved through a three-part curriculum that provides training in one of nine modern languages, and courses in international studies and world business. In addition, many other options are available to broaden and extend a student's international experience. Study abroad is one of these. In addition to its Glendale campus, Thunderbird operates two centers, one in Geneva and one in Tokyo, where students can spend a summer or semester taking courses for credit toward their degree. The School also sponsors learning opportunities which take place all over the world. During summer programs and its three-week Winterim seminars in January, faculty lead groups to Africa, Australia, South America, the Middle East, Europe and Asia to explore the regional business environment and issues in that area related to international business. Students also may earn academic credit through projects they carry out for companies seeking expertise in opening their business in another country, or selling their product internationally. Internships provide another avenue for gaining business experience abroad.

A major new direction for the School is in distance education, and that is also taking place on an international level. A large expansion and investment has been made in technology for the delivery of instruction to an international market. Currently, Thunderbird presents its degree program in Latin America through distance education to students in Mexico and Peru, and this model is one that can be delivered in other parts of the world. Executive Education is also a growing area at Thunderbird and one that is looking abroad for students. Currently the school has initiatives offering business development skills in China, Russia and elsewhere.

Operating in a truly global environment presents special challenges for the library, which provides resources for teaching, learning and research. The International Business Information Centre, or the IBIC, Thunderbird's library on its Glendale campus, provides resources to students and faculty who may be anywhere in the world. For example, in a single week the IBIC may hear from a student in Panama on an internship seeking information on environmental issues related to a business enterprise, a group of students in Czechoslovakia working on a marketing project for an American restaurant chain seeking to open a franchise in Prague, a student at the Tokyo center doing research on the Korean automotive industry, or a faculty member on sabbatical and doing research in Shanghai. This is in addition to handling the needs of the 1,500 students on campus who are also looking for similar kinds of information for courses and other projects, and the 250 enrolled in distance education in Latin America who have the identical kinds of assignments to complete.

To handle this demand, the IBIC has built collections that are specialized and very focused. The IBIC acquires materials on International business, cross-

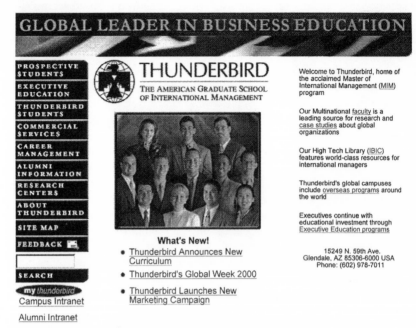

Figure 1. Thunderbird's External Web
Page, Showing Access to My Thunderbird

cultural management, foreign languages and industry-specific materials along
with reference tools relating to topics such as emerging markets, competitive
intelligence, political risk, international business ethics, electronic commerce,
finance, and other areas related to international business. It has also strategically invested in electronic resources and databases, which now number over
50, almost all of which are Internet-based. Because of this decision, the IBIC
has been able to take advantage of the School's unique intranet to provide
resources to users wherever in the world they may be, as long as they have a
computer and an Internet connection. For users, it is an affordable and easily
accessible network.

MY THUNDERBIRD

To support electronic solutions to many teaching and information needs
in a global environment, the School has developed an electronic instructional portal that all Thunderbird community members use to exchange
and share information, including much of that which is traditionally
available in the library. This portal, which is called *My Thunderbird*, is

sed to conduct on-line discussions, post messages and teaching materi-
ls, and access resources. *My Thunderbird* (MTB) is a secure, web-based
ntranet, which the IBIC uses to provide resources and support for its far-
lung users. A web site that requires authentication (user ID and password) for access, MTB provides features and information based on the
ecurity permissions of the user. It configures itself to fit the person who
ogs in so that only the resources appropriate to that user are available.
Designed and built by Thunderbird's Information and Instructional Tech-
lology Department (I&IT), *My Thunderbird* is a unique and elegant electronic solution to support teaching and learning in a worldwide setting
see Figure 1).

Combined with the School's requirement that every student own a laptop
computer, the electronic access students and faculty have is impressive. *My
Thunderbird*'s ability to sort out categories of users allows the School to provide different levels of service to different users. Some of these are students
who have been admitted but not yet enrolled and who may be anywhere in the
world; alumni, some 30,000 strong and also distributed worldwide; those in
internships, executive education programs, overseas and distance education
programs, and those working full-time on degrees—who may be either in
Glendale or abroad. MTB is the system through which faculty post course
pages for reserve readings, announcements, lecture notes and syllabi. It is
where every department has a page where news and announcements, policies,
forms, and contact information can be found. Food Services on campus uses
this to post daily menus of what is available in the cafeteria, for example, and
the Human Resources Department posts positions that are open and the campus telephone directory. Groups may use it for a bulletin board, sharing documents or discussions, because access can easily be restricted to only members
of the group. A team working on a class assignment may form a group, for
example, or a committee assigned to a project may use the system to share
drafts of a document.

My Thunderbird was developed using Microsoft Internet technologies,
but is deliverable to any user's desktop, regardless of the user's hardware
or software. All that is required is a fairly recent browser, and a connection to the Internet. There are some similar projects used at other schools,
but Thunderbird's system has the advantage in that it is usable on any
kind of browser. MTB is wholly database driven, unlike web sites that
depend on extensive text files, allowing for quick update of content in an
organized fashion. It is a portal to the rich information environment of
Thunderbird.

My Thunderbird is completely integrated with the registrar's data system,
which is another very distinctive and critical feature. Because of this union,
registration drives access without additional administrative overhead. There
is no other data entry or input needed, and users gain access (or not) to MTB

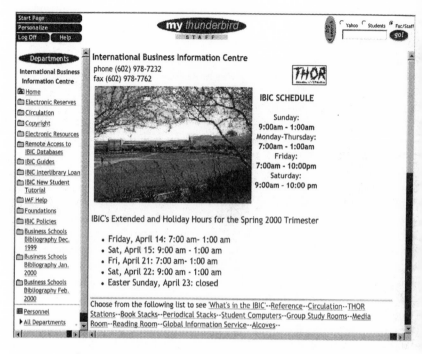

Figure 2.   IBIC Department Page on My Thunderbird

based on current registration. There is also no need for faculty, staff, or students to create web pages, as MTB automatically does this, using a template and information from the registrar's database. All that is left is for the user to add content; an easily accomplished task, because no knowledge of web programming is required.

My Thunderbird supports extensive personalization. I&IT created an information architecture with such a low barrier to entry that its growth was immediate, and this allowed the portal to become content-rich almost overnight. Each campus department and every course, faculty member and student has a page which they could develop. The system creates basic pages that faculty and campus units can adapt to specific needs and use for a variety of purposes. Owners of the pages, instead of a web master, can quickly change and update information. Global changes can be made without editing individual pages. For example, in the event of a course number change, MTB edits all affected courses, faculty, and student pages with minimal human effort required. Students and faculty took to the idea quickly, and, by July 1999, 94 percent of the full-time faculty at the Glendale campus were making use of the new technology. Fourteen percent of instructors are considered high-end users, enhancing their classes with links, files, and discussion groups. *My Thunderbird* has become the place where the most current and accurate campus schedules, announcements, and news are found.

IBIC: THE VIRTUAL LIBRARY

My Thunderbird became the answer to many of the IBIC's needs. Already a gateway to many information sources through its system THOR (Thunderbird On-line Resources), IBIC provides a large selection of databases, an on-line catalog, its web site, and links to other libraries for users. Librarians found they could use MTB for many of their other programs and services. This made an already highly electronic library become even more so, while enhancing remote access. MTB permits the IBIC to provide remote access from anywhere to databases, a student on-line tutorial, library forms and policies, IBIC's web page and catalog, resource guides, the schedule of library instruction classes, hours, directions for using specific databases, and other information. These resources are available to any student, staff or faculty member with a connection to the worldwide web. The IBIC department page provides the complete text of documents, such as the campus copyright guidelines; a guide to services for alumni and the student loan policy are also available to any registered user. Each IBIC staff member's photo and personal page is also found here. What follows is a discussion of some of the uses the IBIC has made of MTB to become a virtual library available to its users worldwide.

Paperless Processes

Internal procedures are easier for both staff and users as a virtual library with electronic services has been created. IBIC staff have changed paper forms to electronic forms, and have found that going paperless offered many benefits (see Figure 2).

Interlibrary Loan

Requests for interlibrary loan are handled electronically so that faculty and students submit them without coming to the IBIC, using a computer instead of a pen. Users may check THOR, the IBIC Catalog, for holdings. If an interlibrary loan is needed, a form is available on-line through MTB which uses question boxes to fill out the necessary information. Clicking the "send" button connects the completed form to the campus e-mail system, and it is automatically transmitted to the interlibrary loan staff for processing. Accuracy and readability of the requests is improved. Paper forms for this purpose, even at the reference desk, have been eliminated. Computers with MTB access are readily available in the IBIC, in every office, and across the campus. Faculty make requests from their offices, and students overseas make particular use of this feature. See Appendix I for a copy of the paperless interlibrary loan form.

Fine Appeals

Students receive overdue notices through the campus e-mail system. Should they wish to file an appeal and begin the process of challenging a fine, a form is available on IBIC's department page on *My Thunderbird*. This is also designed with a question box, and once it is electronically completed, is automatically sent by e-mail. See Appendix II for a copy of the paperless fine appeal form.

Remote Access to Databases

Like most academic libraries, the IBIC has struggled with facilitating remote access to its licensed databases. Part of the solution was accomplished in 1999, when digital subscriber lines, or DSLs, connected the centers in Tokyo and Geneva to the main campus in Arizona. This means that users at the Tokyo and Geneva centers are part of the Thunderbird network. They are assigned Thunderbird Internet Protocol (IP) addresses and access the school's web-based databases without trouble.

The difficulty lies in serving users *outside* the IP range of Thunderbird. Students may be using any Internet service provider, from anywhere in the world. Other users outside the IP range include students living in Arizona, but outside the local calling area; students on internships and projects overseas; and faculty researchers out of town for the weekend or out of the country for a semester. An important group of users, representing Thunderbird's growing international distance education initiative, are the students in the Master of International Management for Latin America (MIMLA) program. Providing library support to students dispersed all over Mexico and in other countries in Latin America, as well as the many others noted above, is resolved by MTB.

While some schools use a proxy server, Thunderbird's I&IT Department decided to try alternate means. Proxy servers are essentially pieces of hardware that stand between a local network and the Internet. Remote users authenticate themselves to the proxy server, which then assigns them a local IP address, thus allowing access to licensed databases. This method sounds simple, but causes several problems. Chief among them is the fact that the user, who may be thousands of miles from campus and using equipment and software unknown to the campus IT staff, must go through a series of steps to con-

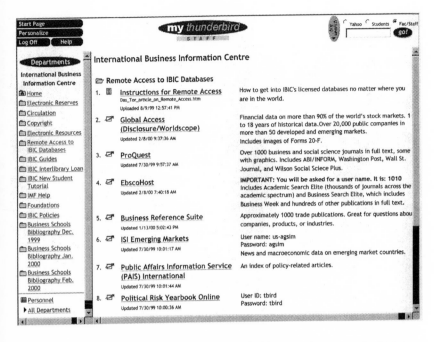

Figure 3.   IBIC Department Page Showing the Remote Access to the Databases

figure their browser for proxy server access. Thunderbird does not always have close contact with its users and technical support of proxy server access would present difficulties.

The staff of the IBIC, together with the school's network administrator, decided to use a method that takes advantage of referral URL, a feature of HTML available for years but rarely used. Thunderbird students and faculty must log into MTB using their student identification number and password. The link to the registrar's database will verify that they are currently enrolled students. This provides the necessary security. Students then must go to a page on the IBIC Department page within MTB, where links take them to various databases. All the database vendors need to know is the URL of the secure page. There is no setup required for the school itself.

Negotiating with vendors of databases for this access produced mixed results. Some vendors were ready and willing to implement referral URL access. For others, when a user clicks on a link a scripted ID and password is sent to the database, invisible to the user. One database, EbscoHost, uses a combination of referral URL and user ID. Still others, including the U.S. Department of Commerce's Stat-USA, will not accommodate remote access. Currently, nine databases are

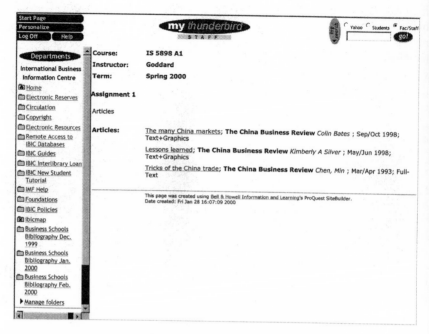

Figure 4. Instructor's Course Page Showing Electronic
Reserve Readings Created Using ProQuest SiteBuilder

available for remote use through the Internet for currently enrolled students and
faculty (see Figure 3).

Electronic Reserves

My Thunderbird was introduced at almost exactly the same time that UMI (now
Bell & Howell) released a major option for use with ProQuest. ProQuest is a database of over 1,600 business and management journals. It provides indexing and
full text for 900 of those titles. The feature, known as SiteBuilder, allows users to
create durable links to individual articles within ProQuest. SiteBuilder also allows
faculty members and librarians to create powerful, complex Boolean searches on
a given topic. An HTML link is created that is placed on a course page. To execute
the search, all the student has to do is click, and the most recent articles are presented. For the first time, it was possible to create secure, dynamic course pages.
Copyright is not an issue, as Bell & Howell owns the rights to the articles and
explicitly gives permission to create the links.

Among instructors, the synthesis of MTB with SiteBuilder created unprecedented interest in the library. Faculty could provide students with electronic read-

ings on course pages, available to them anywhere and anytime. Current bibliographies of articles on topics related to the course could be posted and automatically updated. Courses are offered every semester to show faculty members how to integrate the ProQuest database with MTB. It is not uncommon for these workshops, conducted jointly by the library and the Instructional Services department, to be completely booked within hours of announcement. Because it can be used both on the campus and for distance education, it meets both Thunderbird's goal of using technology to enhance teaching, and its goal to provide resources to dispersed, international users (see Figure 4).

The term "electronic reserves" conjures images of workers feverishly scanning paper documents and uploading them to a course page. With electronic publishing now coming into its own, however, paper-to-byte conversion is less and less necessary. With some publications, scanning and uploading is still required, but MTB facilitates that as well. The library is able to accommodate both the needs of the instructor and the requirements of copyright law, by observing some simple guidelines regarding intellectual property. While discussion of copyright is beyond the scope of this paper, it should be noted that the automatic restrictions in effect on MTB help ensure compliance with the doctrine of Fair Use.

DISTANCE EDUCATION: THE MASTER OF INTERNATIONAL MANAGEMENT LATIN AMERICA (MIMLA) PROGRAM

The Masters of International Management Latin America (MIMLA) program is the first actual distance education program at Thunderbird. Begun in 1998, there are now approximately 240 students enrolled in the program. These students take classes in their home cities of Monterrey, Mexico City, Guadalajara and Querétaro, Mexico and Lima, Peru. The executive education-style program is a partnership between Thunderbird and the Instituto Tecnológico de Estudios Superiores de Monterrey (ITESM). Students work toward a joint Thunderbird-ITESM degree via satellite courses broadcast from both Thunderbird and ITESM. Students are required to have access to a computer and an Internet connection, and the majority of them own laptops. They utilize the Internet to share files and resources and communicate among themselves using MTB. The IBIC librarians are challenged to teach these students in various locations to access the resources they need to complete their graduate-level research. However, in response to the format of their program and technological tools such as MTB, various methods have been devised to communicate with these students throughout the course of the 22-month program.

First, during an initial 10-day on-campus orientation held in Arizona at the Glendale campus, librarians hold sessions with all MIMLA students to introduce them to the primary databases and web sites that they will use. These sessions include a lecture-style presentation and a series of workshops in the computer lab where students ask questions as they learn to access remote resources and perform research. The first class of MIMLA students, who began the program in August of 1998, had access to five databases. Professors, students, and librarians could post announcements, assignments, comments, and questions in an open forum available to participants in the program. The second MIMLA class, which came to campus in August 1999, has access to nine databases and additional features such as file sharing, electronic breakout groups, personal profiles on one another, and web links.

In addition to receiving instruction on remote access and database usage while on campus for orientation, MIMLA students engage in ongoing communication with librarians and instructors via e-mail and the MTB breakout groups. To provide students with more face-to-face follow-up, librarians appear in classes broadcast via satellite to answer students' questions about their research projects and information needs. This interaction virtually emulates face-to-face contact, as it would be in a classroom with an instructor.

The kinds of assignments the MIMLA students are given are similar to those on-campus students might also have. For example, a professor of cross-cultural communication asked his MIMLA students to do group research projects on the cultural issues of doing business in several different countries. Because the members of each group lived in different cities, they conducted all research and communication via the Internet, specifically through MTB (for breakout groups and IBIC databases) and e-mail. The faculty member reported that students felt apprehension at first but that an IBIC presentation made during one of the satellite broadcasts helped allay their fears. The librarian who made the presentation demonstrated how to access and effectively search the databases most useful for this particular project. Additional feedback from faculty indicates that as with students generally, the quality of the research received from students varied based on the amount of effort that they put in to the project.

In the opinion of one of the MIMLA students, the access to information that the IBIC provides allows the students to learn faster and to focus on international business concepts without having to spend too much time searching for information. That is, the IBIC makes the learning process more efficient by putting the right research tools directly into the students' hands. MIMLA students had access to only 9 of the 50 databases available on campus because of licensing restrictions. However, the databases to which they do have access are those which are especially relevant to their research needs (Info LatinoAmerica, ISI Emerging Markets, and ProQuest, to name a few). The students in Mexico also have access to ITESM library resources, which they can access by visiting the local ITESM campus in their city.

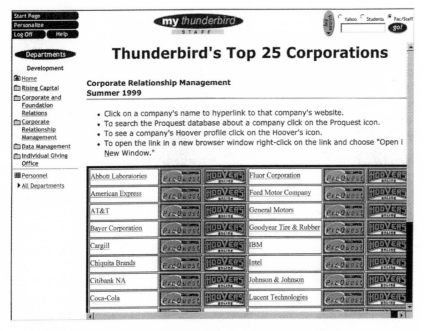

Figure 5. Corporate Relations Management Group
Page Using ProQuest and Hoover's On-line Database

The MIMLA students, all of whom are mature, working professionals, seem to agree that they learn much more from the program than the information that the professors impart in each satellite session. "The virtual learning experience is the future," says one. "We receive knowledge while experiencing real-life [international] business situations around the world. The MIMLA program...prepares you to do the real thing." The success of the MIMLA program, expressed by professors and students alike, has Thunderbird administrators considering this model for other distance education programs around the world. In the meantime, IBIC librarians will continue to locate and evaluate resources that may be used by current students. In addition, they will continue to teach MIMLA students how to access and incorporate information into their unique, international educational program.

CORPORATE RELATIONSHIP MANAGEMENT

Another way Thunderbird uses MTB is for sharing information from library databases among work groups made up of members from different campus units. Because of its ability to admit only specified members of a group, *My Thunderbird* allows people in different locations to have access to information that needs to be available only to a selected number of authorized users. One such project is an effort to organize and coordinate our contacts with the school's corporate partners and clients. These companies may hire Thunderbird graduates, sponsor interns, donate money, fund scholarships, contract with the school for executive education programs or consulting, or use the IBIC's fee-based Business Information Service (BIS) for research and information delivery.

Staff from the various departments involved in these enterprises meet to develop strategies for managing our corporate relationships. Corporate relationship management means specifying what will be developed with or obtained from the company, and creates a focused approach, rather than multiple contacts and requests that might even be in conflict with each other. It also identifies those who are to take responsibility for the goal. Some possible goals that might be set for a relationship with a particular company are that they hire ten of our graduates a year, provide a $25,000 scholarship every year, and/or sponsor five interns plus one group consulting project for an advanced management course.

To succeed, the coordinating group needed a mechanism to track contacts and activity with each company so that each person would know what the other participants were doing. Another need was to be familiar with what the company does and how it works, up-to-date with its activities, and aware of what is happening in its industry. This is accomplished using *My Thunderbird*. IBIC was able to meet the information need for the Corporate Relationship Management group through links to our databases posted in a secure electronic folder. Not only is current information available to all members through computers in individual offices at any time, but it is automatically updated and maintained without staff intervention.

Using 25 companies initially, IBIC created a web page that provided links to specific company information. These included a link to each company's own web page and to company information, including financials, history, competitors, and other background from Hoover's, and current full-text articles from business and management newspapers and journals using the ProQuest database (see Figure 5). The latter can be programmed to search the database regularly to create a bibliography and post new "hits" at the top of the list. By using the web, MTB, and IBIC's databases, information is distributed easily, and once the page is set up, the program becomes effortless on our part. Plans are to expand the list of corporate partners, which librarians can do simply by creating additional links and programming an additional search in ProQuest. Group participants can readily update or refresh their information on a company whenever necessary, check to see who has been in contact with the com-

Foundations| Career Management| Thunderbird A - Z| Library(IBIC)| New Student Home
Thunderbird Home | Orientation Information| Overseas Programs| Foreign Students

Foundations For Global Leadership

Please complete the following readings in preparation for this course.

The staff of the International Business Information Centre (IBIC) at Thunderbird created these "durable links" using a new technology, called SiteBuilder, from UMI. By clicking on a link below, you will be taken directly to the individual article within the ProQuest Direct database.

"Critical success factors for creating superb self-managing teams"
Organizational Dynamics; Summer 1997; Ruth Wageman.

"Developing leaders for the global frontier"
Sloan Management Review; Fall 1998; Hal B Gregersen.

"What makes a leader?"
Harvard Business Review; Nov/Dec 1998; Daniel Goleman.

"The Dark Side of Leadership"
Organizational Dynamics; Autumn 1990; Jay A. Conger.

"The Impact of Type and Level of College Degree on Managerial Communication Competence"
Journal of Education for Business; 73(6):352-357, July 1998; Thaddeus McEwen.

"Speechifying: agony or ecstasy?"
Industry Week; 247(13):22, July 06, 1998;Sal F. Marino.

The IBIC is a high-tech library operated specifically to support your studies at Thunderbird. More than 50 databases, 70,000 books, and 1,600 journals are available. More resources are added each month. These articles are drawn from ABI/INFORM Global, via ProQuest Direct, our premier source of academic business articles. Should you have any difficulty using these links, please contact Wes Edens, Electronic Resources Librarian at the IBIC.

Figure 6. The Readings for New Students in
Thunderbird's Business Foundations Course

pany and what was the result, and log their own activity for other group members. The IBIC was able to provide a new service that enhanced the effectiveness and efficiency of an important campus program.

NEW STUDENT ORIENTATION: THE INFORMATION GAME

The IBIC provides instruction to students on how to find and use information as both a scholastic skill that will help them while they are working on a degree, and a professional skill, which will be an asset to them on the job. A piece of this is accomplished by showing them how to access resources, use databases and the Internet, and *My Thunderbird.* In addition to teaching students to use these specific systems, two other challenges exist for IBIC's instruction program: foreign students rarely arrive with the standard skill set of their American counterparts, and graduate programs provide little opportunity for remedial instruction.

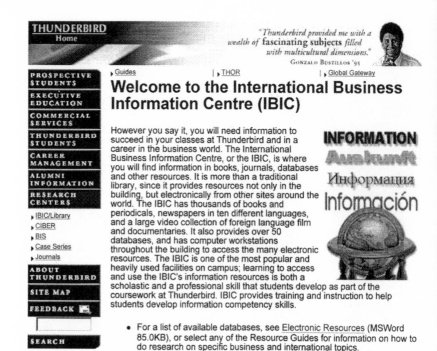

Figure 7. IBIC External Web Page

Library Bibliographic Instruction classes provide special challenges because the cultural, educational, and linguistic backgrounds of the learners are so varied. However, librarians can expect that all Thunderbird students, upon arrival to begin classes, are computer literate, know how to use Microsoft software, and have basic Internet skills (navigating, downloading, and printing.) Many, however, know little about using information databases or finding information resources electronically. Because everyone has some exposure to and knows the Internet platform before they enter Thunderbird, it bridges cultures and learning styles. It is an ideal way to reach new students in the many countries in which they live.

Figure 8. Global Gateway Database, Including the Country Files

At Thunderbird, experience has shown that the ability to cross language and cultural boundaries is enhanced by the incorporation of the technology into the instructional program. The web can, in this situation, deliver general knowledge more effectively than a lecture. For students learning to use English, reading and working at their own pace is easier than listening to a foreign language delivered at the speaker's pace. The option to work at the learner's chosen speed, on an assignment that can be done anywhere with an Internet connection, has real advantages for a library orientation.

To address these unique needs and to help students begin learning to use the IBIC, information competency training begins before the students even arrive.

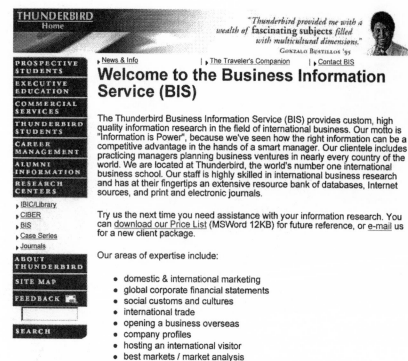

Figure 9.   The Business Information Service Page

Using a transitional technology, a web board, the Internet can carry an emulation of *My Thunderbird* to students, which they use from the time they are accepted until they arrive on campus to enroll. The web board was created to familiarize students with the school and its programs prior to their arrival, thereby easing the transition and adjustment period. The "New Students" link on the School's traditional, open web page is designed specially for incoming students who have not yet set foot on campus. A log-in and password that is sent out in an information packet to the new student limit private access. Before they arrive, the School assigns accepted students to cohort groups and chat rooms with other new students, and a current student who serves as the cohort team leader. To start to prepare them for business courses, business articles are posted, read and discussed electronically. Questions are asked and answered, and personal information and even photos are exchanged electronically. Seeing an opportunity to reach the many new students who literally live all over the world, the IBIC designed an Information Game for this group to do electronically as a bibliographic instruction tool. Using the Internet, students can practice on their own time to gain some of the skills they will need (see Figure 6).

To build the game, IBIC chose a small group of databases, which are available through the New Student web site. All of them are Internet resources or sites freely available on the web, such as IBIC's catalog and web site, the Global Gateway; Hoover's On-line Database and Transium (a full-text marketing journal database.)

The Information Game asks the student a series of five questions, requiring them to perform a typical search in each of the above databases. The students are required to answer a question about their search. The students select from four multiple-choice answers. There is always one correct answer, one answer that is *almost* correct, one answer that is completely wrong and a trick answer, so that the students have to perform the search and cannot just guess to succeed. Once the game is complete the students get results instantly. The game is scored, and the results appear on the web page along with the correct answers to questions that they missed. As the game is played, the information that the students have supplied previously (such as: name, cohort group and Thunderbird admittance date) are recorded for statistical record keeping. The IBIC and the students both know immediately how many have accessed the game, their scores and their entrance information. This allows IBIC to tally the results and collect the data used to tailor the bibliographic instruction to meet students' needs once they arrive on campus. Students are enthusiastic about the Information Game as a learning tool and give it high marks in evaluations of the School's orientation. See Appendix III for a copy of the Information Game.

USE OF THE WORLDWIDE WEB VS. THE CAMPUS INTRANET: OPEN OR RESTRICTED ACCESS

The IBIC also uses traditional web page technology to deliver information to users and to the public through its open architecture on the worldwide web (see Figure 7). These information services supplement and complement those, which are restricted just to Thunderbird students, or those enrolled in a specific class. Two IBIC programs are especially effective using the more open architecture provided by the web. These are the Global Gateway and the Business Information Service.

APPENDIX I.   ILL REQUEST ON-LINE FORM

IBIC INTERLIBRARY LOAN ONLINE BOOK REQUEST FORM

Please read the IBIC Interlibrary Loan policies and copyright notice.
(* means required info)

*NAME John Smith   ***BOX #**   ***PHONE #**

*STATUS Select one   ***DATE**   ***EMAIL** smith@ibic.edu

Item Request

Please check THOR (Thunderbird Online Resources catalog) **first.**

Item is Select one **Material needed by** _(request will be cancelled after this time)_

*BOOK TITLE

AUTHOR

PUBLISHER

EDITION **Need this edition only?** select one

ISBN

MESSAGE

[Submit ILL Request]   [Clear Form]

ILL POLICIES

The International Busienss Information Centre will absorb all reasonable costs (generally not to exceed $10.00) for obtaining your request.

Articles will be delivered by campus mail to the faculty department or campus post office, or may be picked up at the IBIC Circulation Desk if there is a charge (Payment due upon receipt of article.).

You will be contacted to pick up requested books at the IBIC Circulation Desk.

NOTICE: WARNING CONCERNING COPYRIGHT RESTRICTIONS The Copyright Law of the United States (Title 17, U.S. Code) governs the making of photocopies or other reproductions of copyrighted materials. Under certain conditions specified in the law, libraries and archives are authorized to furnish a photocopy or other reproduction. One of these specified conditions is that the photocopy or reproduction is not to be "used for any purpose other than private study, scholarship or research." This institution reserves the right to refuse to accept a copying order if, in its judgment, fulfillment of the order would involve violation of copyright law.

APPENDIX II.   FINE APPEAL ON-LINE FORM

IBIC Fines Appeal Form		
Appeals are normally reviewed every Friday, although a decision may not be made immediately because of the need to investigate the circumstances. The IBIC Director will notify you by e-mail of the outcome. If you are blocked from checking out IBIC materials because of fines, you may request a temporary clearance from the Circulation Supervisor once you have submitted your appeal. The following are not valid reasons to waive fines: • Failure to read e-mail • Ignorance of the fine policy • Inability to pay • Transfer of items to another student for return and their failure to do so • Planned travel that prevented on-time return. There is no provision to excuse the first fine incurred.		
Submitted By:	John Smith	
Email Address:	smith@ibic.edu	
Thunderbird ID #:		
Box #:		
Ammount of Fine:		
Reason for Appeal: Submit Request Clear Request		

THE GLOBAL GATEWAY
www.t-bird.edu/research/ibic/links

One IBIC service provided to the international business community at large is information through the Global Gateway database. Thunderbird student employees, under the guidance of IBIC staff, browse the web in search of sites useful to international business researchers. The sites are carefully evaluated according to accuracy, authority, currency, objectivity, and scope. Sites that pass are entered into a database, available to anyone in the world with Internet access.

The database is structured along the lines of Thunderbird's tripartite program. The main categories are Countries, World Business, International Studies, Modern Languages, News, and Reference. Two more levels of categorization allow users to narrow down a search to World Business/Accounting/Taxes, for instance. Keyword searching is also available.

The Countries category is actually a separate project that was incorporated into the Global Gateway database. Users click on a country, and then can browse the best sites in several subcategories, such as Government, Culture & Language, Companies & Markets, and Education. With the inclusion of the Countries category, users are given the option of searching by geography, rather than subject area (see Figure 8).

Global Gateway is continually updated, in contrast to other web sites that use static, sporadically updated lists of links. Global Gateway uses a live network connection between the IBIC and the database server, and any changes made by IBIC operators are instantaneously reflected in the

APPENDIX III. THE IBIC INFORMATION GAME FOR NEW STUDENTS

Foundations| Career Management| Thunderbird A - Z| Library(IBIC)| New Student Home
Thunderbird Home | Orientation Information| Overseas Programs| Foreign Students

Play the Information Game
The New Student Online Tutorial

Learning to use the IBIC's databases, reference sources and other information resources will not only help you be successful in your classes at Thunderbird, but will give you a professional skill you will use in your career. Knowing how to use research tools will save you time and give you an advantage when you need to find information.

We have picked five resources, available on the Internet, for an exercise to show you some of the kinds of tools you will use as a student. You will be introduced to many more as part of your courses at Thunderbird. Get a headstart with this online tutorial, which will introduce some frequently used research tools and provide an opportunity for you to develop skills in using databases.

> **1- Print this page(or copy the questions)**
> **2- Follow the instructions**
> **3- Use the IBIC Site on the Thunderbird Web page for this exercise**
> **4- Answer THOR**
> **5- Answer five questions**
> **6- Come back to this page and click here to enter your answers**

The five databases demonstrated in this tutorial are:

1- IBIC Online Catalog
2- Global Gateway
3- Northern Light
4- Hoover's
5- Transium Business Intelligence

- **IBIC Online Catalog** - Named for the Norse God of Thunder, THOR also stands for Online Resources and is the gateway to IBIC databases, including the catalog. Use the IBIC catalog to find books, periodicals, videos, and other publications in the IBIC collection.

  Robert Moran is an International Studies professor here at Thunderbird and has written many books about cultures and

APPENDIX III.   CONTINUED

traveling abroad. Do an author search to find the number of books by Professor Moran the IBIC has.

   a. 8
   b. 19
   c. 37
   d. 45

- **Global Gateway -** This is Thunderbird's meta-site for International business information. A meta-site is a website that organizes and categorizes other web pages. These Internet links are maintained by the IBIC Librarians and support the curriculum and needs of faculty, staff, students, and alumni

1. Go to THOR , choose IBIC Websites (the fourth blue box at the top of screen)
2. Do a keyword search for Japan on **Global Gateway Links**

What does JETRO stand for?

   a. Japanese External Trade Organization
   b. Japan Trade Region
   c. Japanese Trade Organization
   d. Japan External Organization

- **Northern Light** - Northern Light is a free Internet site that combines the reach of a World Wide Web search engine with access to 5,300 premium full-text sources previously unavailable except to users of expensive online services like LEXIS-NEXIS, Dow Jones Interactive, and Dialog.

1. Return to THOR, choose IBIC Databases (the fifth blue box at the top of screen)
2. Select Northern Light for Journal and Newspaper Indexes and Articles
3. Do a keyword search for "Mexico and Culture"
4. Choose **"Mexico Online - Mexican Search Engine"** and then choose "Holidays: Official and Religious."

What Mexican holiday occurs on January 6th?

   a. Dia de los San Antonio de Abad
   b. New Years Day
   c. Dia de los Santo Reyes
   d. Christmas

- **Hoover's** - Hoover's is a database to which the IBIC subscribes. A more limited version is available for free through their website. Use Hoover's to search for profiles of companies, their employees, competitors, and

APPENDIX III.   CONTINUED

products. Hoover's covers 11,000 U.S. and foreign companies, both public
and private.

1. Go to THOR
2. Select IBIC Databases (the fifth blue box at the top of screen)
3. Choose **Hoover's** from the "Company Information" databases
4. Do a company name search in toolbox, type: **Swatch**

Who are the top three competitors of this watch company?

     a. Timex/Guess/Fossil
     b. Casio Computer/Citizen Watch/Seiko
     c. Seiko/Swiss Army/Guess
     d. Casio Computer/Guess/Movado

- **Transium Business Intelligence** - Transium Business Intelligence is one
  of the best sites for company research.

1. Return to THOR and choose the Global Gateway
2. Do a search for **"Transium"**
3. Once in the Transium database, do a search for **Walt Disney World**
4. Select **Advertising and Market Research**

How many weddings have been held at WDW to date?

     a. 4,000
     b. 7,000
     c. 10,000
     d. 13,000

This completes the quiz. Go back to the top and click for answers!

product as seen by the public. It also operates with its own search engine,
and conducts searches through a collection of links to produce results,
rather than simply presenting a list.

BUSINESS INFORMATION SERVICE
www.t-bird.edu/BIS

IBIC operates a fee-based information service whose users are the alumni of
the School and other external corporate clients. IBIC promotes and markets the
service in several ways, but the Business Information Service (BIS) web page

represents a major source of new contacts. Those searching for an information broker or research service that specializes in international business are likely to encounter the page on the web. Clients who have used the service may recommend others who then consult the page for prices and a description of what IBIC's librarians can offer through the BIS. The BIS web page is also promoted to participants in Executive Education and other programs as a place to find a currency converter and a time zone converter. While they are using these information tools, the page serves as a reminder about the research service (see Figure 9).

The BIS page is also used to post handouts for courses IBIC librarians teach at alumni seminars and other programs. Instead of paper copies, participants take away with them a web address, which they can access when they return home. It is another way that the IBIC has become a more paperless operation. It is also a mechanism to keep alumni in touch with the School, and create business for the IBIC service.

CONCLUSION

Thunderbird's library has taken advantage of the opportunity offered by the School's intranet to offer users a virtual library with electronic services. Building a virtual library involves many issues, but the foremost is access to the technology that can make it possible. The need for solutions to the many challenges of operating global programs certainly motivated a large investment in technology at Thunderbird. The virtual library is just one outcome from that investment, but without the design and structure provided by MTB, it would not be possible. Besides technology support, some of the other issues include:

- Negotiation of licenses and agreements with vendors for remote access
- Cooperation and teamwork with other campus units, especially IT
- Library Instruction using new methods of delivery to teach the use of a totally electronic resource
- Changing processes, such as the use of forms, for basic services
- Helping faculty design assignments that can be done with available resources
- Developing policies for electronic programs, such as reserves
- Organization and maintenance of electronic collections, such as links on web pages
- Collecting useful data from users to improve systems

While the virtual library on MTB does provide impressive support for programs, books are not available electronically yet, and when a book is the only answer to an information need, it still has be handled in a traditional way. Having access to a system such as MTB, on the other hand, has allowed librarians to deliver many improvements, and reach users whose information needs were not previously addressed. The appeal of easy access to resources has brought new users, such as the fund-raising and development staff, to the IBIC.

With students and faculty involved in learning projects all around the world, *My Thunderbird* provides distributed and remote access to many kinds of traditional library resources. Off-campus students and faculty can now access services and resources that previously they would only have by coming to the IBIC, and the redesign of many services to suit a virtual environment improves on the traditional model. By using technology, Thunderbird has overcome the problems created by distance and some of the multicultural differences in learning.

ACKNOWLEDGMENT

The authors would like to acknowledge the contribution to this article made by Joseph S. McVicker, Director of Application Development in I&IT at Thunderbird, and the creator of *My Thunderbird*.

THE ELECTRONIC GLOBAL LIBRARY OF JONES INTERNATIONAL UNIVERSITY

Kim Dority and Martin Garnar

INTRODUCTION

Jones International University (JIU) was established by Glenn R. Jones in 1993 to provide Internet-delivered, undergraduate and graduate-level courses leading to a Bachelor's or Master's degree in Business Communication. Accredited by the North Central Association of Colleges and Schools (NCA) in March 1999, JIU was designed to meet the needs of students for whom pursuing an education within the traditional higher education structure simply was not feasible.

JIU students are, for the most part, working adults whose time and scheduling constraints make it difficult if not impossible for them to consider pursuing an "on-campus" degree. They are motivated, self-directed learners comfortable with information technology and electronic communications. As part of the requirements for enrolling at JIU, all students have access to computers that support high-speed data exchange (an extremely important consideration in designing access to the library's electronic resources).

During the planning stages for the development of JIU, the advisory board reiterated its commitment to developing an electronic library that would both mirror

Advances in Library Administration and Organization, Volume 17, pages 93-107.

the activities of a campus-based academic library and promote information literacy as a means of supporting lifelong learning. In addition, the library would follow the revised 1998 *ACRL Guidelines for Extended Campus Library Services* to ensure conformity with accepted academic standards.

These guidelines, which stipulate the standards to which libraries for extended campus programs should adhere, were based on the following stated assumption:

> Library resources and services in institutions of higher education must meet the needs of all their faculty, students, and academic support staff, wherever these individuals are located, whether on a main campus, off campus, in distance education or extended campus programs, or in the absence of a campus at all; in courses taken for credit or noncredit; in continuing education programs; in courses attended in person or by means of electronic transmission; or any other means of distance education (ACRL 1998).

The Jones International library, officially named the Electronic Global Library (E-Global Library), was designed to adhere to the various standards identified by ACRL's Extended Campus Library Services Division either immediately or as part of its developmental design. The intent in establishing the electronic library was to provide JIU's students with library services that not only supported their immediate course learning and research needs, but also provided opportunities for further academic and intellectual exploration. The goal was to mirror as closely as possible the best attributes of an on-campus academic library.

DESIGNING CORE SERVICES

Working with several academic librarians, JIU identified five core services provided to students in traditional academic libraries. These were:

> Bibliographic instruction
> Reference and research
> Document delivery
> Interlibrary loan
> Electronic database searching

For each of these services, JIU created a process or program to meet its students' reference and research needs. Following is an overview of how the E-Global Library service was structured to support JIU students.

Bibliographic Instruction

Teaching students both how to use the library's various information resources (indexes, directories, catalogs, on-line databases, etc.) and acquainting them with the specialized subject resources is a key element in the support of independent learners. However, many students not only do not know how to use a library, they are also too embarrassed or intimidated to ask for help.

"Libraries 101" offers students an opportunity to learn all about libraries in an easy, nonintimidating manner. This section of the E-Global Library explains how libraries (both public and academic) are organized, what types of reference and research materials are available and what each is best for, how to frame a question or a research project, and other topics key to using any library effectively. Knowing that remote students occasionally turn to their local public or academic libraries for research needs, "Libraries 101" also discusses how to most courteously and effectively work with their local library. (Understanding the challenge remote students can pose to local librarians, this section stresses realistic expectations, the responsibilities of the student, and the existing priorities of the librarian.)

Reference

On-campus students regularly turn to the library's resources to answer simple questions using ready-reference sources such as almanacs, directories, encyclopedias, or statistics sources. In addition, they may need the reference librarian to help get them started with a research project, direct them toward an appropriate reference tool, or assist them in tracking down an obscure citation. To mirror these activities, the E-Global Library used a two-pronged approach to deliver the reference component of its global library.

First, it created an annotated, Internet-based reference collection comprising more than 500 academic-caliber sites organized by topic and/or format within forty academic disciplines. These sites are grouped within four broad areas: general reference, the social sciences, the humanities, and science and technology. The key points in evaluating potential additions to the collection were academic-level content; completeness, correctness, and objectivity of content; authority and/or subject expertise of the site's author/editor; currency; reliability of host organization; and usefulness to JIU courses of study.

As reference expert Jim Rettig (1996) has pointed out, however, evaluating web sites can quickly become a pretty complex job. In the print world, librarians have traditionally used several key criteria to evaluate reference books before deciding whether to add them to their collections. These criteria focus primarily on questions of content: comprehensiveness, correctness and currency of information, objectivity and lack of bias, the usefulness of supplementary materials such as charts, graphics, or appendices. An important consideration in this evaluation process is the author's subject expertise and authority and the publisher's credibility and reputation. In addition, we look at how effectively the reader can access the information: is there a detailed, well-organized index, are there thoughtful cross-references, can the reader locate information by subject terms as well as by, for example, titles or names of individuals? In the print world, each of these elements is usually readily identifiable and easily evaluated.

The Internet rarely affords such concrete opportunities for analysis. In fact, the Internet reference environment presents overwhelming challenges at an even more basic level: how do librarians find the reference tools that exist on the Internet when the existing tools to do so are so primitive? The language of print reference tools is unreliable on the Internet.

For example, rather than providing the rich and authoritative compendium of topical articles one would expect from a print-based encyclopedia, an Internet site calling itself an "encyclopedia" is frequently simply an extensive, unannotated set of links to other topical sites. An Internet "guide" is often the same thing. "Dictionaries" may be a hobbyist's collection of self-created topical definitions, "handbooks" an advocacy group's editorialized compendium of information. Search engines cannot make these distinctions, so are useless in locating credible research tools among millions of web sites found on the Internet.

Fortunately, many professional and academic groups have attempted to identify and evaluate these sites, and it is from these authoritative sources that the E-Global Library has developed its core reference collection. These sources include, but are not limited to:

> Argus Clearinghouse
> BUBL (Bulletin Board for Librarians)
> C&RL NewsNet Internet Resources
> E-Blast
> Infomine
> Internet Public Library
> Librarian's Index to the Internet
> Michigan Electronic Library (MEL)
> Mining Company
> Rettig on Reference
> Scout Report

Based on the recommendations of these sources, print evaluative tools like *Choice*, *Library Journal*, and *College & Research Libraries News*, and extensive exploration of specialized gateway directories, the E-Global Library evaluated more than 3,000 potential reference sites. Of these, approximately 600 have been selected for inclusion in the virtual library reference collection. This core collection is continually monitored, updated, and expanded to reflect the growing digital content emerging as Internet-based resources.

In addition to the core reference library, the E-Global Library also created topical pathfinders of both print and Internet-based reference material for the three areas of emphasis for IU students: business, communications, and business communications. These are part of the library's web site, and, like the core collection, are continuously updated to ensure currency.

The core reference collection is anchored by the key subscription-based electronic resources familiar to academic librarians. These include, among others, the on-line version of Encyclopaedia Britannica and the Galenet publications: Associations Unlimited, Biography and Genealogy Master Index, Gale Business Resources, Gale Database of Publications and Broadcast Media, and Research Centers and Service Directories.

Second, the E-Global Library contracted with an experienced academic librarian to provide e-mail based reference and research assistance to its students. At this point, JIU has found that given the relatively small number of students it has, one librarian is able to respond quickly to student inquiries with relative ease. However, as JIU student numbers grow, the E-Global Library will work closely with its on-call librarian to add reference staff as necessary.

Document Delivery

Because many remote students cite time constraints as one of the most challenging aspects of taking college courses, it was imperative that JIU students be able to obtain copies of important articles as quickly as possible. Fortunately, there are several excellent alternatives for accomplishing this. Three are Internet-based, the fourth draws on the resources of a nationally known, highly successful provider of information services.

The Internet-based solutions are UnCoverWeb, the database of more than 7,000,000 articles drawn from 17,000 multidisciplinary journals; Northern Light, an on-line business library composed of 5,400 full-text journals, books, magazines, newswires, and reference sources; and ArticleFirst, the OCLC periodical index of 5.5 million articles drawn from 13,000 journals. UnCoverWeb will fax the full text of any of its articles for fees ranging from $10 to $20, with 24-hour turn-around, while Northern Light and Article First will fax or e-mail articles for a similar fee.

For articles not found within the UnCoverWeb database (but identified through other resources), JIU students are able to request document delivery from CTRC, a University of Colorado-based information vendor with whom the E-Global Library has established a relationship. The delivery cost for CTRC article delivery is similar to that of UnCoverWeb's, with a turn-around time of one to three days.

Interlibrary Loan

Although many students (and instructors) prefer the currency of articles for their course research needs, occasionally a need will arise for a document or book not readily available through a JIU student's local resources. To address this situation, the E-Global Library has arranged with CTRC to process its student requests for interlibrary loan. In general, turn-around time will be similar to that experienced with on-campus ILL requests, although CTRC can ship books via more expensive (faster) methods if the student so requests and is willing to absorb the cost.

Electronic Database Searching

A primary component of student research in most academic institutions today is electronic database searching. The E-Global Library consulted with several academic librarians, reviewed the databases provided by numerous colleges and universities, and met with the database expert at BCR, a library service provider and purchasing consortium, to determine which databases would be the most useful for its students. Based on these evaluations, the E-Global Library assembled a collection of research databases that it believes offers both breadth and depth of information. This database core collection includes, but is not limited to:

ComAbstracts
OCLC First Search (WorldCat, ArticleFirst, Contents First, FastDoc, PapersFirst, Proceedings, ERIC, GPO Monthly Catalog, MEDLINE, UMI Periodical Abstracts, and UMI ABI/Inform Abstracts)
The basic Wilson abstracts
Hoovers and General Business File ASAP

In addition, the E-Global Library is currently evaluating several other databases, such as Dissertation Abstracts, Ethnic Newswatch, and Humanities Abstracts, that would be available as part of an expanded First Search package.

JIU believes that by providing its students the library services and research capability described above, it will ensure them the opportunity to move beyond the elements of the course outline into the broader expanse of intellectual exploration.

Teaching Students to Fish

Future plans for the E-Global Library focus not only on expanding the resource base but also (and perhaps even more importantly) expanding the tutorial content available at the library site. We are committed to offering an extensive on-line bibliographic instruction component because we believe that the ability to effectively and knowledgeably use information resources—especially electronic resources—is a key factor in being able to succeed as lifelong learners.

Admittedly, this "teach the student to fish" approach is not one uniformly agreed-upon by distance education librarians. Although a recent survey of the impact of electronic reference resources on academic librarians found an increase in librarians' instructional role, "with more librarians assuming the role of teacher/trainer" (Tenopir and Ennis 1998), distance learners present a somewhat more complex challenge.

Time constrained, juggling multiple roles and personal responsibilities, many if not most distance education students have not used an academic library for years and have little experience with the new electronic resources. Kirk and Bartelstein (1999) note in their overview of distance education and academic libraries that "these returning students, while highly motivated and self-directed, may be insecure about their library skills or lack experience using new technologies."

In fact, some students may be highly resistant to librarians' efforts to promote information "self-sufficiency." Goodson (1997) suggests that this is not necessarily a bad thing:

> I now think that the services we provided to off-campus students are precisely what the majority of users really want and what we ought to be offering them. In other words, not only is distance education the model for higher education in the next millennium, but the kinds of library support services often supplied to off-campus students can and should be the prototype for future library services as well. Research services customized to users' real needs are going to become the norm, rather than the exception, and librarianship as a profession will not survive unless we wake up and recognize that the era in which we could get away with insisting that customers come to our building in order to get our product (not to mention, do it all by themselves!) is nearly over. If we delude ourselves about this much longer, I am certain that people will start finding ways to get their information needs met by others who are more accommodating than we have traditionally been.

Thus the job of teaching these students how to use the wealth of electronic resources literally at their fingertips becomes not just how to, but *whether* to. The E-Global Library response will be to develop the most effective tutorial materials we can, encourage and assist the students with their use, and then move into "provider of information" mode when necessary. The goal will be to help students learn the six core information literacy competencies identified by Lindauer (1998): (1) develop effective search strategies, (2) locate and retrieve information sources, (3) analyze and critically evaluate information, (4) organize and synthesize information, (5) use/apply information, and (6) create awareness and attitude formation about information and information technology.

If the goal is information literacy, the challenge will be instructional methodologies. The learning styles of adult learners differ from those of traditional college-age students, and any on-line bibliographic or research instruction will need to take those differences into consideration. At the same time, however, the electronic surround offers a multitude of possibilities for creating interactive, linked learning components that will enable students to learn in a manner that best suits their particular learning style. Although currently the E-Global Library has a content-rich bibliographic instruction component, the developmental goal for the coming year is to develop the main BI component into a much more extensive, interactive, hypertext module that will be designed to connect with the special learning characteristics of adult students.

We will be closely monitoring not only student usage of the research tools themselves versus their reliance on the E-Global Library librarian to provide relevant information but also their *attitudes* about information self-sufficiency. Also, given convenient on-line access to both electronic database resources and a strong, subject-organized collection of content-rich Internet sites, which will students choose to use?

According to a 1998 survey by the UCLA Higher Education Research Institute (www.uclanews.ucla.edu/Docs/KC010.html), "82.9 percent of new freshman—more than four out of five students—are using the Internet for research or homework."And these were not distance education students, but traditional students with access to an on-campus academic library! If this trend continues to grow, as most of us assume it will, then perhaps our Internet-focused information literacy efforts will need to greatly increase relative to other types of bibliographic instruction.

What About "Victim" Libraries?

It has been the policy of the E-Global Library to "cover all the bases" for its students through its various services, and thus there should be little if any need for JIU students to turn to their local public libraries for research or reference assistance. We provide interlibrary loan and document delivery services through a national vendor, and our on-call librarian responds quickly to any questions students have.

Whenever we mention public libraries (especially in the "How Libraries Work" section of Libraries 101), we have emphasized that their public libraries, although staffed by knowledgeable and helpful professionals, are not specifically designed to respond to distance learners' needs, and therefore any requests for assistance should take this into consideration. We note staffing, resource, and budget constraints, encourage students to respect the librarians' multiple responsibilities, and emphasize the appropriate etiquette involved in asking for assistance from a local public library.

Generally speaking, we do not discourage students from using the local public library because we do not want to create a negative image of them for our students. We attempt instead to offset any need to visit the local library by having all the resources available through the E-Global Library, in order to minimize the impact of our students on their community libraries. We have been very careful to avoid the relationship described so well by Dugan (1997) as "provider and victim libraries," wherein local public and academic libraries bear the brunt of supporting students enrolled in courses provided by remote universities.

Other models exist for remote-campus/local library relationships. In some cases, a college or university with an off-site, but geographically based, degree program may partner with a local public library to provide library services to its students. Britton and Combe (1991) have described such a partnership between the University of Southern California and the Ventura County Library system, which entailed relying on the reference and BI capabilities of the local staff but also supplementing the local collection with books and journal subscriptions appropriate to the university's curriculum. In another approach, Central Michigan University developed a research-methods course module to be undertaken at public libraries located near off-campus CMU class sites (Collier 1991). In this case, CMU librarians traveled to present BI sessions on-site at the local libraries.

In another instance, Denver, Colorado-based Regis University established a cooperative agreement with the Loveland (CO) Public Library to serve as a remote "academic library" for the Regis program delivered to Loveland students, some 75 miles north of the Regis campus (Scrimgeour and Potter 1991; Schmidt 1995). This model included training of public library staff by academic librarians in the use of the Regis library catalog and ILL policies, plus financial support from the Regis library and from grants to increase the holdings in specific subject areas relevant to the off-campus Regis students.

Also, in an especially innovative partnership, the Palm Springs, California public library decided to create a "university" by hosting a virtual university via video conferencing technology and courses from various institutions within the California state higher education system (Levinson 1998). Equipment costs were paid primarily through an LSTA grant supplemented by private foundation and corporate sources.

These and other similar models bring into question the role that public libraries *might* play and the role they *want* to play in engaging with/supporting distance learners: is this an opportunity or a threat, or perhaps both depending on funding and staffing issues? We have sought to minimize the impact of our students on their local public libraries, but is this a good thing in the long run?

As the original peoples' universities, local public libraries could function as key learning coaches for distance education students, but do they want to? Do we want to encourage students to become independent of public libraries or see them as a welcoming community resource? If the goal in an expanding universe of end-user searching is to ensure that the local public library does not become marginalized, what better way to do so than to involve them as key resources in the career-driven lifelong learning goals of the community's adults? We will continue to explore this issue with public library professionals, as well as closely monitoring the extent and impact of JIU students' use of their local public libraries.

DIGITAL CONTENT GROWTH

Headlines, journal articles, conference presentations, an onslaught of company announcements—all make it clear that the digital library in its various iterations is continuing to grow in both technological sophistication and the range of its content offerings. As librarians grapple with the effect a digital future will have on traditional service and staffing assumptions, the number of vendors and nonprofit content suppliers joining the fray continues to grow.

Harvard Business School Publishing and Harvard Business Review have recently announced the availability of 3,200 case studies and 1,000 reprint articles on-line for a fee through a vendor of distance education support services. Octavo (www.octavo.com), the creation of Adobe CEO John Warnock, is digitizing rare books such as Newton's 1704 *Opticks* and Robert Hooke's *Micrographia* to provide fully searchable scholarly content with links to translations and other related material on the Internet. And by now, all librarians are familiar with such excellent and ground-breaking resources as Project Gutenberg, the University of Virginia's Jefferson collection, and the National Digital Library initiative coming out of the Library of Congress.

In addition, Boulder, Colorado-based netLibrary has begun offering academic libraries an opportunity to provide students with copyright-controlled digital "copies" of originally print-based monographs, including textbooks, reference books, and scholarly works, likely to be found in a core academic library collection. Representing content from publishers such as Cambridge University Press, Oxford University Press, MIT Press, University of California Press, ABC-CLIO, Libraries Unlimited, Facts on File and O'Reilly & Associates, netLibrary currently offers about 2,000 titles but has indicated at several recent professional conferences that it intends to be close to 20,000 titles within a year.

Similar efforts to provide digitized, on-line periodical content for students are also being developed through initiatives like JSTOR's retrospective collection (Journal Storage Project; jstor-info@umich.edu) and California's JACC initiative (http://www.co.calstate.edu/irt/seir/), aimed at getting publishers and vendors to provide the California State University system libraries with a database of core titles plus titles customized to the individualized curriculums of each campus.

At the same time, publishers are slowly beginning to explore digitization options themselves, investigating ways to structure "downstream" to port directly into an electronic format. Although issues such as copyright, multiplatform interoperability, and searchability options will need to be addressed, industry analyst Mike Shatzkin (1999) recently noted "There is no doubt that digital technology changes the way publishers and booksellers handle their most basic business process, but the most profound changes ditigal technology will create may be in the marketplace itself." And, we might add, in the libraries of tomorrow.

The result of these and similar efforts and initiatives will be to provide an ever-increasing amount of scholarly content in electronic format that students will be able to access via computer, regardless of whether or not they are sitting in the campus library. For distance-education libraries based primarily on electronic resources, as is the E-Global Library, as well as for traditional academic libraries supporting off-campus students, this trend will mean that more and more content can be made immediately, conveniently accessible to students regardless of time of day or geographic location.

THE RESEARCH AGENDA

Because it will be based primarily on electronic rather than print resources, the E-Global Library will be carefully monitoring the impact of this new model on its students and their learning outcomes. Our goal is to help develop a broader understanding of college students who are distance-based adult learners, and how libraries can most effectively support their reference, research, and learning requirements. There are many important questions related to this issue, including:

- What are the most effective ways to provide successful on-line bibliographic instruction? Is there information that we can gather from other disciplines, for example, media psychology or adult learning methodologies, that will help us craft highly effective solutions?
- How much do distance learners use their local public libraries for assistance? If there is sustained or more than occasional use, what financial models need to be considered to produce an equitable relationship with the local public library?
- What are distance and/or adult learners' attitudes about their local libraries? Do they view them as an important resource in their personal and professional lives, and if not, are there way to encourage this outcome, and would that be desirable for the public libraries?
- If content digitization continues to grow as an option, for example in the work that netLibrary is doing, what will those financial models look like?
- What impact will the Digital Millennium Copyright Act (http://lcweb.loc.gov/copyright/disted) have not just on student access to electronic materials but also on how those materials are read, downloaded, printed, or otherwise manipulated?
- Can e-mail reference service be as responsive to students' needs as face-to-face? Do distance and anonymity diffuse the intimidation factor so many adult learners face in an on-campus library?
- Will distance learners use books for research if they are easily (but not immediately) available, or will they instead opt for the immediacy of whatever electronic resources are available on-line?
- At what times of the day and week are distance learners doing their research? Anecdotal evidence has indicated that midnight Sunday night is a favorite time, but can we determine this information more specifically? This may influence, for example, how many hours a day/week an on-call (via e-mail) librarian needs to be available to help.
- How often are students willing to move beyond the packaged set of information resources provided in the course pack (or now, more than likely, electronic reserves) to investigate a concept or subject further? Are there steps that we can take to encourage this?

- Are distance education faculty more or less cognizant and supportive of the key role the electronic library should play in their course design and presentation?
- What impact will initiatives such as OCLC's NetFirst have on distance-education library support? Will tools geared toward the needs and expectations of librarians be sufficiently user-friendly to work for distance learners as well?
- What partnerships can be explored among vendors, reference and research content developers, and other distance-education providers that will provide the most expansive access to electronic resources possible?
- What roles for librarians will be most effective and useful to students in the distance-learning environment? Coach/facilitator or information provider? High tech or high touch? Academic research tool or lifelong-learning information source? Perhaps equally important, what combination of these roles will draw new professionals into our field?

We believe these are all questions that will be of increasing importance to both the field of distance education and to academic librarianship as a profession, and we look forward to participating in the research initiatives they will necessitate. Answering these questions will enable library schools to do a more informed job of, as Kascus (1997) has suggested, "educating the next generation of librarians, who must be computer literate and sensitized to the special needs of off-campus/ distant learners." Reflecting the realities that Goodson has noted, Kascus further points out that "the curriculum of tomorrow's library schools will need to reflect a new philosophy of service that is user-oriented rather than library-oriented."

THE FUTURE OF DISTANCE EDUCATION

Once considered a poor cousin to traditional, campus-based education, distance education has now become what economists call a "disruptive technology," one that makes us re-think all our assumptions about how we do what we do and, equally important, *why* we do it. It is having the same impact on those academic libraries expected to support their institutions' remote students.

Questions quickly arise about resource allocation, staffing priorities, budget conflicts, and the institution's commitment to supporting the reference and research needs of its distance learners. But new answers are now developing for those critical questions, answers enabled by the growing sophistication of our information and communications technologies. New interactive software, telecommunications options, authoring technologies, electronic publications, Internet-based reference sites, and other education-based services—as these tools are delivered to us, we will need to explore further and faster how to utilize them most effectively for our students.

The "faster" part will become increasingly critical, as distance education continues to grow exponentially and internationally. Although management guru Peter Drucker has gained notoriety among the higher education community for his statements regarding the inevitable demise of traditional higher education, at about the same time he also noted in a *Forbes* article that "the future is outside the traditional campus, outside the traditional classroom. Distance learning is coming on fast" (Gubernick and Eberling 1997).

Statistics bear him out. Experts predict that the number of students enrolled in Internet-based courses will grow from roughly 700,000 in 1998 to an astounding 2 million-plus in 2002 (*Distance Education Report* 1999). Experts predict that up to 50 percent of the enrollments in higher education may be on-line learners by the year 2007 (Kascus 1994).

The growth in the number of higher education institutions that are becoming or intend to become distance education providers is equally stunning: while in 1995 only one-third of American higher education institutions offered courses via distance education, the American Council on Education estimated that by 1998 some 85 percent of "traditional" colleges and universities were either offering or intended to soon offer distance-accessible courses (Kirk and Bartelstein 1999). Furthermore, the latest edition of *Peterson's Guide to Distance Learning Programs 1999*, published in cooperation with the University Continuing Education Association, notes that although there were fewer than 100 institutional listings in its initial 1995 publication, the recent edition includes programs from 850.

The distance education arena reflects a wide diversity of institutions and degree programs, including:

- Stanford University's on-line master's degree program in electrical engineering,
- San Jose State University's School of Library and Information Science,
- University of Illinois at Urbana-Champaign's Master of Science in Library and Information Science,
- UCLA Extension's on-line offering of its more than 100 renowned continuing higher education courses, and
- the Internet-based MBAs of Syracuse University, Duke, Auburn, Case Western Reserve University, Colorado State University, Oklahoma State University, Ohio University, North Carolina State University, Regis University (Denver), and Jones International University.

In addition, state and regional governing bodies are also stepping into the Internet-based degree fray. The New Jersey Virtual University (www.njvu.org), the 18-state Western Governors' University (http://www.wgu.edu), the Southern Regional Electronic Campus (http://www.srec.sreb.org/), and the State University of New York's SUNY Learning Network (http://www.sln1.suny.edu/sln) are but a few of the most notable initiatives underway.

Even corporations, whose primary focus is likely to be on industries entirely unrelated to education, are starting their own "corporate universities." With some 400 corporate universities in the early 1980s, the number of "company colleges" has now jumped to 1,600, including 40 percent of Fortune 500 companies. According to Jeanne Meister, president of Corporate Universities Exchange, if the current growth rate continues, the number of corporate universities will exceed the number of traditional universities by the year 2010, if not sooner (Denning 1999). And that does not even count publishers like McGraw-Hill, Simon & Schuster, and Harcourt Brace who are now exploring ways to turn book "content" into on-line courseware. Where do libraries fit into this picture?

THE LIBRARY ON THE HORIZON

Until fairly recently, on-campus librarians responsible for working with off-campus students have often had difficulty convincing university administration and state legislators that they *do* fit into the picture. The needs among distance education students for research advice, bibliographic instruction, faxed materials, and expedited interlibrary loan service have often been expected to simply be incorporated into the ongoing workflow of the existing staff and resources (Kascus 1994; Stephens and Unwin 1997; Guernsey 1999).

The E-Global Library, on the other hand, was designed to support the learning expectations and outcomes of Jones International University students, *all* of whom are "off-campus." Consequently, all staff and resource funds were dedicated to delivering electronic library services remotely as their primary purpose. In addition, from its inception, E-Global Library has been seen not as an afterthought to the JIU learning experience but as critical to it. Its electronic resources reflect the Internet-based course curriculum and are intended to enable JIU students to move beyond the course reserve readings into the broader arena of intellectual exploration.

Like all academic libraries, the E-Global Library will continually revisit collection development issues, the effectiveness of its bibliographic instruction modules, the convenience and speed of its document delivery and interlibrary loan procedures, and the "user-friendliness" and success of its on-call reference system. We look forward to continuing to expand, enhance, and improve each of these services in response to new technological capabilities, new digitized content options, and most importantly, new knowledge of how adult and distance learners use information resources.

Throughout this learning process, we hope to work with other distance education providers to unabashedly promote where *we think* libraries fit into this picture. For Jones International University, the E-Global Library is a vital component in the lifelong learning commitment articulated in the JIU mission. A member of the Library of Congress's Madison Council, JIU founder Glenn R.

Jones has always believed that learning is about individual exploration and that libraries, the original people's universities, are how that exploration happens.

Consequently, whether that library on the horizon is print-based, electronic, or a wonderfully innovative combination of the two, we believe that it will be the most important companion to tomorrow's lifelong learners.

REFERENCES

Association of College and Research Libraries, Distance Learning Section. 1998. "ACRL Guidelines for Extended Campus Library Services the Final Version, Approved July 1998." *College & Research Libraries News* 59(9): 689-694. (Also available at: http://www.ala.org/acrl/guides/distlrng.html)

Britton, R. and D.B. Combe. 1991. "Providing Off-Campus Library Service Using Academic/Public Library Cooperation and Remote Access to Sophisticated Online Systems." *The Fifth Off-Campus Library Services Conference Proceedings*: 55-63.

Collier, M.H. 1991. "Bibliographic Instruction of Off-Campus Students Using Local Area Libraries." *The Fifth Off-Campus Library Services Conference Proceedings*: 69-72.

Denning, P.J. 1999. "Teaching as a Social Process." *Educom Review* 34(3): 18-22.

Distance Education Report. 1999. "Distance Education Will Keep Growing," 2(4): 8. [www.uclanews.ucla.edu/Docs/KC010.html, cited in *Distance Education Report*, Mar 1998]

Dugan, R.E. 1997. "Distance Education: Provider and Victim Libraries." *The Journal of Academic Librarianship* 23(July): 315-318.

Goodson, C. 1997. "I Have Seen the Future, and It is Us!" *The Journal of Library Services for Distance Education* 1(1), p. 2. (http://www.westga.edu/library/jlsde/vol1/1/CGoodson.html)

Gubernick, L. and A. Ebeling. 1997. "I Got My Degree through E-Mail." *Forbes* 156(2): 84-90.

Guernsey, L. 1999. "College Librarians Plan for Floods of Digital Users." *The Chronicle of Higher Education* 45(11): A28.

Kascus, M. 1994. "What Library Schools Teach about Library Support to Distance Students: A Survey." *American Journal of Distance Education* 8(1): 20-35.

_____. 1997. "Converging Vision of Library Service for Off-Campus/Distance Education." *The Journal of Library Services for Distance Education* 1(1), p. 2. (http://www.westga.edu/library/jlsde)

Kirk, E.E. and A.M. Bartelstein. 1999. "Libraries Close in on Distance Education." *Library Journal* 124(6): 40-42.

Levinson, M. 1998. "Creating a Muniversity: Palm Springs Goes Virtual." *American Libraries* 29(7): 66, 68.

Oberman, C., B.G. Lindauer and B. Wilson. 1998. "Integrating Information Literacy into the Curriculum." *College and Research Libraries News* 59(5): 347-352.

Rettig, J. 1996. "Beyond 'Cool': Analog Models for Reviewing Digital Resources." *Online* 20(5): 52-62.

Schmidt, T. 1995. "Extended Campus Library Services: A Loveland Perspective." *Colorado Libraries* (Spring): 20-21.

Scrimgeour, A.D. and S. Potter. 1991. "The Tie That Binds: The Role and Evolution of Contracts in Interlibrary Cooperation." *The Fifth Off-Campus Library Services Conference Proceedings*: 241-254.

Shatzkin, M. 1999. "Fasten Your High-Tech Seatbelts." *Publisher's Weekly* 246(21): 28-31.

Stephens, K. and L. Unwin. 1997. "The Heart of the Matter: Libraries, Distance Education, and Independent Thinking." *The Journal of Library Services for Distance Education* 1(1), p. 2. (http://www.westga.edu/library/jlsde)

Tenopir, C. and L. Ennis. 1998. "The Impact of Digital Reference on Librarians and Library Users." *Online* 22(6): 84-88.

SENSEMAKING AND
NETWORKED INFORMATION

Mary Lynn Rice-Lively

The task of social science is to make sense out of the senses we make out of life.
—(Carey 1988, p. 44)

INTRODUCTION

Innovations in communication and information services enable the creation of new interactive and information-dense environments. The increased use of tele-communication innovations for communication, information transfer, and peda-gogical purposes mandates systematic research to understand these environments from the perspective of the user. The purpose of this paper is to: (1) explore the interactively complex networked learning environment, (2) identify social sense-making interactions among one group of networked information users, and (3) consider the implications of these observations for networked libraries. The data informing this exploration came from an ethnographic study conducted during the fall of 1995 where the study participants came from two university classes sepa-rated by hundreds of miles, but joined by the technologies of interactive, video teleconferencing and the Internet.

Advances in Library Administration and Organization, Volume 17, pages 109-153.
Copyright © 2000 by JAI Press Inc.
All rights of reproduction in any form reserved.
ISBN: 0-7623-0647-5

A Social and Technological Context

The convergence of telecommunication, information, and media-based technologies provides both the opportunity and a mandate to develop alternative approaches to the study of human information use and sensemaking behavior. As telecomputing options increase "the concept of the library as a corporeal place" to some may recede in importance (LaGuardia 1998, p. viii). What happens to the library's role as a physical place where social interaction has contributed to individual user's "sensemaking?" Clearly, new visualization and communication tools have broadened technological options for information seeking and communication. Nonetheless, these tools may also create barriers to individual and group social interaction and sensemaking. Do such barriers increase with each application of telecommunication technology, as Weick (1985) and others proposed? For example, teleconferencing, e-mail, web sites, remotely accessible full-text databases are all ways to communicate and distribute information. This paper considers the conceptual foundations for social sensemaking as well as reflects on the experiences of a class of networked learners where events and social interactions were systematically observed and documented.

Social interaction, as it is used here, is a situation where one's behaviors influenced the behaviors of others and vice versa. Social interaction may also include related sequences of nonverbal signals and verbal utterances. Through social interaction and social cognition individuals "construct *meaning*" by exchanging ideas, beliefs, and attitudes and by asking questions, arguing, and elaborating on others' ideas (Resnick 1991). Consider for a moment, how the users of networked library information bridge their gaps in understanding and experience to learn to interact effectively using networked technologies? For example, the unpredictable nature of on-line connections often challenges the frustrated networker to puzzle about why a connection cannot be made or what a cryptic message means that appears on their computer screen when a search fails. Is the problem due to the configuration of their personal equipment? Is there trouble at the network level, or is there an error in their search strategy? Unpredictable and, sometimes, inexplicable connections and messages often confuse both the experienced and inexperienced networker. Where does the user go to construct meaning from these events?

The push for use of new technologies coupled with diminished financial resources challenges educators, library and information service providers, and administrators to conduct use-centered studies before implementing networked information systems. During the January 1999 Midwinter conference of the American Library Association the LITA (Library Information Technology Association) Board established a task force with the charge to explore top technology trends in libraries. Among these trends are library users who through their web browsers "expect customization, interactivity, and customer support...Approaches that are library-focused instead of user-focused will be increasingly irrelevant." Another trend is "to put a human face on the virtual library" (see http://www.lita.org/com-mittee/toptech/trendsmw99.htm). On university and college campuses academic computing centers struggle to equip university campuses with fast, broadband networks. Organizations seek to allocate human and financial resources to provide faculty, staff, and students with training and equipment to use and access to networked high end computers and software. Faculty redesign curriculum and adapt teaching styles to appropriately integrate effective use of new technology into teaching and learning activities. Libraries wrestle with the migration of OPACs (on-line public access catalog) and local CD-ROM networks to web-based hypertext information. Systematic user-centered study of these transitions can contribute to focused planning and implementation of networked communication and learning systems informed by the perspective of the computer or network user.

Before proceeding, however, attention must be given to language as it is used here. Certain commonly used words are problematic, because they have meanings that "float at the edge of awareness" (Agar 1994, p. 20). In this paper the potentially problematic, although familiar, words are *culture*, *meaning*, *sense*, and *information*.

Making Sense of Familiar Words

Words, as well as things, can become so familiar that we no longer see them at all. The following examination of the words, *culture*, *meaning*, *sense*, and *information* seeks to move beyond the familiarity of the terms and establish a common interpretation through a brief consideration of each word's origins and usages. The first term to be explored is the foundation for an ethnographic, interpretive common ground, *culture*.

Culture

Culture is a complex construct with current interpretation of the concept drawing from its Latin roots, *cultura*, cultivation or tending, worship and reverential homage (Simpson and Weaver 1984). To some extent, the number of academic disciplines (anthropology, sociology, linguistics, and communication) seeking clarification, agreement, and understanding of the concept of culture illustrates the term's almost limitless, subtle nuances, connotations, and particularized definitions.

Most scholars, however, have agreed that the study of culture seeks to identify and to order patterns and themes of the symbols, rules, and beliefs common to a particular social group. Phrased another way, "a society's culture...consists of whatever it is one has to know or believe in order to operate in a manner acceptable to its members" (Geertz 1973, p. 11). Culture is both something people have and something that happens to them (Agar 1994). For example, social group members learn through experience the rules and customs of the group and behave (or not) according to those behavioral norms.

Before elaborating on the cultural endeavors of this case study, another concept essential to this study requires clarification. What is *meaning*, as used here, and how is it socially constructed?

Meaning

The word meaning is both simple and complex. Literally, the definition of meaning is that which was intended to be or actually was expressed or indicated. Phrased another way, meaning implies the final purpose or significance of something (Flexner and Hauck 1987). In philosophy, the use of meaning conveys the common or standard understanding of an expression, construction, or sentence in a given language, or of a nonlinquistic signal or symbol (e.g., nodding head in agreement or disagreement, waving a hand in greeting, shrugging of shoulders, to name a few). Boulding (1961) offers another perspective by describing meaning as images. One's image of a situation or event results from past experience. With new information messages the individual's image changes. To Boulding (1961, p. 7) "the meaning of a message was the change which it produced in the image."

Contemporary usage of meaning, however, usually focuses on human thoughts, beliefs, and intentions; its focus is on propositional attitudes, rather than on ideas and images. Meaning in this context identifies individual constructs (thoughts, beliefs, and intentions) conveyed in speech and in practice, and influenced by social interactions of speech and experience. In other words, implicitly meaning is an individual construction (an image) made explicit through the cultural understanding of a social group. How then, specifically, is meaning made explicit? Carey (1988) discussed the role of communication in all of its forms in facilitating individual and social construction of meaning (thoughts, beliefs, and intentions expressed in speech and in practice). Through the medium of culture, facilitated by communication, the past history of a society enabled and constrained thinking among members of a social group. For example, members of networked groups communicate to form and distribute ideas, beliefs, and attitudes, a process also called social cognition (Resnick 1991). Social cognition should be distinguished from cognitive science (an interdisciplinary area that includes the study of artificial intelligence, psychology, linguistics, philosophy, anthropology, and neuroscience.) Finally, to continue a discussion of culture and meaning requires clarifying the term *sense*, particularly as it relates to sensemaking in a networked learning environment.

Sense

Meaning, as it is individually and socially constructed, contributes to making sense in a particular context of an event, of a physical object or symbol, and of spoken or written language. Weick (1995) observed that to the novice an explanation of sensemaking is similar to walking into a conversation that had been going on for centuries. The challenge of interpreting sensemaking exists in part due to the word's simultaneous commonality (implying that we all understand the definition of sense) and its complexity. The word sense, from its Latin root *sensus,* conveys perception, feeling, faculty of perception, and meaning.

For our purposes, the use of sense describes actions such as understanding and grasping by using the physical senses and reflections or perceptions. Sensemaking identifies the process of understanding or grasping a situation or information through the use of one's perceptions and reason. In the process of sensemaking individuals construct meaning to bridge gaps of understanding between what they experience and their past "image" of that experience. To bridge gaps of understanding individuals seeks and use *information.*

Information

Information is an essential component of sensemaking. Multiple uses of the word information, however, often cause confusion. For example, information has been described as messages (Boulding 1961), as a physical entity or phenomenon (Wilson 1981), and even by its traits and functions: to inform, activate, instruct, and generate ideas (MacMullin and Taylor 1984). It is Buckland's (1991) categorization of information that proves to be useful in this context: information-as-process, information-as-knowledge, and information-as-thing. The sensemaking process is really "information-as-process." In sensemaking "information-as-knowledge" is intangible, personal, and conceptual. When making sense information-as-knowledge provides an "image" from past experience to begin to understand a phenomenon. Buckland described "information-as-thing" as tangible (e.g., text and documents, objects, and even events.) From information-as-thing individuals receive cues, usually coming from "messages" in their environment that influence their understanding of a phenomenon. Finally, Buckland (1991, p. 356) claimed that: "If anything is, or might be, informative, then everything is, or might well be information. In which case calling something information does little or nothing to define it. If everything is information, then being information is nothing special." Whatever is informing to an individual or to a group is necessary to the process of sensemaking.

The use of information is essential to enable people "to cope with their lives" (Dervin 1977, p. 13) by reducing uncertainty. With information an individual can construct a reality that makes sense, based on internal knowledge (previous experience and individually constructed information) and external knowledge (facts gathered from a situation). Gaps of information in the process of sensemaking occur for two reasons: an individual has no prior experience to draw upon to explain a situation, or environmental circumstances prevent or impede the fact-gathering that might assist in explaining an event. Once an individual can explain the event (accurately or not), sense for that person is made, and action can be taken. In this respect, sensemaking is the process of seeking and using information and involves both cognitive activity (mental process of perception or reasoning) and behavioral activity (acting on the information). The following discussion weaves together concepts of information seeking, meaning-making, and learning as inextricable components of any study of sensemaking.

CONCEPTUAL FRAMEWORK

To explore any social setting one must collect and construct a framework of concepts that can inform and strengthen the inquiry. Concepts of learning and information seeking, technology and learning, and meaning-making all contribute to the system of sensemaking.

Learning and Information Seeking

Few in library and information services would disagree with the assumption that learning is inseparable from the information-seeking process. Learning is a psychological, cognitive, and a social process. One common definition of learning describes the permanent change in a person that has been behaviorally reinforced through experience and practice. Rogers (1969) discussed the idea of learning with the *whole person* in contrast to learning with the mind (e.g., memorization, recitation). Learning with the whole person occurs when an individual makes connections from new information to significant experiences and feelings, a process of individual associations and experiences to construct meaning with regard to new concepts or ideas. Conversation, often a social behavior, contributes significantly to this process. Through conversation individuals can socially negotiate consensus about the meaning of ideas and events. The theoretical interpretations of this and other tools that mediate information seeking and communication at a distance (computer-mediated communication and distance education) all contribute to expanded understanding of sensemaking in networked environments. Attention must also be given to other topics related to information seeking and learning in a networked environment: learning, the social construction of knowledge, and distance learning. Finally, the interplay among the ideas and theory of sensemaking, learning, cognition, and the social construction of knowledge weave together the fabric of sensemaking and networked information.

Bruffee (1993) described "education as a conversation," as the experience of "collaborative learning." In a networked environment information this can take place in many settings. Information seeking and learning can be mediated or disintermediated. They can also occur in face-to-face settings or remotely with individuals linked through compressed video and a T-1 connection or communicating through Internet-based media such as e-mail and the World Wide Web. The user of our networked information systems emerge within a telecommunications infra-structure that may include separate physical places (classrooms, universities, and cities) where individuals live, work, and study, as well as through the conversa-tions (formal/informal and on-line/off-line) among information users. "Human thought is consummately social: social in its origins, social in its functions, social in its forms, social in its applications" (Geertz 1973, p. 360). Although Geertz offered only one interpretation of the thought process, this interpretation seems to be consistent with studies related to networked environments. The array of social behavior in both face-to-face and networked settings often includes the social construction of knowledge, the process where individuals, as members of a social group synthesized their thoughts through a process of negotiation. To negotiate the meaning of an event or idea networked information users may need to ask questions, to confirm perceptions and ideas, to interpret events, and, generally, to reach consensus on the meaning of an event or idea. Academic institutions, librar-ies in particular, must consider how individuals socially construct knowledge in a technology-mediated environment. To broaden understanding of the meaning of networked interactions the researcher consulted among other topics theoretical works on sensemaking.

Sensemaking

The work of two sensemaking scholars influenced the thinking of this author: Brenda Dervin, a communications scholar, and Karl Weick, an industrial psychol-ogist. While Dervin's research primarily focused on individual sensemaking, Weick approached it from an organizational or social perspective. To Weick sen-semaking involves both individual and group sensemaking processes and behav-iors. Significant differences and similarities exist between Dervin's and Weick's research. Both scholars, however, focused on events in which the people involved suddenly, and often deeply come to feel that their universe is no longer a rational, orderly system. To illustrate, consider this hypothetical example of such a sense-making event involving university students.

Today most university students develop (from past experiences) a routine for beginning an information search at a library. They enter the physical library, retrieve handouts, read signs, and turn to the librarian for specific directions on how to proceed. What happens, however, when the librarian is not physically available but present only as "on-line help?" Networked information users often experience "gaps" in their understanding of how to proceed with their informa-tion-seeking activities. Imagine sensemaking in the next generation of OPACs where OPACs "will be virtual in that they'll exist only during a particular use and they won't look the same to any two users ... Users will determine the interface" (Sanders 1996, pp. 13-14).

A social sensemaking event begins when the networked user does not receive the expected response and continues as that computer user speculates to whomever might be available on the absence of the expected response. Such an incident exemplifies a sensemaking event where the messages (information-as-thing) that inform the individual on how to proceed were unavailable, when the on-line system mediating the interaction offered no information. As is often the case in networked settings, there are either no clues to assist the user in discovering how to proceed or the clues given do not make sense within the experience of this particular person. Perhaps, this example emphasizes the need to better understand social sensemaking behavior in a networked environment, where networked information users must often reinvent their communication, interaction, and learning behavior.

Sensemaking, as described by Dervin (1992), is a set of metatheoretic assumptions about the nature of information, the nature of human use of information itself, and the nature of human communication. The term "sensemaking" describes both a theory and a process. Dervin, a communications scholar, explained that the theoretical view of sensemaking considers information as a human construction to bridge gaps or discontinuities in reality (Kelly 1955; Carter 1973). The sensemaking process creates bridges that connect information from past experience or from cues from the environment to understanding or reality. An individual's construction of meaning or sense does not occur in a vacuum but is influenced by his or her physiological, social or cultural context. Many academic disciplines, including philosophy, cognitive science, psychology, and education, embrace the constructivist perspective that meaning, sense, reality, learning, personality, and knowledge were constructed both individually and socially.

Sensemaking owes a theoretical debt to philosophy and to cognitive and behavioral science. Within networked environments social sensemaking becomes more difficult because individuals must make sense of electronic text or images that exist independently of space and time (Zuboff 1984). The process of networked sensemaking begins when common sense (grasping or understanding) is inadequate to explain or navigate through a problem situation. A loss of the use of individual common sense, knowledge that guided everyday life (Berger and Luckmann 1966), occurs when the networked environment replaces face-to-face interaction and disturbs the day-to-day reality for network users. Weick's (1995) consideration of "social sensemaking" (as opposed to individual sensemaking) identified behaviors that include both internal (e.g., thinking, grasping, and understanding) and external processes (e.g., social information seeking through conversations and storytelling) to reduce ambiguity. Notably, both Dervin's (individual sensemaking) and Weick's (social or organizational sensemaking) perspectives shape this author's understanding. Dervin's emphasis on the communication process as it related to sensemaking directs our attention to communication behaviors in both off-line and on-line environments. On the other hand, Weick's more holistic approach to sensemaking events broadens the understanding of the social sensemaking process that involves a problem, people, and a variety of social interactions.

How, then, does sensemaking research differ from other research approaches to information seeking and use? One assumption of sensemaking is that "information is not a thing that exists independent of and external to human beings, but rather is a product of human observing" (Dervin 1983, p. 4). This view of information is controversial in that alternative views exist about the nature of information from thermo-dynamics, quantum physics, artificial intelligence, and other disciplines. Furthermore, Dervin's assumptions about information differ from those generally found in library and information science research. The author acknowledges the complexity of defining information, but generally treats information as a product of human interpretation in order to be consistent with the sensemaking approach employed herein. The process of sensemaking, seeking and using information in response to changing situations, rooted in individual and group experiences, past, present, and future, is best understood from the constructivist perspective. Savolainen's (1993) overview of sensemaking research clarified the distinction between information seeking from the traditional and the constructivist's research approach. Traditional research on information seeking and use began from the system-centered or institution-centered (library) approach. Zweizig and Dervin (1977) proposed that, instead of asking "who is using the library or how much the library is used," the research focus should move to individual information seeking and use. Among others, Dervin's contributions to the sensemaking theory offer an alternative to information- or system-centered studies that considered the individual's approach to the study of information seeking and understanding.

In the overview of sensemaking, Savolainen (1993) critically reviewed sensemaking theory in library and information science research by considering user-centered approaches to information seeking and use, as opposed to system-centered studies. The review acknowledged information seeking and sensemaking's debt to the contributions of Bruner (1973) on how people construct meaning and of Carter (1973) on discontinuity, instances where people must construct sense as life's events change individual reality. The study reported here, however, charted a research course different from previous sensemaking research because ethnographic research techniques aim to capture a holistic view of the culture of a social group (the networked seminar participants). Previous sensemaking studies conducted by Dervin and, to some extent, Weick focused on the events and processes (individual and social) of sensemaking without systematic consideration of the cultural context in which the sensemaking occurred.

Kuhlthau (1993) suggested that, when individuals attempted to make sense of a phenomenon, people gathered information, seeking meaning rather than answers. The role of information in the sensemaking process was significant, because information seeking, constructing meaning from information, and using information to act were central to making sense of a problem or a subject. Drawing from

Shannon and Weaver's (1949) information theory, Dervin viewed information as reducing uncertainty. Rather than just viewing information-as-a-thing, Dervin (1983, p. 5) assumed that information seeking and use were "constructing activities—as personal creating of sense.... Sense-making assumes that this constructing is what is involved in information sharing interactions...the successive modifications of internal pictures of reality—a series of constructings and reconstructings."

Dervin's approach to sensemaking research considered the study of "information use as construction" in contrast to "information use as transmission," as explored in information theory. Information use as transmission assumed that information had an existence apart from individual construction of information. In this sense, sensemaking served as a "theoretic net" for information and communication theories developed to study people making sense (the informal usage as understanding or grasping) in their everyday lives. As a process, sensemaking was a day-to-day event, where individuals navigated through problematic situations or bridge information gaps (Dervin 1977). For the present study the researcher turned to other approaches to sensemaking research that investigated and described social or organizational efforts of sensemaking.

Social and organizational sensemaking studies appeared most extensively in the work of Karl Weick, as well as the research of others who followed Weick's theoretical and methodological approaches. Weick's view of sensemaking suggested that people try to make things rationally accountable to themselves and others by relating events to what has been experienced or known. He contends that there were times when people suddenly and deeply felt that the universe was no longer a rational, orderly system. What made such an episode so shattering was that both the sense (understanding or grasping) of what was occurring and the means to rebuild that sense (meaning) collapsed (Weick 1993). While Dervin studied sensemaking in everyday life, Weick considered more extreme organizational or social incidents.

In one study Weick (1993) described social sensemaking among firefighters who fought the Mann Gulch forest fire. To construct this case study Weick used interviews, archival records, observation, and personal experience of the firefighters. During the disaster 13 experienced firefighters lost their lives due to the disintegration of role structure and sensemaking. The firefighting crew, accustomed to using a series of routines and habituated patterns to fight a blaze, discovered that the roles and rules that usually governed efficient firefighting failed them. The fire-burning pattern and its rapid spread presented the firefighters with an event that did not fit their experience. Previously acquired knowledge and firefighting strategies no longer made sense in this context. According to Weick, the surviving firefighters repressed habituated behavior and created innovative responses to the fire through the use of informative cues from their environment. They used these cues to gather contextual information such as how the fire *actually was burning*, as opposed to how the fire *was supposed to burn* to protect themselves from the fire. From this case study, Weick observed that even organizations (e.g., transitory organizations like the firefighters' work crew) that were good at decision making might still be deficient in sensemaking or constructing meaning from new situations.

To better understand the tools mediating social interaction and learning in networked information environments the author turned to the literature of computer-mediated communication (CMC), technology-assisted instruction, and distance education (DE). Each of these tools mediating the social interactions of communication and learning introduce, to some extent, an additional level of complexity to social and communication interactions.

TOOLS MEDIATING NETWORKED LEARNING

To explore questions raised by increased use of teleconferencing and computer-mediated communication (CMC) as they relate to networked learning and information seeking, one must consult the theoretical foundations for the use of the tools mediating learning in this setting: computer-mediated communication, technology-assisted instruction, and andragogical distance learning. Sensemaking theory provides a user-centered lens through which these new information and communication environments could be understood. Theoretical contributions to the areas of cognition and the social construction of knowledge (ways of thinking) also informed this exploration.

Analysis of the research literature confirmed a lack of well-developed user-centered concepts to explain the complexities of the interrelationship between technology and individuals (Goodman, Griffith and Fenner 1990; Palmquist 1992). Notably, the technologies that linked campuses, individuals, and information delivery could support social interaction in networked learning environments, but not without introducing new levels of interactive complexity. Research in the areas of CMC, technology-assisted instruction (computers and Internet), and the delivery of distance education, the tools of networked information, facilitates an enhanced understanding of networked sensemaking and learning.

Computer-mediated Communication

The current trend to provide instructional and information services through electronic media demands increased attention to the behavior of information users within these new environments. Computer-mediated communication (CMC), an umbrella term for communication facilitated through the use of computers, software programs, and telecommunications, was developed approximately 25 years ago. Participants in networked environments often discover that they must use new "intellective skills" that demand new conceptual and cognitive aptitudes (Zuboff 1984). Researchers explained that the use of these new skills is necessary because CMC creates an "interactively" complex social and information environment where groups exchanged information at different rates and at different times than in face-to-face settings (Walther and Burgoon 1992).

Following the implementation of networked communication in the military and scientific research community, the corporate world began to install networks with e-mail communication by the early 1980s. With the spread of CMC to corporate settings, researchers began to study social aspects of this communication medium (Hiltz and Turoff 1993; Sproull and Kiesler 1986; Steinfield 1986; Rice and Love 1987). While the use of CMC removes some barriers of time and distance, communication lacks dramaturgical, emotional, and status cues (Kiesler, Siegel and McGuire 1984). Williams' (1977) review of research about communication via electronic media noted the loss of intimacy in CMC. Furthermore, some researchers argued that new users of electronic communication also perceived a loss of message content. For example, Chapanis (1975) observed that speakers using the voice mode of communication delivered eight times as many messages, eight times as many sentences, five times as many words, and twice as many words than persons using teletypewriting. The absence of important social context cues influencing a perceptual distrust of the content could inhibit the development of relationships, particularly with regard to reciprocity and trust (Williams 1975; Short, Williams and Christie 1976; Sproull and Kiesler 1986; Walther and Burgoon 1992). The loss of social context cues, resulting from technology-mediated interactions proved particularly significant in this study.

There is an extensive literature on CMC (Hiltz 1990; Garton and Wellman 1995), and it continues to grow. A second generation of CMC research considered the socio-emotional interactions that can inhibit or enhance work and social interactions. Researchers reported at that time that CMC was no longer a novelty and that the medium continued to evolve (Walther and Burgoon 1992; December 1995). For instance, Newby (1993) observed that the norms for the use of CMC had matured, with networked communities creating standards for acceptable and effective communication behavior. Experienced CMC users have created new communication alternatives for decision making, discussion, and information sharing in an asynchronous mode without face-to-face interaction. Weick (1990) wrote that one effect of CMC was that the work environments and the understanding of social groups (organizations) within these environments become more complex. CMC messages often are flawed and incomplete, devoid of social context cues necessary for accurate interpretation. Nonetheless, CMC systems offer new forms of technology-mediated human communication for work and for social purposes (Santoro 1995). Additionally, Internet-based CMC offered new communication alternatives for creating "virtual spaces" for activities such as communication for scholarly activity and research and for social activity, group interaction, and education (December 1995). Although the use, development, and characteristics of CMC have been considered in numerous studies, this research identified none that specifically considered sensemaking in networked learning environments.

Technology-assisted Instruction

Computers have been tools for education for over 25 years, but scholars have only just begun to understand cognitive processes and the effects of computer technology on teaching and learning (Rutkowska and Crook 1987). Used to mimic a variety of teaching practices, some good and some bad, computing innovations have increased the understanding of learning and thinking processes and have contributed to changes in the classroom and in pedagogical methodologies (Lesgold and Reif 1983). Increasingly libraries providing on-line information services have turned to on-line tutorials to extend the reach of library instructional services beyond the walls of the physical library. For example, the University of Texas (UT) System's TeleCampus, its equivalent to an emerging virtual university, has constructed its own virtual library for students taking courses at a distance. Within the UT System Digital Library, students can access links to system-component libraries, external supporting libraries and projects, web-based reference resources, article databases (mostly limited to students from UT system schools), and a web-based information literacy tutorial (http://www.uol.com/tele-campus).

Networking, telecommunications, and computing all continue to develop as instructional vehicles in the college classroom. Hiltz (1990) noted that communication via electronic media could successfully facilitate teaching and learning. The use of computer conferencing allowed the content (subject) of the message to become the primary focus, an ideal condition for instructional purposes (Mason and Kaye 1990). Numerous educators corroborated the extraordinary value of using electronic communication (either e-mail or newsgroups) to facilitate on-line learning by extending the classroom beyond the confines of a physical space (Hiltz 1990; Harris 1993; Ellsworth 1995). In recent years the focus of human computer interaction (HCI) research has grown beyond the study of "interaction between the user and the computer to a larger context of interaction of human beings with their environment. Humans interacting with their environment transcended the user interface to a reality beyond the 'human-computer' system" (Kapetelinin 1996). In distance learning, unlike computer-assisted instruction (CAI), significant communication and human interaction must accompany the use of computing and interactive technologies.

Distance Education

Distance education (DE) consists of all arrangements for providing instruction through print or electronic communication media to persons engaged in planned learning in a place or time different from that of the instruction (Moore 1990).

Furthermore, based on a study of research in DE, instructors agreed that the absence of the common resources of a classroom, library, and even recreational areas were characteristic of distance education (Keegan 1986). Innovations in telecommunication and information technologies, perhaps, changed this definition because today in networked environments, non-place-dependent digital resources could be made accessible.

Over a century ago (1887) the University of London first provided non-place-dependent education through correspondence courses. By the 1930s telecommunications had enhanced correspondence-based distance teaching through the use of radio. In time, educators could choose to offer instructional services using television broadcasting, audio and video recording, and, now, computer modems, satellite, and microwave systems (Moore 1990).

Dede (1992) suggested that technology evolves in waves of innovation and consolidation. Recognizing the growth of distance education, as well as the need for systematic study and a conceptual foundation, Moore (1973) issued a call for research to build a theoretical framework for this form of education. This call, however, has been largely unheeded. Most research in distance education has been practical in its orientation rather than theoretical (Keegan 1986). Later, Hiemstra (1982, p. 883) encouraged DE research to focus on interactions in the use of mediated communication in instruction, rather than on "attention to task effectiveness, user attitudes, or simple objective measures of communication." Distance education research, however, continues to be primarily evaluative and prescriptive, not theoretical. The absence of a theoretical framework contributed to negative opinions of distance education among educators, because theoretical foundations guide practical applications and subsequent research (Glaser and Strauss 1967).

In recent years research focusing on the social aspects of distance or networked learning has increased. Bruce et al. (1993, p. 15) reminded the DE educator that: The design of any technology must be understood not simply as the construction of a physical artifact to meet a functional specification, but as a process in which relations among people are realized.

Numerous studies explored social interactions in teleconferencing settings. Moore (1973) considered factors affecting the student. Moore concluded first that to succeed, the student must work autonomously, and be self-directed, self-motivated, and capable of working alone. Second, geographic distance often separated the student and the instructor. Finally, in most distance education settings, the learner was alone and had to exercise a greater degree of control over his or her learning and to discover on their own relevant resources to support learning.

New telecommunications technology can support synchronous video and audio linking classes separated by distance. To some extent, the use of CMC eliminated some of the inconvenience and isolation of distance and facilitates wider sharing of resources. Williams (1978) noted that teleconferencing might be better than no communication at all, but it does not adequately replace face-to-face interaction in most learning environments. As bandwidth narrows from face-to-face interaction to technology-mediated interaction, communication is likely to be viewed as less friendly, emotional, and personal and more serious, business-like, depersonalized and task-oriented (Hiemstra 1982).

Based on this review of the DE literature and observations made during this inquiry, it is apparent that distance learning settings must incorporate social interaction opportunities for socially validating new learning. During collaborative interactions students interacted socially contributing to the formation of new knowledge within a class setting. Students cannot simply assimilate knowledge as it is presented. To understand what is being said, "students must make sense of it or put it all together in a way that is personally meaningful.... An optimum context for learning provides learners with frequent opportunities to create thoughts, to share thoughts with others, and to hear other's reactions" (Bouton and Garth 1983, pp. 76-77). Although Bouton and Garth might have overgeneralized about students' ability to "assimilate knowledge," distance learning must facilitate "education as a conversation." It was through conversations, technology-mediated or not, that individuals as members of a social group began to synthesize thoughts or negotiate reality or meaning. Through conversations social groups reached consensus contributing to individual and social knowledge.

In summary, conceptual foundations of an analysis of distance learning environments draws from the theory and literature about technological tools (CMC and teleconferencing) that mediate discourse and distance learning in this setting, the conceptual topics (activity theory) related to learning in a networked environment, and the interplay between the ideas and theory of sensemaking, learning, cognition, and the social construction of knowledge. Bruner (1979, p. 20) reminded us that "all forms of effective surprise grow out of combinatorial activity—a placing of things in new perspectives." Educational and information service institutions must strive to experiment with the "combinatorial activity of placing things in new perspectives" to design and provide access to resources that facilitate learning and sensemaking in networked environments.

LISTENING TO THE USERS: ETHNOGRAPHIC RESEARCH

This section describes the ethnographic research process as it was applied to this case study. The research techniques described in the next section illustrate how the researcher sought to place the events, activities, and interactions of seminar participants in a new perspectives. Complex issues require creative investigative approaches. The application of ethnographic research methods to the study of networked sensemaking offers a noncontrolling, holistic, and case-oriented approach to the study of complex social processes, as well as a user-centered approach to data collection and analysis. Although there is a growing number of qualitative studies exploring information seeking (e.g., Fidel 1993), most examples of this kind of study of information seeking considered information retrieval. A qualitative or naturalistic inquiry places the inquirer in a "lifespace" situation using a variety of data collection techniques to gain a "holistic" overview of the culture of the social group and to collect mundane as well as unusual events through the eyes and voices of the social group under study. The study of sensemaking using naturalistic data collection strategies in the context of networked learning offered a user-centered alternative to much of the "administrative research" published on distance education. Administrative research, as used here, refers to those studies conducted for experimentation with and evaluation of new technologies. Examples of administrative research have included policy formation, cost analysis, descriptions of delivery systems and teaching methods, or program administration and evaluation of programs. Although the study of distance education did not come of age until the early 1990s (Harry, John and Keegan 1993), a survey of teleconferencing and distance education literature suggested the relative infancy of distance education research and emphasized the need for the use of in-depth and user-centered research methodologies to study distance education. This section describes the qualitative and user-centered research techniques used to investigate the use of teleconferencing and Internet-based communications in an on-line classroom.

A Research Setting for Networked Sensemaking

As libraries (particularly academic libraries) redirect their attention and services to on-line remote users, it is critical that service planners begin to understand how their users make sense of the networked information they access. While the case study reported here was set in a university-level distance education class, the experiences of class participants provide glimpses of sensemaking in a networked environment that can shape creation of user-oriented on-line information services.

The Researcher Role of the Ethnographer

New educational settings dependent on complex information and communication technology infrastructures are particularly well-suited to an inductive research strategy. First, qualitative research facilitates understanding and explaining interactions in a complex social and technological environment because the research strategies are user-centered and empirically based. Second, the interactive nature of communication technologies are ill-suited to positivist, linear research models that often miss important contextual and phenomenological information characteristics of social settings. "Simple effects cannot be studied when the uses of the new media are complexly variable for each individual participant in a communication system" (Williams, Rice and Rogers 1988, p. 25). For example, networked information users are diverse in their cultural orientation to communication and in their communication technology skills. Finally, ethnographic research techniques provide a systematic way to collect and use data from a socially and technologically complex setting. In the case of this study the users were a community of learners linked through their educational and sensemaking experiences. Sensemaking was both the subject of the study (the culture of networked sensemaking) and an essential tool for ethnographic research. Ethnographic research requires the researcher to "make sense" of the events, beliefs, and social patterns of the study group.

Data for qualitative research typically come from fieldwork, where the researcher, as the research instrument, spends time in the study setting. Wolcott (1994) suggested that everything in a naturalistic study had the potential to be data. It is the researcher, however, who intervenes in a social setting and decides to make and take note of some things and not of others.

Researchers must be aware of the challenges of conducting fieldwork in multiple physical settings, and balance skill, competence, and rigor with flexibility, insight and tacit knowledge (Guba and Lincoln 1981). For example, in conducting a study of two university classes separated by hundreds of miles and linked by teleconferencing, e-mail, and the web, the researcher's goal, as an ethnographer, was to identify and describe the culture of the social group under study by documenting symbols, rules, and beliefs manifested in behavior and communication among participants. Through ethnographic techniques the researcher sought to describe what was seen and heard in the social group, grounding the observations in the context of study participants' view of reality as expressed in interviews (Fetterman 1989). For this task the ethnographer had to combine the skills of an artist and a scientist, and in these roles was required to describe the culture(s) of the study group. Through the use of a vivid narrative, thick with description (Geertz 1973), the researcher as artist-ethnographer enables the reader to experience the *culture* (symbols, rules, beliefs, and experiences) of the study group. Such a description draws from the data collected by the researcher as the scientist-ethnographer who systematically observed, documented, and analyzed the interactions, events, and behavior of the social group. The story described the emergent culture of a learning community linked by networked communication and information. Such a story can provide insight to library system planners and managers, as well as educators developing networked-based classes.

Rigorous study of networked environments, as seen through the eyes of its users, can contribute to a broader view of how individuals and groups seek to understand events and information mediated within electronic contexts. Do users of electronically transmitted messages (whether text or compressed video) find them flawed, as purported by some (e.g., Weick 1985)? Weick proposed that such messages contain only what can be collected and processed through machines, and omits socio-emotional cues important to communication. Does the exclusion of sensory messages (intuitive and perceptual senses) such as feelings, intuitions, and contextual, information impede individual and social interactions and sense-making?

Traveling back and forth between the two remote classrooms was the only way for the researcher to discover the people and beliefs behind interactions distorted by the technologies of teleconferencing and e-mail. As the human research instrument, using innate abilities for cognition, intuition, and flexibility, the researcher sought "to discover the flesh and blood" behind the observations of the seminar, the interior texture rather than the external form (Zuboff 1984, p. xiv) of participant interactions. The researcher was well-placed to observe and understand the context of events or individual behavior and to interview students to discover what they were thinking or how they responded to particular situations. As a restrained participant-observer, the ethnographer-researcher engaged in activities observing and documenting class activities, behaviors, and physical aspects of the social situation.

In this study the ethnographer-researcher moved back and forth between the roles of "professional stranger" (Agar 1980) and "participant." Never functioning as a full participant in the class community, the researcher attended class and, on occasion, contributed to discussions and activities.

Research Setting

The Mexico-United States border was the home of Borderland University (BU), with the Heartland University (HU) located hundreds of miles away in the same state. (Note: in keeping with the ethics of qualitative research these are fictional names of these universities.) The two sections of the class (27 students, with 13 at one site and 14 at the other) were at separate higher education institutions and used high-end teleconferencing and Internet-based technologies to conduct weekly sessions and to communicate during the intervening days. Facilitating the course were two instructors, one from each institution, who collaboratively developed syllabi (each site used its own syllabus) to explore "Communication Issues Related to NAFTA and the United States-Mexico Border."

The students in both sections brought a variety of backgrounds to the class activities. While the BU section included a mix of 10 undergraduates and four graduate students, the HU group included 13 students all studying at either a master's or doctoral level. This interactive complexity of the study setting contributed to the researcher's interest in the site. First, class instruction and communication used a variety of communication technologies such as teleconferencing, e-mail, e-mail distribution lists, fax, and worldwide web pages. Furthermore, the ethnic and cultural diversity of the students complicated class interactions, because the BU students were mostly Latino (four Mexican citizens) and the HU class included students from Brazil, Korea, Mexico, Taiwan, and Peru. The mix of student rank (graduate and undergraduate students), different fields of study, different levels and types of computing and networking skills, and wide range of knowledge (technical and topical) all contributed to the complexity of the research setting. Complex social settings required flexible research methods. For this reason, the use of qualitative research methodologies provided the researcher with the flexibility of using multimethod data collection techniques, alternatives for data validation, and the flexibility of the intuitive, experienced human research instrument.

Based on observations and experiences during a pilot study, this inquiry aimed to understand how students interacted to interpret and understand what they thought they saw and experienced in their networked learning environment (teleconferencing, e-mail, and the web). The group's use of networking and teleconferencing communication media provided a rich data source for observing and documenting social sensemaking behavior.

Data Collection Sources and Techniques

Ethnography typically employs multiple data collection techniques (Fetterman 1989). For example, in this study the researcher used face-to-face observation, interviews (individual and group), and focus groups, as well as archived e-mail messages. Additionally, two questionnaires distributed to class members gathered data on student networking skills and attitudes toward networking technologies. The receipt of copies of the learning journals offered by three Borderland students, as well as class observation notes shared by a BU graduate student conducting his thesis research in the Borderland classroom, were unexpected data sources.

Observation of the Study Group. Data collection techniques included 60 contact hours with study participants. "Description, in its everyday sense is at the heart of qualitative inquiry…. It is an intuitive as well as an objectifying act" (Wolcott 1994, p. 55-56). The researcher entered each social situation to engage in activities as appropriate and to observe all aspects and participants in the activities. As a participant-observer placed in the social situation, the researcher can be aware of the contextual variables present as the processes and meanings of events unfold (Wilson 1977). Students in the face-to-face and remote classrooms provided clues to their interactive styles through their "apparent" attention or inattention to the class activities at hand.

The researcher audiotaped the interactions in the class meeting, making every effort to capture conversations in the face-to-face classroom, as well as those transmitted through the video monitor. Recording clear, understandable audio is always a challenge, but making audiotape recordings in this setting was particularly difficult for a number of reasons. Among the challenges to useful audiotaping was the uneven quality of audio transmission during the teleconferencing.

Through the telling of stories seminar participants reaffirmed their experiences, modified their perspective, and inspired new stories. Storytelling encourages a social validation of an event (Reason 1994), because through stories listeners receive both an explanation of the event, as well as historical patterns that contribute to understanding the event (Weick 1995). Social sensemaking actions, of which explanations of social events were a part, often contributed to the construction of knowledge shared among members of a social group. The collection and analysis of the narratives of study participants provided data to complement the researcher's own observations and interpretations to develop a cultural description of this social group.

Interviews and the Study Role of the Informants. Interviews with study participants involved face-to-face interactions, usually with one study participant at a time and several telephone interviews. During these "conversations with a purpose" (Kahn and Cannell, cited in Marshall and Rossman 1995, p. 80), the researcher and a member of the study group discussed questions introduced by the researcher or comments made by the respondent. Occasionally, the researcher followed these interviews with the researcher-initiated e-mail messages that included more questions and requests for confirmation of particular interpretations of statements previously offered by the respondent or to verify a phrase or a statement made in earlier exchanges. These requests for confirmation or verification contributed to the trustworthiness of the study and exemplified the researcher's efforts to "member-check" data judged important to the study. Some of the interview sessions (conducted with individuals and groups) were formal and prearranged through appointments, while other interviews were more opportunistic, taking advantage of the availability and willingness of a student to be interviewed. All of these interviews provided contact hours with study participants outside of the scheduled class time.

Each informant served as another set of eyes and ears, joining the eyes and ears of the researcher to make sense of class events. Initially, the researcher encouraged the informants to provide weekly e-mail messages to the researcher, as a journaling activity to document individual reflections on and observations of class events and interactions. As the semester progressed, however, the researcher also used e-mail messages to ask specific questions relating to the previous class and as a way to facilitate informants' reflection on the seminar experience. Informants' responses to questions confirmed or refuted the researcher's observations of class sessions.

Face-to-face interactions were particularly important at the border site. First, the researcher had little time, except in class, to build rapport and trust with student informants. Second, each of the BU informants expressed a preference for face-to-face interaction instead of e-mail.

Questions Asked of Study Participants. Ethnographic interviews focus on eliciting respondents' interpretations of events and behaviors drawing from their firsthand experiences with the culture of the social group under study (Marshall and Rossman 1995). Interviews with BU and HU class participants evolved into a pattern of conversation usually beginning with informal, personal exchanges such as, "How are things going?" or "Have you been busy?" This personal exchange set the respondent at ease, established rapport, and eventually led the informant's readiness to respond to questions from the researcher. Normally, the researcher came to an interview with three or four questions relating to observations of recent class events or interactions. On some occasions, however, the natural flow of the conversation moved into unanticipated areas that proved interesting and, ultimately, relevant to the study focus. Often such questions spontaneously emerged during the conversation from comments or an idea expressed by the respondent. For example, during an interview with two Borderlanders, Arturo and Antonio (undergraduate students in communication and rhetoric and composition, respectively, whose names have been changed for this report) the discussion focused on the formality of student interactions during teleconferencing. Antonio interrupted the conversation with his own question for the researcher, "Do you know our way of communicating [during a teleconferencing discussion]? When seeing a 'no' headshake, he replied, 'We write notes…in Spanish'!" This admission of a form of communication unnoticed by the researcher introduced a new direction for questioning, as well as an unconsidered alternative for sensemaking. Practicing flexibility in the control of the direction of interaction between the researcher and the respondent during "a conversation with a purpose" was a strength of using the qualitative research approach.

A challenge to any researcher studying sensemaking is to craft interview questions relating to the researcher's topical interest in sensemaking, but at the same time allow the respondent's perspective to unfold (Marshall and Rossman 1995). The following questions asked of each of the informants evolved as a result of the advice of other scholars experienced in sensemaking research: "What helps or what hinders your learning or understanding of what is happening in the class?" "Can you recall during the last class an instance when you were confused? If so how did you respond?" "What did you do? What helped? What hindered your understanding?" For example, when asked to observe and reflect on the confusion or "sensemaking" behaviors of their colleagues, each respondent appeared at ease in identifying these situations, and usually his or her conversation led to fruitful discussions of their own sensemaking events and behaviors. Notably, this preference for reporting on the social, as opposed to individual, sensemaking activities had important implications for this study.

Other Data Sources: Electronic Communication and Questionnaires. An early assumption of the researcher was that e-mail archives would provide a rich data source that could be searched for "trigger words" to identify sensemaking events. Trigger words might have included "wonder," "question," "why," "how," "confuse," and "surprise." As reported below and in later sections of this study, class e-mail did not become a place for individual or group sensemaking. Instead, e-mail messages had more practical purposes such as discussing class assignments, verifying web site addresses, and article citations. E-mail did not include exploratory or creative discussions of the implications of in-class discussion topics or presentations.

Additional data were derived from two questionnaires (one distributed the fourth week of the semester and one distributed at the final class) that sought to identify individual attributes, characteristics and attitudes, as well as individual expectations for and perceptions of the seminar. The questionnaires combined attitudinal measures, such as seven-point Likert scales, with open-ended questions.

Several questions gathered class demographic information and other questions aimed to trigger reflection on sensemaking and information seeking. For example, questions asked, "If something in class discussions or activities is confusing to you, how do you clarify or 'unconfuse' the situation? Can you provide an example from the class?" The return rate for both questionnaires was 100 percent from the Heartlanders, with Borderland students returning 60 percent (9) of the first questionnaires and 47 percent (7) of the final questionnaires. Marshall and Rossman (1995) warned of the disadvantages of survey research, particularly with regard to accuracy of measurement and generalizability.

The use of multiple data collection techniques including attitudes and characteristics reported in the questionnaires augmented observational and interview data. In a research study, normally, the step following data collection is data analysis. The following section explains the process of data analysis in ethnographic research.

Data Analysis

Ethnographic data analysis occurred continuously and simultaneously, as the researcher chose one type of data over another or reformulated questions as appropriate to the context of the study setting. Agar explained that the iterative process of collecting data included analysis, evaluation, using information to collect more data, and refining the data through interpretation. This process was a dialectic rather than a linear process (Agar 1980). Spradley's (1980) prescriptive, ethnographic data analysis provided the map for the cyclical research process to identify behavior patterns of sensemaking culture of this social group. Because ethnography is inherently iterative and analytical, simultaneous data collection and analysis enabled the researcher to decide which methods to use next and how to use them (Fetterman 1989).

A primary analytical tool for the ethnographer was the ability to confront enormous amounts of information and to make sense of it. Fetterman described the initial stages of analysis as selective perception, whereby the researcher identified an event or a comment and begins to piece together the puzzle of understanding this particular social group. Unlike the pieces of a jigsaw puzzle designed to come

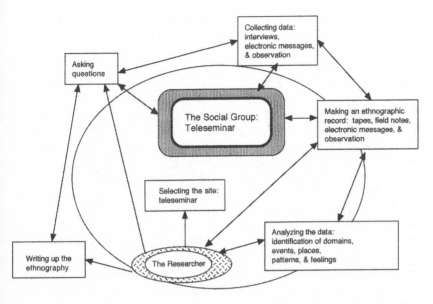

Figure 1. Ethnographic Research Cycle

together in one pattern, the recombinant nature of ethnographic data offered a variety of configurations. For the formal analysis the researcher reviewed all of the data collected (field notes, transcripts and on-line transactions) a minimum of three times. Spradley's model for ethnographic analysis provided methodological guidance. The process of using formal ethnographic analysis facilitated "making systematic examination of something to determine its parts, the relationship among parts, and their relationship to the whole" (Spradley 1980, p. 85). Additionally, throughout the study the researcher noted in a field journal events or observations relating to the study including dates of interviews and significant research events, as well as introspective reflections (tightly or loosely coupled to the study; see Figure 1).

The primary analytical goal of the ethnographer was to search for patterns that existed in the research data. For example, to develop a description of the culture of this class the researcher first descriptively reconstructed individual social situations such as a particular class or an event within that class. The social situation became "the stream of behavior (activities) carried out by people (actors) in a particular location (place)" (Spradley 1980, p. 86). To analyze a social situation, the researcher considered the semantic relationships of words describing and classifying terminology unique to the study group. By reviewing transcripts, all field notes, and the field journal the researcher began to identify recurring patterns of study participants' thoughts and behavior. Cover terms, general terminology selected by the researcher to classify an entity, served as a way to analyze, organize, and reconfigure units of data to discover descriptive patterns and interconnecting threads in the culture of the social group. For example, the physical room where each face-to-face class met was a kind of place. In this place there were people (teacher, students, observers, and guests), equipment (a teleconferencing system, computers, and telephone), furniture (tables and chairs), and instructional material (overhead transparencies, photocopies of articles, and books). The on-line classroom space included both the Borderland and the Heartland classrooms and spanned a distance of hundreds of miles. In this setting the "cover terms" also included types of communication tools, types of media, types of equipment, as well as types of participants. These examples illustrated some of the variables contributing to a "thick and rich" description of the seminar classroom. The recurrent themes emerging during this study shaped the description of the class. These themes included: (1) communication, (2) technologies mediating communication, and (3) social interaction. Data analysis was a nonlinear process of seeing a pattern, returning to the data or the classroom, and exploring or confirming the pattern or an observation with an informant. In an ethnographic study "analysis facilitated the identification of essential features and the systematic description of interrelationships among them—in short how things work" (Wolcott 1994, p. 12). The final product, the ethnographic report, identified and interconnected the themes to tell the story of the networked seminar.

The process of piecing together the story of the on-line seminar moved from data analysis to identifying significant patterns and themes in the events and behaviors of the social setting. The formal and informal analytical techniques resulted in the identification of three distinct class cultures. In each face-to-face section (the BU and the HU groups) and in the networked classroom unique patterns of behavior emerged. Through the process of reading and rereading study transcripts, field notes, and journal entries, overlapping patterns and themes emerged from conversations among participants and from observations. Use of Spradley's (1980) various analytical techniques to systematize the data "teased" out interconnecting topics and themes. The analytical process broke events, behavior, and conversations into smaller and smaller parts, only to bring them back together in new configurations. The themes emerging comprised "the systems of meaning" (Mead 1962, p. 52) giving form, order, and direction to the seminar culture. Dominating these study data and contributing to the description of the cultures of the seminar were the people, places, events (social and instructional), and the tools of the group.

Trustworthiness and Triangulation of the Data

Traditionally, validity and reliability of measurements are the underpinnings for good research. In this qualitative inquiry, the researcher sought to demonstrate the trustworthiness of the inquiry rather than the validity of its measures, based on an assumption of naturalistic research that there exists a variety of personal constructs of reality in social settings. To meet the criteria for trustworthiness, the researcher demonstrated credibility through prolonged engagement with the research setting. Persistent observation of and prolonged engagement in the seminar setting, as well as the monitoring of on-line interactions, contributed to the trustworthiness and credibility of the data. The researcher, as the research instrument, aimed to complement her personal biases concerning networked learning with the use of observation of behavior patterns and verbatim participant statements. Phrased another way, the researcher used "the tension between participant data and observer analysis to constantly refine [her] theory" (Wilson 1977, p. 250). In this study the understanding of social sensemaking as a part of sensemaking theory emerged from and was grounded in the data.

Triangulation. Triangulation, a basic component of ethnographic research, uses different information sources to seek contextual validation of findings (Denzin 1978). For example, the use of different data collection methods contributed to data triangulation (e.g., observation, e-mail logs, interviews, focus groups, and students' learning journals). The identification of particular themes and patterns in numerous data sources improved the quality of the data. Additionally, the researcher supplemented these data sources with field notes and entries in a reflexive journal documenting dates, times, and places of events and interesting discoveries or insights into group interactions. The reflexive journal, in combination with field notes, ensured the confirmability of the study by providing an audit trail for the data collection activities. The researcher also triangulated the data by confirming a particular perception or an event made by one informant with other students or with her peer debriefers. Another technique applied to confirm the meaning of particular statements was the use of member checking.

Member Checking. Although the researcher made every effort to record events accurately and to member check, she sought contextual validation by verifying portions of typed interview transcriptions. "Seeking contextual validation" contributed to the credibility of the study by confirming descriptions of particular class events or the implications of group interactions. Member checking embedded the data in the study setting, thereby strengthening the trustworthiness of a description or interpretation. In this study the researcher used several methods to member check interpretations or records of comments: sharing print copies of sections of transcripts with informants or quoting comments either in a follow-up interview or, when possible, using e-mail to verify the accuracy or the meaning of remarks.

Peer Debriefers. Efforts to establish credibility also included the use of peer debriefers, a process of exposing research activities and observations to the searching questions of experienced protagonists (Lincoln and Guba 1985). During the study two peer debriefers offered invaluable counsel to the researcher. The researcher shared frequent, focused conversations with one peer debriefer, a doctoral student in Library and Information Science, well-read and experienced in qualitative research methodologies. The second peer debriefer, the BU master's also conducting thesis research in the seminar, provided another valuable interpretation of seminar events and interactions.

The Product of the Research. By using a variety of data collection techniques, the researcher created a "holistic" overview of mundane as well as unusual events, through the eyes and voices of members of the social group under study. The description and understanding of the culture of the seminar drew from observations of class activities and from the conversations of study participants. The use of ethnographic research techniques, described in the previous section, facilitated a systematic "breaking apart" and "putting back together" of the puzzle pieces of social interactions and social sensemaking. During these interactions students attempted to span the barriers of distance, technology, demography, and time. The data collected and analyzed from this inquiry gave life to the stories, events, and interactions of the members of the networked learning group. Storytelling, vivid with the use of metaphors and personal experiences, enabled the researcher to make sense of or understand what was learned from in the seminar. Schön (1983) observed that through the medium of stories understanding can be transformed by metaphors that carry familiar ideas to less familiar settings. The interpretations of the events and experiences of a social group as told in their stories are characteristic of ethnographic writing. The description of seminar events observed "through the looking glass" of the video monitor sought to inform future design and implementation of learning communities and information services, communities and services that seek to facilitate rather than impede social sensemaking processes.

INTERPRETATION OF NETWORKED
LEARNING AND INTERACTIONS

The interpretation of qualitative research data begins at the "threshold in thinking and writing at which the researcher transcends factual data and cautious analyses and begins to probe into what is to be made of them" (Wolcott 1994, p. 37). To begin an exploration of "what was to be made" of the activities and events of one networked class, it is useful to revisit the questions motivating the inquiry.

- How did communication technologies such as teleconferencing contribute to or detract from social interaction in the networked classroom?

- Did barriers to communication and learning increase with each application of a telecommunication technology, as Weick and others proposed (e.g., teleconferencing, e-mail, and web sites)?
- Did users of electronically transmitted messages (whether text or compressed video) find such messages flawed or incomplete? Or, phrased another way, if there were "gaps of understanding" in the use of technology-mediated communication, how did social groups bridge these "gaps"? What were the inhibitors to bridging "information gaps" in teleconferencing technology-mediated communication?
- How and where did students make sense of their experiences and of new knowledge in a networked learning environment?
- How did teleconferencing's exclusion of sensory (intuitive and perceptual senses) information such as feelings, intuitions, and contextual information affect sensemaking?

Weick (1995) wrote that perceptions of information technology (IT) might undermine the ability of the technology to facilitate sensemaking, implying that an individual's perceptions of the quality and utility of IT affect the individual's use of and individual receptivity to IT tools. The following interpretations of sensemaking in this networked learning environment are those of the author, as well as of the study informants.

Networked Technologies, Social Interaction, and Social Sensemaking

This networked learning environment offered examples of both positive and negative effects of teleconferencing and other technology-based communication media on learning and social interaction. The inquiry, however, sought to understand the culture of a networked seminar by focusing on social cognition and social sensemaking interactions among seminar participants. Social sensemaking, a facet of social interaction, depended on unimpeded communication. How, then, did communication technologies such as teleconferencing contribute to or detract from social interaction in the classroom?

Earlier in this paper a discussion of the role of communication reflected on its forms in facilitating individual and social construction of *meaning* (thoughts, beliefs, and intentions expressed in speech and in practice). The "ritual of communication...linked to terms such as *sharing, participation, association, fellowship*, and the *possession of a common faith*" (Carey 1988, p. 18) cemented the cultural patterns of behavior, rules, and beliefs common to the social group. These "webs of culture that humans spin" (Mead 1962, p. 5) enabled and constrained thinking among members of the seminar group. Despite the distance separating the two campuses, students had a number of options available for communication to build "social cognition," to exchange experiences, to ask questions, and to tell stories arguing with and elaborating on each other's comments. For this class, the communication options included teleconferencing, e-mail, telephone, and fax. Notably, few students made extensive use of these alternative media, leaving teleconferencing as the primary medium for cross-class interaction because the medium was essential to conducting class.

Weick (1995, p. 110) reminded us that the substance of sensemaking starts with three elements: a frame, a cue, and a connection. Frames were past moments of socialization, and cues tended to be present in moments of experience. If an individual could construct a relation between these two moments, then meaning was created. The seminar participants interacted using frames (past experience) and cues (present moments) to make sense of and to act on newly created and understood information. These interactions led to social sensemaking events and included conversations, whispering, and note writing. Turner (1988) described social interaction as interaction that was reorganized and influenced by the behaviors of others. In this study social sensemaking, one component of social interaction, involved the process where individuals interacted in a social group with the purpose of understanding or grasping the meaning of a situation or event.

In the networked classroom that emerged when the two classes were on-line, social interaction differed from that in the off-line, face-to-face classrooms. For example, several students complained that the technological setting changed, even depersonalized, social interactions. The respondents speculated that the aggravation of unclear audio or imprecise images impeded social interaction. Although teleconferencing interaction (transmitted sound and image) appeared synchronous, much information was missing from the images of remote class members. One student described viewing classmates on the video monitor as the "tiny head phenomenon." Unless the camera focused on one person, all that remote viewers could see of their peers were tiny heads and shoulders. Teleconferencing's compression of sound and image for transmission created "noise" (audio static or visual distortions of space or action) that interfered with the exchange of important, although subtle, interactive information. Such interactive information included important communication signals such as body language, facial expressions, sighs, and shrugs signaling disagreement, approval, boredom, or anger. The visual information projected through the video monitor was incomplete because teleconferencing transmission distorted contextual information important to sensemaking. Nonverbal reactions to ideas, comments, or opinions were lost to the remote group. Gendlin (1964) described the concept of "felt-meaning," a reaction that de Kerckhove (1995) called "sub-muscularization." This response was "the equivalent of hundreds of thousands of cognitive operations performed in a split second by the body in response to stimuli" (de Kerckhove 1995, p. 12). During teleconferencing in the present study the distortion of visual information also distorted or incompletely conveyed the viewer's "felt-meaning."

Technology-mediated communication affected individual communication styles and, therefore, social interaction. One student observed: "You feel like you have to talk well all the time, not make mistakes, and I think it is stiffer than a regular class, where you are more relaxed. We have this idea of being in a common room, with the other side being a mirror, where there would be a screen." Even among the more adept teleconferencing communicators in the group, teleconference-mediated interactions consistently were more formal and tailored to the medium than interactions observed in the face-to-face classroom. For example, on-line the instructors spoke slowly and distinctly with a raised and modulated voice, and repeated statements. The teleconferencing technology imposed a formality on social interactions. The necessity to request permission from the teleconferencing console operator to have the attention of the camera exemplified this formality. The speaker often had to stand to access a microphone. Lost in these interactions were communication responses expressed through body language, facial expressions, and nods. Unless the camera focused on a head shot of a remote classmate, the subtle nods of agreement or disagreement were lost from discussions. The combination of class participants' unfamiliarity with effective teleconferencing communication and uncertainty in response to incomplete interactive information stifled spontaneous, natural, cross-class interactions. Furthermore, the absence of "natural communication" in most cases inhibited or diffused opportunities for the divergent discussions necessary for "deep" learning, social cognition, and social sensemaking between the two class groups.

Students from both classes reflected on their perceptions of social interactions when teleconferencing. Another student observed that, "The content [of social interaction] is not visual in any way…[In the class] it is all presentation. We are geared much more to presentation." A young woman commented in an e-mail message to the author on the diminishing conversation in class:

> We [the HU class] are spending less and less time in conversation. A problem of [the] teleconferencing course is our interaction and communication should not depend on and be limited by technologies. In order to make everything clear, people on both sides should spend time for extra-communication [implying communication that is off-line and face-to-face]. In a face-to-face class, if we are not satisfied with a class, we blame the instructor. Maybe we blame the technology here.

Both of these reflections illustrated the discomfort felt by networked class participants concerning "differences" between student interaction in the teleconferencing and face-to-face classrooms.

A challenge for instructors teaching in teleconferencing classrooms is to train students prior to going on-line in effective communication using the teleconferencing tools. For effective interactive teleconferencing communication students had to learn to speak more slowly, modulating their voices to decrease feedback from the audio on the other side. It was also necessary to pause longer than in face-to-face communication for a response. Teleconferencing participants also should be encouraged to address both the camera and the face-to-face group so as not to appear as if they were giving a presentation. In this study the students at one campus rarely turned to address their classmates instead focusing their comments on the camera, while students at the other campus seemed to address their attention to the face-to-face class glancing only occasionally at the camera. With training and experience, however, most participants could use the teleconferencing technology more effectively. Interestingly, certain seminar participants quickly mastered effective teleconferencing communication styles. The most intensive and effective examples of interaction were those times when the camera's eye focused on a head-shot of interaction between two speakers (one in each class). Seeking to overcome the loss of socio-emotional cues during interaction with their remote classmates, the students unanimously preferred closeup shots of individuals to wide-angle shots, because closeups provided a clearer view of facial expressions simulating proximity.

As noted earlier in this report, the effects of camera-shyness and behavior in front of the television camera pointed to the "the physical gap caused by the television that requires new mechanisms to integrate sites and create communities of affinity" (Nahl 1993, p. 207). The narrowing of teleconferencing bandwidth from that of face-to-face interaction could make interactions seem less friendly, more serious and business-like, and depersonalized and task-oriented. Scholars reported that depersonalization by the medium manifested itself in the use of politeness strategies among teleconferencing communicators in order to show regard for "face" (Hiemstra 1982). Interviews with study participants confirmed the perception of the depersonalizing effects of teleconferencing. Teleconferencing planners and participants must discover strategies to optimize and personalize the context for learning creating frequent opportunities to think, to share thoughts with others, and to hear other's reactions (Bouton and Garth 1983). In the seminar the free-flowing exchange of ideas might have increased had students participated in cross-class discussions using e-mail.

Technology can dramatize and exaggerate behaviors and attitudes, leading to misunderstandings, even conflict. For example, the incomplete, flawed information transmitted by teleconferencing technology could distort the perception of remote class behaviors and actions, losing contextual information (e.g., smells, sounds, and touch) usually gathered through the physical senses. Examples noted by seminar participants included moments when the lens of the camera focused momentarily on a student cleaning out her purse or on two students conducting their own conversation. When viewed by a remote class member, the actions seemed rude and inattentive. Missing from this interpretation was contextual information that might have explained the behavior. Perhaps the student cleaning out her purse was only looking for a pencil or getting an aspirin. Other instances of misinterpretation or exaggeration of the actions of students in the remote section included times when one class muted the audio transmission to permit a face-to-face section to conduct a private conversation. Some participants often construed such actions as negative or exclusionary, when the intention actually might have been different. The previous examples illustrated instances when important contextual information available in face-to-face relationships was absent in technology-mediated interactions.

The development of face-to-face relationships and the information that accompanied such relationships empowered these individuals to "go beyond the information given" by the teleconferencing tools and inform their interactions by referencing their "image" of the individual. The most relaxed teleconferencing interactions occurred among a few individuals. The seminar participants who exemplified spontaneous and natural teleconferencing interaction were those individuals who had a prior relationship or those who deliberately developed a new relationship through face-to-face and telephone interaction.

Accommodating social sensemaking in teleconferencing interactions requires meeting several criteria. First, participants had to become comfortable and proficient in use of the technologies to communicate. Second, they had to develop or establish relationships with the person(s) with whom they were communicating. Third, individuals had to build a level of trust face-to-face that carried over to teleconferencing. It was not just "first make friends, then do business," but first make friends face-to-face then do business. Finally, individuals chose the medium most appropriate for a particular message or communication exchange. For example, fax, mail, or even web sites were best for sending lengthy narrative or statistical information. If face-to-face interaction was not available, then a combination of telephone conversations and e-mail messages were preferable for negotiating details of collaborative work. In my peer debriefing sessions with a master's student conducting his thesis research in the same class, we agreed early in the semester that, after face-to-face communication, telephone conversations were most satisfactory for our own post-class sensemaking. The observation that communication and social sensemaking relationships were enhanced by face-to-face communication introduced the idea of distance or proximity in social relationships. Or as Thibaut and Kelley (1959) phrased it, the propinquity effect.

Some contact or acquaintance between a pair of people is, of course, an essential precondition for the formation of a relationship between them.... The physical distance between people and the more in the course of their daily activities their required paths cross, the more likely they develop social visiting relationships. Presumably, this is so because contacts between people depend upon the ecological factors of distance and pathways.... Our analysis suggests the further possibility that distance might contribute to the costs of a relationship.... From the law of least action, we would expect propinquity to have a positive effect on relationship formation (pp. 39-40).

Teleconferencing might be an improvement on no communication; currently, however, it did not adequately replace face-to-face interaction.

Bruce et al. (1993) reminded distance educators that the design of any technology must take into consideration people and interactions. Developers of teleconferencing technologies must create systems which support easy, individually accessible equipment. Some teleconferencing systems allowed speakers to push a button when they wanted to comment. Sensitive "cameras and microphones" facilitate an automatic response to the "voice" speaking and focus on the face of the speaker. One student, in response to a video on new technologies shown during class, offered the following suggestions concerning effective use of new communication technologies:

> Without a solid education or a way to think critically about what you are doing with the technology, it really starts to deal with you rather than you with it. Easier doesn't necessarily make things better. The best technology is when there is symmetry [of awareness and appropriate use] to the technology architecture.

Through training and experience instructors and students could learn how to appropriately use teleconferencing technology to their communication and sensemaking advantage. The design of distance learning classrooms and instructional goals must be accomplished through a process of continuous experimentation and alignment of the components of technology, facilities, and task to support communication and interaction. This process is critical when planning for social learning and interaction in a networked environment.

Social Sensemaking

In a networked communication setting social sensemaking is the process where individuals, confused or uncertain about a situation, interacted socially to understand or grasp the meaning of a phenomenon. An individual's confusion or uncertainty occurs for two reasons: the absence of prior experience (a frame) to draw upon to explain a situation, or environmental impediments to fact gathering (cues) that might have assisted in explaining a situation or event. During social sensemaking a group negotiates reality by thinking as a social process (social cognition). Such group negotiations might normally include asking questions, confirming and correcting observations, and interpreting confusing events or observations. Connections are made and verbalized in individuals' exchanges of their "frames" and "cues." The social sensemaking process involves internal (individual sensemaking) and external processes (social thinking and communication). How might these interactions occur in a networked information environment? In this study social sensemaking primarily occurred in small groups in the face-to-face setting. Examples included note writing, whispering, and conversations outside of the range of the camera and the microphones. Perhaps in the teleconferencing classroom social sensemaking would more likely occur when the individuals interacting have developed, even reinvented communication styles appropriate to teleconferencing interaction. This reinvented communication style included interaction that was characterized as:

- aggressive—interrupting a conversation, if necessary;

- motivated—the individual moved physically to access and use the tools of teleconferencing technologies (camera and microphone);
- developed and/or maintained by prior face-to-face relationships; or
- self-confident—publicly acknowledging a lack of understanding or comprehension.

As the communication and interactive demands of teleconferencing changed so did their communication techniques. For example, when there was delayed audio transmission or feedback, these individuals experimented with techniques for effective teleconferencing interaction. When appropriate they addressed by name the person in the remote site with whom they were interacting. In some instances these individuals were quick to suggest that a remote speaker talk more loudly or move closer to the microphone, while at other times they deliberated before interacting, making the most of their time on-line. Effective teleconferencing communicators were able to reinvent their communication style and their social interactions to fit the moment or the circumstances.

Among the examples of potential on-line social sensemaking were those occasions of storytelling when the speaker used broad, and often inexact descriptions of an experience relevant (or not) to the topic at hand. Stories offered a medium for social sensemaking, potentially transforming group understanding with rich metaphors, and carrying familiar ideas to less familiar settings. Storytelling (whether accurate or not, or even directly relevant or not to an activity) was important to the process of students' constructing individual meaning around confusing or uncertain topics. With very few exceptions every seminar student who chose to participate in a teleconferencing discussion told a story. These stories attempted to confirm an event or phenomenon or to add understanding to the topic of the discussion. The storytelling styles of participants varied with individual styles emerging for each person. Their stories, part of their own sensemaking exercise, had consistent patterns. They:

- drew from past experience (the frame),
- emphasized their "personal experience" with topic at hand (the cue), and
- ended with personal opinion based on emotional reaction or observations (a connection or a statement of understanding or action).

Absent from these individual sensemaking-through-storytelling events in the on-line classroom were the listeners' contributions to the stories to confirm, revise, or otherwise develop the story.

For social sensemaking to occur, first, teleconferencing participants in social sensemaking had to become comfortable with and understand their surroundings, minimizing the impediments to gathering cues from their environment. Next the participant had to develop a sense of trust among members of the

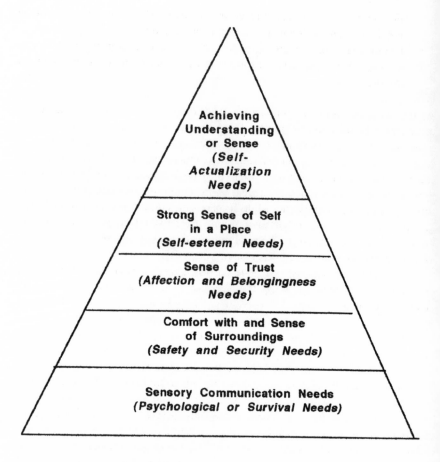

Figure 2.   Hierarchical View of Social Sensemaking

social group, a process of developing an interpersonal rapport with members of the group. Then the individuals had to build as a social group a strong sense of self, understanding who they were within a particular context in a particular place. In the group studied, each participant had to develop a strong sense of self within his or her place in the teleconferencing environment. Finally, movement through the development stages brought an individual to the point of action where they participated in social interactions with confidence in the importance of their contribution to the group's understanding. Attaining this level of social interaction in the teleconferencing environment required experimentation and trial and error, a continuous process of movement up and down the hierarchy of social sensemaking needs. Figure 2 portrays another view of the interactive nature of the social sensemaking cycle.

Social Sensemaking When Technology is Opaque

In the study reported here the irregular use of cross-class e-mail teleconferencing, the primary technology used for communication in the seminar proved to be both opaque and transparent. Turkle (1995, p. 23) discussed how early computing technologies prepared us for "taking things at interface value" by presenting themselves as open, as transparent. According to the conventional definition of the term, an object "is transparent if it lets the way it works be seen through its physical structure...[Things appear] opaque when they hid their structure while performing miracles of complex functions" (Turkle 1995, p. 79).

In some ways the introduction of the Macintosh computer's iconic style, however, prepared us for new opaque (not transparent or easily understandable) interfaces which simulated a space (e.g., a desktop with a trash can). Implicit in opaque technology was the technology user's loss of awareness of the workings of the technology and their role in facilitating the use of the technology (e.g., compressed video, T-1 network connections, electricity, and sound amplification). The invisibility of system workings contributed to the perception of an opaque interface. When users of opaque technology reflected on the opacity of a particular technology, such as teleconferencing, they began to question and became confused by the effects of the technology on human interactions. The networked seminar presented numerous examples when participants communicating within their opaque, technology-mediated environment sought to overcome gaps in information and to interact socially.

During those instances of "technological opacity" class members exhibited confusion concerning their communication and interactional behavior with a remote classmate. One student described experiences with opaque technology as "cognitive disconnects." The psychological literature, however, referred to this phenomenon as cognitive dissonance, instances where an individual's choice or action appeared inconsistent (dissonant) with his or her values or experience. During instances of "cognitive dissonance" the invisible operations of the technology disappeared (or became opaque) with all aspects of teleconferencing functioning properly (clear audio and clear, synchronous video). Although several examples illustrated confusion resulting from the opacity of the teleconferencing technology, a particular incident of this confusion occurred near the end of the semester. The timing of these occurrences suggested that seminar participants had become more comfortable in communicating and interacting in the teleconferencing environment.

This confusion often led to a kind of social sensemaking when the sensemaker turned to his or her environment (in these examples the environment of the physical and the virtual classroom) to gather more facts to understand and respond to the situation, only to have these cues inhibited by the technology. Frequently, the actions following such incidents included embarrassed comments to a neighboring classmate, jokes or puzzlement over how such confused behavior could have happened. In another such instance there was confusion about the physical location of the students in the combined classes.

The "gaps of understanding" alluded to above resulted from two confusions. First, confusion occurred when individuals were not able to distinguish where one communication space ended and the other began; in other words the participants had difficulty distinguishing between face-to-face or technology-mediated communication. Second, the confusion resulted when the lack of previous teleconferencing experience impeded the seminar participants' understanding of a situation. The environmental circumstances (technologically induced cognitive dissonance) impeded fact-gathering and, therefore, sensemaking. Weick (1995) observed that sensemaking becomes a challenge in those instances when there is disparity between the speed and complexity of information technology and the ability of humans to comprehend the outputs of the technology. Apparently, the speed and complexity of the teleconferencing technologies confused the actions (behavioral and social interactions) of seminar participants. Users of the opaque teleconferencing technology began to question and become confused by the effects of the technology on their human interactions. Furthermore, when the social environment was uncertain or confusing, levels of socially interactive spontaneity and creativity diminished. The physical, social, and technological environment all influenced social sensemaking or understanding in this setting. When the dynamics of the teleconferencing technology became opaque, participants became confused in interactions with the remote group and with their physical environment.

Social Sensemaking When Teleconferencing Technology is Transparent

Transparent teleconferencing technology, as interpreted by Turkle, also affected social interaction between classes. When technology was transparent, technology users became aware of the need for and use of certain tools, the microphone or the camera, to communicate. The workings or operations of the teleconferencing systems became transparent. Participants were conscious of the tool mediating interaction. The transparency of the teleconferencing technology occurred when individuals became aware of the necessity to use tools (a microphone or the camera) to mediate interaction. The use of the tools interfered causing frustration because individuals must exert more effort than usual (e.g., face-to-face or on the telephone) to communicate and interact. Such incidents usually occurred at those times of inconvenient or nonfunctional access to teleconferencing tools. For example, inconveniently located microphones, inappropriate focus of the cameras, or malfunctioning T-1 lines all made participants aware of the necessity for all parts of the teleconferencing system to work.

Students described their frustration, even fatigue, on those occasions when they wanted to participate in a discussion, but the awkward configuration of microphones and video cameras impeded them from responding spontaneously.

I mention that it gets tiring on the listener when the [audio] levels aren't set right. You have to like adjust the distortion in your head, decipher it. It is almost like listening to a foreign language. It wears you out. You have to concentrate that much more.

In situations such as those that Jon described, individuals wishing to participate in cross-class communication (dialogue, discussion, and question-asking and -answering) had to exert extra effort to act on their communication impulses. The subtle nodding of a head, frowning, or other behaviors signaling the entrance of an individual into a discussion were insufficient to draw the attention of the camera or to get access to the microphone. To facilitate natural communication the interference or "noise" of the transparent technologies must be filtered out. Maria observed during an interview that, "We are still not used to the mediums [sic] so much. It is still too tangible for us. It is not like a telephone. On the telephone you don't care if your voice is like this or that." More natural, unimpeded interaction occurred in teleconferencing when all the components of the teleconferencing system functioned and the tools mediating the interaction were used appropriately. To interact, participants had to swiftly adapt their communication styles or format to accommodate the transient environmental changes (loss of or static in audio) in teleconferencing's delivery and transmission. Participants had to become accustomed to using the tools and resources at hand to interact socially and to satisfy their individual needs for interaction and sensemaking. Teleconferencing participants had to become bricoleurs because social interaction changed in response to transparent technology.

RECOMMENDATIONS FOR NETWORKED TEACHING AND LEARNING

Networked teaching, while different from teaching in a face-to-face classroom, can enable new behaviors and skills among participants. For example, the "rhythm of teaching and learning" changes because of changed rates and means of communication. The use of teleconferencing in networked learning environments can both empower and pacify students. Many of the examples of participants' experiences in the seminar explored in this study identified some of the current technological impediments to interacting and sensemaking in the networked classroom. It should not be forgotten, however, that both of the seminar instructors viewed the networked class as exploratory and experimental. Throughout the semester all participants in the networked classroom, including instructors, students, and the researcher, experimented with techniques for the effective use of the technologies. Those participants empowered by the technologies chose to master effective use of the technologies through experimentation, trial and error. The result was a bricolage, the product of their mastery.

The bricoleur is a "Jack of all trades" who can perform a large number of tasks using the tools at hand. The bricolage is not considered a project. Instead, a bricolage is that which is accomplished or created using tools or resources collected by the bricoleur for use when they might "come in handy." Class participants collected skills and understanding that facilitated inventing a style of communication to satisfy needs for interaction and sensemaking as the technological or environmental resources change. Communication and social interaction in the teleconferencing setting demanded effort from teleconference participants. Other less aggressive learner-communicators appeared to be passive, even paralyzed by their inability to communicate and interact in the teleconferencing environment. Educators must continue to discover and experiment with tailoring learning experiences in the networked environment. Innovations in networked learning environments must be designed to accommodate: (1) individual learning and information-seeking styles, (2) appropriate use of time and place, and (3) social interaction and social sensemaking.

To effectively incorporate technology-mediated communication into instruction the use of different communication media must have specific instructional purposes. For example, the purposes might include the use of e-mail for the distribution of class logistical information, skill development activities, and continuation of discussions outside the classroom, as well as socialization of a student to CMC. The importance of predetermining instructional goals for technology-mediated communication could significantly alter not only the quantity and the quality of communication between people, but deepen and broaden learning in the classroom.

In computer-assisted instructional settings the opportunity arises for the student to be forced to actively participate, "rather than passively listen (or doodle or sleep or stare out the window)" (Hiltz 1990, p. 21). Teleconferencing instructors, however, must discover ways to encourage students to experiment with and use the available tools for interactions, rather than to passively accept the feeling of powerlessness. One instructor observed that teaching in the teleconferencing classroom could be similar to teaching large classes with similar losses of spontaneity and individuality. Several students suggested making each evening's class agenda available before class, because, with an advance agenda, students could begin to consider their contributions. The suggestion for more structure to the on-line sessions, perhaps, was in response to the perceived sense of loss of control or power caused by the mediating technologies. Additionally, facilitating opportunities for personalized learning, interactions, and discussion among members of the face-to-face group was crucial to social interaction and sensemaking. Such learning activities should include face-to-face discussions for each class. Communication should not be completely dependent on and limited by the technologies. Teleconferencing instructors must make assignment and project expectations explicit in the face-to-face class setting (if possible), using off-line time to supplement and to clarify class activities or assignments through the students' questions and discussion.

Ethnography and Sensemaking	• Reconstruct sensemaking events by reflecting retrospectively
	
	 • Identify points of confusion or puzzlement, sensemaking events
	
	 • Identify inhibitors in the environment or in social interactions to social interaction and therefore social sensemaking
	
	 • Establish trust and rapport with the researcher
	
	 • Use skills as bricoleur to
	
	    - construct meaning around new experiences
	
	    - participate in cross-class social interaction
	
	    - find a ways and places for social sensemaking

Figure 3. Study Implications for Teleconferencing and Sensemaking

Unquestionably, the social interactions among study participants contributed to learning. In this networked setting students and instructors had to "invent" new opportunities for social sensemaking. Based on the data collected during this inquiry, we could conclude that the technological tools that mediated discourse and distance learning could impede social interaction, social sensemaking, and, ultimately, the social construction of knowledge. Educators teaching in networked learning environments should explore instruction techniques that deliberately facilitate:

- social interaction,
- divergent conversation,
- personalization of interaction (use of names, sharing of biographical information),
- convenient access to microphones,
- responsive use of cameras to capture as quickly and accurately as possible the faces and expressions of students during discussion, and
- informative camera sweeps of the group.

Ethnography and sensemaking

- Reconstruct sensemaking events by reflecting retrospectively

- Identify points of confusion or puzzlement, sensemaking events

- Identify inhibitors in the environment or in social interactions to social interaction and therefore social sensemaking

- Establish trust and rapport with the researcher

- Use skills as bricoleur to

  - construct meaning around new experiences

  - participate in cross-class social interaction

  - find a ways and places for social sensemaking

Figure 4. Implication for Study Participants

Accommodation of social interaction in a networked environment could require adjustments as simple as reconfiguring the teleconferencing equipment and fur-niture arrangement. On the other hand, facilitating social interaction also could be as challenging as fitting the instructional goals and communication behaviors to the social sensemaking needs of the people involved in a specific situation.

STUDY IMPLICATIONS FOR
NETWORKED INFORMATION SPACES

Teaching and learning in networked classrooms demands a balance of innova-tion and caution. While a single case did not result in generalizations, it did offer insights that are transferable to other similar situations. A strength of this study was that its empirically based findings contributed to a further under-standing of the study's theoretical underpinnings. First, the study discovered that the tools that mediated distance learning in this setting (computer-mediated communication and the provision of distance education) can impede social interaction and social sensemaking. To facilitate learning and information seeking, networked environment activities must be developed that encourage social interaction to build collaborative relationships and discussions to interpret new learning, and time must be taken for questions. Figure 3 displays the study implications for social sensemaking during teleconferencing. Second, the study identified the interplay among sensemaking, learning, cognition, and the social construction of knowledge, all of which are a part of social sensemaking. Third, the study developed Weick's exploration of organizational sensemaking by considering, through the use of ethnographic research techniques, the cultural context for social interaction for sensemaking. Figure 4 further describes the study implications for participants. In conclusion, the following capsulizes the implications of this inquiry for those who facilitate and participate in teleconferencing.

Communication technologies, such as the teleconferencing used in this study, detracted from social interaction, and ultimately, social sensemaking in the classroom setting. Teleconferencing-mediated interaction increased the barriers to communication, and, ultimately, to social interaction. Barriers to social interaction increased when questions were not heard and passed unanswered. Formal and presentation-like cross-class interactions replaced creative, divergent thinking important to learning and intellectual development. Library planners must expand upon the "on-line help desk" concept to facilitate social interaction and sensemaking among information service providers and their users.

The participants in teleconferencing (interactive, compressed video) perceived the teleconferencing messages of cross-class social interaction and communication as flawed or incomplete. Gaps of understanding, as well as uncertainty and ambiguity, occurred as a result of either the transparency or the opacity of the technology. Telecommunication technologies dramatized and exaggerated behaviors and attitudes, leading to misunderstandings and conflict. The exclusion of sensory (intuitive and perceptual senses) information such as feelings, intuitions, and contextual information affected seminar participants' ability to grasp the context in which events or behaviors were occurring. Library designed networked information spaces must experiment with user-modifiable interfaces to ameliorate "flawed messages" and barriers to social interaction.

Participants in teleconferencing used their skills as "bricoleurs" to facilitate social interaction and social sensemaking. Individuals invented more effective communication styles for teleconferencing interaction. They also sought interaction in small groups in the face-to-face setting for social sensemaking through conversations beyond the reach of the microphone or the camera, through whispering, and through note passing.

Educators using technology-mediated tools in the classroom and library networked information service planners must develop a scaffolding that permits, even encourages, social interaction. Through conversations, one part of social interaction, students must have opportunities to negotiate consensus on understanding new ideas and experiences. These negotiations shape and are shaped by the emergent culture of the social group of users. In this inquiry the culture of this networked learning environment not only mediated thought and social learning, but also influenced the forum for negotiated meanings. Whether a participant is making sense of events and activities in a networked learning environment or an ethnographer is seeking to make sense of a particular social group, each of us has to discover and cultivate our skills as a bricoleur and each of us has to become adept at performing a large number of tasks to respond with flexibility to our changing environments.

REFERENCES

Agar, M. 1980. *The Professional Stranger: An Introduction to Ethnography.* New York: Academic Press.

———. 1994. *Language Shock: Understanding the Culture of Conversation.* New York: William Morrow.

Berger, P.L. and T. Luckmann. 1966. *Social Construction of Reality: A Treatise in the Sociology of Knowledge.* New York: Anchor.

Boulding, K.E. 1961. *The Image.* Ann Arbor, MI: Ann Arbor Paperbacks.

Bouton, C. and R.Y. Garth. 1983. *Learning in Groups. New Directions in Teaching and Learning,* No. 14. San Francisco, CA: Jossey-Bass.

Bruce, B., J.K. Peyton and T. Batson. 1993. *Networked-based Classrooms.* New York: Cambridge University Press.

Bruffee, K.A. 1993. *Collaborative Learning: Higher Education, Interdependence, and the Authority of Knowledge.* Baltimore, MD: The Johns Hopkins University Press.

Bruner, J. 1973. *Beyond the Information Given: Studies in the Psychology of Knowing.* New York: W.W. Norton.

———. 1979. *On Knowing: Essays for the Left Hand.* Cambridge, MA: Harvard University Press.

Buckland, M. 1991. "Information as Thing." *Journal of the American Society of Information Science* 45(5): 351-360.

Carey, J.W. 1988. *Communication as Culture: Essays on Media and Society.* Boston: Unwin Hyman.

Carter, R.F. 1973. "Communication as Behavior." Paper presented at the annual meeting of the Association for Education in Journalism, Fort Collins, CO.

Chapanis, A. 1975. "Interactive Human Communication." *Scientific American* 232: 36-42.

December, J. 1995. "Transitions in Studying Computer-mediated Communication." *Computer-Mediated Communication Magazine* 2(1). Available on-line: http://www.december.com/cmc/mag/current/toc.html

Dede, C.J. 1992. "The Future of Multimedia: Bridging to Virtual Worlds." *Educational Technology* 32(5): 55-60.

Denzin, N.K. 1978. *Sociological Methods.* New York: McGraw-Hill.

Dervin, B. 1977. "Useful Theory for Librarianship: Communication Not Information." *Drexel Library Quarterly* 13: 16-22.

———. 1983. "An Overview of Sense-making Research: Concepts, Methods, and Results to Date." Paper presented at International Communication Association Annual Meeting, Dallas, TX.

_____. 1992. "From the Mind's Eye of the 'User': The Sense-Making Qualitative-Quantitative Methodology." Pp. 61-84 in *Qualitative Research in Information Management*, edited by J.D. Glazier and R.R. Powell. Englewood Cliffs, CO: Libraries Unlimited.

Ellsworth, J.H. 1995. "Using Computer-mediated Communication in Teaching University Courses." Pp. 11-27 in Computer-mediated Communication and the Online Classroom: Overview and Perspectives, Vol. 1, edited by Z.L. Berge and M.P. Collins. Cresskill, NJ: Hampton Press.

Fetterman, D.M. 1989. *Ethnography Step by Step*. Newbury Park, CA: Sage.

Fidel, R. 1993. "Qualitative Methods in Information Retrieval Research." *Library and Information Science Research* 15: 219-247.

Flexner, S.B. and L.C. Hauck. 1987. *The Random House Dictionary of the English Language*, 2nd ed. unabridged. New York: Random House.

Garton, L. and B. Wellman. 1995. "Social Impacts of Electronic Mail in Organizations: A Review of the Research Literature." *Communication Yearbook* 18: 434-453.

Geertz, C. 1973. *The Interpretation of Cultures*. New York: Basic Books.

Gendlin, E.T. 1964. *Experience and the Creation of Meaning*. New York: Free Press.

Glaser, B.G. and A.L. Strauss. 1967. *The Discovery of Grounded Theory*. Chicago: Aldine.

Goodman, P.S., T.L. Griffith and D.B. Fenner. 1990. "Understanding Technology and the Individual in an Organizational Context." Pp. 45-83 in *Technology and Organizations*, edited by P.S. Goodman, L.S. Sproull and Associates. San Francisco, CA: Jossey-Bass.

Guba, E.G. and Y.S. Lincoln. 1981. *Effective Evaluation: Improving the Usefulness of Evaluation Results through Responsive and Naturalistic Approaches*. San Francisco, CA: Jossey-Bass.

Harris, J.B. 1993. "An Internet-based Graduate Telecomputing Course: Practicing What We Preach." Pp. 641-645 in *Technology and Teacher Education Annual*, edited by D. Carey et al. Charlottesville, VA: Association for the Advancement of Computing in Education.

Harry, K., M. John and D. Keegan. 1993. *Distance Education: New Perspectives*. London: Routledge.

Hiemstra, G. 1982. "Teleconferencing, Concern for Face, and Organizational Culture." *Communication Yearbook* 6: 874-904.

Hiltz, S.R. 1990. "Evaluating the Virtual Classroom." Pp. 133-183 in *On-line Education: Perspectives on a New Environment*, edited by L.M. Harasim. New York: Praeger.

Hiltz, S.R. and M. Turoff. 1993. *Networked Nation*. Cambridge, MA: MIT Press.

Kapetelinin, V. (1996). "Computer-mediated Activity: Functional Organs in Social and Developmental Contexts." Pp. 45-68 in *Context and Consciousness: Activity Theory and Human-computer Interaction*, edited by B.A. Nardi. Cambridge, MA: MIT Press.

Keegan, D. 1986. *Foundations of Distance Education*, 2nd ed. London: Routledge.

Kelly, G. 1955. *The Psychology of Personal Constructs*, Vols. 1-2. New York: Norton.

de Kerckhove, D. 1995. *The Skin of Culture: Investigating the New Electronic Reality*. Toronto: Somerville House Publishing.

Kiesler, S., J. Siegel and T.W. McGuire. 1984. "Social Psychological Aspects of Computer Mediated Communication." *American Psychologist* 39(10): 1123-1134.

Kuhlthau, C.C. 1993. *Seeking Meaning: A Process Approach to Library and Information Services*. Norwood, NJ: Ablex.

LaGuardia, C. 1998. *Recreating the Academic Library: Breaking Virtual Ground*. New York: Neal Schulman Publishers.

Lesgold, A.M. and F. Reif. 1983. *Computers in Education: Realizing the Potential*. Washington, DC: U.S. Dept. of Education, Office of Educational Research and Improvement.

Lincoln, Y.S. and E.G. Guba. 1985. *Naturalistic Inquiry*. Newbury Park, CA: Sage.

LITA Board. 1999. "Top Technology Trends." Available on-line: http://www.lita.org/committee/toptech/trendsmw99.htm

MacMullin, S.E. and R.S. Taylor. 1984. "Problem Dimensions and Information Traits." *The Information Society* 3(1): 91-111.

Marshall, C. and G.B. Rossman. 1995. *Designing Qualitative Research*. Thousand Oaks, CA: Sage.

Mason, R. and T. Kaye. 1990. "Toward a New Paradigm for Distance Education." Pp. 15-30 in *On-line Education: Perspectives On a New Environment*, edited by L.M. Harasim. New York: Praeger.

Mead, G.H. 1962. *Mind, Self, and Sciety from the Standpoint of a Social Behaviorist*. Chicago: Chicago University Press.

Moore, M.G. 1973. "Toward a Theory of Independent Learning and Teaching." *Journal of Higher Education* 44(9): 661-679.

————. 1990. *Contemporary Issues in American Distance Education*. Oxford: Pergamon.

Nahl, D. 1993. "Communication Dynamics of Live, Interactive Television System for Distance Education." *Journal of the Association of Library and Information Science Educators* 34(3): 200-217.

Newby, G. 1993. "The Maturation of Norms for Computer-mediated Communication." *Internet Research* 3(4): 30-38.

Palmquist, R.A. 1992. "The Impact of Information Technology on the Individual." Pp. 3-42 in *Annual Review of Information Science and Technology*, Vol. 27, edited by M.E. Williams. Medford, NJ: Learned Information.

Reason, P. 1994. "Three Approaches to Participative Inquiry." Pp. 324-339 in *Handbook of Qualitative Research*, edited by N.K. Denzin and Y.S. Lincoln. Thousand Oaks, CA: Sage.

Resnick, L.B. 1991. "Shared Cognition: Thinking as Social Practice." Pp. 1-20 in *Perspectives on Socially Shared Cognition*, edited by L.B. Resnick, J.M. Levine and S.D. Teasley. Washington, DC: American Psychological Association.

Rice, R.E. and G. Love. 1987. "Electronic Emotion: Socioemotional Content in a Computer-mediated Communication Network." *Communication Research* 14(1): 85-108.

Rogers, C. 1969. *Freedom to Learn*. Columbus Ohio: Charles E. Merrill.

Rutkowska, J.C. and C. Crook. 1987. *Computers, Cognition and Development: Issues for Psychology and Education*. New York: John Wiley and Sons.

Sanders, L.M., ed. 1996. *The Evolving Virtual Library: Visions and Case Studies*. Medford, NJ: Information Today.

Santoro, G.M. 1995. "What is Computer-mediated Communication?" Pp. 11-27 in *Computer-mediated Communication and the Online Classroom: Overview and Perspectives*, Vol. 1, edited by Z.L. Berge and M.P. Collins. Cresskill, NJ: Hampton Press.

Savolainen, R. 1993. "The Sense-making Theory: Reviewing the Interests of a User-centered Approach to Information Seeking and Use." *Information Processing & Management* 29(1): 13-28.

Schön, D.A. 1983. *The Reflective Practioner: How Professionals Think in Action*. New York: Basic Books.

Shannon, C.E. and W. Weaver. 1949. *The Mathematical Theory of Communication*. Urbana: University of Illinois Press.

Short, J., E. Williams and B. Christie. 1976. *The Social Psychology of Telecommunication*. London: Wiley.

Simpson, J.A. and E.S.C. Weaver, eds. 1984. *Oxford English Dictionary*, 2nd ed. Oxford: Clarendon Press.

Spradley, J.P. 1980. *Participant Observation*. New York: Harcourt, Brace, Jovanovich.

Sproull, L. and S. Kiesler. 1986. "Reducing Social Context Cues: Electronic Mail in Organizational Communication." *Management Science* 32(11): 1492-1512.

Steinfield, C. 1986. "Computer-mediated Communication in an Organizational Setting: Explaining Task-related and Socioemotional Uses." *Communication Yearbook* 9: 777-803.

Thibaut, J.W. and H.H. Kelley. 1959. *The Social Psychology of Groups*. New York: John Wiley and Sons.

Turkle, S. 1995. *Life on the Screen: Identity in the Age of the Internet*. New York: Simon and Schuster.

Turner, J.H. 1988. *A Theory of Social Interaction*. Stanford, CA: Stanford University Press.

Walther, J.B. and J.K. Burgoon. 1992. "Relational Communication in Computer-mediated Interaction." *Human Communication Research* 19(1): 50-88.

Weick, K.E. 1985. "Cosmos vs. Chaos: Sense and Nonsense in Electronic Contexts." *Organizational Dynamics* 14: 50-64.

_____. 1990. "Technology as Equivoque: Sensemaking in New Technologies." Pp. 1-43 in *Technology and Organizations*, edited by P.S. Goodman, L.S. Sproull and Associates. San Francisco, CA: Jossey-Bass.

_____. 1993. "Collapse of Sensemaking in Organizations: The Mann Gulch Disaster." *Administrative Science Quarterly* 38: 628-652.

_____. 1995. *Sensemaking in Organizations.* Thousand Oaks, CA: Sage.

Williams, E. 1975. "Coalition Formation over Telecommunication Media." *European Journal of Social Psychology* 5: 503-507.

_____. 1977. "Experimental Comparisons of Face-to-face and Mediated Communication: A Review." *Psychological Bulletin* 84(5): 963-976.

_____. 1979. "Teleconferencing: Social and Psychological Factors." *Journal of Communication* 28: 125-131.

Williams, F., R.E. Rice and E.M. Rogers. 1988. *Research Methods and the New Media.* New York: The Free Press.

Wilson, S. 1977. The Use of Ethnographic Techniques in Educational Research. *Review of Educational Research* 47(1): 245-265.

Wilson, T.D. 1981. "On User Studies and Information Needs." *The Journal of Documentation* 37(1): 3-15.

Wolcott, H.F. 1994. *Transforming Qualitative Data.* Thousand Oaks, CA: Sage.

Zweizig, D. and B. Dervin. 1977. "Public Library Use, Users, Uses: Advances in Knowledge of the Characteristics and Needs of the Adult Clientele of American Public Lbraries." Pp. 231-255 in *Advances in Librarianship*, Vol. 77, edited by M.J. Voigt and M.K. Harris. New York: Academic Press.

Zuboff, S. 1984. *In the Age of the Smart Machine: The Future of Work and Power.* New York: Basic Books.

THE CHANGING ROLE OF THE
CHIEF INFORMATION OFFICER
IN HIGHER EDUCATION

Jon P. O'Donnell and Isadore Newman

INTRODUCTION

The use of information technology (IT) in higher education has received tremendous attention from researchers, educators, administrators, politicians, and others, in part because of the resources that have been dedicated to it. Hogue (1995) estimated that over $4 billion are spent annually on IT in higher education. This study concentrated on how that investment in technology is administered and supported, and more specifically, with the predictions made by Synnott and Gruber (1981) concerning the creation of the chief information officer (CIO) position.

THE LITERATURE

Synnott and Gruber (1981, p. 66) defined the CIO as a "senior executive responsible for establishing corporate information policy, standards, and management

Advances in Library Administration and Organization, Volume 17, pages 155-185.
Copyright © 2000 by JAI Press Inc.
All rights of reproduction in any form reserved.
ISBN: 0-7623-0647-5

control over all corporate information resources." The CIO should be able to provide centralized management and control over information processing and utilization even though it may be distributed geographically and functionally throughout the organization. According to these authors, organizations that fail to implement the CIO position will suffer from an opportunity cost associated with not treating information as a resource that must be managed as a total entity. They predicted that leading-edge information managers would gradually evolve into the role of a CIO as they integrate technology more effectively into the core of the business and that they would move up the corporate ladder and be recognized as their organization's CIO.

The use of technology in higher education was initially limited to administrative support functions such as payroll, accounting, and registration (Ryland 1989). Today, technology has pervaded almost every functional area of higher education. The Internet has led to nearly ubiquitous access to electronic information. In the early 1990s this was mainly limited to individual researchers sharing information via electronic mail and later included topical subject forums and bulletin boards. Today, many faculty consider the Internet to be their most valuable research tool and can electronically publish any form of information including text, graphics, video, and audio; and make it immediately accessible to millions of people.

This is leading to a more computer literate employee population that, in turn, demands more access to information. Campus libraries are becoming more driven by technology. A growing number of journals and periodicals are available in electronic form. Many of the index and search engines are accessible via the Internet and have been expanded to include information concerning library holdings and links to related items. Some information providers are even maintaining repositories of past articles and other (non-published) information sources that are only accessible in electronic form, and libraries expect to provide more journals only on-line.

Technology is also changing the way faculty fulfill their responsibilities beyond teaching and research. Electronic access is often available to departmental budget and enrollment figures. It is difficult for a CIO to explain to a faculty member that, although they can access U.S. census information and images from the Hubbell Telescope, they are not allowed to access student records for advising purposes.

Technology is also playing a major role in providing alternative methods of instructional delivery. Distance learning has received increased attention in recent years and has been fueled by the Clinton Administration's desire to make at least two years of college education available to every citizen. Some people are even questioning the need for physical university campuses in the future.

According to Mara (1994), the user population for information technology at Cornell University has grown from a few hundred central office staff to over 20,000 members of the university community. Newcome (1995) stated that, in tough financial times, there is a tendency for the administration to turn to technology for solutions. Has this infusion of technology been accompanied by changes in the organizational structure to maximize its effectiveness as predicted by Synnott and Gruber (1981)?

As technology continues to pervade every facet of higher education, the need for an individual to plan for, oversee, and coordinate this technology grows. The rise of the role of the CIO in higher education has been predicted in the past. Woodsworth (1987) and Penrod, Dolence and Douglas (1990) showed that the position was appearing in greater numbers between 1986 and 1989. A study by Pitkin (1993) showed some conflicting results.

Woodsworth (1987) provided the initial work in describing CIO positions in higher education, including the demographics and qualifications of incumbents, profiles of responsibilities, and organizational structures. In her recommendations for further research, she calls for a broad-based longitudinal study that could provide information about the effects of the size of the institution on the reporting levels of the CIO position.

A longitudinal study would also provide information about the changing qualifications required for and expectations of CIOs. Woodsworth, Gapen and Pollock (1987) speculated that as the pace of technological change stabilizes, the CIO of today will be tomorrow's "Model T" and that the CIO of the future will need a less technical background. Several respondents in the 1986 study projected that their positions would become broader in scope and include more functions in the future, but at least one respondent speculated that the position would entirely disappear as technology becomes absorbed into the fabric of all areas in the university.

Higher education is notoriously resistant to change. If the role of the CIO is becoming more prominent then other roles may be becoming less prominent. If there is a trend toward implementing CIO positions and aligning all technology units under them, then this should affect the entire organizational structure.

In these times of limited resources and increased competition in higher education there is a greater need to maximize the return on investments. Colleges and universities are investing heavily in information technology. Is somebody responsible for optimizing this investment or are institutions suffering from the opportunity cost associated with the inefficiencies of decentralized control of information technology?

The CIO is a businessman first and technologist second and is responsible for maximizing the benefits of using technology to solve core business problems. Teaching and research are the core of the higher education business. In the last five years, technology has had dramatic effects on these areas. The Colorado Community College system already offers associate degrees that can be completed over the Internet without ever physically seeing an instructor or even entering the state. Has this integration of technology into the core business of higher education been accompanied by an expanding role of the CIO position in higher education?

Is support of the academic mission receiving increased attention as evidenced by changing staffing patterns between academic computing and administrative computing? Is the CIO role more prominent where this occurs? Are CIOs more prominent in institutions that dedicate a greater percentage of their technology budget to academic instead of administrative support functions? Is there a relationship between the percentage of the general budget dedicated to technology and the prominence of the CIO?

There is a lot of debate over whether the library should report to a CIO instead of the chief academic officer. How many institutions have their head of libraries reporting to a CIO? Are institutions changing to this organization as more of the information in the library is available in digital form? In institutions where the library reports to the CIO, is it more likely for the CIO to report to the chief academic officer than the president?

Many factors can affect the role of the CIO on campus. Woodsworth (1987) indicated a need to study the relationship between institution size and the CIO role. Is the CIO position emerging more in research institutions than in community colleges of similar sizes? Are public institutions more likely to have CIOs than private institutions? Are larger institutions more likely to have CIOs than smaller institutions?

Synnott and Gruber (1981) stated that the ultimate goal of the new breed of information manager should be to become recognized as the CIO by top management. They identified some strategies for information managers to use to progress toward this goal. One such strategy was to take a lead role in information management planning and institution-wide strategic planning. Are campuses with a formal strategic planning process more likely to have a prominent CIO position? Are the CIOs being recognized as CIOs by their institutions?

This longitudinal study tested Synnott and Gruber's predictions as well as provided answers to the conflicts reported in Pitkin's study. In addition, by following the same institutions for three years, it provided an opportunity to identify trends in the changing role of the CIO in higher education. This was the first study that applied a consistent definition and measurement of the degree to which the CIO concept evolves in institutions over time.

REVIEW OF THE LITERATURE

The CIO concept originated in the business environment. Synnott and Gruber (1981, p. 66) provided the first comprehensive description of the role and responsibilities of the CIO in the corporate world. They defined the CIO as a "senior executive responsible for establishing corporate information policy, standards, and management control over all corporate information resources." They identified nine roles that CIOs must perform to be effective executive officers and described a number of strategies for information managers to employ in order to evolve their positions into CIOs.

Synnott (1987) described the CIO as the highest ranking executive with primary responsibility for information management. Ganz (1985) and Dillman and Hicks (1990) support this idea of the CIO being an executive-level position. Turner (1984) and Augustson (1989) add to this definition the responsibility for long-range planning.

Anne Woodsworth (1987) provided the initial descriptive research on the role of the CIO in American universities. She later (1991) provided a three-tiered scale based on span of control to describe the degree to which the CIO concept had been implemented in higher education as follows.

1. Total CIO. Responsibility for academic computing, administrative computing, libraries, telecommunications, instructional resources, graphics, printing and copying services, and surface mail.
2. Almost Complete CIO. The most common model. Gives the CIO in colleges and universities a good portion of the responsibilities outlined above, most typically academic computing, administrative systems, and telecommunications (both voice and data). The single element most often missing from the portfolio of the almost complete CIO is the library. The most common configuration of a job for the CIO at present is the one that omits libraries, printing, copying, mail services, and other like areas.
3. Staff Role. This is a rare model. Without the power to directly implement policies, these CIOs must coordinate, cajole, coerce, or otherwise handle managers of various information units and guide them toward common goals and policies.

Penrod, Dolence and Douglas (1990) conducted another study of the CIO position in Higher Education. They identified a three-tiered scale that describes the degree to which the CIO concept is implemented based primarily on the reporting level of the CIO and the corresponding implications in terms of budget and policy control as well as interactions with executive officers.

1. Vice President Level. The position normally reports directly to the Chief Executive Officer of the institution or at least to the Provost or Executive Vice President. These individuals often function as executive officers of the institution and have either line responsibility or policy-setting authority for most information technology resources in the institution and often control funding for technology.
2. Associate Vice President Level. This type of CIO is also a policy officer but most likely reports to the Provost or Executive Vice President. The CIO has line responsibility for many of the IT resources but does not control funding for technology.

3. Director Level. This position generally reports to a vice president or associate vice president, is not an executive officer, and has limited policy authority. Contact with executive officers of the institution is limited to technical issues and it is unlikely that an institutional technology plan even exists.

Horgan (1996, p. 1), President of the CAUSE constituent group for CIOs, emphasized that the CIO must take the enterprise view and maintain an institutional focus rather than a narrower technology perspective. She defined the term CIO in higher education in the following way.

> The term "chief information officer" in higher education does not have a clear functional definition. For some, a CIO is a senior-level administrator who participates on the institution's executive council and who is responsible for institution-wide information resources management (including central computing and networking, the library, telecommunications, multimedia, printing, and so forth). For others, a CIO is a senior information technology officer who provides high-level oversight for information technology related operations and who works in partnership with the college or university library head and advisory groups in planning for institution-wide investment in information resources—technology, services, and information.

Purpose of the CIO Position

Synnott and Gruber (1981, p. 12) begin with the premise that information is an ingredient vital to good management. They suggest that the decreasing cost and increasing performance of new technologies have created very real opportunities for improvement in the effectiveness of organizations but that these opportunities are not easy to exploit. They aptly describe the challenges facing the CIO as follows:

> Information management is like drinking out of a fire hydrant. The flow of new technologies is so strong that it is difficult to control consumption. There are a large number of serious issues in the management of information resources, and the length of the list of difficult problems is increasing rapidly. Responding to these rapid changes in the information age will require information managers who can manage by plan rather than by crisis....

> The problems today in the information systems field are legion, but I cite only a few: the need to prioritize the huge resources that are being pumped into information systems development; the need to integrate the various pieces; the difficulties that nonspecialists are finding in working with new technologies; the conflicts between the information specialists and the users of information; and the lack of education of top management as to the key opportunities.

These challenges can all be restated today because they stem from rapid changes in technology and the decisions concerning the integration of that technology into the organization. According to Synnott and Gruber (1981, pp. 67, 76), the main purpose for creating a CIO position is to avoid paying the opportunity costs associated with not treating information as a corporate resource. They believe in the need for someone to act as the architect of the organization's information capabilities in a conscious effort to allocate scarce resources where they will do the most good for the organization. In their words,

> What needs to be sold is not the CIO role but an understanding and acceptance of the fact that information is a valuable corporate resource that must be managed as a total entity, and that the role of the manager of information resources must be that of CIO in order to exert a broad corporate perspective and a leadership role in bringing together and managing information as a corporate resource.

> If knowledge is power, then information is power, because knowledge is information. Companies can't run without it; managers can't manage without it. Yet, organizations are only just beginning to recognize the value of their corporate information resources.

Woodsworth, Gapen and Pollock (1987, p. 3) described the need for integration and coordination among the different technology units as a major reason for the creation of the CIO position in higher education. It was not uncommon to have separate directors of the library, media center, telecommunications department, and computer center all performing some similar tasks and moving in similar directions with little planning and much replication of effort.

> One of the major reasons for creating a CIO position in academic institutions is that information services and technologies are increasingly viewed as a utility, providing "power" to a broad spectrum of the academic community. This utility must be developed effectively and efficiently, and plans must be made to cope with the inevitable changes in information technology, so that an institution can incorporate them in a cost-effective manner.

Barone (1989) and Penrod (1985) believe the key reason for the creation of the CIO position in higher education is based on the need for planning a solid infrastructure for computing technology and services. The CIO would be responsible for bridging the gap between the information technology plan and the institutional goals. Battin (1989) suggests that distributed computing only exacerbated the need for a centralized infrastructure that was globally coordinated to support the decentralization of computing power.

Past Predictions on the Rise of the CIO Position

According to Turner (1984), only 20 higher education institutions had CIOs prior to 1984. Penrod, Dolence and Douglas (1990) and Woodsworth (1991) revealed that the number of higher education institutions that have implemented either the first or second category of CIO has doubled every two years between 1986 and 1990 as a replacement for the third category. Even after this rapid rise, Penrod, Dolence and Douglas (1990) asserted that no more than one-third of all higher education institutions had either instituted the CIO position by 1990 or offered the potential for CIO positions. They predicted that over the next decade, this potential may grow to close to one-half of the colleges and universities in the country.

Woodsworth (1987) stated that several of the CIOs participating in her study projected that their positions would become broader in scope and include more functions in the future, while at least one person speculated that the position would entirely disappear as technology becomes absorbed into the fabric of all areas in the university.

Temares (1991) predicted that the forces that caused a rise in the implementation of CIOs in the corporate sector have corresponding counterparts in higher education. These forces were identified as satisfying the information needs of students and faculty, a participatory approach to management, and aligning information technology with the goals of the organization. Responding to these forces will require the coordination and direction provided by a CIO.

Not everyone agreed with either the need for a CIO or predicted that their role would be expanded. B.L. Hawkins (Pitkin 1993, p. 10) contends that most higher education institutions created the position out of panic without planning because it appeared to solve problems in the private sector. Burch (1989) considers CIOs as nothing more than title inflation and Freedman (1987) suggested that the idea of strategic information technology is just an academic exercise that has provided a new way to sell senior management on bigger information systems budgets. Fleit (1989) considers the idea of "chief" anything as being foreign to higher education because there is a notorious lack of formal authority.

Prior Studies

Woodsworth (1987) conducted the initial descriptive study on the CIO position in higher education. She interviewed 28 of the 32 CIOs that were found in a prior study (Woodsworth 1986) among the 91 institutions that were members of the Association of Research Libraries. Information was collected concerning levels of responsibility of the CIO for information technology units, levels of participation in decision making about the IT units, reporting level of the CIO, and biographical information. The results of the study indicated that CIOs reported equally to presidents and provosts and that they tended to have responsibility for academic computing, administrative systems and telecommunications but only a minor responsibility for library automation.

Penrod, Dolence and Douglas (1990) conducted a national survey in which they identified more than 150 individuals that appeared to be serving as CIOs based on position titles attained from the 1988 Higher Education Directory and attendance lists of the 1988 national conferences of CAUSE and EDUCOM. They looked for titles containing a combination of a senior management designation (such as vice president) and a reference to technology. They also acknowledged that small colleges and community colleges were underrepresented on their original lists. They then collected and analyzed 58 usable responses, of which over one-half were from research universities. Nearly 40 percent of the respondents reported to the CEO, 19 percent reported to the provost/CAO, and 36 percent reported to another vice president. Data communications reported to the CIO in 96 percent of the responses, administrative computing in 89 percent, academic computing in 86 percent, voice communications in 69 percent, planning in 32 percent, institutional research in 19 percent, the library in 15 percent, and media services in 15 percent. CIOs who reported to the president were more likely to supervise institutional research and CIOs who considered themselves executive officers of the institution were more likely to oversee voice communications.

Penrod, Dolence and Douglas (1990) compared their findings with those of Woodsworth (1987) and concluded that the CIO positions in higher education were "maturing." They based their conclusion on the fact that nearly 40 percent of the CIOs in their survey reported to the president compared to under 30 percent in the Woodsworth (1987) study. In addition, the CIOs in the 1990 study were more likely to have a policy committee and less likely to hold degrees in computing, engineering, or physics. However, their conclusions may be questionable given the fact that they surveyed two entirely different populations and that the 1990 study used the title of the CIO in determining the population it included.

Pitkin (1993) conducted a study primarily aimed at determining whether the role of the CIO position in higher education is characteristic of the role in the business sector. In addition, this study collected demographic characteristics including reporting relationships of the CIOs and reported them by type of institution. Pitkin (1993) concluded that the trends cited by Woodsworth (1986, 1991) and Penrod, Dolence and Douglas (1990) were reversing.

Pitkin's study was also limited to institutions that already employed a CIO. The primary source of this list was the 1991 edition of *Institutions with a Recognized CIO* produced by CAUSE, although the 1990 edition of *Peterson's Register of Higher Education* (Wells, Henne and Harrigan 1989) was also used. Surveys were sent to 200 institutions, and 153 usable responses were received with over one-half of these coming from doctoral granting institutions. Pitkin's study found that 26 percent of the respondents reported to the CEO, 30 percent reported to the provost/CAO, 37 percent reported to some other vice president, and the remaining 6 percent reported to other positions. Data communications reported to the CIO in 92 percent of the responses, administrative computing in 91 percent, academic computing in 80 percent, voice communications in 62 percent, planning in 19 percent, institutional research in 22 percent, the library in 11 percent, and media services in 14 percent.

Using the same logic employed by Penrod, Dolence and Douglas (1990), Pitkin's findings refute the claim that the CIO position in higher education was "maturing." Penrod, Dolence and Douglas based their claim in part on the fact that the number of CIOs that report to the president increased from only 28 percent in Woodsworth's study to nearly 40 percent. In Pitkin's study, this number dropped to 26 percent. In addition, areas of responsibility for the CIO dropped off significantly in all cases except administrative computing.

There are many possible reasons for these conflicting results. Although advances in technology have occurred constantly over the life of these studies, the implementation of these technologies does not occur at a steady rate. The IBM PC was first introduced in 1981 and local area networks began to appear in the mid-1980s, but it was not until the early 1990s that they were implemented in mass in higher education. These technologies have played a key part in enabling decentralized computing and may lead to a weakening of the CIO role if one measures the number of things that person controls. If this is the case, the near ubiquitous access to the Internet in higher education and the network infrastructure required to support it would likely lead to a continued erosion of the role of the CIO.

The differing populations of the studies provide another possible explanation for the conflicts. Woodsworth's (1987) study consisted entirely of institutions belonging to the Association of Research Libraries which indicate a research focus. Penrod, Dolence and Douglas included all types of institutions in their study, but they acknowledged that smaller institutions were underrepresented. Pitkin's (1993) study was the only one which broke down results concerning areas of responsibility based on institution type (doctoral, master's, or undergraduate) and control (public or private). Pitkin's results showed that the most prominent CIO positions occurred in the private undergraduate institutions with the doctoral institutions also scoring high.

Rivet (1997) conducted a study to investigate the relationship between the CIO and CEO at small colleges in the United States based on the perceptions of CEOs. To be eligible, an institution had to have between 500 and 3,000 full-time students and offer at least baccalaureate degrees. One factor studied was the relationship between the administrative reporting level of the CIO and the CIO's role in campus decision making. The reporting level was measured based on the distance between the CIO and CEO.

The results of Rivet's (1997) study showed that the administrative distance between the CIO and CEO and the CEO's personal view of the importance of campus technology were nearly equally strong as predictors of the technology leader's role in campus decision making. She concluded that the institutionalization of technology and the role of the CIO on the small college campus appears to still be emerging. Although more presidents are recognizing the value of technology, many have still not acknowledged their CIOs as strategic campus decision makers.

Organizational Structure Issues

The CAUSE Current Issues Committee is responsible for proposing a list of current or developing issues and trends that are important to the future of information resources management and use in higher education. The list, published in the

Spring 1997 issue of CAUSE/EFFECT, included the issue of Information Resources Organization and Job Restructuring. The effects of technology on organizational structures is not limited to administrative offices. Information resources organizations are expected to have a natural organizational agility to adapt to technological change yet are often constrained by rigid job classification schemes.

Branin, D'Elia and Lund (1994) have noted that the organizational rather than technological challenges have been most difficult for CIOs to deal with and cited the continued disagreements about whether centralized or decentralized structures work best in higher education. It is important to note that an institution's IT organization could theoretically be completely centralized or decentralized, but most institutions will fall somewhere along the continuum in between.

Some authors would argue that the need for a CIO is greatest in a decentralized organization to maximize effectiveness. Battin (1989, pp. 369-370) describes this as follows: "The paradox of information technology is that it makes possible an unprecedented decentralization of technical power to individual option while at the same time it requires a globally coordinated infrastructure to permit the effective individual exercise of that power."

Other authors call for abandoning the hierarchical organizational structures of the industrial age in favor of more networked management or project-oriented approaches. Donovan (1988) suggests that the best organization for IT would be a network of individuals, systems, and databases organized around a strategic set of functions. Network structures tend to have fewer organizational levels with wider spans of control and are characterized by flexibility and a reduction in organizational barriers. Barone (1987) believes that this allows success to be measured in strategic terms and focuses attention on institutional goals.

The microcomputer revolution of the 1980s provided the means for individual units on campus to take control of computing in their offices. According to Solomon (1994), many believed this was the answer to the frustrating bureaucracy of central computing services and their seeming indifference to departmental needs. Although it could be argued that a well-run centralized operation could provide all the advantages of a decentralized organization, the root of the difference stems from the organizational distance between the operational "line" personnel and the technical support staff.

Reporting Level

The organizational level to which the CIO reports has been used in nearly every definition of a CIO to date (Synnott and Gruber 1981; Synnott 1987; Ganz 1985; Turner 1984; Augustson 1989; Dillman and Hicks 1990; Heterick and Sanders 1993). Whether in a hierarchical or networked organizational structure, the presumption is that reporting directly to the CEO provides more direct contact with executive-level management and more participation in campus-wide decision making. Rivet (1997) showed a strong correlation between these factors, as did Penrod, Dolence and Douglas (1990).

According to Heterick and Sanders (1993), because the responsibilities of a CIO necessarily cross organizational boundaries and the IT resources must be viewed as available to the entire campus, the CIO must remain politically neutral. Rivet (1997) suggests that, if the CIO is administratively subordinate to either a purely academic or administrative division on campus, there is a risk of violating this neutrality. Caffrey and Mosmann (1967) believe that reporting to the CEO is an indication of the CEO's willingness to intervene as arbitrator when disputes arise over technology allocations. These arguments lead Rivet (1997, p. 6) to conclude that

> certainly, then, the alliance of the president's position on the campus with that of the organizational placement of the campus technology leader (i.e., the chief information officer) can be a critical element in the success of campus technology initiatives and the effectiveness of the chief information officer as a campus administrator.

Synnott and Gruber (1981, p. 29) make a number of references to the reporting level of the CIO position. Their premise is that being a successful business manager in addition to understanding emerging technologies will provide the CIO with the means to bridge the technology with the business goals and result in making the CIO a part of the senior management of the firm. They stated this most clearly in the following passage.

> Another important point is the location of the information management function in the company hierarchy. It is important that it have a position in the organization of equal stature with other major functions of the business. Why? Because IM is a corporate-wide activity, and making it subservient to another function could deprive the company of the real potential of its scarce (and expensive) resources.

Span of Control

The span of control for a CIO is determined by the number of information technology functions that are overseen by the CIO position. In some cases the CIO is directly responsible for the function, and in others there is a responsible line officer that reports to the CIO. Using the span of control in the definition of the prominence of the CIO does imply that more prominent CIOs come from more centralized organizations. However, even in distributed models there tends to be centralized planning, policy, and support structures.

Synnott and Gruber (1981, p. 50) suggest that the CIO must be able to provide this centralized planning and control over information technology functions even though they may be distributed geographically and functionally throughout the organization. They use the term "coalescence planning" to refer to the process of determining which functions in the organization are properly a part of the information technology unit. Their views on the relationship between centralized and distributed models is best described in the following passage.

> The spread of sophisticated and expensive technical resources throughout the company will require extra care in the management of these resources. Operations can be distributed, even systems development can be distributed, but management control must never be distributed because such distribution would create decentralized chaos.

The advantages and disadvantages of a centralized versus a decentralized structure for IT have been debated for many years. Authors such as Solomon (1994) would argue that a centralized structure is more efficient based on reducing redundancies, setting standards, and pooling expertise. Mulhollan (1989) argues that the development and implementation of a strategic plan can only be done in a centralized structure. On the other hand, arguments in support of a decentralized approach were outlined by Kettinger (1990) and stem from benefits associated with keeping the control of the technologies close to the problems that they address without much concern for the "baggage" attached to large centralized services.

McClure (1992) proposed that two factors affecting the kinds of organizational structures used in IT departments in higher education were the convergence of digital technologies and the organizational culture of the institution. Technological trends have led to a number of areas providing traditional services in new ways. An examination of the services and people who provide them led to questions of duplication and turf wars. At the heart of the convergence of services is the concentration on the network as a means of providing solutions. McClure (1992) identified the following areas of overlap between traditionally separate units.

1. The most obvious overlap is that the missions of both computer centers and libraries concentrate on sharing information. Books and journals were once the library's domain and computer files were the computer center's domain. The more that library information is available electronically, without the user ever stepping into the building, the more it appears to be just another computer application.

2. Voice, data, and video traffic may now all share the same physical wires. If these functions report through different vice presidents, which should be responsible for this infrastructure?

3. Academic and administrative computing were traditionally separated by the differences in the needs of administrators and faculty. With widespread uses of PCs and local area networks in both environments this separation can lead to conflicting standards and recommendations.

4. The office of media services was traditionally responsible for slide projectors and televisions, but, now that instructional technology involves presen-

tation software and distance learning over the Internet, it overlaps with academic computing.

5. Advances in high-speed laser printers and desktop publishing software create some overlap between the computer center, printing services, and copy centers.

McClure (1992) also identified a number of organizational strategies from simple reorganization to a full merger and vertical integration of technology units possibly accompanied by downsizing. One of the organizational strategies involved the creation of a CIO position to centralize IT leadership and possibly shift unit reporting lines to this office. This strategy is consistent with Pflueger's (1996) description of California Lutheran University and Chan's (1995) description of DePaul University as well as the latest reorganization at The University of Akron. Another strategy was to establish some type of formal coordinating council, possibly in conjunction with a CIO position similar to Nelson and Davenport's (1996) description of Central Michigan University.

As stated earlier, most institutions fall somewhere between the fully distributed and completely centralized models. Eleey (1993) described the organizational structure at The University of Pennsylvania and its Wharton Business School as distributed support with central management. Payton and Mueller (1992) described the organizational structure at Stanford University as consisting of a centralized data center for accounting and personnel systems but a decentralized approach to many other systems. Payton and Mueller (1992) agreed that it was more difficult to do strategic planning, enforce standards, integrate systems across business lines, and provide career paths for technical staff in decentralized units, but they believed that they had advantages of offering a more intense commitment to their department and advanced business knowledge and that those far outweighed these negative factors.

Conrad, Rome and Wasileski (1994) describe the organizational structure of information technology at Arizona State University as being similar to that of The University of Pennsylvania as described by Eleey (1993). They use a central management structure but physically distribute the support functions while reserving 20 percent of the staff time for central meetings and training. These authors charge centralized organizations with providing technical solutions with no business needs, allowing huge backlogs just to lobby for more resources, and being reluctant to empower nontechnical staff.

Merging of Libraries and Computer Services

Many authors have called for a closer alignment between the library and computer center citing better control, coordination, funding, and efficiency as reasons (Battin 1984; Jones 1995; West and Katz 1990). Reorganizations lead to changing individual roles and a blending of cultures. This appears to be especially problematic when library and computing centers are joined under a CIO. One initial problem is that the director of libraries and/or the computer center director could consider this a demotion. Sharrow (1995) identified nine barriers to library and IT cooperation. West and Smith (1996) concentrated on the cultural differences between these offices, calling their merger a potential "clash of titans."

Widner and Lawlor (1994) identified three barriers to cooperation between libraries and computer centers that seem to provide a good summary. The first was the autonomy that both computer center directors and library directors enjoy due to the specialized functions they serve. Neither a provost nor vice president of business is expected to understand their day-to-day operations and tend to defer to their decisions and recommendations.

A second barrier to cooperation is based on cultural differences between library and computer staff. Library staff consider themselves to be faculty, require academic credentials (usually an MLS), and often hold faculty rank. They see their role as direct service to the research and instructional mission of the college. Computer staff see themselves outside this mission and are more impressed by technical expertise than credentials. As experts, they tend to have a different philosophy toward service to their "users" than librarians have toward their "patrons." West and Smith (1996) consider librarians to have a feminine culture and computer center staff to have a masculine culture.

The third barrier to cooperation identified by Widner and Lawlor (1994) is the overlap in functions performed by staff in each office. Technology issues have become core to the role of librarians as their job changes from showing patrons where to find information to showing them how to find information. Until the definition of the roles and responsibilities of the staff become clear there will be some tension between personnel on both sides. This is especially true when the compensation structures definitely favor one over the other.

Having a CIO oversee both the library and computer services seems to directly address the first barrier because the CIO is expected to have some knowledge of both operations as well as how each fits into the strategic plans of the institution. The next two issues are based on the clarity and distinction of personnel roles. Creation of a CIO is often accompanied by a reorganization into functional units that may lead to reclassifications of positions. Woodsworth (1991) addresses this issue calling for more generic position descriptions such as Information Technologist and moving away from specializations.

Institution Size, Control, and Type

Woodsworth (1987), in her recommendations for further research, called for a closer investigation into the role of CIOs in different sizes of institutions. Woodsworth's study was limited to research institutions. Pitkin (1993) completed the only study investigated that reported some of its results by institution type and control. The effects, if any, that institution size, type, and control may play in the prominence of the CIO position may be based on the governance models most prevalent in these institutions.

Birnbaum (1988) described four prominent organizational governance models in higher education and offered a fifth more comprehensive model that blends the others. Bolman and Deal (1984) suggest that every manager uses a personal model of organizations when making decisions. Although none of these models fits all aspects of any institution all of the time, all models fit some aspects of all institutions some of the time (Birnbaum 1988). It is, therefore, important to keep in mind that situational factors must be considered in all decision making and that elements that are prevalent in one type of institution will occur in microcosms of other types of institutions.

The collegial model is most closely associated with small, private, residential, selective liberal arts colleges. Most faculty and staff live close to campus and the campus is the center of their social lives. A collegial system is made up of a community of equals in which individual status differences are de-emphasized and there is a mutual respect for the opinions of all. Organizational structure in a collegium is not very important and most communication occurs on an informal basis with little need to commit agreements to paper. Decisions are ultimately made by a consensus that requires open discussions so that all parties feel that they have had a chance to speak in support of an issue. This may require an extended amount of time for major decisions. There is little accountability in decision making because no individual is charged with making the decision.

Ringle and Smallen (1996) identified some differences on technology issues between small colleges and larger universities. Small colleges often emphasize teaching over research and publication, and their budgets are usually tuition-based and do not allow for major technology investments. Therefore, they tend to be prone to collaborative relationships with other institutions and are not as quick to emphasize the values of technology. Funding for IT in the collegium is likely to be considered a price that all must bear in support of the quality of their institution and be covered from a centralized pool of funds.

The bureaucratic model is most commonly found in public undergraduate institutions that emphasize low cost, access, community needs, and career preparation. The faculty as well as the students may spend little time on campus outside of the classroom. Although there remains some collegial interaction within the subunits, rules and regulations create the framework within which most interaction between units occurs. The underlying premise in bureaucratic institutions is that the day-to-day functioning of the institution can occur in a more efficient and effective manner with less reliance on judgments made by administrators through rules and standard operating procedures. Most bureaucracies are characterized by an organization chart that maps out the official interactions that are to occur.

The political model is prevalent in medium to large public comprehensive universities with extensive mission statements that appear to be connected to many programs beyond teaching, research and community service. The campus is characterized by diversity. In political institutions, the complex organization is broken into many subgroups based on characteristics such as work groups (departments), work type (faculty, staff, or student), age, ethnicity, or sex. Individuals belong to many of these subgroups, and each subgroup has different goals and values. Each group must compete for influence and resources which often requires joining with other groups to compromise and bargain.

The organized anarchy model is most prevalent in large, complex, graduate, research institutions. It is similar to the political model in that there are many subgroups and subcultures. Three characteristics of an organized anarchy are unclear goals, unclear technology, and unclear participation. When goals are unclear, it is difficult to decide on what is right or wrong. Technologies refer to how organizations turn inputs into outputs. It is difficult to say exactly what happens to a student from the time he or she enrolls until graduation. Unclear participation refers to the many forums in which issues may be aired and debated. People tend to move into and out of these forums based on the time they have available.

RESEARCH METHOD

This study employed an ex post facto research design with repeated measures that was guided by past and present theoretical and empirical data and specific research hypotheses. It tested the previously stated hypothetical relationships between the prominence of the CIO position and the alignment of technology with the core business of higher education. Although ex post facto research has relatively low internal validity, the ability to use large sample sizes often increases its external validity.

The CAUSE member institution survey database was used for the study. Surveys were sent out in 1994, 1995, and 1996. Although there were 462 responses in 1994, 425 responses in 1995, and 345 responses in 1996, only 131 institutional members responded to all three surveys, and the results of this study are based on those institutions.

The major weakness in prior studies has been that they took a single snapshot of the CIO position from many institutions and then made comparisons between institutions. This study was mainly focused on changes in the CIO position and the associated organizational structure over time. An institution with no clear CIO in 1994 that created the position in 1995 or 1996 would indicate a rise in the prominence of the CIO position. Another institution may have abandoned the CIO concept and completely decentralized all management of information technology over this same period. Investigating these factors required tracking this progression at specific institutions to determine whether the roles have changed from year to year.

The instruments were developed by the Information Resources Committee at CAUSE in an attempt to provide benchmark information to help member institutions compare themselves to other similar institutions. Multiple linear regression (the general linear model) was used to test 15 specific research hypotheses. A regression model was written for the specific research hypotheses, and the full and restricted models were then tested to see if each specific research hypothesis would be accepted or rejected.

Each of the 131 institutions was measured three times, providing a total of 393 observations. Statistical analysis assumes that all observations are independent and this assumption would be violated if the study did not control for the individual differences between institutions (McNeil, Newman and Kelly 1996). Multiple linear regression was chosen as the statistical method in this study to provide the means to control for these differences.

All of the specific research hypotheses were directional except for those dealing with the relationship between the prominence of the CIO position and the institution's size, Carnegie classification, and control. An F test was used to determine if the R^2 of the full and restricted models were significantly different at an alpha level of .05.

Power is the ability of the statistical analysis to find significance if in fact significance exists (McNeil, Newman and Kelly 1996). Using an alpha level of .05 and the N size of 393, the power can be calculated for different effect sizes. Cohen (1977) arbitrarily defined three effect sizes: large (> .35), medium (.15 to .35), and small (< .15). Using an effect size of .15, the ability of this study to detect significance if it exists is over 99 percent. Using an effect size of .05 will still yield a power of almost 95 percent.

Assumptions and Limitations

Several assumptions underlie this study. First of all, it is based on information collected from institutions that are members of CAUSE. CAUSE was The Association for the Management of Information Technology in Higher Education and the publisher of CAUSE/EFFECT. CAUSE's mission was to be an indispensable partner in enabling the transformational changes occurring in higher education through the effective management and use of information resources—technology, services, and information. In 1997 more than 1,300 colleges and universities in the United States and abroad were members of CAUSE. Institutional members came from every state in the United States and from every type of institution: from the small liberal arts college to the largest state systems. In 1998, CAUSE and EDUCOM merged to form EDUCAUSE. Any ability to generalize these findings to all institutions is based on the assumption that institutions that joined CAUSE are not significantly different from other institutions.

Other assumptions are based on the timing of the survey instruments. Because this is a longitudinal study, it is assumed that any bias or errors from the participants in self-reported information were randomly distributed between surveys. Although the CAUSE member institution survey was designed by practicing professionals who were responding to the needs of their fellow constituents, completion of the surveys was not required and the length of the survey may have been a deterrent to some CIOs. No analysis is available to determine how different the institutions which responded to the survey are from those that did not.

There is no precise definition of exactly what constitutes a CIO (Horgan 1996) so the two indicators chosen in this study were designed to cover both primary schools of thought as well as to provide some ability to compare its results to those of earlier studies. The instruments were filled out by the CAUSE member at each institution. It is likely that some of these individuals changed between the beginning and end of this study, and the results could be affected by their personal opinions. Because this study is focused on changes at individual institutions over time and the instrument was often sent to the same individuals, it is likely that these individuals reported consistently.

RESULTS OF THE STUDY

CIO Prominence Trends

The first question addressed by this study was based on the predictions by Synnott and Gruber (1981) that the new breed of information managers are moving out of the back shop and into business manager roles and climbing the corporate ladder as their company's CIO. They suggest that one of the main reasons for the creation of a CIO position is to provide centralized management and planning to optimize the potential benefits of major investments in information management. Synnott and Gruber state that it is important that information management have a position in the organization of equal stature with other major functions of the business so that no part of the organization will be deprived of its scarce and expensive resources.

Synnott and Gruber (1981) and others predicted a rise in the prominence of the CIO position as the strategic importance of information is recognized by top management. A single, composite score representing the prominence of the CIO position was calculated based on descriptions of the CIO position from Synnott and Gruber (1981), Penrod, Dolence and Douglas (1990), Woodsworth (1991) and others. This score was determined by adding together the CIO's reporting level score and the span of control score.

The reporting level is an indication of the CIO's participation in executive-level management and decision making (Rivet 1997) and is used in virtually every definition of a CIO. It is based on the number of management levels between the CIO and CEO and operationally defined as follows. A scale of one through seven was chosen so that the reporting level would have equal weight, and the span of control was the measure used to determine the overall prominence of the CIO score (see Table 1).

Table 1.   Reporting Level Scores

Officer to Whom CIO Reports	Score
Chief Executive Officer	7
Chief Academic Officer	5
Administrative Vice President, Chief Financial Officer, or Executive Vice President	3
Dean or Other	1

The span of control is also included in many definitions of a CIO and is an indicator of the degree of centralization of control over the information technology units. According to Woodsworth (1991), a total CIO would have primary reporting responsibility for academic computing, administrative computing, networking, telecommunications, data administration, libraries, and institutional research. The span of control in this study was operationally defined by scoring one point for each of the functions which reports to the CIO, for a maximum possible score of seven. One point would be scored even if there was no clear CIO because any one of the unit department heads could be chosen.

The reporting level, span of control, and prominence of the CIO were tested to see if they increased significantly each year over the three years studied while holding the individual differences between institutions constant. Although the results are inconclusive using all institutions (probability < .1), the predictions of Synnott and Gruber (1981) held true (probability < .0261) when the analysis was restricted to private institutions.

The reporting level at private institutions increased during this period with .76 percent of the variance uniquely accounted for by the change in years, independent of institution size, Carnegie classification, control, and the differences between the institutions. Similarly, the span of control at private institutions increased during this period with .69 percent of the variance uniquely accounted for by the change in years, independent of institution size, Carnegie classification, control, and the differences between the institutions. Because the prominence score is a summation of the span of control and reporting level scores, it is not surprising that it increased during the same period with .93 percent of the variance uniquely accounted for by the year while holding the same predictor variable constant.

These predictor variables account for only a small amount of unique variance, but this is not surprising when one considers that the differences between the 131 institutions were controlled for and only the changes due to the passage of time were measured. In all these cases the differences between the institutions accounted for over 80 percent of the total variance. This means that between 5 and 10 percent of the remaining variance was predicted by the passage of time.

Institution Size, Carnegie Classification, and Control

Woodsworth (1987) called for a closer investigation into the role of CIOs at different sizes of institutions. In general, doctoral granting institutions are larger than master's granting institutions, and master's granting institutions are larger than undergraduate institutions. In addition, public institutions in each Carnegie classification are larger on average than the corresponding private institutions. Therefore, any investigation into the role of institution size must also investigate the effects of Carnegie classification and institutional control (public or private).

Pitkin (1993) showed reporting relationships by Carnegie classification and institution control. The Carnegie classification system was compressed for the purpose of this study into undergraduate, master's, and doctoral institutions to aid in comparisons to information provided by Pitkin (1993) and to future studies. The Carnegie classification, control and FTE were all reported on the instrument.

There was a positive linear relationship between institution size and the prominence of the CIO at a probability of .0063. The size of the institution uniquely accounted for 1.84 percent of the variance in CIO prominence independent from Carnegie classification and institution control. Larger institutions had more prominent CIOs on average than smaller institutions, and this difference was especially significant in the reporting level component of the prominence.

The relationship between Carnegie classification and CIO prominence was also tested. The results for all institutions were not significant but when the analysis was restricted to include only the public institutions, significance was found. At public institutions 2.48 percent of the variance in CIO prominence was uniquely accounted for by Carnegie classification independent from institution size and control. On average, public doctoral granting institutions have more prominent CIOs than public master's granting institutions and public master's granting institutions have more prominent CIOs than public undergraduate institutions. When controlling for the effects of institution size and institution control (public or private), the master's granting institutions had a positive effect (parameter weight = +1.3124) on CIO prominence followed by doctoral granting (parameter weight = −0.2179) and undergraduate institutions (parameter weight = −1.331).

The relationship between institutional control (public or private) and CIO prominence was also tested and was found to be significant at a probability of .0041. The institution control uniquely accounted for 2.03 percent of the variance in CIO prominence independent from Carnegie classification and institution size. Private institutions had more prominent CIOs on average than public institutions (parameter weight +1.128) and this difference was especially significant in the reporting level component of the prominence. In addition, the trend of increasing prominence of CIOs was significant in private institutions between 1994 and 1996. The studies by Woodsworth (1987) and Penrod, Dolence and Douglas (1990) showed a rise in the implementation of the CIO concept on American campuses. Pitkin's (1993) study concluded that the most prominent CIO positions occurred in private undergraduate institutions, but stated that the CIO position overall was on the decline. The data in this study refute Pitkin's findings, at least for private institutions, and support the trends cited by Woodsworth (1987) and Penrod, Dolence and Douglas (1990).

CIO Recognition

Synnott and Gruber (1981) stated that the ultimate goal of information managers should be to become recognized by top management as the CIO of their firm. With this recognition would come participation in senior-level decision making and the treatment of information as a corporate resource. The survey included a question which asked if the institution had an individual who was functioning as a CIO and then asked if this person was recognized as a CIO.

This prediction was tested by comparing the prominence of CIOs that were recognized by top management as CIOs against the prominence of CIOs that were acting as a CIO but were not recognized. The 95 responses that indicated no clear CIO were not included in the analysis. This positive relationship (parameter weight = +1.69) was significant at a probability of .0001. The recognition of the CIO uniquely accounted for 2.03 percent of the variance in CIO prominence independent from institution size, Carnegie classification, institution control, and whether or not the CIO was acting as a CIO.

The reporting level, span of control, and prominence all showed a significant relationship on this test. A post hoc analysis was conducted to determine if the predictor variables accounted for unique variance when holding one of the criterion variables constant as recommended by Newman and McNeil (1972). The span of control continued to show a significant relationship even when the variance due to the reporting level was held constant (probability = .0001). The reporting level did not show a significant relationship when holding constant the span of control.

The study also tested to see if the number of institutions that recognize an individual as their CIO was increasing. Although the number of recognized CIOs at public institutions increased by two and the number at private institutions increased by one during the three-year period, this change was not statistically significant (probability = .2069). This lack of significance could be due to the short reporting period. Higher education is notoriously resistant to change and more time may be needed for this change in attitudes to be measurable. In addition, individual personalities may play a role in the reluctance of top management to welcome the old computer center director or Dean of Libraries onto the executive management team.

Strategic Planning

Penrod, Dolence and Douglas (1990) found that institutions which fully implemented the CIO concept were more likely to value planning throughout the institution and required the CIO to maintain a strategic plan for information
technology. Synnott and Gruber (1981) believe that information managers must
be a catalyst for planning throughout the organization and by doing this they will
gain recognition as the CIO of the organization. The relationship between the
prominence of the CIO and the institution's commitment to strategic planning
was tested. The commitment to strategic planning was measured on an ordinal
scale from zero to five by adding one point for each of the following processes
that were implemented on the campus.

- There is an overall campus strategic plan.
- There is a strategic plan for information technology.
- The information technology plan is part of the overall strategic plan.
- The information technology plan is linked to the budget.
- The information technology plan is updated regularly.

The results of the test showed a positive relationship (parameter weight =
+.4018) that was significant at a probability of .0001. The commitment to strategic
planning uniquely accounted for .05 percent of the variance in CIO prominence
independent from institution size, Carnegie classification, and institution control.
The reporting level, span of control, and prominence all showed a significant relationship on this test. A post hoc analysis was conducted to determine if the predictor
variables accounted for unique variance when holding one of the criterion variables
constant. The span of control continued to show a significant relationship even
when the variance due to the reporting level was held constant (probability =
.0001). The reporting level did not show a significant relationship when holding
constant the span of control.

Dedication of Resources

One of the main reasons that Synnott and Gruber (1981) and others called for
the creation of CIO positions was to manage and coordinate the use of the tremendous resources dedicated to information technology. If this has merit, a rise in the
prominence of the CIO position may be indicated by the commitment of
resources. This commitment was measured in this study as a percentage of the
educational and general budget dedicated to information technology. This value
was determined differently for each reporting year. The 1996 figure was determined by summing the spending on all hardware, software, networks, operations,
maintenance, training, personnel, and other information resource units and dividing this total by the reported institutional education and general budget. The 1995

figures were reported on the instrument as a percentage. The 1994 figures were calculated by adding the reported total values for academic computing, administrative computing, and telecommunications and dividing this sum by the reported total educational and general budget.

The relationship between the percentage of the budget dedicated to IT and CIO prominence was found to be positive, and this relationship was almost significant, with a probability of .0680. One reason for this lack of significance could be based on the difficulty in determining actual budget figures and then consistently identifying them as to whether or not they relate to technology. Some institutions may allocate all technology purchases from a single budget pool and others may distribute this money to individual departments with other equipment and supply funds. In addition, determining personnel costs may be difficult at institutions where salary information is not publicly available. It is also possible that some of the significance of this relationship was lost in the process of disaggregating and aggregating these budget figures.

Alignment with Academic Mission

The essence of Synnott and Gruber's (1981) prediction is based on the need for the information manager to shed the label of technologist and take on the role of a general business manager. The key to this transformation is the successful alignment of information technology with the core of the business instead of just supporting the automation of ancillary functions. Information technology in higher education has traditionally been focused on the administrative functions of accounting, payroll, and registration (Ryland 1989). Following the logic of Synnott and Gruber, as information technology in higher education is aligned with teaching, learning, and research, there should be a corresponding rise in the prominence of the CIO position.

This alignment can be measured in a number of ways. An extension of the last research question would be to follow the money. The 1995 survey included the spending on academic support functions as a percentage of the total IT budget. A higher percentage dedicated to academic support would indicate a greater alignment with teaching, learning, and research and, therefore, predict a more prominent CIO. This relationship was not found to be significant and if anything, the relationship between these variables appeared to be negative.

This measurement was based on the assumption that academic computing is more closely aligned with the support of teaching, learning, and research than is administrative computing, networking, or telecommunications. Some institutions have abandoned the structural separation between academic and administrative computing support. At least part of this difference could be explained by the difficulty in reporting budget figures and the value judgments that must be made in deciding what constitutes academic spending versus administrative spending. For example, if a university operates a help desk designed to answer any question from the campus community, is this an academic or an administrative expense? Which category receives the expense for a large mainframe computer that is used for both academic and administrative purposes?

The wide disparity between what was expected and what was found in this case may indicate more than a problem with the collection of data. Another likely explanation is that the prominence of the CIO position may be based more on the culture and governance model of the institution and the role that technology plays in the institution's mission. A bureaucratic campus may reward a CIO for greater support of administrative functions. In very large multipurpose institutions there are often conflicting goals that indicate a lack of agreement on the mission of the institution.

Alignment with teaching, learning, and research can also be measured in terms of a dedication of staff. The total full-time equivalence of staff dedicated to academic computing, administrative computing, networking, and telecommunications was reported for 1994, 1995, and 1996. Institutions with a greater percentage of their IT staff dedicated to academic computing could be considered to have information technology more aligned with teaching, learning and research. A shifting of staffing patterns to academic computing is an indication of realignment with the academic mission and may be accompanied by a rise in the prominence of the CIO. Synnott and Gruber (1981) predicted that organizations would recognize the value of strategic information technology and encourage this proliferation.

The study tested to see if there was a significant rise in the percentage of information technology staff time dedicated to academic support during the three years studied. The results of this test indicate that there has been little change in staffing patterns between academic and administrative support staff. The study also tested to see if there was a positive linear relationship between CIO prominence and the dedication of technology staff time to academic support. Although this test was not significant using all institutions, the expected relationship was found to be significant when restricted to public institutions.

Although it is easier to determine the allocation of staff time than it is to determine spending amounts, the problem of allocating these figures between academic and administrative functions still exists. For example, the individuals that staff a university help desk serve both academic and administrative clients and the computer operators that run the university's mainframe could potentially be allocated either way. As long as all institutions responded with consistent definitions then the results would be valuable. This problem is minimized in institutions where academic and administrative computing functions are staffed separately. Although some individuals may serve diverse clients, the reporting of staff time would most likely follow the organizational reporting lines. One reason that public institutions showed a significant relationship could be based on their propensity for bureaucratic governance models with more formal organizational structures.

Reporting Relationship of the Library

The university library is one information technology office that enjoys an academic reputation. The head of the library often holds the title of Dean and has traditionally reported to the chief academic officer. Many authors have called for a closer alignment between the library and computer center, citing better control, coordination, funding, and efficiency as reasons (Battin 1984; Jones 1995; West and Katz 1990). The library has always enjoyed an academic image especially in research-oriented institutions. The placement of the academic library under a CIO could be an indication of top management's acceptance of the CIO as more than a technologist. Some people do not even consider an information manager to be a CIO unless they have reporting responsibility for both computer services and the library. The merging of the technologies used for computing and information retrieval have provided the potential for these two powerful information providers to clash.

This study tested to see if there was an increase in the number of institutions in which the CIO has reporting responsibility for the library over the reporting period. Although there was a slight increase in both public and private institutions, this increase was not significant. This is not surprising, because there was only a three-year reporting period and the differences between the 131 institutions was controlled for Carnegie classification and institution control in addition to size. Also, personnel reorganizations are costly and can lead to personality conflicts so they may be less likely to occur in the short run.

The study also tested to see if there was a positive relationship between CIO prominence and whether the CIO had reporting responsibility for the library. Because the prominence and span of control scores were influenced by the reporting relationship of the library, both were adjusted to remove these effects. The results showed that there was an increase in CIO prominence when the CIO had reporting responsibility for the library, and this positive relationship (parameter weight = +3.548) was significant at a probability of .0001. The reporting relationship of the library accounted for 9.92 percent of the variance in CIO prominence independent of institution size, Carnegie classification, and institution control.

As expected, there was a significant positive relationship indicating that CIOs with reporting responsibility for the library are more prominent, have a higher reporting level, and a greater span of control than those without responsibility for the library. A post hoc analysis was run to determine if the predictor variables accounted for unique variance when holding one of the criterion variables constant. The span of control and reporting level each account for significant variance when holding the other constant.

SUMMARY AND IMPLICATIONS

The use of technology in higher education is no longer limited to the administrative support functions of accounting, registration, and payroll. With distance learning programs, computer-aided instruction, electronic journals, and the collaboration fostered by the Internet, technology is being used to aid in the core functions of teaching, learning, and research. As technology pervades every facet of higher education, the need for an individual to plan for, oversee, and coordinate this technology grows. The major focus of this study was to determine whether or not the role of the CIO was becoming more prominent with these changes in technology as predicted by Synnott and Gruber (1981).

This study differed from previous studies in that:

- it did not limit the list of participating institutions to those with recognized CIOs;
- it was longitudinal and repeatedly measured the same institutions over time;
- it used a consistent measurement of the prominence of the CIO; and
- the specific research hypotheses controlled for the confounding variables of institution size, Carnegie classification, and control (public or private).

Comparisons of specific numbers between this study and prior studies is difficult because of these implementation factors. One of the strengths of this study was the application of consistent measurements to the same institutions over time. Because prior studies eliminated institutions that did not have a CIO and each study identified the existence of a CIO differently, comparisons between the studies have to be treated skeptically.

The results of the study generally confirmed the predictions by Synnott and Gruber (1981), especially at private institutions. In private institutions there was a trend to consolidate more technology units under a CIO and a corresponding rise in the CIO's reporting level. CIOs at larger institutions were more prominent than those at smaller institutions and CIOs at private institutions are more prominent than those at public institutions. The recognition of the CIO by top management was an indicator of CIO prominence as was an institution's commitment to strategic planning.

The most significant indication of CIO prominence was the reporting relationship of the library. When the library and other information technology units reported to a CIO, it indicated a rise in reporting level and span of control as predicted. The next most significant indication of CIO prominence was the recognition of the CIO by top management. Together these relationships get at the heart of the predictions made by Synnott and Gruber (1981). They stated that the primary goal of information managers should be to gain recognition as their organization's CIO. With this recognition comes inclusion in the executive management team and the treatment of information as a strategic resource.

One important finding was that there appeared to be little relationship between the resources dedicated to information technology and the prominence of the CIO. Because IT spending was unrelated to CIO prominence, it was not surprising that the dedication of resources to academic computing over administrative functions was also not significant. It is impossible to determine how much of this difference was related to the difficulties in obtaining these figures and consistently discerning the difference between academic and administrative uses. One possible explanation is that the need to more efficiently use limited resources countered the effects of the need to coordinate and plan the use of greater expenditures on technology.

If the measurement of the dedication of resources is treated as unreliable, alignment of information technology with the academic mission is best measured by the reporting relationship of the library. Because there is such a strong relationship between the reporting relationship of the library and CIO prominence, there does appear to be a positive relationship between the alignment of technology with the core of the business and the prominence of the CIO.

CIOs at larger institutions were more prominent on average than those in smaller institutions. Because the prominence included the reporting level and the reporting level was inversely related to the number of management layers between the CIO and CEO, it would seem logical that CIOs at smaller institutions would have fewer intervening layers due to the smaller organization size. There are a number of potential reasons to explain why this was not the case in this study. This may be because larger institutions have attained some critical mass in which technology expenses can be justified by the size of the benefited population. This may also be due to the level of specialization afforded by larger institutions and the need for a coordinating level of management.

At first glance it may appear that the findings in this study are unimportant because they are based on small effect sizes. Although statistical significance was found in the positive relationship between CIO prominence and year in private institutions, this relationship uniquely accounted for only .93 percent of the total variance. This is not surprising because the differences between the institutions was controlled for and they accounted for a total of 87.52 percent of the variance. This means that knowing the year accounts for 7.45 percent of the remaining 12.48 percent of variance. It would have been possible to create the illusion of larger effects by not holding constant the extensive influence of the individual differences between institutions, but that would have defeated the purpose of this study.

ACKNOWLEDGMENTS

This paper is a summary of a dissertation with the same title completed at The University of Akron in 1998. The author was Jon O'Donnell and the co-advisors were Dr. Isadore

Newman and Dr. Robert Dubick. Please refer to that document for a more detailed description of the research method and statistics. This study would not have been possible without the help of Jane Ryland and Janet Munson at CAUSE. I would also like to thank the late Dr. Robert Dubick who provided the patience and guidance to see this study through to completion.

REFERENCES

Augustson, J.G. 1989. "Strategies for Financial Planning." In *Organizing and Managing Information Resources on Campus*, edited by B.L. Hawkins. McKinney, TX: Academic Computing Publications.

Barone, C. 1987. "Converging Technologies Require Flexible Organizations." *CAUSE/EFFECT* 5(1): 20-25.

_____. 1989. "Planning and the Changing Role of the CIO in Higher Education." *Information Management Review* 24.

Battin, P. 1984. "The Electronic Library—A Vision for the Future." *EDUCOM Bulletin* 19(2): 12-34.

_____. 1989. "New Ways of Thinking About Financing Information Services." In *Organizing and Managing Iinformation Resources on Campus*, edited by B.L. Hawkins. McKinney, TX: Academic Computing Publications.

Birnbaum, R. 1988. *How Colleges Work*. San Francisco, CA: Jossey-Bass.

Bolman, L. and T. Deal. 1984. *Modern Approaches to Understanding and Managing Organizations*. San Francisco, CA: Jossey-Bass.

Branin, J., G. D'Elia and D. Lund. 1994. "Integrating Information Services in an Academic Setting: The Organizational and Technical Challenge." *CAUSE/EFFECT* 17(3): 26-31.

Burch, J.G. 1989. "CIO: Indian or Chief?" *Information Strategy: The Executive's Journal* 5(6).

Caffrey, J. and C.J. Mosmann. 1967. *Computers on Campus*. Washington, DC: American Council on Education.

Chan, S.S. 1995. "Strategies for Restructuring IT Organizations." *CAUSE/EFFECT* 18(3): 13-19.

Cohen, J. 1977. *Statistical Power Analysis for the Behavioral Sciences,* 2nd ed.. New York: Academic Press.

Conrad, L., J. Rome and J. Wasileski. 1994. "Will the Last Central IT Person Please Turn Off the Lights." Paper presented at the CAUSE Conference, Dallas, Texas.

Dillman, H.L. and M.A. Hicks. 1990. "Reorganizing for Information Technology Management on Campus." *CAUSE/EFFECT* 13(3): 4-6.

Donovan, J.J. 1988. "Beyond Chief Information Officer to Network Manager." *Harvard Business Review* (September): 134-140.

Eleey, M. 1993. "Managing to Change: The Wharton School's Distributed Staff Model for Computing Support." *Penn Printout* (March).

Fleit, L.H. 1989. "The Myth of the Computer Czar—Revisited." In *Organizing and Managing Information Resources on Campus*, edited by B.L. Hawkins. McKinney, TX: Academic Computing Publications.

Freedman, D.H. 1987. "Are We Expecting too Much from Strategic IS?" *Information Systems* (January): 22-24.

Ganz, B. 1985. "A Model for Organizational Analysis for Community Colleges: A Contingency Approach." Unpublished doctoral dissertation, Northern Arizona University.

Heterick, R.C. and W.H. Sanders. 1993. "From Plutocracy to Pluralism: Managing the Emerging Technostructure." *EDUCOM Review* 28(5): 22-28.

Hogue, W.F. 1995. "Reorganizing Information and Technology Resources: Diffusion and Decision Processes in One University." Unpublished doctoral dissertation, Harvard University.

Horgan, B. 1996. "CAUSE's CIO Constituent Group: Sharing Experience and Expertise." *CAUSE/ EFFECT* 19(2): 1.

Jones, C.L. 1995. "Academic Libraries and Computing: A Time of Change." *EDUCOM Bulletin* 12.

Kettinger, W.J. 1990. "The Decentralization of Academic Computing: Defining Future Roles." *CAUSE/EFFECT* (Fall): 15-23.

Mara, M. 1994. "Implementing Distributed Computing at Cornell University." *Managing Information Technology as a Catalyst of Change*. Proceedings of the 1993 CAUSE Annual Conference, Boulder, CO.

McClure, P.A. 1992. "Organizing Information Technology—Integration or Disintegration?" *CAUSE/ EFFECT* 15(3): 3-5.

McNeil, K., I. Newman and F. Kelly. 1996. *Testing Research Hypotheses with the General Linear Model*. Carbondale and Edwardsville: Southern Illinois University Press.

Mulhollan, P. 1989. "Information Resource Management: Why Centralize?" In *Information Technology—Can it All Fit?* (Professional Paper Series Number 2). Boulder, CO: CAUSE.

Nelson, K.R. and R.W. Davenport. 1996. "A Planning Process Addresses an Organizational and Support Crisis in Information Technology." *CAUSE/EFFECT* 19(2): 26-33.

Newcome, T. 1995. "The CIO—Lightning Rod for IT Troubles?" *Government Technology* 58(October): 9-10.

Newman, I. and K. McNeil. 1972. "A Note on the Variance of Each Criterion in a Set." *Multiple Linear Regression Viewpoints* 3(2): 58-60.

Payton, M. and A. Mueller. 1992. "A Success Story for Decentralization." Paper presented at the CAUSE Conference, Dallas, TX.

Penrod, J.I. 1985. *Creating CIO Positions*. Proceedings of the 1985 CAUSE National Conference, Boulder, CO.

Penrod, J.I., M.G. Dolence and J.V. Douglas. 1990. *The Chief Information Officer in Higher Education* (Professional Paper Series No. 4). Boulder, CO: CAUSE.

Pflueger, K. 1996. "Moving Beyond Re-organization to Integration: A New Structure for Information Services." Paper presented at the CUMREC conference.

Pitkin, G.M. 1993. "The Chief Information Officer in Higher Education." Unpublished doctoral dissertation, University of Northern Colorado.

Ringle, M.D. and D.L. Smallen. 1996. "Structures, Plans, and Policies: Do They Make a Difference? An Initial Assessment." *CAUSE/EFFECT* 19(3): 35-39.

Rivet, E.A. 1997. "The College President and the Technology Leader: Defining a New Role in Campus Planning." Unpublished doctoral dissertation, University of New Hampshire.

Ryland, J. 1989. "Organizing and Managing Information Technology in Higher Education: A Historical Perspective." In *Organizing and Managing Information Resources on Campus*, edited by B.L. Hawkins. McKinney, TX: Academic Computing Publications.

Sharrow, M. 1995. "Library and IT Collaboration Projects: Nine Challenges." *CAUSE/EFFECT* 18(4): 55-56.

Solomon, M.B. 1994. "The Need to Rethink Decentralized Computing in Higher Education." *CAUSE/ EFFECT* 17(4).

Synnott, W.R. 1987. *The Information Weapon: Winning Customers and Markets with Technology*. New York: John Wiley and Sons.

Synnott, W.R. and W.H. Gruber. 1981. *Information Resource Management: Opportunities and Strategies for the 1980s*. New York: John Wiley and Sons.

Temares, M.L. 1991. *Future Directions in Higher Education: A CIO's Perspective*. Proceedings of the 1990 CAUSE National Conference, Boulder, CO.

Turner, J.A. 1984. "As Use of Computers Sweeps Campuses, Colleges Vie for Czars to Manage Them." *Chronicle of Higher Education* 28(14): 1, 14.

Wells, J., R. Henne and D. Harrigan, eds. 1989. *Peterson's Register of Higher Education, 1990*. Princeton, NJ: Peterson's Guides.

West, R. and R. Katz. 1990. "Implementing the Vision: A Framework and Agenda for Investing in Academic Computing." *EDUCOM Review* 32-38.

West, S.M. and S. Smith. 1996. "Library and Computing Merger: Clash of Titans or Golden Opportunity." In *Realizing the Potential of Information Resources: Information, Technology, and Services.* Track 8: Academic Computing and Libraries. Boulder, CO: CAUSE. (ERIC Document Reporductions No. ED 392342)

Widner, J. and A. Lawlor. 1994. "Library/Computing Center Relations: A Comprehensive State University View." *CAUSE/EFFECT* 17(3): 45-46.

Woodsworth, A. 1986. *The Roles and Responsibilities of the Senior Information Manager at Selected American Universities. Final report to the Council on Library Resources.* Washington, DC. (ERIC Document Reproduction Service No. ED 279 343)

_____. 1987. "The Chief Information Officer's Role in American Research Universities." Unpublished doctoral dissertation, University of Pittsburgh.

_____. 1991. *Patterns and Options for Managing Information Technology on Campus.* Chicago: American Library Association.

Woodsworth, A., D.K. Gapen and K. Pollock. 1987. *Chief Information Officers on Campus. EDU-COM Bulletin* 22(2): 2-4.

ASSESSING THE GEORGIA LIBRARY LEARNING ON-LINE (GALILEO) PROJECT

David P. Bunnell

DESCRIPTION OF THE GALILEO PROJECT

Georgia Library Learning On-line (GALILEO) began as the vision of Ralph Russell, then Director of Georgia State University's Pullen Library and William Potter, University Librarian at the University of Georgia. It was initially envisioned as the beginning steps toward the establishment of a statewide library for the citizens of Georgia. The plan gained support from University System Chancellor Stephen Portch and, most importantly, Governor Zell Miller. The political support of Governor Miller was instrumental in securing Georgia Lottery funds to support the program. GALILEO, one of the first statewide virtual library projects, became a reality in the fall of 1995.

GALILEO began as a University System of Georgia project, but since its inception a number of Georgia library consortia have formed to join the family of GALILEO users. The consortia joined the GALILEO project as follows:

Phase I (September 21, 1995–June, 1996)
    34 University System of Georgia institutions
Phase II (July, 1996–June, 1997)

Advances in Library Administration and Organization, Volume 17, pages 187-197.
Copyright © 2000 by JAI Press Inc.
ISBN: 0-7623-0647-5

56 regional public libraries
34 technical institutes
41 private colleges and universities
Phase III (July 1997 to date)
101 additional public libraries
180 public school districts (representing 1,800+ K-12 schools)

The increase in the number of libraries joining the project has helped keep political support strong. GALILEO has become a highly valued information resource throughout the Georgia library community.

The GALILEO system has been implemented as a worldwide web-based server offering access for participating institutions to over 100 bibliographic databases indexing thousands of periodicals and scholarly journals. Over 2,000 journal titles are provided in full text. Other resources include two encyclopedias, business directories, and government documents from the state of Georgia. The GALILEO web site also provides links to the on-line catalogs of member institutions and a collection of links to web resources by subject.

Users who access the GALILEO web site from the campus networks of member institutions are identified by their Internet address and are given a list of databases to which their home institution subscribes. Users who access GALILEO from off-campus are given a password that allows them to use their home institution's database collection. Every member institution subscribes to a core set of databases and then arranges with their consortium for access to additional resources that fit their needs.

BEGINNINGS OF THE ASSESSMENT EFFORT

The first version of the GALILEO web interface included the ability to get usage statistics by database, institution, and time period. While these basic statistics were useful, they were of limited use in assessing the GALILEO project. During the first year of operation the GALILEO Steering Committee decided to appoint an Assessment Committee composed of one representative from each consortia to evaluate GALILEO's effectiveness and gauge user satisfaction. The Assessment Committee has grown as the number consortia has increased and now consists of ten consortia representatives and a representative from GALILEO's technical administration.

Assessing a project this large and with such a diverse constituency is a daunting task. The Assessment Committee decided that the first assessment effort should include three components: (a) usage statistics, (b) on-line user surveys, and (c) surveys of University System library directors and staff. As a result, a total of five surveys have been conducted by the Assessment Committee since 1995. This paper will focus on the strengths and weaknesses of the surveys given thus far, possible changes that could be made to make the surveys more effective, and future assessment efforts being contemplated by the Committee.

LIBRARY DIRECTOR AND LIBRARY STAFF SURVEYS

The first survey was given in 1995 to test the survey instrument, this survey became the model for further library director and staff surveys (Appendix A). The second survey was the first to produce usable results. It was sent to the 34 University System library directors in October 1996. These initial surveys were designed to determine what variables library directors thought were most essential to the success of GALILEO and how well library directors thought GALILEO was performing. The instrument used included 10 elements of success ranked on a scale of 1 to 5 with 5 being the highest. The results were ranked by how essential the directors felt each element was to the success of GALILEO (Appendix B) and how well the directors thought GALILEO was performing in that area (Appendix C). As these tables show, reliability tied for first as the most essential variable, but also had the lowest achievement rating. Cost/value benefit also tied for first as the most essential variable but also had the highest achievement rating. This first survey to the membership served as a good predictor of what would be the most vexing problem with GALILEO, namely, the performance of the search engine over the web. It logged more complaints about system downtime, slow Internet connections, slow computers, and times of high usage than about anything else relating to user experiences during the first two years of GALILEO.

In the second section of this survey the directors were asked to give their opinions on what they believed were the most positive outcomes and most critical problems relating to GALILEO for three different user groups: library users, the general public, and library faculty and staff. The positive outcomes for library users and the general public were "access to resources" and "full-text availability." The critical problems cited for library users and the general public were "reliability" and "slow response time." The positive outcomes for library faculty and staff where identified as "expanded access to new resources" and "availability of new technologies." The critical problems noted were "reliability" and "training users." When asked to identify one addition or change they would recommend for GALILEO, the library directors responded with "more full-text" and "additional databases."

The third survey administered in the assessment effort was given to the University System library faculty and staff in February 1997. It utilized essentially the same instrument that had been given to the library directors the previous year. A total of 237 usable surveys were returned (Appendix D). The University System library faculty and staff indicated that "credible search results" and "reliability" were the most essential variables in gauging the success of the system. "Credible search results" had the second highest rating in terms of GALILEO's achievements but, "reliability" lagged, receiving the second lowest rating among the variables listed.

The surveys of library directors, faculty, and staff were helpful in developing plans for system improvements. They showed two themes that would carry through all of the GALILEO user surveys: the desire for full-text resources and the need to keep reliability high. One of the weaknesses noted in these surveys stemmed from the differences in technology used at the various University System libraries. While some of the reliability problems stemmed from the fact that the GALILEO servers were sometimes off-line, dissatisfaction arose at least as often because there was no consistency in the speed of the local computers or in their data connections to the Internet. It was difficult in the assessment effort to filter out these factors to get an idea of what improvements could be made at the GALILEO systems level to overcome these problems and increase reliability.

GALILEO USER SURVEYS

The fourth survey was conducted through a web form on the GALILEO home page during April 1997. The survey was open to any GALILEO user and participation was voluntary. There were 543 usable commentary responses and a total of 503 fully completed surveys. Through this survey the Assessment Committee sought to identify the type of GALILEO users completing the survey (i.e., undergraduate, graduate, faculty, staff, or other); their institutional affiliation; how frequently they used GALILEO; and most important of all, how well GALILEO met their needs.

Users were asked to respond with "yes," "usually," or "no" to the following six statements.

1. The GALILEO system is easy to use.
2. Using GALILEO databases saved me time.
3. GALILEO is an effective service.
4. GALILEO response time is acceptable.
5. GALILEO results met my information needs.
6. I would recommend GALILEO to a friend.

Users were also asked to comment on how they believed the GALILEO service could be improved. The results of the survey were generally very positive (Appendix E). It indicated that an overwhelming majority of users had come to believe that the GALILEO system was easy to use, saved the user time, was effective, and that they would recommend it to others. However, there were mixed results on response time and meeting the information needs of the user. These comments reflected the ambiguous relationship between GALILEO's technical performance and database availability.

The free form comments were analyzed and then grouped into ten comment types, reflecting the concerns expressed. The comment types ranked by number of responses were:

1. "Make Easier to Use"
2. "More Full-Text"
3. "Faster Response Time"
4. "More Databases"

5. "Positive Comments"
6. "Better Reliability"
7. "More Workstations"
8. "Better Holdings Information"
9. "More Multimedia."

The results of this first on-line user survey led to changes in the survey form. A wider scale of responses was created to permit more in-depth analysis of results. A question on whether or not the respondent had previous training in the use of GALI-LEO was added, as were additional questions designed to identify the respondent and his/her institutional affiliation. The revised survey was administered during October 1998.

The results to this survey were similar to those of the first on-line user survey and were generally positive overall (Appendix F). There were high marks for ease of use, saving the user time, system effectiveness, and users indicated that they would still recommend it to others. The low scores again related to the speed of the system and its capacity to meet the information needs of the user. The Likert scale used in the second survey was easier to interpret and gave a clearer picture of the views of user populations provided by respondents.

The comments provide by respondents were also similar to the previous year. The comment types ranked by number of responses were:

1. "More Full-Text"
2. "Faster Response Time"
3. "More Databases"
4. "Make Easier to Use"
5. "Positive Comments"
6. "Better Reliability"
7. "More Workstations"
8. "Better Holdings Information"
9. "Access to Databases from Off-Campus."

However, the comments were more difficult to categorize this time because of the larger number of respondents and greater diversity of the population that was surveyed.

The most interesting part of the 1998 survey comments was the drop in position for comments classed under "Maker Easier to Use" and the appearance of comments related to the need for greater access for databases from off-campus. This new type of comment related to the fact that access to the Lexis-Nexis Academic Universe has, at once, become very popular and is restricted to use on the campuses of member institutions. There is currently no way by license to get the Lexis-Nexis database through the standard GALILEO password used for off-campus access, and this has presented a concern for many patrons.

It is expected that changes in the GALILEO system will make the next on-line survey different from the last two. The GALILEO Steering Committee has decided to have more gateway access to vendor databases and less local loading of databases using the standard GALILEO interface. The complete analysis of the 1997 and 1998 GALILEO user surveys can be viewed on the web at: http://www.galileo.peachnet.edu; go to the "About GALILEO" link.

FUTURE GALILEO ASSESSMENT METHODS

There is great value in the survey method of assessment. It is a valuable tool to measure the pulse of the GALILEO user community over time. The user survey is now in its second consecutive year of administration and has shown the GALILEO Steering Committee the popularity of the system as well as its weaknesses. The value of the survey will be in its continued use over a long period of time. The Assessment Committee understands the need to keep the survey consistent across years and will make very few changes to future survey instruments.

The Assessment Committee has also recognized the need to again survey the library directors and staff. The GALILEO participants have increased in number and in diversity of library type. A new survey of directors and staff would be a good benchmark for future GALILEO planning.

The weakness of the survey method is its limited capability to follow up with users and get details on their problems with the system. The GALILEO user surveys are more akin to popularity polls then scientific surveys. The Assessment Committee has discussed the need for more rigorous study of the impact of the virtual library on Georgia library users.

The Assessment Committee has considered a cost/benefit analysis. However, the diversity in the types of libraries that participate in GALILEO makes a true cost/benefit analysis impractical. It is possible for individual institutions to do an analysis for their libraries, but this method of assessment has limited use to the GALILEO project. There is also a feeling in the Assessment Committee that the focus group method of assessment holds a great deal of promise for understanding the needs of GALILEO users. Focus groups would allow for more in-depth answers, immediate follow-up on a particular problem, and create a friendlier environment for users to express their experiences.

Assessing a virtual library's performance will be a continuing challenge as more large projects such as GALILEO are developed. It will be important in the future for the administrators of these large projects to share their ideas on assessment and help each other through the pitfalls.

APPENDIX A.   EXAMPLE LIBRARY DIRECTOR SURVEY

---

1. Everything considered, the overall GALILEO program (all eight components) does a good job.
_____ No   _____ Yes

2. Various factors have been identified as critical indicators of customer satisfaction in serves industries. Assuming these are applicable for users of the GALILEO *online* databases as well, please rate the service you receive from GALILEO for the factors listed below. You may write in an additional indicator not covered in the list. Circle how essential the factor is to you (with 1 being low and 5 high) and then how GALILEO rates (with 1 being low and 5 being high).

How Essential to You? Low — High	Factors GALILEO *Online* Services	How Does GALILEO Rate? Low — High
1 2 3 4 5	Availability of the system is reliable.	1 2 3 4 5
1 2 3 4 5	Access to the databases is convenient.	1 2 3 4 5
1 2 3 4 5	Follow-up on problems/suggestions is responsive.	1 2 3 4 5
1 2 3 4 5	Communication is good about changes that effect GALILEO.	1 2 3 4 5
1 2 3 4 5	GALILEO databases meet the needs of my library users.	1 2 3 4 5
1 2 3 4 5	Search results are credible (can be trusted).	1 2 3 4 5
1 2 3 4 5	Remote access security is good.	1 2 3 4 5
1 2 3 4 5	My staff feel competent in helping library customers use GALILEO databases.	1 2 3 4 5
1 2 3 4 5	Search screens are easy to use.	1 2 3 4 5
1 2 3 4 5	The cost/benefit of GALILEO provides value to my library.	1 2 3 4 5
1 2 3 4 5	I feel comfortable raising issues/concerns about GALILEO.	1 2 3 4 5
1 2 3 4 5	other (specify) _____	1 2 3 4 5

3. Overall the *online* GALILEO system does a good job.

_____ No   _____ Yes

(continued)

APPENDIX A.   (CONTINUED)

4. GALILEO was implemented in Sept. 1995. Thinking about the year since its inception, identify the one most positive outcome for each of the user groups identified below; identify the one most critical problem experienced by each of the user groups identified.

User Group	Most Positive Outcome	Most Critical Problem
A. Library users		
B. General public users		
C. Library faculty/staff		

5. If you could add to or change one thing about GALILEO, what would it be?

6. The GALILEO assessment initially includes three components: a) usage statistics (some available online), b) online user surveys, and c) surveys of University System library directors and staff. What additional information/data about GALILEO should be reported as part of the assessment process for use for institutional/management decision-making?

7. Questions on this survey may be used on future surveys (e.g., library users, library staff). Were there any questions that were confusion to you or that is revised/added?

8. Comments

Name(optional)_____
Institution_____

APPENDIX B.   ELEMENTS DEEMED MOST ESSENTIAL TO GALILEO SUCCESS (OCTOBER 1996)

Of the ten elements identified as quite essential to the success of the online GALILEO system, ratings are listed below, highest to lowest by mean score. Totals are included for ratings of "outstanding" (5) and "excellent" (4+5). There were 33 responses to all but 1 ranked question, which had 32 and is indicated by an asterisk.

How Essential? (most to least)	Score		Very Essential (ranking = 5)		Quite Essential (4 + 5)	
	Mean	Median	Number	Percent	Number	Percent
Reliability	4.94	5	30	94%	32	100%
Cost/Value Benefit	4.94	5	30	94%	32	100%
Staff Feel Competent	4.84	5	27	84%	32	100%
Credible Search Results	4.84	5	27	84%	32	100%
Convenience	4.81	5	26	81%	32	100%
Search Screens Easy to Use	4.78	5	25	78%	32	100%
Databases Meet Needs	4.75	5	25	78%	31	97%

(continued)

APPENDIX B.   (CONTINUED)

Comfortable Raising Issues	4.75	5	25	78%	32	97%
Responsive on Suggestions	4.72	5	23	72%	32	100%
Communication About Changes	4.69	5	22	69%	32	100%
Remote Security is Good[*]	3.79	4	7/28	25%	17/28	61%

APPENDIX C.   GALILEO (ONLINE) RATINGS ON ESSENTIAL ELEMENTS (OCTOBER 1996)

To determine which elements were considered essential to the success of GALILEO 12 elements were surveyed. Following from most to least is the ranking. A scale of 1 to 5 was used with 1 being the lowest and 5 being the highest. Totals are included for "outstanding" (3) and "excellent" (4+5), N = 237.

Ratings (highest to lowest)	Score		Outstanding		Excellent (4 + 5)	
	Mean	Median	Number	Percent	Number	Percent
Cost/Value Benefit	4.82	5	29	88%	31	94%
Comfortable Raising Issues	4.63	5	23	70%	31	94%
Responsive on Suggestions	4.27	4	16	48%	27	82%
Staff Feel Competent	4.27	4	11	42%	25	76%
Credible search Results	4.24	4	16	48%	25	76%
Databases Meet Needs	4.12	4	9	27%	29	88%
Convenience	4.09	4	9	27%	27	92%
Communication About Changes	4.03	4	14	42%	25	76%
Search Screens Easy to Use[*]	4.00	4	7/32	22%	26/32	81%
Reliability	3.39	3	1	3%	15	45%

APPENDIX D.   ELEMENTS DEEMED MOST ESSENTIAL TO GALILEO SUCCESS (FEBRUARY 1997)

Of the twelve elements surveyed, ratings are listed below, highest to lowest. Totals are included for "outstanding" (5) and "excellent" (4 + 5), N 237.

How Essential? (most to least)	Very/Quite Essential (4 + 5)
Credible Search Results	96.92%
Reliability	96.04%

(continued)

APPENDIX D.   (CONTINUED)

Meets Needs of Users	95.56%
Screens Easy to Use	95.54%
Staff Feel Competent	94.00%
Cost/Value Benefit	90.43%
Communication About Changes	87.50%
Follow-Up on Suggestions	86.60%
Comfortable Raising Technical Issues	74.41%
Convenience	73.00%
Ideas Taken Into Consideration	72.12%
Remote Security is Good	59.0%

APPENDIX E.   GALILEO ONLINE USER SURVEY 1997 (ALL RESPONDENTS)

Question	Yes	Usually	No
The GALILEO system is easy to use	291	186	26
	57.8%	37.0%	5.2%
Using GALILEO databases saved me time	342	129	32
	68.0 %	25.6%	6.4%
GALILEO is an effective service	386	99	18
	76.7%	19.7%	3.6%
GALILEO response time is acceptable	204	242	57
	40.6%	48.1%	11.3%
GALILEO results met my information needs	223	247	32
	44.3%	49.1%	6.4%
I would recommend GALILEO to a friend	425	56	22
	84.5%	11.1%	4.4%

APPENDIX F.   GALILEO ONLINE USER SURVEY 1998 (ALL RESPONDENTS)

Question	Mean Response
The GALILEO system is easy to use	3.02
Using GALILEO databases saved me time	3.15
GALILEO is an effective service	3.36
GALILEO response time is acceptable	2.88
GALILEO results met my information needs	2.89
I would recommend GALILEO to a friend	3.22

ACKNOWLEDGMENTS

The author would like to acknowledge the significant contribution of Bill Richards, Library Director at Georgia College and State University in Milledgeville, Georgia. Mr. Richards coauthored a paper and copresented the results of the GALILEO Assessment Committee for the Georgia Chapter of the ACRL at the 1998 Georgia Library Association Annual Conference in Macon, Georgia [D.P. Bunnell and W.A. Richards, 1999, "User Survey Assessment of GALILEO" (Georgia Library Learning On-line), *The Georgia Library Quarterly* 36(1): 6-12]. The author would also like to thank the past and current members of the GALILEO Assessment Committee, especially the Chair, Bill Nelson, Library Director of Augusta State University and Dr. Judy Kelley, Director of Virtual Library Development for the University System of Georgia.

EXPLORING THE VIABILITY OF ESTABLISHING AN ADVISORY COMMITTEE AND THE ROLE, FUNCTION, AND EFFECTIVENESS OF SUCH AN ADVISORY COMMITTEE IN ADDRESSING ISSUES FACING A COMMUNITY COLLEGE LIBRARY

John C. Painter

PURPOSE OF THE STUDY

Owens Campus librarians were isolated in their efforts to improve library services and programs. The librarians needed a broad base of support to address such library issues as: (1) adequate funding, (2) technological expansion efforts, and (3) administrative support for needed library resources. The early phases of this study established the feasibility of using an advisory committee to meet those needs.

Advances in Library Administration and Organization, Volume 17, pages 199-241.

It was felt that an advisory committee could provide the change force required by Owens Campus library personnel to help them adequately address the changing library environment that occurred at the community college level. Exploring the merits of advisory committees in relation to library improvement warranted an in-depth investigation and analysis.

Thus, the purpose of this study was to explore the viability of establishing an advisory committee and to determine the role, function, and structure of such an advisory committee in addressing issues facing a community college library. When found to be feasible, an advisory committee similar in structure to the advisory committees currently serving the instructional units at the Owens Campus of Delaware Technical & Community College was recommended.

The value of advisory committees to community college instructional and administrative divisions had previously been established (Dieffenderfer et al. 1977). The author believed that a similar advisory committee structure would contribute to the institution's library system. In order to confirm that belief, this study addressed the following questions.

1. What is the structure, role, and function of advisory committees currently serving instructional departments at Delaware Technical & Community College, Owens Campus?
2. What are the roles and functions of community college libraries specifically and of libraries at higher education institutions in general?
3. What are the needs of the Delaware Technical & Community College, Owens Campus, Library, in terms of services to be provided, resource requirements, and level of internal and external support required?
4. What do the important stakeholders perceive to be the major role and function of the Delaware Technical & Community College, Owens Campus, Library?
5. Is an advisory committee to the Delaware Technical & Community College, Owens Campus Library, feasible and desirable?
6. What should be the structure, role, and function of a library advisory committee?
7. Can an advisory committee address library issues such as: technological development, collection development, staff development, adequate funding, strategic planning, plus other needs as identified?

ROLE, AND FUNCTION OF ADVISORY COMMITTEES IN COMMUNITY COLLEGES

Community colleges have long recognized advisory committees as an integral component of the collegiate structure and process for planning and continuous improvement (Minnesota State Council 1991). According to Oen (1985), an advisory committee's major function is to provide advice in determining general policies and types of occupational programs or clusters that are needed in the community or region.

Services and functions that advisory committees offer to technical/vocational institutions are contained in materials published by the Nebraska Council on Vocational Education (1994), the Alabama Council on Vocational and Technical Education (1990), and the Delaware Advisory Council on Career and Vocational Education (1989). The following is a selected compilation of services and functions, based on materials generated by these three organizations, that advisory committees provide in various locales:

1. advise the school authorities on the development of its long-range and annual plans for vocational education;
2. assist the school authorities in identifying the vocational education needs of individuals and the community;
3. review budget requests for labs, equipment, and supplies;
4. evaluate adequacy of facilities and equipment;
5. make recommendations to school officials and Boards of Education;
6. determine community needs by conducting surveys and labor market trends;
7. assist in conducting clinics and in-service training for teachers;
8. assist in making cost studies for specialized programs/courses;
9. assist in the review of legislation affecting vocational education;
10. provide objective, periodic evaluations, with recommendations presented to proper authorities;
11. share their expertise on new and developing areas;
12. act as an agent of change to increase the relevance of the programs;
13. assist in long-term regional planning; and
14. participate in needs assessment for new occupational training programs in the community.

Advisory committee structure, which includes such issues as (1) membership recruitment, (2) term length, (3) committee responsibility, (4) job description, (5) orientation, (6) committee reports, (7) organization structure, (8) membership composition, and (9) by-laws, appears to be limited only by the imagination of the institution interested in forming external support groups and the relationship between the institution and the community (Ditzenberger and Morkey 1985).

Due to the rapid change of occupational patterns and technological improvements, community colleges must seek reliable input as to how they can develop, adapt, revise, and update their programs and services. Advisory committees, their structure, purpose, and role unite vocational/technical-based education programs to the needs of the business and industrial community. This connection encourages accountability and positive development for both the community and the educational institution.

ROLE OF THE COMMUNITY COLLEGE LIBRARY

Change is everywhere in today's library environment (Curzon 1989). Community College libraries are no exception. Kalick (1992) reports that life in the community college in general and in the library in particular is one of change, contrasts, and activity. Curzon (1989) summarized the milieu with the following.

> Twentieth-century librarianship has witnessed significant change in the last years. The variety of services and formats provided, the professionalism of the profession, and the automation of many processes are some of the modern developments that affect the daily lives of library and information managers... This global informational network creates a complex and intense dimension for librarians unknown to their predecessors. The amount, diversity, and speed of information available through state-of-the-art technology has surrounded library managers with a continual flow of new directions and opportunities. Today, the manager of even the smallest library or agency faces what may seem an insurmountable task of managing constant change in the library and information environment (p. 13).

With library reassessment comes examination of the role of the community college library. The Association for College and Research Libraries (ACRL; 1994) states that the role of a community college library must be consistent with the stated mission of the institution. The ACRL goes on to note that the structure and function of a learning resources program is obviously determined by the role assigned within the institutional structure.

Sacks and Whildin (1993) define the community college library role through the eyes of higher education accrediting associations. Sacks and the higher education accrediting associations view the academic libraries' role in relation to the parent institution's mission and purpose. Sacks and Whildin (1993) indicate that a library and its effectiveness should be judged using the following criteria:

1. the library's importance as an instructional resource;
2. the importance of mission, goals, and objectives in supporting the library's constituencies;
3. the relationship of the library's resources and services to its parent institution's instructional program, research goals, and programs;
4. the quality (nature, scope, and size) of collections, staff, and physical facilities;
5. the availability of access services enabling the user to locate and use information not locally available;
6. reference, library instruction, and referral assistance to enable the user to identify, select, and use information resources;
7. the nature and extent of collections and services;
8. the financial and organizational abilities to support the faculty and student needs; and
9. The mechanisms used to communicate with the constituents (pp. 11-12).

In contrast to Sacks traditional and accepted roles for postsecondary libraries, Steuart (1990) looks to the future by stating that postsecondary libraries must be charged with providing library resources to an international electronic network for scholars. Such a network emphasizes the concept of service rather than a physical building. The library's role in this scenario is to select and disseminate information, serving as an intermediary between the user in need of specific information and the sources of that information.

Higher education libraries enhance and support the goals of the parent institution. They effect and support the quality of teaching and learning. Subsequently, the library is directly linked with the instructional process and, hence, the success of the students (Commission on Higher Education 1989).

The Commission on Higher Education in conjunction with the Middle States Association of Colleges and Schools (1989) asserts the role of the community college library as:

> A library/learning resources center is of paramount importance to the educational program and to the research of students and faculty. The types and variety of books and other materials depend on the nature of the institution; therefore, collection development must relate realistically to the institution's educational mission, goals, curricula, size, complexity and degree level, and the diversity of its teaching, learning, and research requirements (pp. 34-35).

Both the Association for College and Research Libraries and the Middle States Accreditation Association agree that the community college library role and purpose must be consistent with the stated mission of the institution. Library standards (both the *1995 College Library Standards* and the *Standards for Community, Junior, and Technical College Learning Resource Programs*) were primarily created to address developing concerns in college libraries. These concerns include collections, personnel, budget, media, services and networking. The Association for Educational Communications Technology and ACRL (1994) state that the standards are intended to assist in evaluating and developing learning resources/library programs. Library standards promote excellence in libraries and a means to measure library effectiveness.

National standards developed and adopted by the American Library Association/Association for College Research Libraries for Community, Junior, and Technical College Library/Learning Resource Programs were intended to assist in evaluating and developing learning resources/library programs. The national standards are divided into seven sections: (1) objectives, (2) organization and administration, (3) staff, (4) budget, (5) user services, (6) collections, and (7) facilities. These standards are viewed by community college librarians as guidelines and a basis to provide both quantitative and qualitative data for assessment purposes as well as goals to strive toward.

The *1995 College Library Standards*, written by an Association of College Research Libraries' Task Force Committee, were developed for addressing concerns in academic libraries. Because the Owens Campus Library serves three,

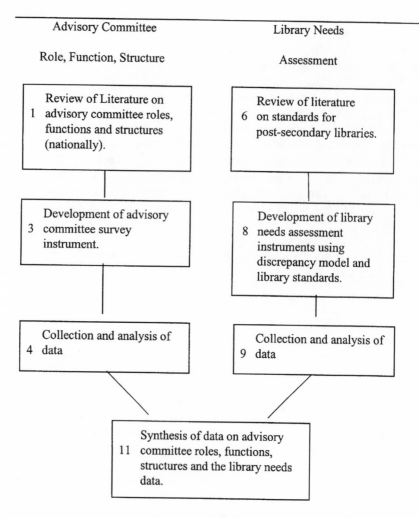

Figure 1. Study Processes

four-year Delaware academic institutions, in addition to addressing its own two-year curriculum obligation, it was necessary to investigate the library standards for four-year colleges as well. Those standards include data and guidelines on such areas as collections and staff formulae, budget, audiovisual collections and services, networking, and cooperative associations (Association of College and Research Libraries 1994).

Both the Middle States Commission on Higher Education and the Association for College Research Libraries describe the importance of the community college

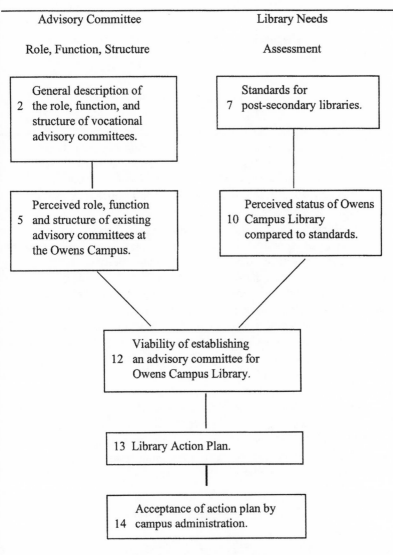

Figure 2. Study Outcomes

library's role to the parent institution. It was intended that this study blend the two entities, community college libraries and advisory committees, into a union that: further clarifies the campus library role to constituents; demonstrates how the library administration can strategically involve campus stakeholders in decision making and other aspects of library development and advancement; involves the library administration in the campus information gathering process; and sequentially makes the campus library better able to serve the comprehensive diverse educational programs available at the Owens Campus of Delaware Technical & Community College.

RESEARCH DESIGN

This study employed both qualitative and quantitative methods to address the research questions outlined previously. Data gathering and analysis techniques characteristic of qualitative research, as described by Merriam (1988), were emphasized. However, as advocated by Miles (1994), the qualitative study linked with and utilized distinct types of quantitative data to provide a complete and exhaustive study about the research subject.

The study is displayed graphically in Figures 1 and 2. This mode of describing the basic design was chosen because the study included several interconnecting components (the number in each box demonstrates the linkage between each component). Figure 1 describes the processes or activities that were utilized in the study. Figure 2 details the outcomes from the various steps in the study. The two diagrams demonstrate the two major threads that ran parallel and flowed through the entire study. One thread focused on the role, function, and structure of advisory committees while the second related to conducting a needs assessment of the library. The merging of these two major threads, the synthesis of data from the components, led ultimately to the development of the library action plan for the Owens Campus.

Data collection for both components occurred during the fall 1995 semester. A discrepancy model was utilized for the needs assessment component. As suggested by Merriam (1988), the study was designed primarily to provide insight, discovery, and interpretation about the data in relation to the research topic rather than attempting a single hypothesis testing or discovery.

ANALYSIS OF THE DATA

Data were collected from 13 different groups at the Owens Campus in order to determine the viability of establishing an advisory committee to the library and to determine the role and function that such a committee would fill. To facilitate the presentation and analysis of the data there are four sections structured according to the major research questions addressed by this study.

The first section provides data and results obtained from the samples of individuals who responded to the advisory committee survey designed to answer research question 1. The second section focuses on the roles and functions of college libraries through the literature review findings. The third section provides data and results from the ten groups who responded to the library needs assessment instrument. The fourth section provides data and related analyses regarding the fourth question on the feasibility and desirability of establishing a library advisory committee.

Advisory Committees

A 37-item survey (see Appendix A) was designed, based on the literature review, to determine the structure, role, and function of advisory committees currently operating at the Owens Campus. The instrument had two sections. The first 26 items asked respondents to indicate their perceptions of the importance of specific roles or functions an advisory committee could perform. These 26 items used a 5-point Likert scale response format, ranging from "Very Important" (1) to "Very Unimportant" (5). The intent was to determine the most important and least important roles or functions of an advisory committee as perceived by various stakeholders. The remaining 11 items were open-ended questions designed to elicit information on the structure and operating procedures of existing advisory committees.

The advisory committee survey was sent to 15 Owens Campus instructional department chairs, 5 campus administrators (approximately one-half of the total administrative staff) and 35 members of advisory committees. The final tally of completed surveys was as follows: 15 (100%) department chairs, 5 (100%) campus administrators, and 8 (23%) advisory committee members. Thus, the results for staff members can be considered to be representative but the low response rate from advisory committee members makes those data somewhat suspect.

The responses from the 28 individuals who completed the items on the first part of the advisory committee survey were entered into a computer database and a statistical package, SYSTAT, was used to perform the required analyses. The first step in the analysis was to determine the internal consistency of the items in that first section of the survey. The task was completed by computing a Cronbach Alpha Coefficient across the entire 26 items for the 27 respondents who responded to all items. (One respondent answered only 25 items.) The value of alpha obtained, 0.907, indicated an acceptable level of internal consistency or reliability for the first 26 items in the instrument. As noted previously, the content validity of the items had been established by the fact that they were drawn from various literature sources developed and published by different state advisory councils on vocational/technical education.

The next step in the analysis involved computing the usual descriptive statistics used with survey data—the mean, standard deviation, and frequency distribution of responses for each item for each of the three subgroups of respondents and for the total group of 28 respondents. The frequency tabulations indicated that many of the cells in the two-way tables (response by subgroup) had frequencies of less

Table 1. Advisory Committee Survey

	Frequency					Overall	
Item	1	2	3	4	5	Mean	Std. Dev.
a.	11	13	1	1	2	1.92	1.12
b.	13	12	1	0	2	1.78	1.06
c.	2	6	8	9	3	3.17	1.12
d.	7	14	3	2	1	2.11	1.01
e.	9	12	3	3	0	2.00	.96
f.	13	11	1	2	0	1.70	.86
g.	3	15	7	1	1	2.33	.87
h.	3	12	5	5	2	2.66	1.14
i.	3	16	6	2	0	2.25	.76
j.	0	7	5	12	3	3.40	1.01
k.	4	8	8	6	2	2.78	1.16
l.	1	18	2	4	3	2.64	1.12
m.	0	8	7	10	2	3.28	1.01
n.	2	11	3	9	3	3.00	1.21
o.	4	12	3	7	2	2.67	1.21
p.	4	23	0	1	0	1.92	.53
q.	0	8	8	9	3	3.25	1.00
r.	0	2	10	12	4	3.64	.82
s.	2	16	6	3	1	2.46	.92
t.	4	15	4	3	2	2.42	1.10
u.	11	17	0	0	0	1.60	.49
v.	0	10	9	7	2	3.03	.96
w.	10	13	5	0	0	1.82	.72
x.	8	18	1	0	1	1.85	.80
y.	5	16	5	1	1	2.17	.90
z.	5	19	3	1	0	2.00	.66

Table 2. Advisory Committee Survey Items
Ranked by Order of Most Importance

Item	Survey Statement	Mean	Std. Dev.
u.	Share expertise	1.60	.49
f.	Review curriculum	1.70	.86
b.	Identify technical needs	1.78	1.06
w.	Identify new occupational training programs	1.82	.72
x.	Act as a change agent	1.85	.80
a.	Advise on long-range plan	1.92	1.12
p.	Develop educational objectives	1.92	.53
z.	Assist in long-range plan	2.00	.66
e.	Establish standards for students	2.00	.96

Table 3. Advisory Committee Survey
Items Ranked by Order of Least Importance

Item	Survey Statement	Mean	StdDv
r.	Secure funds for meetings, workshops, etc.	3.64	.82
j.	Planning field trips	3.40	1.01
m.	Application for funds	3.28	1.01
q.	Cost studies for programs	3.25	1.00
c.	Review budget requests	3.17	1.12
v.	Priorities for budget items	3.03	.96
n.	Scholarship and financial assistance	3.00	1.21

Table 4. Summary of Advisory Committee Members Survey Data Items

Survey Question	Response (Follows Question)
1.	How should members be selected? Appointees should be related to field of study.
2.	What is the optimum number of members? Eight to 15 persons.
3.	Types of individuals to include on committee? Professional, non-professional, citizens, students, employers, business leaders.
4.	Length of term for members? Serve three years.
5.	How to choose officers for committee? Select democratically.
6.	Should by-laws and operating procedures be established? Not necessary
7.	Number of meetings held annually? Two to three.
8.	To whom should the committee report? Department chair.
9.	How frequently should committee meet? Two to three times per year.
10.	Should committee be divided into subcommittees? Yes, a curriculum committee.
11.	Should minutes be kept for meetings? Yes.

than five, thus making statistical testing of differences in response patterns between the three subgroups untenable (Ferguson 1971).

The results for all 28 respondents are displayed in Table 1. The first five columns provide the number of respondents who selected each of the possible five responses for each item. The average response and standard deviation for each item across the 28 respondents are given in the remaining two columns of Table 1. Items with a small mean value are those considered most important by the respondents, those which are least important have the highest mean values. Table 2 provides a listing of those items which received a mean rating of 2.00 or less, that is, the items judged by the respondents to be the most important functions or activities of advisory committees.

The data in Table 3 can be used to identify the roles or functions that were judged least important or inappropriate for an advisory committee to fulfill. Of particular interest was the fact that six out of seven items listed in Table 3 relate to funding issues. Investigating this finding further led to the conclusion that items *r, m, q, c, v,* and *n* received a higher mean value from the advisory committee members' subgroup than the other two subgroups—department chairs and administrators. Thus, even though the statistical sample is small, it appears that advisory committee members consider departmental funding matters less important or perhaps not their responsibility.

The data from the 11 open-ended questions on the structure and organization of advisory committees were manually tabulated and summarized. Those data are displayed in summary form in Table 4.

While there appeared to be some differences between the three subgroups in their views of the important roles of advisory committees, the more important finding was the level of agreement across the entire set of respondents about the important and unimportant roles and functions of an advisory committee. The data from the survey indicated the kinds of functions that should be incorporated into the mission or charge of an advisory committee. The data also indicated what roles an advisory committee to the library might perform when such a committee is established.

The data on the structure and operational issues concerning advisory committees indicated that the three subgroups were generally in accord with one another but some differences do exist. However, the differences appeared to be based more on how the three subgroups perceive structure and function rather then significant philosophical differences. Also, the differences that did exist appeared to be between the advisory committee subgroup and the other two subgroups—campus administration and department chairs—rather than between all three subgroups.

Library Role and Function

The role and function of a community college library was addressed by a thorough review of the literature. The library literature, specifically the *Standards for Community, Junior, and Technical College Learning Resource Programs* and the *ACRL 1995 College Library Standards* state that the role of postsecondary libraries are determined by the role assigned by the institutional organization. The learning resources program for these postsecondary institutions must be consistent with the stated mission of the institution, its educational goals, curricula, size, complexity and that diverse resources must be available to accommodate diverse learning styles.

The *Standards for College Libraries*, 1995 edition, also states that college libraries effectively support the institution's curriculum and scholarly and creative accomplishments of students and faculty (Kaser 1982). These standards were used as the criteria for what a library should be and how it should operate. They were also rephrased slightly and became the items used in the needs assessment component of the study.

Library Needs Assessment

Three needs assessment survey instruments (see Appendices B, C, and D) were designed, based on library standards from the Association for Educational Communications and Technology and the Community and Junior College National Library Association and the Association for College Research Libraries (ACRL), to determine the strengths and weaknesses of the Owens Campus Library based on the specific criteria cited in the different sets of library standards. Three different instruments were developed because it was felt that only certain subgroups in the sample would have knowledge necessary to respond to many of the items included on the survey forms. The needs assessment instrument completed by library staff and college administrators contained 43 items, all of which had a 5-point Likert response scale. The response choices ranged from "Strongly Agree" (1) to "Strongly Disagree" (5) and requested information about the library in seven areas, including the following: objectives, organization, staff, user services, budget, collection, and facilities.

The instrument completed by faculty of the Owens Campus and faculty from University of Delaware, Delaware State University, and Wilmington College, which share the facility and utilize the services of the library, contained 18 items. All items used the same 5-point Likert response scale as that used in the administrator library staff form. The areas contained on this survey were limited to the following three: user services, collections, and facilities.

The instrument completed by students of the Owens Campus and students from the University of Delaware, Delaware State University, and Wilmington College contained 16 items. All items used the same 5-point Likert response scale as that used in the other two survey forms. The areas contained on the survey were limited to the following three: user services, collections, and facilities.

The needs assessment survey was completed by 134 students, 47 faculty, 8 administrators, and 8 library personnel. Student participants were randomly selected from official matriculated student lists by assigning random numbers taken from a chart located in a general statistics textbook.

The final tally of completed surveys, with response rates in parentheses, was as follows: 92 (74%) Owens Campus students, 42 (88%) partnership students, 8 (100%) Owens Campus administrators, 8 (100%) Owens Campus Library personnel, 17 (56%) partnership faculty, and 30 (42%) full-time Owens Campus faculty members. It would appear, based on the responses, that the results for the above groups overall can be considered to be representative of the total Campus population and their responses indicative of the total population served by the Owens Campus Library.

The response from the 197 individuals who completed the library needs assessment survey or portions thereof were entered into a computer database and a statistical package, MYSTAT, was used to perform the required analyses. The first step in the analysis was to determine the internal consistency—

Table 5. Library Assessment Survey

Survey Question		Frequency					Overall	
		1	2	3	4	5	Mean	Std. Dev.
Obj	1	7	8	1			1.62	.61
Obj	2	3	6	3			2.25	.77
	3	5	6	5			2.00	.81
	4	5	4	7			2.12	.88
	5	9	6	1			1.50	.63
Org	1	9	7				1.43	.51
	2	8	5	3			1.68	.79
	3	9	6	1			1.50	.63
	4	5	7	4			1.93	.77
	5	2	9	4	1		2.25	.77
	6	5	6	3	2		2.12	1.02
	7	3	12	1			1.87	.50
Staf	1	6	4	1	5		2.31	1.30
	2	4	7	2	2	1	2.31	1.19
	3	3	9	3	1		2.12	.80
	4	6	2	2			1.75	.68
	5	7	3	6			1.93	.92
	6	11	4		1		1.43	.81
	7	4	8	2	2		2.12	.95
User	1	36	117	36	4	4	2.10	.78
	2	41	102	43	8	3	2.13	.84
	3	20	108	46	18	5	2.39	.88
	4	30	104	46	14	3	2.26	.85
	5	7	45	77	3	2	2.55	.69
	6	6	38	85	3	2	2.61	.72
	7	22	90	54	9	6	2.37	.88
	8	18	81	68	9	5	2.45	.84
	9	17	83	68	8	5	2.45	.83
Budg	1	4	6	5	1		2.18	.91
	2	1	6	6	3		2.68	.87
	3	7	1	7	1		2.12	1.08
	4	8	4	4			1.75	.85
	5	2	6	6	2		2.50	.89
	6	9	2	5			1.75	.93
Coll	1	41	98	49	6	3	2.14	.83
	2	8	15	39	1		2.52	.73
	3	19	20	22	2		2.11	.88
	4	3	7	2	3	1	2.61	1.04
	5	4	5	7			2.73	.67
	6	25	112	45	10	5	2.27	.84
Faci	1	43	102	38	10	4	2.13	.88
	2	52	106	33	3	3	1.98	.79
	3	21	25	8	5	4	2.14	1.16
	4	4	6	2	4		2.37	1.14
	5	12	4				1.25	.44
	6	1	2	3	7	2	3.46	1.12
	7	25	75	20	11	3	2.19	.91

Table 6.   Needs Assessment Data Ranked by Most Important
Needs (Highest Mean Value) of the Owens Campus Library

Rank	Item	Survey Statement	Mean
1	6 (Facility)	Learning resources space restricted to function	3.46
2	5 (Collection)	Obsolete materials policy	2.73
3	2 (Budget)	An ample and stable budget	2.68
4	4 (Collection)	Collection is of sufficient scope	2.61
5	4 (User Serv)	Information literacy program for students	2.61
6	5 (User Serv)	Provision for instructional suppport production	2.55
7	2 (Collection)	A collection development policy exists	2.52

reliability—of the instruments. The task was completed by computing a Cronbach Alpha Coefficient based on each group of respondents completing the three different survey forms—the library personnel and administration sample, the faculty sample, and the student sample. The Cronbach Alpha Coefficient for group one (library personnel and administrators) who completed a 43-item survey was .855. The Cronbach Alpha Coefficient for the second group (faculty sample) who completed an 18-item survey form was .843. The computed Cronbach Alpha Coefficient for the third group (student sample) who completed a 16-item survey form was .918. The values of alpha obtained for these three groups indicated an acceptable level of internal consistency and reliability for the total items listed on the three different surveys. As noted previously, the content validity of the surveys had been established because items were drawn from library standards developed and adopted by the Community and Junior College National Library Association and the Association of College and Research Libraries.

The next step in the analysis involved computing the usual descriptive statistics used with survey data—the mean, median, standard deviation, and frequency distribution of responses for each different survey completed by the three subgroups and for the total sample. The frequency tabulations of response by subgroup indicated that nearly one-half of the cells had frequencies of less than five. This made statistical testing of differences between subgroups somewhat suspect. For that reason, the interpretation of the results focused on the total sample, although results for each group were examined and reported.

The results for all 197 respondents are displayed in Table 5. The first five columns provide the number of respondents who selected each of the possible five responses for each item. The average response and standard deviation for each item across the respondents are given in the remaining two columns. Items with a small mean value are those with which the respondents agree strongly. Those items with which the respondents disagreed most strongly have the highest mean values.

Table 6 provides a listing of those items on the library assessment survey with the highest mean values; all were 2.50 or higher. That is, the respondents felt that these standards were least well met by the Owens Campus Library.

1.   Item 6 in the Facilities section stated: "Space assigned to learning resources is restricted to the functions for which it is designed." This item had an overall mean value of 3.46 indicating that respondents did not agree with the statement. The median for that same item was 4.00, reinforcing the high mean value respondents recorded for this statement. Nine of 15 respondents responded "Disagree" or Strongly Disagree" with the statement. These responses indicated that Campus Library and Administrative personnel should carefully monitor how the library facility is utilized and that future use should be restricted to library services and purposes.

2.   The next highest overall mean value was 2.73. Survey participants gave that value to the statement: "Obsolete, worn-out, and inappropriate materials are removed based on a policy statement." The standard deviation for this item was .67, indicating a high level of consistency among respondents. The high mean value indicated concern from library users about obsolete materials. Seven of the 16 respondents chose the "Don't Know" category. These responses indicated that library personnel should update resources on a regular basis, work with instructional cohorts in discarding obsolete resources, and pay particular attention to replacing obsolete and inappropriate technical resources.

3.   The next highest overall mean value was 2.68, which related to a budget item. The statement, "An ample and stable budget are based either on percentage of educational and general budget totals for the institution or based on a dollar amount per full-time student equivalent" received a 2.68 mean rating from the 16 respondents. That relatively high mean value signifies concern about budget allocation. Three respondents were "Undecided." This response indicated that the respondent observed that the library budget might not be adequate to provide the resources and services needed for the number of academic programs served.

4.   Under the "Collections" category, when asked to consider the following statement, "The collection is of sufficient scope and currency to support the curriculum as well as meet individual information needs of students and faculty," the respondents provided an overall mean value of 2.61, indicating some concern about this item. Four (24%) respondents gave this item a 4 or 5 "Disagree" or "Strongly Disagree" rating, and two respondents marked "Don't Know." This response indicated that collection currency is important to the Campus community. Combining this finding with the previous concern of an ample and stable budget, the conclusion could be drawn that library users expect the library collection to be sufficient for their curricula and personal needs.

5.   Under the category labeled "User Service," when given the statement "An information literacy program for students is provided through a variety of techniques," the respondents also provided an overall 2.61 mean value indicating

some concern. However, this concern or high mean value was probably due to the number of respondents (85) who marked the choice "Don't Know" as opposed to actually "Disagreeing" that there is a problem with the information literacy program.

6.   Under "User Service" statement 5, "Provision is made for instructional support production services," respondents rated this item with a 2.55 overall mean value, indicating some concern. However, 77 respondents chose "Don't Know," thus again perhaps raising the total mean value. The median, perhaps a better statistical indicator for this particular statement, was 3.00. This response indicates that Owens Campus Library personnel may not be adequately informing their constituents about the services and resources available to them.

7.   Under "Collections" category, statement 2, "A collection development policy statement serves as the basis for selection and acquisition of material," rated an overall mean value of 2.52 which also signaled some concern. Forty respondents out of 63 marked this statement as "Don't Know" or "Disagree." Perhaps this response also indicated a lack of knowledge or information about library services available to users. This particular item and the previous item indicated that Owens Campus Library personnel might want to examine how information about library services is provided to the community.

Because the needs assessment data were available for the individual subgroups as well as the total sample, it was possible to compare certain survey item responses between the three different subgroups. This was especially true in the "User Services" section where similar statements were listed on the three different surveys. Because students were important library users, the researcher was particularly interested in that subgroup's responses relating to the needs of the Owens Campus Library. The student sample survey data, which included 92 Owens Campus students and 42 partnership institution's students, offered the following findings regarding their concerns and needs for the Owens Campus Library.

1.   Statement 6 in the Users Section of the student survey stated, "An information literacy program for students is provided through a variety of techniques." Students rated this statement a mean value of 2.67 and a median of 3.00. The standard deviation was .66 indicating consistency among the responses. Eighty-five out 134 respondents marked "Don't Know," thus indicating lack of knowledge about any literacy program available at the Owens Campus.

2.   The next highest mean value rating by students was 2.61 for statement 5 under the heading "User Services" which stated "Provision is made for instructional support production services." The median for this question was 3.00 and the standard deviation was .69. Seventy-seven respondents out of 132 marked "Don't Know" on the survey, thus again indicating their lack of knowledge about this particular service.

3. Statement 8 under "User Services" related to interlibrary loan services: "The Owens Campus interlibrary loan system is accessible, efficient, and adequately serves the needs of the campus community." The student median for this question was 3.00, mean value 2.59, and standard deviation .82. Comparing the mean value of 2.08, the median of 2.00, and standard deviation of .80 of this statement given by the faculty sample to the student statistical responses, suggested a substantial difference in perception between the two subgroups on the quality of interlibrary loan service provided by the Owens Campus Library.

4. Statement 9 under the "Users Section" stated: "The Owens Campus learning resources program provides easy access for students, faculty, staff, and administration in the instruction of electronic databases." The student mean value for this statement was 2.53 and the standard deviation .82. Once again, comparing the faculty responses, mean value of 2.21, and standard deviation of .80 to the student's statistical responses for this particular statement, a difference between the two subgroup's perceptions about the quality of library instruction on electronic databases occurring at the Owens Campus Library was apparent.

5. Statement 7 under "User Services," "The Owens Campus material loan period is sufficient for the diverse needs of the campus communitym" received a 2.50 mean value and a standard deviation of .90 from the student sample. When the student responses were compared to the faculty responses (mean value response of 2.02, standard deviation of .70), it appeared that the students were not as satisfied with the Owens Campus loan period as the Campus faculty members.

The survey responses for the above cited statements from the three different subgroups (16 Owens Campus library personnel and administrators, 47 Owens Campus and partnership faculty, and 134 Owens Campus and partnership students) illustrated some of the notable differences between the three subgroups in "User Services" provided at the Owens Campus Library. The differences in the level of responses by the three different subgroups to identical survey statements provided multiple checks on the quality of service available at the Owens Campus Library. Owens Campus Library personnel tended to believe that equal service was provided to all library users; however, the data showed a different perception among the student respondents.

When comparing certain statistical survey data obtained from student and faculty survey samples, the two subgroups differed, at times substantially, in their responses to the identical survey items. Student survey responses to the identical survey items provided a higher mean value to the identical items than the mean values given by the faculty survey sample. Such differences, in conjunction with the additional findings outlined in this section, indicated that the Owens Campus Library leaders may want to explore and implement other alternatives to improve "User Services" programs needing improvement as revealed in the needs assessment described in this study.

Library Advisory Committee Feasibility and Desirability

This section provides data and related analyses on research question number 4: "Is an advisory committee to the Delaware Technical & Community College, Owens Campus Library, feasible and desirable?" The answer to this question was based on data compiled from survey instruments developed and utilized to answer research questions 1 and 3. Research question 1 focused on the role, structure, and function of advisory committees in existence at the Owens Campus. Research question 3 was answered with three library needs assessment survey instruments administered to Campus samples—administrators and library personnel, Owens Campus and Partnership faculty, and Owens Campus and Partnership students—to collect needs assessment data from the Owens Campus Library community.

Data obtained from the above-cited sources indicated that advisory committees were effective change agents. Specifically, Campus department chairs, administrators, and advisory committee members confirmed that advisory committees were excellent sources for information, assistance, and support in achieving academic department program goals and objectives. Such a committee was most useful for providing expert advice on updating and developing new programs; reviewing relevancy of curricula to the needs of the community; assisting in identifying technical needs of students and the community; assisting and participating in needs assessment studies for new technical training programs; acting as a change agent in making instructional programs relevant to community needs; assisting and advising college authorities on long-range planning for technical education needs; assisting in the development of educational objectives for the institution; assisting college officials with long-range planning efforts; and assisting faculty with establishing proficiency standards for students.

Utilizing the literature on the function of college libraries, a needs assessment of the Owens Campus Library was constructed and conducted. The needs assessment revealed that: the library users were concerned about utilizing assigned library space for purposes other than library services; the library collection included obsolete materials; the library's budget was ample and stable enough to serve the diverse user group; the library's holdings were of sufficient scope to meet the needs of its clientele; there existed a collection development policy statement; and there was a provision for instructional support production services.

The above library findings provide invaluable insight about the needs of the library as well as a course of action for library personnel to pursue. Valid input from campus constituents about the library is vital to its effectiveness. Corrective measures applied to these findings can perhaps be a beginning for the Campus Library to become a more effective and relevant department to meet the informational needs of the instructional departments.

The Owens Campus Library assessment study disclosed that library users are concerned about utilizing assigned library space and facilities for purposes other than library services. Clearly, a library advisory committee could address such a concern. Study findings revealed that advisory committees are effective change agents. With the support of an advisory committee the Owens Campus Library leaders could share this concern about the use and purpose of library facilities with college authorities and the two forces present a collaborative position that library space and facilities be retained for the use of library services and staff only.

Assisting library staff in establishing an ample and stable budget might also be addressed by a library advisory committee. However, this item would need to be addressed with a great deal of care because the advisory committee survey indicated that current advisory committee members felt that financial matters were really not in their purview.

Library collection development could also benefit from advisory committee input. Developing a collection to support the diverse curricula available at the Owens Campus is an enormous task for library personnel. A library advisory committee representing the diverse college community could provide valuable and needed input for identifying resources needed by the divergent instructional programs, especially because advice on planning, developing objectives and acting as change agents were advisory strengths identified on the advisory committee survey.

In addition to the above issues that clearly fall within the purview of a library advisory committee, the following concerns which have begun to surface in the general postsecondary library community, and at the Owens Campus Library as well, could be presented for consideration by an established library advisory committee.

A library advisory committee could assist library staff in conveying information to the college community about existing and newly developed programs available at the Campus Library. Study findings indicated that survey respondents were unfamiliar with the library information literacy and instructional support services available to them. If such services were first presented and shared with advisory committee members, perhaps those persons could take such information back to their colleagues, classmates, students, and community friends, thus informing them about such services available from the library.

Advisory committees may also be able to assist library staff members with long-range planning policy development in managing technological developments. The Owens Campus Library installed a million dollar automation system in late 1996. This automated system will require the four Delaware Tech Campus libraries to merge public catalogs, revise acquisition procedures, revise and update interlibrary loan procedures, cooperate on cataloging operations, and examine other library operations and programs which were previously under the direction of each independent campus library. A library advisory committee could be an extremely valuable partner to the library staff in approaching that challenging venture.

Library technological resources allow library users to see and know what resources other libraries own. How to access, borrow, and receive those items for library users is of the utmost importance. An advisory committee could assist library personnel in developing new policies related to obtaining and utilizing these electronic resources.

Study findings also revealed that Owens Campus students were concerned about the amount of time library materials could be borrowed. An advisory committee could assist library officials in determining the most efficient and effective loan period for students, thus making such policies more relevant to borrower's needs.

These additional issues, although not a direct finding from the survey data, present authentic concerns and problems to the Owens Campus Library staff. By involving other sources, such as a library advisory committee, library staff could better resolve such pending library concerns.

Based on the needs identified in the needs assessment component of the study and given the roles and functions that existing instructional advisory committees feel that they can best perform, it is clear that an advisory committee to support and assist library staff is both feasible and desirable.

CONCLUSIONS

The purpose of this study was to explore the viability of establishing an advisory committee to determine the role and function and structure of such an advisory committee in addressing issues facing a postsecondary library. Therefore, this study was designed to gather data on advisory committees, including their role, function, and structure to determine if such a resource could be applied toward addressing community college library issues.

Sample data results from 15 instructional department chairs, 5 campus administrators, and 8 advisory committee members, about the role, function, and structure of advisory committees indicated advisory committees were considered valuable resources for Owens Campus instructional departments.

Although advisory committees had been in existence at the Owens Campus since its inception in 1967, no valid attempt had ever been made to analyze or evaluate their actual role or function. The data collected from the three sample subgroups were a first attempt at formally analyzing advisory committees role, function, and structure. The reason for such an investigative undertaking was to determine if an advisory committee was worth establishing and implementing at the Owens Campus Library.

Data obtained from the multiple campus sources were consistent with the advisory committee literature, which reported that advisory committees could provide much needed support and strength to postsecondary instructional departments. Both descriptive and anecdotal data obtained from the study's subgroups, department chairs, administrators, and advisory committee members, indicated advisory committees assist both instructional and administrative staff in developing goals, objectives, curricula update, and provide support and assistance toward numerous worthwhile endeavors appropriate for a specified department. Such findings suggested that an advisory committee could play a similar role in assisting library personnel in developing and obtaining goals and objectives, updating and improving programs, planning technology development, assisting in the improvement of library operations and functions, and other pursuits common to a community college library setting.

A library needs assessment, based on standards promulgated by the Association of College and Research Libraries, indicated that certain services of the Owens Campus Library were not present at the anticipated or expected level. These results, based on a sample of 134 students, 47 faculty, 8 administrators, and 8 library personnel indicated that room existed for improvement.

The data on advisory committees coupled with the needs assessment data indicated that an advisory committee was feasible, desirable, and appropriate for the Owens Campus Library. A plan to establish such an advisory committee was prepared and presented to the Owens Campus administration in 1996. The plan for an Owens Campus Library Advisory Committee was accepted and endorsed by the Campus Administration in 1996.

APPENDIX A

Survey Instrument Relating to Structure, Role, and Function
of Advisory Committees at the Owens Campus of Delaware
Technical & Community College for Department Chairs,
Administrators, and Advisory Committee Members

The following questions relate to your opinions about the structure, role, and function of advisory committees currently in place at the Owens Campus of Delaware Technical & Community College, Georgetown, Delaware.

Classification: Dept. Chair___. Administrator___. Advisory Comm. Member___.
(Please place check mark in appropriate space. Thank you).

1. Please circle the number corresponding to your opinion about the importance of the role advisory committees play in each of the following functions at DT&CC, Owens Campus.

a. Advise college authorities on the development of long-range and annual plans for technical education

Very Important	Important	Undecided	Unimportant	Very Unimportant
1	2	3	4	5

b. Assist college authorities in identifying technical education needs of individuals and the community

Very Important	Important	Undecided	Unimportant	Very Unimportant
1	2	3	4	5

c. Review budget requests for labs, equipment, supplies

Very Important	Important	Undecided	Unimportant	Very Unimportant
1	2	3	4	5

d. Evaluate adequacy of facilities and equipment

Very Important	Important	Undecided	Unimportant	Very Unimportant
1	2	3	4	5

e. Assist in establishing proficiency standards for students

Very Important	Important	Undecided	Unimportant	Very Unimportant
1	2	3	4	5

f. Review curriculum to ensure relevancy

Very Important	Important	Undecided	Unimportant	Very Unimportant
1	2	3	4	5

g. Assist in development of skill improvement classes for industry employees

Very Important	Important	Undecided	Unimportant	Very Unimportant
1	2	3	4	5

h. Recommend instructors for program and desirable instructor qualification

Very Important	Important	Undecided	Unimportant	Very Unimportant
1	2	3	4	5

i. Serve as a source for speakers or obtain speakers for class meetings

Very Important	Important	Undecided	Unimportant	Very Unimportant
1	2	3	4	5

j. Assist in planning and conducting field trips

Very Important	Important	Undecided	Unimportant	Very Unimportant
1	2	3	4	5

k. Make recommendations to college officials and Board of Trustee members

Very Important	Important	Undecided	Unimportant	Very Unimportant
1	2	3	4	5

l. Assist in determining community needs by conducting surveys and labor market trend studies

Very Important	Important	Undecided	Unimportant	Very Unimportant
1	2	3	4	5

m. Assist in the development of application for funds

Very Important	Important	Undecided	Unimportant	Very Unimportant
1	2	3	4	5

n. Provide scholarships and other financial assistance for students and graduates

Very Important	Important	Undecided	Unimportant	Very Unimportant
1	2	3	4	5

o. Assist in conducting clinics and in-service training for instructors

Very Important	Important	Undecided	Unimportant	Very Unimportant
1	2	3	4	5

p. Assist in developing educational objectives

Very Important	Important	Undecided	Unimportant	Very Unimportant
1	2	3	4	5

q. Assist in cost studies for program/course

Very Important	Important	Undecided	Unimportant	Very Unimportant
1	2	3	4	5

r. Secure funding for instructors to attend meetings, workshops, seminars

Very Important	Important	Undecided	Unimportant	Very Unimportant
1	2	3	4	5

s. Assist in the review of legislation affecting technical education

Very Important	Important	Undecided	Unimportant	Very Unimportant
1	2	3	4	5

t. Provide objective, periodic evaluations with recommendations presented to proper authorities

Very Important	Important	Undecided	Unimportant	Very Unimportant
1	2	3	4	5

u. Share their expertise on new and developing areas

Very Important	Important	Undecided	Unimportant	Very Unimportant
1	2	3	4	5

v.   Assist departments to set priorities for budgetary expenditures

Very Important	Important	Undecided	Unimportant	Very Unimportant
1	2	3	4	5

w.   Participate in needs assessment for new occupational training programs in the community

Very Important	Important	Undecided	Unimportant	Very Unimportant
1	2	3	4	5

x.   Act as an agent of change to increase relevancy of program

Very Important	Important	Undecided	Unimportant	Very Unimportant
1	2	3	4	5

y.   Keep community informed on current specific needs and changes in labor market

Very Important	Important	Undecided	Unimportant	Very Unimportant
1	2	3	4	5

z.   Assist in long-term regional planning

Very Important	Important	Undecided	Unimportant	Very Unimportant
1	2	3	4	5

2.   Please respond to the following questions regarding the structure and operations of advisory committees based on your knowledge and/or experience of advisory committees at the Southern Campus, DT&CC.

a.   How do you believe advisory committee members should be selected?
b.   What is the optimum number for an effective advisory committee?
c.   What types of individuals do you believe should serve on advisory committees?
d.   What do you believe should be the length of terms for advisory committee members?
e.   Once advisory committee members are selected and agree to serve how should officers be chosen?

f. Do you believe formal by-laws and operating procedures should be established for directing the operations of advisory committees?
g. How many committee meetings should be held annually?
h. To whom should the advisory committee report?
i. How frequently should advisory committees meet?
    Monthly___ Bi-Monthly___ Twice a Year___
    Once a Year___ Not at All___
j. Should the advisory committee be divided into subcommittees? If answered yes, can you give an example? Yes___ No___
    Example (Please elaborate)
k. Do you recommend that minutes be kept for each meeting?
    Yes___ No___

APPENDIX B

Owens Campus Library Needs Assessment
Survey Instrument for Library Staff and Administrators

The following statements pertain to the operations and functions at the Owens Campus Library. Please circle the number which, in your opinion, reflects to what degree you agree or disagree with each statement.

If you feel you are unfamiliar with certain portions, please mark "Don't Know" rather than skipping that portion. However, please, only use this category when you absolutely know very little about the statement. Thank you.

Classification: Owens Campus Administrator_____. Owens Campus Library Staff_____. Thank you.

Objectives

1. Owens Campus Library has a comprehensive mission statement for the learning resources program based on the nature and purpose of the institution.

Strongly Agree	Agree	Don't Know	Disagree	Strongly Disagree
1	2	3	4	5

2. The mission statement was developed by the learning resources staff in consultation with the widest possible representation of the college community and is viewed periodically.

Strongly Agree	Agree	Don't Know	Disagree	Strongly Disagree
1	2	3	4	5

3. The mission statement is used, along with institutional educational goals, in the annual planning process.

Strongly Agree	Agree	Don't Know	Disagree	Strongly Disagree
1	2	3	4	5

4. All component units located at the Owens Campus learning resources program, whether administered centrally or by campus units, are clearly defined.

Strongly Agree	Agree	Don't Know	Disagree	Strongly Disagree
1	2	3	4	5

5. The learning resources program is an integral part of the institution's process for the improvement of instruction.

Strongly Agree	Agree	Don't Know	Disagree	Strongly Disagree
1	2	3	4	5

Organization and Administration

1. The responsibilities and functions of the Owens Campus Library are clearly defined within the institutional structure of Delaware Technical & Community College.

Strongly Agree	Agree	Don't Know	Disagree	Strongly Disagree
1	2	3	4	5

2. The duties and responsibilities of the chief administrator of the Owens Campus learning resources program are clearly defined within the institutional structure.

Strongly Agree	Agree	Don't Know	Disagree	Strongly Disagree
1	2	3	4	5

3. The learning resources program administrator is professionally trained and knowledgeable about learning resources, information, and/or media materials and services.

Strongly Agree	Agree	Don't Know	Disagree	Strongly Disagree
1	2	3	4	5

4. The comprehensive learning resources program includes a variety of services which are organized into functional units.

Strongly Agree	Agree	Don't Know	Disagree	Strongly Disagree
1	2	3	4	5

5. The administrator and professional staff are involved in all areas and all levels of academic activities and institutional planning.

Strongly Agree	Agree	Don't Know	Disagree	Strongly Disagree
1	2	3	4	5

6. Advisory committees are available to provide essential information to the staff and to serve as a link with users.

Strongly Agree	Agree	Don't Know	Disagree	Strongly Disagree
1	2	3	4	5

7. Administration of the learning resources program is based on staff participation and consensus.

Strongly Agree	Agree	Don't Know	Disagree	Strongly Disagree
1	2	3	4	5

Staff

1. Sufficient and qualified professional and support staff are available to implement the services for which the program is responsible.

Strongly Agree	Agree	Don't Know	Disagree	Strongly Disagree
1	2	3	4	5

2. Professional staff members have a graduate degree from an accredited institution, faculty status, benefits, and obligations or the equivalent.

Strongly Agree	Agree	Don't Know	Disagree	Strongly Disagree
1	2	3	4	5

3. Professional staff belong to and participate in library, learning resources, media, and other appropriate associations. Professional development is encouraged through direct financial support of attendance and participation in local, state, and national organizations.

Strongly Agree	Agree	Don't Know	Disagree	Strongly Disagree
1	2	3	4	5

4. The changing nature of learning resources programs and ongoing changes in technology mandate regular staff participation in continuing education.

Strongly Agree	Agree	Don't Know	Disagree	Strongly Disagree
1	2	3	4	5

5. Technical and classified personnel have appropriate specialized training or experience. Classification, status, and salary are equivalent to those provided for other institutional employees with similar qualifications.

Strongly Agree	Agree	Don't Know	Disagree	Strongly Disagree
1	2	3	4	5

6. Student assistants perform a variety of tasks that assist and complement professional staff, clerical staff, and technicians. Student assistant programs offer work opportunities and career exploration for student workers.

Strongly Agree	Agree	Don't Know	Disagree	Strongly Disagree
1	2	3	4	5

7. The support staff represents at least 65% of the total library staff, not including student assistants.

Strongly Agree	Agree	Don't Know	Disagree	Strongly Disagree
1	2	3	4	5

Budget

1. The mission statement forms the basis for the program budget and is part of the institutional planning process; annual objectives are developed by the learning resources staff.

Strongly Agree	Agree	Don't Know	Disagree	Strongly Disagree
1	2	3	4	5

2. An ample and stable budget are based either on a percentage of educational and general budget totals for the institution or based on a dollar amount per full-time student equivalent.

Strongly Agree	Agree	Don't Know	Disagree	Strongly Disagree
1	2	3	4	5

3. Local processes are developed so that all expenditures originate within the learning resources program and are reviewed by the chief administrator.

Strongly Agree	Agree	Don't Know	Disagree	Strongly Disagree
1	2	3	4	5

4. Internal accounts are maintained for evaluating the flow of expenditures, monitoring encumbrances, and approving payment of invoices.

Strongly Agree	Agree	Don't Know	Disagree	Strongly Disagree
1	2	3	4	5

5. The learning resources budget provides stable funding for contractual services, equipment and materials replacement, and for maintenance of automated public and technical services.

Strongly Agree	Agree	Don't Know	Disagree	Strongly Disagree
1	2	3	4	5

6. All directly related revenues such as fines, payments for lost and damaged materials, sale of unneeded items, and student use fees are used solely for the support of collections, services, and activities of learning resources programs.

Strongly Agree	Agree	Don't Know	Disagree	Strongly Disagree
1	2	3	4	5

User Services

1. The learning resources program provides a variety of services that support and expand the instructional capabilities of the institution.

Strongly Agree	Agree	Don't Know	Disagree	Strongly Disagree
1	2	3	4	5

2. The learning resources program seeks to enlarge access to the academic services available at the college and in the community in accordance with the college mission through networking, resource sharing, on-line information services, and technological advances.

Strongly Agree	Agree	Don't Know	Disagree	Strongly Disagree
1	2	3	4	5

3. Services provided meet the instructional and informational needs of students, faculty, staff, and administration; provide professional assistance; and include a minimum of information access provision for students in off-campus locations.

Strongly Agree	Agree	Don't Know	Disagree	Strongly Disagree
1	2	3	4	5

4. Necessary equipment to access information and to assist instruction is available and efficiently managed.

Strongly Agree	Agree	Don't Know	Disagree	Strongly Disagree
1	2	3	4	5

5. Provision is made for instructional support production services.

Strongly Agree	Agree	Don't Know	Disagree	Strongly Disagree
1	2	3	4	5

6. An information literacy program for students is provided through a variety of techniques.

Strongly Agree	Agree	Don't Know	Disagree	Strongly Disagree
1	2	3	4	5

Collections

1. The learning resources program makes available an organized collection of materials and information in diversified formats including print and nonprint media, computer software, optical storage technologies, and other.

Strongly Agree	Agree	Don't Know	Disagree	Strongly Disagree
1	2	3	4	5

2. A collection development policy statement serves as the basis for selection and acquisition of material.

Strongly Agree	Agree	Don't Know	Disagree	Strongly Disagree
1	2	3	4	5

3. The selection of materials is coordinated by the professional staff, working closely with the campus community. Final management decisions, as to the order in which materials are to be purchased and what gifts should be accepted and processed, are the responsibility of the program administrator.

Strongly Agree	Agree	Don't Know	Disagree	Strongly Disagree
1	2	3	4	5

4. The collection is of sufficient scope and currency to support the curriculum as well as meet individual information needs of students and faculty.

Strongly Agree	Agree	Don't Know	Disagree	Strongly Disagree
1	2	3	4	5

5. Obsolete, worn-out, and inappropriate materials are removed based on a policy statement.

Strongly Agree	Agree	Don't Know	Disagree	Strongly Disagree
1	2	3	4	5

6. The reference collection includes a wide selection of standard works, with subject bibliographies and periodical indexes in print and electronic formats.

Strongly Agree	Agree	Don't Know	Disagree	Strongly Disagree
1	2	3	4	5

Facilities

1. The learning resources program provides adequate space for housing collections in a variety of formats, for study and research, for public service activities, for staff workrooms and offices, and for basic production.

Strongly Agree	Agree	Don't Know	Disagree	Strongly Disagree
1	2	3	4	5

2. Student seating approximates a minimum of 10% of the FTE enrollment. The space for user activities accommodates a wide variety of learning styles and study situations, attractive, comfortable, and designed to encourage use. Different types of seating arrangements are offered, including: (1) individual carrels, (2) tables for four, (3) computers and workstations, (4) microfilm reader stations, (5) small group study rooms.

Strongly Agree	Agree	Don't Know	Disagree	Strongly Disagree
1	2	3	4	5

3. The generally accepted formula for books and other bound collections is calculated at 10 bound volumes per assignable square foot. This number is double to 20 volumes per square foot if compact shelving is used. Other materials such as audiovisual, software, microforms, maps, archives, etc. are to be converted to volume equivalents by using one of the existing conversion tables available in the literature and should be included in the total stack estimate. Anticipated growth of the collection should be factored into the calculation.

Strongly Agree	Agree	Don't Know	Disagree	Strongly Disagree
1	2	3	4	5

4. Staff space for workrooms, offices, equipment areas, etc. are in compliance with state and institutional guidelines. A minimum of 175 square feet per staff member to accommodate new technologies, equipment, and hardware is desirable. Individual offices for professional staff and administrators are figured at 200 square feet per person.

Strongly Agree	Agree	Don't Know	Disagree	Strongly Disagree
1	2	3	4	5

5. New construction and remodeling projects are to be in compliance with the Americans with Disabilities Act (ADA).

Strongly Agree	Agree	Don't Know	Disagree	Strongly Disagree
1	2	3	4	5

6. Space assigned to learning resources is restricted to the functions for which it is designed.

Strongly Agree	Agree	Don't Know	Disagree	Strongly Disagree
1	2	3	4	5

APPENDIX C

Owens Campus Library Needs Assessment Survey Instrument for Students

The following statements pertain to the operations and functions at the Owens Campus Library. Please circle the number which, in your opinion, reflects to what degree you agree or disagree with each statement.

If you feel that you are unfamiliar with certain portions, please mark "Don't Know" rather than skipping that portion. However, please, only use this category when you absolutely know very little about the statement. Thank you.

Classification: Owens Campus Student____. Wilmington College Student____. University of Delaware Student____. Delaware State University Student____. Thank you.

1. The learning resources (Library) program provides a variety of services that support and expand the instructional capabilities of the institution.

Strongly Agree	Agree	Don't Know	Disagree	Strongly Disagree
1	2	3	4	5

2. The learning resources (Library) program seeks to enlarge access to the academic services available at the Owens Campus and in the community in accordance with the college mission through networking, resource sharing, on-line information services, and technological advances.

Strongly Agree	Agree	Don't Know	Disagree	Strongly Disagree
1	2	3	4	5

3. Services provided meet the instructional and informational needs of students, faculty, staff, and administration; provide professional assistance; and include a minimum of information access provision for students in off-campus locations.

Strongly Agree	Agree	Don't Know	Disagree	Strongly Disagree
1	2	3	4	5

4. Necessary equipment to access information and to assist instruction is available and efficiently managed.

Strongly Agree	Agree	Don't Know	Disagree	Strongly Disagree
1	2	3	4	5

5. Provision is made for instructional support production services.

Strongly Agree	Agree	Don't Know	Disagree	Strongly Disagree
1	2	3	4	5

6. An information literacy program for students is provided through a variety of techniques.

Strongly Agree	Agree	Don't Know	Disagree	Strongly Disagree
1	2	3	4	5

7. The Owens Campus material loan period is sufficient for the diverse needs of the campus community.

Strongly Agree	Agree	Don't Know	Disagree	Strongly Disagree
1	2	3	4	5

8. The Owens Campus interlibrary loan system is accessible, efficient, and adequately serves the needs of the campus community.

Strongly Agree	Agree	Don't Know	Disagree	Strongly Disagree
1	2	3	4	5

9. The Owens Campus learning resources program provides easy access for students, faculty, staff, and administration in the instruction of electronic database resources.

Strongly Agree	Agree	Don't Know	Disagree	Strongly Disagree
1	2	3	4	5

Collections

1. The learning resources program makes available an organized collection of materials and information in diversified formats including print and nonprint media, computer software, optical storage technologies, and other.

Strongly Agree	Agree	Don't Know	Disagree	Strongly Disagree
1	2	3	4	5

2. The collection is of sufficient scope and currency to support the curriculum as well as meet individual information needs of students and faculty.

Strongly Agree	Agree	Don't Know	Disagree	Strongly Disagree
1	2	3	4	5

3. Obsolete, worn-out, and inappropriate materials are removed based on a policy statement.

Strongly Agree	Agree	Don't Know	Disagree	Strongly Disagree
1	2	3	4	5

4. The reference collection includes a wide selection of standard works, with subject bibliographies and periodical indexes in print and electronic formats.

Strongly Agree	Agree	Don't Know	Disagree	Strongly Disagree
1	2	3	4	5

Facilities

1. The learning resources program provides adequate space for housing collections in a variety of formats, for study and research, for public service activities, for staff workrooms and offices, and for basic production.

Strongly Agree	Agree	Don't Know	Disagree	Strongly Disagree
1	2	3	4	5

2. Student seating approximates a minimum of 10% of the FTE enrollment. The space for user activities accommodates a wide variety of learning styles and study situations, attractive, comfortable, and designed to encourage use. Different types of seating arrangements are offered, including: (1) individual carrels, (2) tables for four, (3) computers and workstations, (4) microfilm reader stations, (5) small group study rooms.

Strongly Agree	Agree	Don't Know	Disagree	Strongly Disagree
1	2	3	4	5

3. The Owens Campus Library provides convenient and sufficient hours to utilize and borrow resources.

Strongly Agree	Agree	Don't Know	Disagree	Strongly Disagree
1	2	3	4	5

APPENDIX D

Owens Campus Library Needs Assessment
Survey Instrument for Faculty and Staff

The following statements pertain to the operations and functions at the Owens Campus Library. Please circle the number which, in your opinion, reflects to what degree you agree or disagree with each statement.

If you feel you are unfamiliar with certain statements, please mark "Don't Know" rather than skipping that portion. However, please, only use this category when you absolutely know very little about the statement. Thank you.

Classification: Owens Campus Faculty____. Wilmington College Faculty or Staff____. Univ. of Delaware Faculty or Staff____. Delaware State Univ. Faculty or Staff____.

User Services

1. The learning resources (Library) program provides a variety of services that support and expand the instructional capabilities of the institution.

Strongly Agree	Agree	Don't Know	Disagree	Strongly Disagree
1	2	3	4	5

2. The learning resources (Library) program seeks to enlarge access to the academic services available at the Owens Campus and in the community in accordance with the college mission through networking, resource sharing, on-line information services, and technological advances.

Strongly Agree	Agree	Don't Know	Disagree	Strongly Disagree
1	2	3	4	5

3. Services provided meet the instructional and informational needs of students, faculty, staff, and administration; provide professional assistance;

and include a minimum of information access provision for students in off-campus locations.

Strongly Agree	Agree	Don't Know	Disagree	Strongly Disagree
1	2	3	4	5

4. Necessary equipment to access information and to assist instruction is available and efficiently managed.

Strongly Agree	Agree	Don't Know	Disagree	Strongly Disagree
1	2	3	4	5

5. Provision is made for support of instructional production services.

Strongly Agree	Agree	Don't Know	Disagree	Strongly Disagree
1	2	3	4	5

6. An information literacy program for students is provided through a variety of techniques.

Strongly Agree	Agree	Don't Know	Disagree	Strongly Disagree
1	2	3	4	5

7. The Owens Campus material loan period is sufficient for the diverse needs of the Campus community.

Strongly Agree	Agree	Don't Know	Disagree	Strongly Disagree
1	2	3	4	5

8. The Owens Campus interlibrary loan system is accessible, efficient, and adequately serves the needs of the Campus community.

Strongly Agree	Agree	Don't Know	Disagree	Strongly Disagree
1	2	3	4	5

9. The Owens Campus learning resources program provides easy access for students, faculty, staff, and administration in the instruction of electronic database resources.

Strongly Agree	Agree	Don't Know	Disagree	Strongly Disagree
1	2	3	4	5

Collections

1. The learning resources program makes available an organized collection of materials and information in diversified formats including print and nonprint media, computer software, optical storage technologies, and other.

Strongly Agree	Agree	Don't Know	Disagree	Strongly Disagree
1	2	3	4	5

2. A collection development policy statement serves as the basis for selection and acquisition of material.

Strongly Agree	Agree	Don't Know	Disagree	Strongly Disagree
1	2	3	4	5

3. The selection of materials is coordinated by the professional staff, working closely with the campus community. Final management decisions, as to the order in which materials are to be purchased and what gifts should be accepted and processed, are the responsibility of the program administrator.

Strongly Agree	Agree	Don't Know	Disagree	Strongly Disagree
1	2	3	4	5

4. The collection is of sufficient scope and currency to support the curriculum as well as meet individual information needs of students and faculty.

Strongly Agree	Agree	Don't Know	Disagree	Strongly Disagree
1	2	3	4	5

5. Obsolete, worn-out, and inappropriate materials are removed based on a policy statement.

Strongly Agree	Agree	Don't Know	Disagree	Strongly Disagree
1	2	3	4	5

6. The reference collection includes a wide selection of standard works, with subject bibliographies and periodical indexes in print and electronic formats.

Strongly Agree	Agree	Don't Know	Disagree	Strongly Disagree
1	2	3	4	5

Facilities

1. The learning resources program provides adequate space for housing collections in a variety of formats, for study and research, for public service activities, for staff workrooms and offices, and for basic production.

Strongly Agree	Agree	Don't Know	Disagree	Strongly Disagree
1	2	3	4	5

2. Student seating approximates a minimum of 10% of the FTE enrollment. The space for user activities accommodates a wide variety of learning styles and study situations, attractive, comfortable, and designed to encourage use. Different types of seating arrangements are offered, including: (1) individual carrels, (2) tables for four, (3) computers and workstations, (4) microfilm reader stations, (5) small group study rooms.

Strongly Agree	Agree	Don't Know	Disagree	Strongly Disagree
1	2	3	4	5

3. The Owens Campus Library provides adequate and sufficient hours to utilize and borrow resources.

Strongly Agree	Agree	Don't Know	Disagree	Strongly Disagree
1	2	3	4	5

REFERENCES

Alabama Department of Education, The Division of Vocational Education Services & The Alabama Council on Vocational & Technical Education. 1990. "Vocational Technical Advisory Committees: A Guide for Their Effective Use."

Association for Higher Education-ERIC. 1994. *The Advisory Committee Advantage: Creating an Effective Strategy for Programmatic Improvement.* ASHE-ERIC Higher Education Washington, DC Reports.

Association of College & Research Libraries. 1994. *Standards for Community, Junior, and Technical College Learning Resources Programs.* Chicago: Joint committee of the Association for Education Communication and Technology (AECT) and ACRL.

Commission on Higher Education, Middle States Association of Colleges and Schools. 1989. *Characteristics of Excellence in Higher Education: Standards for Accreditation*, rev.ed. Philadelphia, PA.

Curzon, S.C. 1989. *Managing Change: A How-to-do-it Manual for Planning, Implementing, and Evaluating Change in Libraries.* New York: Neal-Schuman.

Delaware Advisory Council on Career and Vocational Education. 1989. *Local Advisory Councils on Vocational Education...A Members Guide.* Prepared by the National Institute for Curriculum Evaluation, Dover, DE.

Dieffenderfer, R., L. Kopp and O. Cap. 1977. *Advisory Committees: Utilizing Business, Industry, Labor Advisory Committees.* Columbus: The Center for Vocational Education, Ohio State University.

Ditzenberger, R. and R. Morkey. 1985. *Establishing an Advisory Committee. Work Experience Module Number 10. Work Experience System.* University of Northern Iowa, Iowa Department of Public Instruction.

Ferguson, G.A. 1971. *Statistical Analysis in Psychology and Education.* New York: McGraw-Hill.

Kalick, R., ed. 1992. *Community College Libraries: Centers for Lifelong Learning.* Metuchen, NJ: Scarecrow Press.

Kaser, D. 1982. "Standards for College Libraries." *Library Trends* 31(1): 7-19.

Merriam, S.B. 1988. *Case Study Research in Education: A Qualitative Approach.* San Francisco, CA: Jossey-Bass.

Miles, M.B. and A.M. Huberman. 1994. *An Expanded Sourcebook: Qualitative Data Analysis*, 2nd ed. Thousand Oaks, CA: Sage.

Minnesota State Council on Vocational Technical Education. 1991. *Effective Advisory Committees Project. Fifty Indices of Effectiveness Regarding the Program Advisory Committee in Minnesota's Technical Colleges: A Working Paper.* St. Paul, MN: Author.

Nebraska Council on Vocational Education. 1994. *Resource Handbook for Developing a Local Advisory Committee.*

Oen, U.T. 1985. Establish and conduct meetings of general and specialized occupational advisory committees. Grayslake: Illinois Competency Based Vocational Education Project, Lake County Area Vocational Center.

Sacks, P.A. and S.L. Whildin. 1993. *Preparing for Accreditation: A Handbook for Academic Libraries.* Chicago: American Library Association.

Stueart, R.D. 1990. "The Liberal Arts College Library: Paradox or Panacea." *College and Research Libraries* 51(6): 524-529.

ASSESSING TECHNICAL EFFICIENCY OF RESEARCH LIBRARIES

Wonsik Shim

INTRODUCTION

Performance Evaluation in Academic Libraries

Higher education has come under increasing pressure to demonstrate its value and performance (Council for Aid to Education 1997; Michalko 1993). As a result many universities and colleges have begun to look at a wide array of performance and accountability measures. These institutions are not only interested in their own (absolute) accomplishments but also want to know how well they perform when compared to peer institutions.

An interesting experiment in this direction is the NACUBO (National Association of College and University Business Officers) benchmark program.[1] Started in 1991, the program now has more than 300 members who regularly report data on predefined functional areas (the library is one of them) and in return receive periodic updates on the best practices, so that they can bring changes to current practices to improve services.

Advances in Library Administration and Organization, Volume 17, pages 243-339.
Copyright © 2000 by JAI Press Inc.
All rights of reproduction in any form reserved.
ISBN: 0-7623-0647-5

As a subunit or department in universities, academic libraries "feel the pressures" (Kyrillidou 1998, p. 4) from the parent institutions to produce evidence on (1) how well the resources are utilized in terms of producing meaningful outputs, and (2) how well the library compares or competes with other libraries within some peer group. Researchers have developed measures for two broad aspects of evaluating library performance. One aspect of library performance is called effectiveness and the other efficiency. Effectiveness here means the extent to which library services meet the expectations or goals set by the organization. McDonald and Micikas (1994) identify at least three additional dimensions of effectiveness based on system resources: (1) how successful the library is in securing required inputs, (2) internal processes and procedures, and (3) constituency satisfaction. In the library field, there has been a strong desire to measure effectiveness in relation to the impact of library services on their users.

Examples of user-centered approaches to the measurement of library effectiveness range from simple user satisfaction surveys to studies on the impacts of using library services (Griffiths and King 1993; Saracevic and Kantor 1997a, 1997b). Material availability, first proposed by De Prospo, Altman and Beasley (1973) and later given a theoretical foundation as "availability" analysis by Buckland (1975) and Kantor (1976, 1984), recognizes that for users, getting what they want is one of the most important aspects of user satisfaction. Material availability spurred a series of research studies (Chaudhry and Ashoor 1994; Ciliberti, Casserly, Hegg and Mitchell 1987; Jacobs and Young 1995; Mitchell et al. 1994; Rashid 1990; Rehman 1993; Revill 1987). Standard library evaluation manuals (e.g., Van House, Weil and McClure 1990) list techniques that generally deal with user assessment.

Out of four dimensions of effectiveness identified by McDonald and Micikas (1994), three—goal-based, system resource-based, and constituency-based—are related to the view of the decision makers at the parent organization. Usually the goals are set by the parent institution. Resources are to be justified to the administrators at the university; and the library must satisfy those who pay for it. Therefore, the library administrators should be mindful of the criteria that the administrators at the parent institution use when attempting to improve the library's effectiveness.

The second aspect of library performance measurement is called "efficiency," here meaning the library's ability to transform its inputs (resources) into optimal production of outputs (services), or to produce the given level of outputs with the minimum amount of inputs. The efficiency aspect of library performance has received less attention in the library literature, although it is an immediate concern for decision makers at the parent institution.

Library statistics usually include some ratios as indicators of efficiency. For instance, ARL provides 30 ratios based on the data reported in its annual statistics. There are numerous cost studies of various services. Many of the studies looked at one particular service area such as references (Cable 1980; Spencer 1980;

High Effectiveness

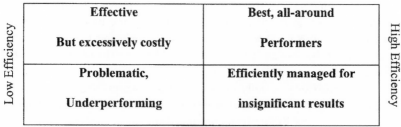

	Effective But excessively costly	Best, all-around Performers	
Low Efficiency	Problematic, Underperforming	Efficiently managed for insignificant results	High Efficiency

Low Effectiveness

Figure 1.   Library Performance Matrix Using the
Levels of Effectiveness and Efficiency as Two Dimensions

Cochrane and Warmann 1989; Robinson and Robinson 1994) or interlibrary loans (Ferguson and Kehoe 1993; Gossen and Kaczor 1997; Palmour, Bryant, Caldwell and Gray 1972; Roche 1993). A few studies attempted to account for multiple user services (Kantor 1986; Mitchell, Tanis and Jaffe 1978).

Like other organizations, the success of the library depends on its ability to behave both effectively and efficiently. It is possible that a library might increase the effectiveness of its services at the expense of the measured efficiency. Or it might increase its measured efficiency at the expense of the service effectiveness. Both situations are clearly not desirable. For instance, the pursuit of cost containment as an end in itself is rarely meaningful. We can put these two dimensions of library performance in a 2 by 2 matrix shown in Figure 1.

Performance improvement requires constant and careful monitoring and assessment of library activities and operating environments. This, in turn, requires the development of proper measurement tools or devices. This study assesses the *technical efficiency* of academic research libraries that are members of the Association of Research Libraries using a complex tool called DEA (Data Envelopment Analysis; Charnes, Cooper and Rhodes 1978). Technical efficiency refers to the conversion of inputs into outputs. The technical efficiency of the organization is based on comparing a ratio for that organization to the corresponding ratio attained by best practice in some comparison set. An organization is technically efficient if there is no waste of inputs in producing the given level of outputs or if there is no example of greater output with the given level of inputs. While the development of effectiveness is, of course, important too, this study is focused on measuring library efficiency.

DEA incorporates the idea of benchmarking and extends it to situations with many resources and services, called "inputs" and "outputs," respectively. Furthermore, it may prove to be a useful tool for the self-evaluation that is often required in the institutional accreditation process.

The goal of this study is to assess the potential of DEA as a tool for studying technical efficiency at research libraries by investigating its (1) feasibility, (2) reliability, (3) relation to other criteria or measures applicable to libraries, and (4) characterization (by data analyses) of efficient libraries. The results of the study have both practical and research significance.

The second part of this study introduces DEA concepts and techniques. We contrast DEA with currently available measures of efficiency. Various DEA models and extensions are discussed and illustrated with examples. The third section of the study presents the research questions for this study and describes the research methodology. It explains data collection, variable selection, and procedures required for data analysis. Finally, we present the results of data analysis. At the end of this section, we provide a summary of results on each research question and conclude with a discussion of the technique and its applicability to the research libraries.

Significance of the Research

This study evaluates a technique for providing research libraries with much needed information regarding their relative efficiency of operation. While none of the currently available evaluation methods, including DEA, can claim to reveal the full nature of a library's efficiency, DEA seems to have advantages over traditional approaches in that it provides library administrators with information about how their libraries compare with peer libraries. Contrary to traditional statistical approaches such as regression analysis, where a library's performance is compared against average performance, DEA identifies a group of "best performing" libraries so that inefficient libraries can examine the policies and procedures of these libraries for areas of improvement. Furthermore, with the results obtained from such a study, libraries may be able to respond to requests from parent organizations regarding performance benchmarking in a solid, quantitative manner. The study will also contribute to the growing body of literature in DEA, not only by applying the technique in a new field but also by offering new insights or observations that can be gained though this study.

DATA ENVELOPMENT ANALYSIS

Previous Approaches to Measuring Efficiency

Ratio analysis and multiple regression are commonly used to measure efficiency. We briefly explain what they are, discuss the advantages and disadvantages associated with each measure, and finally suggest what DEA can contribute to the measurement of efficiency.

Ratio Analysis

Ratios, or partial productivity measures, have been widely used because they are easy to calculate and easy to understand. They summarize the relationship between an output variable and an input variable. For example, the manager of a bank branch might compute the average number of transactions processed by each teller working at the branch. Cost per unit of output is another ratio that is widely used. For example, the same manager might compute the ratio between the total cost incurred by a teller in given period and the total number of transactions that the person handled during the period. Once the ratios or unit costs are computed, they may be compared to the average of either the organization or the industry. Alternatively, they are compared against the goals that are already set by the organization or by some consensus of involved stakeholders.

For organizations like academic research libraries, which involve multiple inputs and outputs, using ratios faces a number of limitations. First, ratios only make sense if the nature of output is to be proportional to input. Ratios ignore the potential economies of scale present in the industry (e.g., ARL libraries) or in a particular library (see Cooper 1984). Second, because they only describe the relationship between one input and one output, it is very difficult to combine multiple ratios to summarize the performance of the library. Finally, the ratios that have in fact been developed concentrate on pairs of input variables, giving little attention to the relationship between an input and an output (e.g., the thirty performance indicators ratios developed by the ARL[2]).

Multiple Linear Regression

Multiple linear regression techniques have been widely used to estimate the relationship between one dependent variable and a host of independent, predictor variables. They model the output level of an organization in terms of a set of input variables, or estimate cost relationships. Multiple linear regression can be a nominal predicting tool in that it projects the marginal change of the dependent variable with unit changes in independent variables. Unlike ratios, regression analysis can easily handle multiple input variables.

Typically the estimation function derived from a multiple regression analysis serves as a yardstick of efficiency. If the observed output of an organization is above the predicted output, then it is considered relatively efficient. The assumption here is that the regression equation defines the efficiency threshold.

Multiple regression analysis is typically applied to one dependent variable. In library applications, typically this is the total operating expenditure (Baumol and Marcus 1973; Cooper 1983, 1984; Kantor 1981a, 1981b) which represents all of the inputs lumped together. Second, regression analysis describes efficiency in terms of average performance rather than in terms of best performance. Finally, regression analysis requires reasonable specification of the relationship among variables (Berry and Feldman 1985). For example, if the underlying relationship between variables is actually nonlinear but a linear function is assumed, then the results will be misleading.[3] Therefore, regression technique has limited value in situations where such specification error can occur.

DEA: Introduction

Data Envelopment Analysis (DEA) measures the relative efficiencies of organizations having multiple inputs and multiple outputs (Charnes et al. 1978). The individual organizations, teams, or units analyzed are called the decision-making units, or "DMUs." The basic concept of DEA is, first of all, to identify the so-called efficient frontier in the comparison set of DMUs. All units on this frontier are said to be operating at 100 percent efficiency. DEA provides an efficiency score for each of the other (inefficient) units, and identifies a benchmark set of efficient units that led to that conclusion. The results of the DEA analysis can be used in performance measurement of academic research libraries, especially for benchmarking purpose.

The term decision-making unit (DMU) carries two implications. First, it emphasizes that the DEA technique can be applied to any level or unit within a managed organization, from an entire firm, to a plant, and down to a single operation such as the shipping room, as long as the DMUs are comparable in the sense that they use a similar mix of inputs and produce comparable outputs. Second, it implies that for any DEA analysis to be meaningful, the DMUs must have some level of control over their resources. In the current study, the unit of analysis or DMU is an entire academic research library.

Since the DEA technique was first developed by Charnes, Cooper and Rhodes in 1978, it has been widely applied to industries as diverse as health care (Chilingerian 1994; Dittman, Capettini and Morey 1991; Nunamaker 1983), finance (Barr, Seiford and Siems 1993; Ferrier and Lovell 1990), education (Ahn, Charnes and Cooper 1988; Bessent, Bessent, Kennington and Regan 1982) and transportation (Cook, Kazakov and Roll 1994; Forsund and Hemaes 1994). It has even been applied to evaluate professional athletes (Mazur 1994). The technique is well documented in both the operations research (Banker, Charnes and Cooper 1984; Cooper, Thompson and Thrall 1996; Dyson and Thanassoulis 1988; Golany and Roll 1989) and economics literature (Banker and Maindiratta 1988; Leibenstein and Maital 1992; Seiford and Thrall 1990; Sengupta 1987). The DEA bibliography compiled by Seiford (1994) includes more than 400 articles, books and dissertations between 1978 and 1992.[4]

In a nutshell, DEA measures the relative efficiency of the DMUs under consideration when each DMU is allowed to be best represented in its mix of both inputs and outputs. According to Charnes, Cooper, Lewin and Seiford (1994), the relative efficiency is calculated "by forming the ratio of a weighted sum of outputs (virtual output) to a weighted sum of inputs (virtual input), when the weights (multipliers) for both outputs and inputs are to be selected in a manner that calculates the Pareto efficiency measure of each DMU subject to the constraint that no DMU can have a relative efficiency score greater than the unity" (p. 6).

In DEA calculations, through mathematical optimization, each DMU is assigned the weights that maximize its efficiency score. In doing so, DEA gives all the other DMUs "the benefit of the doubt" by allowing them to apply the same weights to see if any of them looks better than the library being evaluated (which is called the "focus" DMU). If the focus DMU looks at least as good as any other DMU, it receives an efficiency score of 1. But if some other DMU looks better than the focus DMU, even when the weights are calculated in a way that is most favorable to the focus, then it will receive an efficiency score less than 1. Thus in DEA, a separate complete calculation is done for each DMU.

The weights should not be interpreted as the values of each input and output in any economic sense. Basic DEA calculations are value free. This is particularly attractive in evaluating nonprofit organizations, because it is very difficult to determine the relative value of inputs and outputs. Furthermore, the value system will vary by institution because each may have different goals and objectives. In DEA, the weights represent those multipliers for each input and output which together maximize the efficiency score of a "target" DMU. DEA does not require any specification of how the inputs and outputs are aggregated. In particular, they can be in wildly different scales of measure.

The selection of the weights must, however, meet two conditions. First, they cannot be negative or greater than one. Second, once a DMU has selected a set of weights, it must allow other DMUs in the comparison set to use the same weights. Selection of the weights might be considered as choosing a particular production function from a pool of available production possibilities. In DEA, each unit is free to choose whatever production function (i.e., a particular mix of inputs and outputs) makes the unit look its best.

In general, DMUs are likely to assign bigger weights to the least used inputs and to the outputs that are produced most (Sexton 1986). Units assigning zero weights to some of the inputs and outputs are not uncommon in DEA analysis. This situation is not quite desirable in academic libraries where the production of outputs (services) is not exactly market driven, and substitution among outputs or among inputs is not feasible.[5] Several weight restriction schemes have been proposed by Charnes, Cooper and Li (1989), Dyson and Thanassoulis (1988), and Thompson, Langemeier, Lee, Lee and Thrall (1990). The specific scheme used for the study will be explained in the *Derivation of Constraints and Their Effects* section.

We should distinguish two kinds of efficiencies that might be identified in standard DEA analysis: *technical efficiency* and *scale efficiency* (Banker, Charnes and Cooper 1984). An organization is said to be technically inefficient if there is a potential to increase the level of outputs with given input or to reduce the level of inputs while producing the same amount of output. Scale efficiency has to do with whether an organization is taking advantage of varying returns to scale by adjusting the size of its operation to optimal scale. The measure of scale efficiency of a DMU is the difference between its efficiency at the optimal scale and its efficiency under constant returns to scale. In this study, we focus on the pure technical efficiency.

DEA contributes to the measurement of efficiency in the following ways. First, in the multiple input–output situations, DEA produces a single technical efficiency score for each unit relative to all other units in the comparison population. If a DMU is operating at 100 percent efficiency, then there is no evidence, at least in the given data, to demonstrate that any other DMU can do better. Second, for each DMU evaluated as less than 100 percent efficient, DEA provides a set of DMUs, which we call the benchmark set, that define the corresponding best practices in the sample. The units included in the benchmark set are efficient, by the DEA definition, and can be used as potential peers from which lessons can be learned. In addition, DEA provides specific recommendations as to how much reduction of inputs or augmentation of outputs (a form of efficiency gain) would be required to make a unit efficient. It should be noted that the inefficiencies calculated by DEA must be regarded as "potential." Improvement in the efficiency may not be possible due to factors such as significant difference in the service quality or different external operating environments in the organizations compared. To sum up, unlike previous approaches to measuring efficiency, which tend to focus on average performance, DEA provides a viable alternative where efficiency is defined by units that seem to perform best.

DEA, like other evaluation methods, is not without limitations. First, because the definition of the efficiency score is based on extreme individual observations, the results can be very sensitive to measurement error. Second, the efficiency scores are quite sensitive to variable specification and the size of the comparison set (Dyson, Thanassoulis and Boussofiane 1990). As the number of variables increases, the proportion of efficient DMUs will rise as well. Because the efficiency scores are determined by the choice of optimal weights, more units will be evaluated as efficient simply by becoming a specialist in one input or one output. Dyson et al. (1990) suggest that to ensure enough discriminating power in the analysis, the number of DMUs in the comparison set should be larger than the product of the number of input and output variables. Third, in DEA a unit can appear efficient simply by adjusting its weights in a way that has no relation to reality. Because basic DEA places no restriction on the weights, they may not reflect the true relative value of inputs and outputs. In a sense, DEA provides us with a baseline efficiency evaluation. If a unit is evaluated as inefficient even if it is allowed to make itself look as good as possible, it is then quite likely that the unit really is inefficient unless it is producing an unmeasured output. However, the case for the converse is weaker.

Still, the efficiency score calculated in DEA is a construct which attempts to capture the inherent efficiency in the organization. Unfortunately, DEA tends to be very difficult to understand, especially in its employment of weighting and its mathematical formulation. There are certain subtleties that are difficult to understand unless one is familiar with the computational aspects. Caution is always needed to interpret the results; otherwise, it can become merely "a method of handing out medals," as correctly observed by one of the early pioneers (Farrell 1957). However, properly used, DEA seems to have diffused to a wide range of applications and was even described in the business press such as *Fortune* (Norton 1994).

We have shown that DEA promises to overcome certain limitations in the previous approaches to the measurement of efficiency. In addition, DEA may provide a new way of organizing and analyzing complex data. It will be particularly important to compare the results from DEA analysis to the existing measures of efficiency. We anticipate that different techniques may complement each other, each providing additional information about the efficiency of the organization examined. This kind of triangulation will be quite desirable for both practice and research.

Graphic Illustration

Suppose, for the sake of illustration, we have seven libraries or DMUs which each have only one input and output. We assign these libraries to the coordinate values associated with the points L1 through L7 in Figure 2 where the input is represented on the horizontal axis (X) and the output along the vertical axis (Y).

For example, Library 1 (L1) uses two units of input and produces 2 units of output. Library 2 (L2) uses 3 units of input to produce 5 units of output. The best a library can do is up somewhere in the northwest in the graph where it costs very little and produces lots of output. What DEA does with given data is to identify a set of units in the comparison set (our 7 libraries) whose efficiency score equals 1. In the figure, these are the libraries 1 through 4 (L1-L4) because there is nothing northwest of them. These libraries are called the efficient frontier and define the limits of what a library can achieve in the given situation. In DEA, determination of whether a unit is part of the efficient frontier is based on the units included in the analysis. The heavy line connecting the efficient libraries is called the "envelopment surface" because it envelops all the cases, thus giving the name "Data Envelopment Analysis." Notice also the regression line (thin line shown in Figure

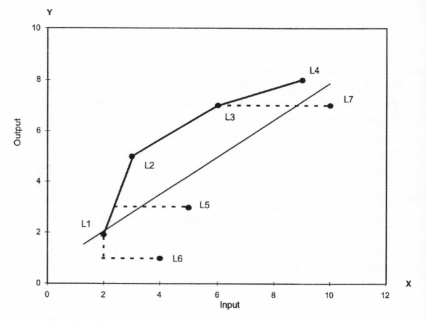

Source: Adapted from Chanes et al. (1994, p. 33).

Figure 2. Envelopment Surface

2) which represents the average relationship between the input (independent variable) and output (dependent variable).

DMUs L5 through L7 are not on the envelopment surface and thus are evaluated as inefficient in the DEA analysis. There are two ways to explain their weakness. One is to say that, for example, Library 5 (L5) could be imagined to produce as much output as it does but with less input. This could be accomplished by moving horizontally until it hits the line between L1 and L2. It should stop there because with this data there is no evidence that any unit can do better than that.

One of the assumptions here is that if L1 and L2 can be attained in the real world, then any point between L1 and L2 is also possible. This is called "convexity" which is almost always assumed in economic theory (Farrell 1957). Mathematically, any point between L1 and L2 represent the weighted average of the two.

Libraries 1 and 2 (L1 and L2) are called the benchmark set and are interpreted as peers for L5 in DEA. Therefore, the term "peers" has a special meaning. It is the set of efficient frontiers with which an inefficient unit is compared. We can also say that the units are compared against a *virtual* DMU on the envelopment surface which produces the same output as the unit being evaluated (which we call "focus DMU") but with less input. If DEA finds such a DMU, either a real unit or a weighted average of several units, then the focus DMU is regarded as inefficient. If there is no evidence for a given focus DMU that such a better virtual DMU exists, the unit is evaluated "technically" efficient because there is no waste of input.

There is a completely different way of looking at efficiency, which is to say that Library 5 could produce more output, consuming the same amount of input. This could be accomplished by moving up vertically until it hits the envelopment surface between L2 and L3. Again for the same reason, it should stop there. This time libraries 2 and 3 become peer libraries for Library 5.

We see that there are two possible definitions of inefficiency depending on the purpose of the evaluation. One might be interested in possible reduction of inputs (in DEA this is called the input orientation) or augmentation of outputs (the output orientation) in achieving technical efficiency. One thing to note is that no matter how efficiency is defined here, Library 5 is not efficient. Depending on the purpose of the evaluation, the analysis provides different sets of peer groups to learn from. In the input orientation, the efficiency score is the (proportional) reduction of input required to move a unit onto the envelopment surface in input-oriented evaluation. In the output-oriented evaluation DEA software reports the (proportional) augmentation of output that achieves the same purpose.

However, there are times when reduction of inputs or augmentation of outputs is not sufficient. In our example, even when Library 6 reduces its input from 4 units to 2, there is still a gap between it and its peer Library 1 in the amount of one unit of output. In DEA, this is called the "slack" which means excess input or missing output that exists even after the proportional change in the input or the outputs.

One could argue that instead of taking either input or output orientation, a DMU could be compared to its peer in the nearest point on the envelopment surface. Recently Frei and Harker (1996) investigated this type of optimal projection of inefficient units on to the envelopment hyperplane. The definition of "nearest" requires establishing a relative importance of inputs and outputs. This approach will not be explored further here.

DEA Formulation

The previous section has presented several key concepts in DEA. As an evaluation technique, DEA is fairly easy to understand on the abstract level. However, some of its main subtleties are only appreciated if one examines its computational aspects. At present, various software packages are available to facilitate the complex computation required in DEA applications.[6] While these tools alleviate the need for setting up complicated DEA programming runs, some familiarity with basic DEA model (Charnes et al. 1978) will be useful for further discussion of DEA application in the libraries.

The CCR Ratio Model[7]

Essentially the CCR ratio model (Charnes et al. 1978) can be thought of as an extension of the simple efficiency ratio (ouput/input) to situations with multiple inputs and outputs. The efficiency score for a DMU was previously defined as the ratio of the weighted sum of outputs (virtual output) to the weighted sum of inputs. Suppose DMU (j) consumes a vector $X_j = \{x_{ij}\}$ of inputs $(i = 1,...,m)$ and produces a vector $Y_j = \{y_{rj}\}$ of outputs $(r = 1,...,s)$, the score for the particular DMU labeled by j_o can be expressed as follows:

$$\max h_o = \frac{\sum_r u_r y_{rj_o}}{\sum_r v_i x_{ij_o}}$$

where the maximization is over the weights μ_r and v_i, to calculate a measure of efficiency (h_o) for DMU o. In the formula, μ_r represents a set of weights for the outputs and v_i a set of weights for the inputs. As it was mentioned in the *DEA Introduction* section, there are two constraints on the model:

1. $h_o \leq 1$ for $j = 1, ..., n$ (n = number of DMUs)
2. $\mu_r, v_i \geq 0$.

As we can see, the model is expressed in a fractional form which has an infinite number of solutions. For any optimal solution (μ^*, v^*), any multiple of it still satisfies the constraints. Charnes and Cooper (1962) developed a transformation technique that converts linear fractional optimization into a linear programming (LP) problem.

$$\max_{\mu,v} h_o = \sum_r \mu_r y_{rj_o}$$

subject to

$$\sum_i v_i x_{ij_o} = 1$$

$$\sum_r \mu_r y_{rj} - \sum_i v_r x_{ij} \leq 0; j = 1,...,n$$

$$\mu_r, v_i \geq 0$$

In linear programming, there is an objective function which serves as the goal to achieve, most often expressed in terms of either maximizing benefits or minimizing costs. Here, the objective function (the first formula) seeks the maximum score of the weighted output. The constraints that accompany the objective function are intended to limit the possible range of the weights (μ_r, v_i), so that the solution is not out of bounds.

DEA calculation requires the solution of n (the number of DMUs) such linear programming problems in the form of a set of m input and s output weights. For each solution, there are $n + m + s + 1$ constraints to be satisfied. For an analysis of a small number of DMUs, spreadsheet programs such as Microsoft Excel can be used to do the calculations.

For each such a linear programming problem (which is called the primal), there is a complementary problem that is calculated from the so-called dual of the problem (Hillier and Lieberman 1986). Therefore, the above primal can be converted to:

$$\min_{\theta, \lambda} z_o = \theta$$

subject to

$$\sum_j \lambda_j y_{rj} \geq y_{rj_o}$$

$$\theta \cdot x_{ij_o} - \sum_j \lambda_j x_{ij} \geq 0$$

$$\lambda_j \geq 0, \theta \; unconstrained$$

While both linear programming formulations have equivalent solutions, there are several reasons why solving the dual problem is useful. First, there are only $m + s$ (the number of variables) constraints in the dual problem compared to $n + m + s + 1$ (the number of variables plus number of DMUs plus one) in the primal problem. So when the analysis involves a large number of DMUs (n), solving the dual is computationally efficient. Second, the variables in the dual have nice interpretations. When a DMU(j_o) is efficient, both θ and λ_{jo} are equal to 1 leaving all the other variables equal to zero. Therefore, θ is the efficiency score for the DMU and tells us that the DMU j_o is efficient. If a DMU is inefficient, then the value for θ will be a positive value less than 1 and the unit will have positive λ values for a set of the other DMUs. In fact, those other DMUs with positive λ are the peers that form the benchmark set for the focus DMU.

Table 1.   Inputs and Outputs of Illustrative Libraries

Library	Reference (000s)	Circulation (000s)	Books (000s)	Staff
A	27	40	15	10
B	20	35	25	13
C	18	25	18	7

Illustrative Example

Here we illustrate DEA by means of a small example. Consider three libraries that all have two output measures (number of annual reference transactions and total annual circulation) and two input measures (size of collection and number of staff). The data reported by the libraries are shown in Table 1.

Without any formal evaluation method, we can easily see that Library B is clearly less productive than Library A because it consumes more of every input with less of every output. For Library C, the situation is a little bit tricky. While it consumes less input, it produces less output.

Our concern is to identify any possible reduction of inputs. For each library, DEA assigns weights to each measure so that the library looks as good as possible when the same weights are applied to all libraries. In DEA, the weighted sum of input values is called the *virtual input*. The *virtual output* is calculated similarly.

Following the primal and dual formula presented in the previous section, we now can calculate the efficiency scores of the libraries, as well as the weights, using linear programs.

(Primal)[8]

> *Library A:*
> max $27\mu_1 + 40\mu_2$
> $15v_1 + 10v_2 = 1$
> $27\mu_1 + 40\mu_2 - 15v_1 - 10v_2 \leq 0$
> $20\mu_1 + 35\mu_2 - 25v_1 - 13v_2 \leq 0$
> $18\mu_1 + 25\mu_2 - 18v_1 - 7v_2 \leq 0$
> $\mu_1, \mu_2, v_1, v_2 \geq 0$
>
> *Library B:*
> max $20\mu_1 + 35\mu_2$
> $25v_1 + 13v_2 = 1$
> $27\mu_1 + 40\mu_2 - 15v_1 - 10v_2 \leq 0$
> $20\mu_1 + 35\mu_2 - 25v_1 - 13v_2 \leq 0$
> $18\mu_1 + 25\mu_2 - 18v_1 - 7v_2 \leq 0$
> $\mu_1, \mu_2, v_1, v_2 \geq 0$

Library C:

max $18\mu_1 + 25\mu_2$

$18v_1 + 7v_2 = 1$

$27\mu_1 + 40\mu_2 - 15v_1 - 10v_2 \leq 0$

$20\mu_1 + 35\mu_2 - 25v_1 - 13v_2 \leq 0$

$18\mu_1 + 25\mu_2 - 18v_1 - 7v_2 \leq 0$

$\mu_1, \mu_2, v_1, v_2 \geq 0$

(Dual)[9]

Library A:

Min θ

$27\lambda_A + 20\lambda_B + 18\lambda_C \geq 27$

$40\lambda_A + 35\lambda_B + 25\lambda_C \geq 40$

$15\theta - 15\lambda_A - 25\lambda_B - 18\lambda_C \geq 0$

$10\theta - 10\lambda_A - 13\lambda_B - 7\lambda_C \geq 0$

$\lambda_A, \lambda_B, \lambda_C \geq 0$

Library B:

Min θ

$27\lambda_A + 20\lambda_B + 18\lambda_C \geq 27$

$40\lambda_A + 35\lambda_B + 25\lambda_C \geq 40$

$15\theta - 15\lambda_A - 25\lambda_B - 18\lambda_C \geq 0$

$10\theta - 10\lambda_A - 13\lambda_B - 7\lambda_C \geq 0$

$\lambda_A, \lambda_B, \lambda_C \geq 0$

Library C:

Min θ

$27\lambda_A + 20\lambda_B + 18\lambda_C \geq 27$

$40\lambda_A + 35\lambda_B + 25\lambda_C \geq 40$

$15\theta - 15\lambda_A - 25\lambda_B - 18\lambda_C \geq 0$

$10\theta - 10\lambda_A - 13\lambda_B - 7\lambda_C \geq 0$

$\lambda_A, \lambda_B, \lambda_C \geq 0$

Using Microsoft Excel's ('97 version) Solver tool, we have the following solutions as shown in Table 2. When we look at the theta (θ) scores, only Library A was evaluated efficient because it has $\theta = 1$. Libraries B and C have the efficiency scores of 0.67308 and 0.95238, respectively. Efficient DMUs will have the lambda (λ) value (the weighted average of a "virtual peer") of 1 only for themselves, and 0 for other DMUs. Libraries B and C each have a positive λ_A score which indicates the dominance of Library A in the comparison set. In other words, Library A is the efficient frontier as well as the benchmark peer.

Table 2.   DEA Solutions for Illustrative Libraries

Library	θ	λ_A	λ_B	λ_C	μ_1	μ_2	v_1	v_2
A	1.00000	1.000	0.000	0.000	0.03704	0.02500	0.06667	0.10000
B	0.67308	0.875	0.000	0.000	0.05000	0.02857	0.04000	0.18929
C	0.95238	0.667	0.000	0.000	0.05556	0.04000	0.05556	0.22667

Table 3.   Projected Inputs and Outputs for Illustrative Library C

Variable	Data (f1)	Projected (f2)	Inefficiency (f2) – (f1)	Proportional Reduction (f1) * (1 – θ)	Slack or Waste
Reference	18	18.00	0.00	n/a	0.00
Circulation	25	26.67	1.67	n/a	1.67
Books	18	10.00	−8.00	.86	7.14
Staff	7	6.67	−0.33	.33	0.00

Note: n/a = not applicable because we are concerned about the possible reduction of inputs in this case (input oriented).

The weights determine the virtual input and output and for the DMU. The virtual output is calculated by weighting a library's observed output values. For Library C, we can verify that:

$$0.05556*18 + 0.04000*25 = 2.00$$

Similarly, the virtual input is calculated by weighting the observed input values.

With the solution from the linear programming problems, we can now calculate the optimal input and output levels for the inefficient DMUs. We have pointed out that each inefficient unit will have some set of benchmark peer libraries. This is accomplished by projecting an inefficient unit onto the envelopment surface. For Library C, it has a lambda A (λ_A) value of 0.667 which means for Library C, the virtual peer is in the form of a weighted average of Library A and no library at all, that is, two-thirds of A. Therefore, we can calculate the projected input and output levels as follows:

$$0.667 * (27, 40, 15, 10) = (18.00, 26.67, 10.00, 6.67)$$

In addition, we can obtain the following information for Library C as shown in Table 3. The observed differences between the projected values and the data are identified as inefficiencies for Library C. Some portion of the inefficiencies can be removed by the proportional reduction of inputs in the amount of 1 minus the efficiency score

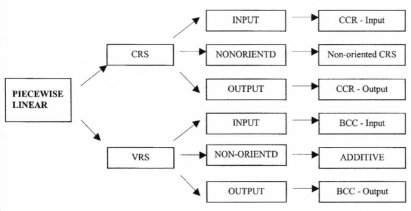

Source: Ali (1994, p. 33).

Figure 3.   Classification of DEA Models.

(θ, it is 0.95238). Even after the proportional reduction of inputs, there are still inefficiencies (slack) in one output (circulation) and in one input (books).

Notice that we have not imposed any constraints on the weights (μ_1, μ_1, v_1, v_1). That is, if we look at the weights optimized for Library B, we accept that one reference transaction is worth about twice (more precisely, 0.05000/0.02857) as much as one circulation transaction. But if we look at the weights optimized for Library C, there is not much difference in the weights assigned for reference transaction (0.05556) and for a circulation transaction (0.04000). In some sense, DEA allows each library to apply its own "worldview" in assessing its efficiency score. Of course, this worldview is an artificial construct that simply optimizes the library reflecting only the given data. It needs not reflect the realistic situation of the library.

This example demonstrates the formulation of the linear programming problems for the DEA analysis with multiple inputs and outputs. We see that the analysis not only provides a single summary measure of efficiency but also other potentially useful information for decision makers.

Taxonomy of DEA Models

DEA models can be classified according to three characteristics: how they treat the issue of *returns to scale* (variable vs. constant); how they set the shape of the benchmark or envelopment surface (*linear vs. nonlinear*); and how they are *oriented* (to reducing input or to increasing output). If we select the piecewise linear class of models, the benchmark envelopment surface will be made of straight lines, and their generalizations will not be curved in any way. Figure 3 classifies the piecewise linear DEA models by treatment of returns to scale and orientation.

For example, the original DEA formulation (CCR model; Charnes et al. 1978) assumes constant returns to scale. While this may be true in certain ranges of inputs and outputs, we do not expect that library operation, in general, exhibits constant returns to scale. The CCR model identifies both technical and scale inefficiencies. On the other hand, the Banker, Charnes, Cooper model (BCC model; Banker et al. 1984) assumes variable returns to scale (VRS). Variable returns to scale can appear in two forms. If an operation can achieve certain economies of scale by increasing its size, we say it has increasing returns to scale. On the other hand, if there are diseconomies of scale, it has decreasing returns to scale. While economies of scale can exist over a range of size in the same operation, the BCC model identifies only technical inefficiency that is not affected by the size of operation. Generally, the constant return to scale (CRS) models will identify a smaller number of efficient units than the variable return to scale (VRS) models because the inefficiencies calculated in CRS include scale efficiencies as well as technical efficiencies.

Because the selected DEA model has to reflect the operational environment of libraries and has an impact on how the results are interpreted and applied, selecting the appropriate, relevant model is an important part of the study. *We have decided to use the BCC, VRS input-oriented model* for the following reasons.

First, we believe that libraries are pressed to know how much potential reduction of inputs is possible. DEA can be used as an initial analysis tool before further information is collected. Second, we are interested in knowing the technical efficiencies in the libraries analyzed, and this model is formulated to identify only the pure technical inefficiencies. Technical efficiency is believed to have to do with managerial practices of the organization, not the size of the operation (Charnes, Cooper and Rhodes 1981). Unlike manufacturing plants, libraries, even if there is some evidence that there are increasing returns to scale, cannot increase their size to take advantage of the situation. Usually, economies of scale in libraries are realized, if at all, in the various consortia in which they participate. Economies of scale are also possible within individual units in the library. Third, we do not expect that libraries will have constant returns to scale. Finally, both because the functional form of the library production properties is not known and because there is a lack of previous studies, we assume a linear envelopment surface as in the majority of DEA applications. The other form of envelopment surface is the Cobb–Douglas form. Further study might suggest the use of such a nonlinear form.

In fact, the application of nonlinear functions is not unprecedented in the library evaluation literature, although none in DEA context. For example, Hayes, Pollack and Nordhous (1983), in their regression analysis, used the log-linear form of the Cobb–Douglas model to determine various production functions in the ARL libraries and the institutions. In the first analysis, they used public service staff as labor and collection size as capital and tried to see how much the combination of this labor and capital explains the production of libraries. They also tested institutional production using the faculty of the institution as labor and the size of library collection as capital. The production was measured by two alternatives: PhDs produced and publications. It would be reasonable to say that both production models seem overly simplistic and have little to offer for the current study. In addition, the number and the kind of variables included in the model is too limited.

Kantor (1981a, 1981b) studied costs in a sample of 65 scientific and technical libraries. He tested several econometric cost functions to find out what can best explain the level of library service. Using what he calls the capacity model, he found that, regardless of the library size, the unit cost of circulation was 99 percent of the cost of an hour of in-house use and the unit cost of a reference transaction was 216 percent of the cost of an hour of in-house use. His model explains 72 percent of the variation in the total operating budget at the 95 percent confidence level.

Application of DEA in the Library Context

It appears that Easun's (1992) dissertation is the only study in the United States that has applied DEA in the library context. Her study was intended to measure the technical efficiency with which school media centers transform resources into a number of library- and school-related outcomes.

The study adopted a multistage procedure whereby outputs from previous runs were used as inputs for the following evaluation model. Two kinds of intermediate outputs were tested in the study: school library services variables and school library use variables. The study also investigated the effect of grouping libraries by expenditure model. The study may be overly aggressive in the sense that it includes school-related outcomes that are outside the context of the DMUs (media centers) under consideration.

In a related work, Johnes and Johnes (1992) used DEA to measure the technical efficiency of U.K. university departments of economics as producers of research. There has not yet been any study applying DEA to measuring library efficiency per se.

RESEARCH METHODOLOGY AND QUESTIONS

1. *Can DEA be applied for evaluating library efficiency?*
    DEA promises a significant improvement over the existing measures of efficiency. This research question is mainly concerned with the task of setting up a relevant DEA study model with proper input and output selection (operationalization). The issue was partly answered in a related project report prepared for the Council on Library and Information Resources (Shim and Kantor 1998a). Yet the question of what inputs and outputs should be included has not been fully answered. Therefore, we use techniques such as sensitivity analysis used to

obtain more information about the size of the number of variables that can be used effectively.

Another important consideration is the selection of the applicable DEA model. Each model entails a set of assumptions regarding the returns to scale (constant vs. variable), orientation (input vs. output), and linearity of the relationship between variables (linear vs. nonlinear). We will answer this question in the research methodology section.

The other aspect of applying DEA has to do with whether the analysis provides meaningful results—evidence that shows that the technique has been successfully applied to various types of organizations. Eventually the results from DEA analysis should be compared with previous measures of library efficiency. In case of disagreement, the results should be justified using the available data.

2. *What are the relevant criteria in determining constraints on weights?*

The choice of weights, as we mentioned in the previous section, determines the technical efficiency of DMUs. For the results of DEA analysis to be reasonable and meaningful in an academic research library environment, there needs to be some constraints on the selection of weights. This requires some investigation of the relationship among input variables and among output variables. In the study, the boundaries set on the weights are derived from published studies, and the ARL statistics are used as starting points. In the research methodology section, there is further discussion about the approach that we take in the study.

3. *Are the efficiency scores stable over a period of time?*

This question deals with the reliability of the method. The ARL statistics we choose to use have two years' data on the selected variables. Assuming that library statistics tend to be quite stable, it is reasonable to expect that the resulting efficiency scores show some level of consistency. Any idiosyncrasies should be explained by the change of data itself or the environment in which the library is operating.

4. *Can we tell, with given results, what distinguishes (or determines) technically efficient libraries from inefficient ones as determined by DEA?*

This relates to the characterization of efficient libraries. The task will seek relations between the results of DEA study and the results from other efficiency measures such as the ratios reported by the ARL itself and multiple regression. Specifically, we seek correlation between the efficiency score and various ratio measures. With multiple regression, we again take the efficiency score as the dependent variable and test the existing set of predictor variables to see what portion of the efficiency score can be explained by the variables. This validation process is extremely important for DEA to be accepted as a viable tool for measuring efficiency in the library arena.

5. *Are the optimal weights characteristics of the library?*

The weights calculated for the inputs and outputs are supposed to be optimized for individual libraries, to make the efficiency score as high as possible. We want to know whether these weights are reasonable and consistent enough to be used as tools for characterizing libraries.

Selection of Data

It is fortunate that the ARL statistics lend themselves to DEA analysis. The data are widely used by member libraries and by other researchers in the field. There are several specific reasons why we use these statistics for the current research. First, compared to other library statistics, the ARL data are considered more reliable. Since 1961/1962, ARL has collected and published statistics on its member libraries. The fact that library rankings and other performance measures are based on the data suggests that the data get considerable use by the library administrators and decision makers at the parent institutions. Second, compared to other sets of library statistics, the ARL statistics are more complete and provide a wide range of information on both inputs and outputs. Third, the data are readily accessible from the ARL at its Internet web site.[10] Thus, the results can be easily replicated and widely used. It is also easy to obtain and transform the data into a format suitable for spreadsheet programs (e.g., Lotus 1-2-3 or Microsoft Excel) and statistical programs (e.g., SPSS).

Currently the statistics include data on collections (13 variables), services (8), staffing (5), expenditure (12), and library (3) and university characteristics (7). The number of university libraries reported in the current statistics is 108, including 13 Canadian ones. For the purpose of this study, we will limit the data to only U.S. institutions ($n = 95$).

As is acknowledged in the guide to the ARL statistics (Stubbs 1996), the majority of variables reported in the data still represent input measures such as collection, staff, and expenditures. These are useful for describing the traditional characteristics of research libraries, but not for assessing emerging uses of technology in providing alternative or new services. Because the data were gathered through self-reporting by member libraries, there are well-known questions about the accuracy and consistency in the way participating libraries entered the numbers. However, the data are generally consistent, and certainly will serve to illustrate the principles of DEA in the research library setting.

We apply the DEA technique for two consecutive years (1995–1996 and 1996–1997) to investigate the stability (and, if libraries are presumed stable, the reliability) of evaluation using DEA. If DEA is revealing a stable characteristic of the libraries, and is measuring it reliably, then the efficiency scores of each should be similar from one year to the next.

The Issue of Comparability

To apply the concept of the efficiency used in DEA, libraries should share the following characteristics.

1. They should share common goals and objectives.
2. They should use comparable sets of resources (inputs) and produce comparable sets of services (outputs).
3. The decision makers (that is, library directors) at the institutions should have a certain level of control over the resources, so that once inefficiency is identified, efforts can be made either to change the mix of inputs or to modify the operational processes.

The libraries included in the analysis are academic research libraries in the United States ($n = 95$) that are members of the Association of Research Libraries (ARL). This population seems to satisfy these three requirements. The similarity of these libraries and of their parent institutions are in part ensured through an explicit, written membership requirement (ARL 1994). The requirement specifies that the parent institution of a university library must be classified as a Research University I or II in the Carnegie Classification. The minimum requirement for Research University II status is that the institution must award 50 or more doctoral degrees annually and receive more than \$15.5 million in yearly federal support.

These libraries use similar inputs and provide rather standardized lines of service, although with different production procedures and varying mixes of input. The levels of inputs, both monetary and in their natural units of measure, and the outputs of all member libraries are compiled in the ARL annual statistics.

However, it is quite well known that there are some differences in the way libraries in the privately funded universities behave, in comparison to their counterparts in the publicly funded universities (Baumol and Marcus 1973; Chressanthis 1995; Lubans and Anspaugh 1990). Baumol and Marcus (1973) found that the relationship between selected library characteristics and selected institution characteristics were stronger at private than at public institutions. Chressanthis (1995) reviewed the studies that investigated the variations in the operating costs of research universities, especially in regard to the variations due to the private vs. public distinction. The existence of greater regulatory control, higher ratio of undergraduate students to total student population resulting in high degree of cross-subsidization, more complex organizational structure, and a much bigger pool of constituencies are listed as possible reasons why public institutions and their libraries are quite likely to appear less efficient than their private counterparts.

Lubans and Anspaugh (1990) comment, drawing on their own experience, that the budget in the libraries at the privately funded institutions differs significantly from that of the libraries at the publicly funded universities both technically and politically. For example, they note that the private institution's bottom line approach to financial matters gives more room for flexibility than there is at public institutions, which normally adopt a line item approach. Another significant difference, they claim, is that private institutions allow greater access to reallocation of salary savings due to vacant staff positions. The above arguments lead us to the conclusion that libraries in the ARL study population should be further broken down into two groups: public ($n = 65$) and private ($n = 30$).

Selection of Variables

The logical starting point in any DEA study is to decide (1) which DMUs are to be evaluated together, and (2) which inputs and outputs best represent the operations of the DMUs. We want to evaluate the technical efficiency of U.S. academic research libraries and believe that libraries at publicly funded institutions and privately funded institutions form two distinct economic groups. We believe that within each group these libraries have sufficiently similar objectives and functions, so that they qualify for joint DEA evaluation.

Selecting inputs and outputs is a more complicated task. In fact, sometimes it is not clear whether a particular variable is an input or an output. For example, the number of volumes added can be regarded as an input, because having more books can increase circulation or interlibrary transactions. But if we regard the number of volumes added as a result of the work done by collection development and cataloging librarians, it might be classified as an output. Similarly, the number of students can be considered either as an input (because if there are more students, output measures such as circulation and reference transactions will go up) or as a constraint (because we cannot change the number of students: it is given).

The analysis is limited by the available (or given) data set. The current study is based on the use of the following variables.[11] This list serves as an initial list. We try to find out the effective number of input and output variables by comparing the efficiencies from various combinations of variables. Table 4 summarizes the descriptive statistics for the 1995–1996 data.

Output Variables (5)
- Total number of interlibrary lending transactions filled (ILLTOT)
- Total number of interlibrary borrowing transactions filled (ILBTOT)
- Number of people who participated in group presentations or instructions (LIBINST)

Table 4.   Summary of Descriptive Statistics of Variables (1995–1996)

Category	Variable	Mean	s.d.	Max.	Min.[a]	Kurtosis	Skewness
Input	VOLS*	3,377	1,966	13,143	1,607	6.7	2.3
	VOLSADN*	74	39	248	22	3.6	1.6
	MONO*	30	25	138	0	4.6	1.7
	CURRSER*	29	19	96	10	4.0	2.0
	PRFSTF	87	48	402	36	18.5	3.3
	NPRFSTF	155	81	589	53	8.0	2.2
	STUDAST	79	39	222	6	1.5	1.1
	TOTSTU*	19	9	53	4	1.6	1.0
	GRADSTU	4,516	2,390	11,592	1,198	0.8	1.1
	FAC	1,387	567	3,186	390	0.8	0.8
Output	ILLTOT*	34	30	249	2	29.1	4.4
	ILBTOT*	17	10	75	2	13.7	2.9
	LIBINST*	11	8	42	0	1.9	1.3
	REFTRANS*	195	184	116	0	9.5	2.6
	TOTCIRC*	673	452	269	0	4.0	1.8

Notes: *Variables in thousands (000s) of units.
§Variables whose minimum value is 0 have missing data.

- Number of reference transactions excluding directional questions (REFTRANS)
- Total number of circulation including renewals (TOTCIRC)

Input Variables (10)

Collection Characteristics (discretionary)
- Total volumes held (VOLS)
- Net volumes added during the period (VOLSADN)
- Monographs purchased, in volumes (MONO)
- Total number of current serial copies (CURRSER)

Staff Characteristics (discretionary)
- Number of full-time professional staff (PRFSTF)
- Number of full-time support staff (NPRFSTF)
- Number of full-time equivalents of hourly student employees (STUDAST)

University Characteristics (nondiscretionary)
- Total full-time student enrollment (TOTSTU)
- Total full-time graduate student enrollment (GRADSTU)
- Total full-time instructional faculty (FAC)

Scaling of Data

As we can see in the descriptive statistics in Table 4, the data values are in wide ranges: volumes held are in the millions, whereas the numbers of professional

Table 5. Scaling of Data

Category	Variable Name	Original Data (1995) High	Low	Applied Scale	After Scaling (1995) High	Low
Input	VOLS	13,143,330	1,606,642	200,000	65.72	8.03
	VOLSADN	248,156	22,381	3,000	82.72	7.46
	MONO	138,406	—	2,000	69.20	0.00
	CURRSER	96,353	10,284	1,000	96.35	10.28
	PRFSTF	402	36	5	80.40	7.20
	NPRFSTF	589	53	8	73.63	6.63
	STUDAST	222	6	3	74.00	2.00
	TOTSTU	52,637	3,988	600	87.73	6.65
	GRADSTU	11,592	1,198	150	77.28	7.99
	FAC	3,186	390	40	79.65	9.75
Output	ILLTOT	248,741	1,988	3,000	82.91	0.66
	ILBTOT	74,598	1,702	1,000	74.60	1.70
	LIBINST	42,222	—	1,000	42.22	0.00
	REFTRANS	1,161,212	—	15,000	77.41	0.00
	TOTCIRC	2,690,871	—	30,000	89.70	0.00

staff and student assistants are in the hundreds or in the tens. We also observe this wide range of values in a particular variable: for most variables the largest ARL member libraries are no more than 10 times larger than the smallest of the ARL libraries and the interlibrary loan activity (ILLTOT) varies by a factor of over 100 from the largest to the smallest. The wide range of values—in one input and output, or in a particular variable across the units—can produce a so-called ill-conditioned matrix that causes computational difficulties (Ali 1994).

Therefore, we applied scale changes for each variable, so that the scaled data fall below 100, with the highest value falling above 40. Table 5 shows the ranges of each variable before and after scaling. We applied the same scaling to both 1995 and 1996 data.

Ali (1994) warns of two possible consequences due to scaling. The main drawback is that reducing to more comparable numbers may decrease the discriminating power of the analysis. This can be a big threat if there was a small number of variables in the analysis. We expect that the existence of a fair number of variables can mitigate the effect of low resolution. The other drawback is that sometimes scaling does not remove all sources of ill-conditioning. Fortunately, in our case, the above scaling did remove all ill-conditioned matrix errors that existed before scaling.

The Constraints on Weights[12]

Because DEA allows the weights of both the inputs and the outputs of each DMU to vary until it gives the best possible combination for the focus library, we would not expect that the resulting weights will always make much sense. To make the DEA analysis more reasonable, there should be some boundary (technically called a constraint) to limit the relative weight or importance of various inputs, and of various outputs.

In the DEA literature, Charnes et al. (1989), Dyson and Thanassoulis (1988), and Thompson et al. (1990) applied various schemes for restricting the relative size of the possible weights. We follow the "Assurance Region" approach developed by Thompson et al. (1990). In this approach, instead of imposing a single set of weights, which is unrealistic, a range of weights in the form of the ratios between the weights is applied to the weight selection process. This will effectively limit the movement of the weights in a more realistic range and potentially improve the validity of the DEA analysis. The introduction of the constraints on the weights is expected to decrease the number of efficient DMUs.

Halme, Joro, Korhonen, Salo and Wallenius (1999) argued against the use of constraints on the weights, and proposed instead to use the explicit preferences of the decision makers. This would make sense in a situation where the DMUs included in the comparison set are all under the control of the same centralized decision makers. However, this is not applicable to our study population because we do not have the information regarding the preferences of library directors or decision makers at the universities on the proposed inputs and outputs.

Basis for Setting Constraints

While DEA permits each library to "rearrange the world" so that it looks as efficient as possible, there are nonetheless some limitations on the distortions that are permitted. For example, if a staff person costs $40,000/year (the person's yearly salary), and a book costs $50 (purchasing), it would be unreasonable to let the DEA program set their weights or multipliers equal in determining the combined virtual input. A sensible approach might be to examine available data, and allow a large, but not outrageous variation around the median value reported in the literature. For example, the numbers given would lead to a nominal ratio of 40,000/ 50 = 800. In applying this ratio, we will adopt two approaches. One is to permit a range from 200 (one-quarter of the observed value) to 3,200 (four times the observed value). We call this the *fourfold range*. This seems extremely generous. Under a twofold range this ratio would be allowed to vary from a low of 400 (one-half of the observed value) to a high of 1,600 (two times the observed value). The justification for varying degrees of range is based on the reports in the benchmarking literature that the observed performance difference among different organizations could be as large as a factor of several hundredfold (Boxwell 1994; Zairi 1996).

The twofold range gives a tighter boundary in the weight selection and is expected to identify a smaller number of efficient units than the fourfold range. We admit that imposing a weight restriction creates some arbitrariness in the analysis. On the other hand, the results are expected to be more realistic and meaningful than the analysis without such restriction. In addition, by applying two kinds of ranges we will be able to study the changes in the efficiency scores as we tighten boundaries.

For outputs, we cannot give the same argument. The coefficients multiplying outputs are supposed to represent the relative value of the specific services. Thus, forming a combined output measure of (3*Reference) + (1*Circulation) [the * represents multiplication] amounts to saying that one unit of reference service is worth as much as 3 units of circulation. The issue of how much a library service is "worth" is an extremely complex one.[13] Following the lead of the economist Morris Hamburg in his landmark study of public libraries (Hamburg, Ramist and Bommer 1972), we will use the ratio of costs as a surrogate for the (unknown) ratio of values. As before, some amount of variation must be allowed. In this case, the justification is not that libraries vary in efficiency. Instead, the justification is that the contexts of libraries vary enormously, and it is quite conceivable that the relative value of say, reference and circulation, might differ by a factor of 4 or even 16 from one setting to another.

Data Analysis

We use a special DEA program called IDEAS from 1 Consulting Co.[14] Using IDEAS, the efficiency scores of libraries will be generated and summarized in tabular form. We analyze the overall pattern of library efficiency scores, both overall and between groupings, to capture any important insights.

After getting results from the DEA technique, we employ various other statistical techniques (multivariate analyses) to corroborate the results and to draw insights. We also investigate the possibility of using weights as parameters characterizing libraries. In DEA, each library is compared against a set of comparable peer libraries. The imposition of the grouping is intended to make this comparison valid and more meaningful. One of the objectives of the study will be to study the ways in which libraries included in the comparison set over the two-year span can be compared and summarized.

Results to be Treated as Confidential

We have made every attempt to make sure that the identity of individual libraries is not revealed by their code or label or any publicly identifiable data (such as collection size, institutional enrollment, etc.).[15] To avoid this problem, we randomly assigned a unique code for each library. In the analysis of the results, we have not referred to the table of codes, and so remain blinded to features of the libraries not present in the data themselves.

ANALYSIS OF RESULTS

In addition to efficiency scores of the libraries included in the analysis, DEA provides the following information for each library.

1. Weights (sometimes called prices or multipliers) attached to each variable. These weights are the primary vehicles in DEA analyses to optimize the efficiency scores of the units included in the comparison population. When there is no constraint on the choice of weights, the weights are calculated following mathematical optimization. However, the weights may be regarded, implicitly, as the importance associated with a particular input (cost) or an output (value), *generated by the evaluation system on hand without any a priori knowledge about which variable is more important than the others.* We can create a binding environment by imposing certain restrictions or boundaries on the assignment of the weights. However, the primary purpose of imposing constraints on the weights is not so much to improve the interpretability of the weights but to strengthen the applicability of the results.

2. A set of benchmark (efficient) libraries. When a library is evaluated as less than 100 percent efficient, DEA provides a set of libraries, which as a combination, represent an efficient competitor for the library. By definition, the libraries included in the benchmark set are 100 percent efficient. The inefficient library might find better ways of doing things if it studies the libraries included in the benchmark set. This information might also be very useful to target a manageable set of a few libraries to learn from, in other words for benchmarking.

3. Amount of reduction of inputs, as we use an input-oriented model, that may be required to place an inefficient library "on par" with its efficient peers in the benchmark comparison set. This reduction of inputs is in proportion to the efficiency score. Thus, for example, if the efficiency score of Library A is .80, then it should have been able to produce its current level of outputs with 80 percent of its inputs or resources. DEA calculates that 20 percent $(1 - .80)$ of Library A may need to be reduced. Nondiscretionary variables are not subject to this proportional reduction because they are beyond the control of the decision makers. As it was mentioned in Section 2.3, there still may be excess inputs or additional outputs (called slack). DEA captures that information as well.

While all of the above information will be useful when one tries to analyze individual libraries, we focus primarily here on the distribution of efficiency scores and the magnitude of the changes as we modify the evaluation environments and add some control variables.

Table 6. Distribution of Efficiency Scores Without Constraints

Efficiency Score	Number of Libraries			
	Public (n = 65)		Private (n = 30)	
	1995	1996	1995	1996
1	47	49	27	29
.91-.99	5	7	2	0
.81-.90	9	4	0	0
.71-.80	3	3	0	0
.61-.70	0	1	0	1
< .60	1	1	1	0
Average	0.96	0.96	0.98	0.99
Number of libraries evaluated inefficient	18	16	3	1

Efficiency Scores without Imposing Constraints

As we mentioned, the libraries are compared to their peer libraries operating in similar conditions or constraints: libraries at the publicly funded universities ($n = 65$) are compared against their peers in the publicly funded universities, and libraries at the privately funded universities ($n = 30$) compete among themselves. Without imposing any constraints on the weights (the mu's and the nu's), we obtained the following results summarized in Table 6.

Table 6 shows that most of the libraries are deemed to be efficient. For example, in 1995, among libraries at the publicly funded universities, more than 72 percent (= 47/65) of the libraries in the group were evaluated by DEA as efficient. In the private group, in 1996, only one library out of 30 was evaluated inefficient. The average efficiency scores in all categories are extremely high, all in the upper .90's. The fact that many libraries are evaluated efficient with high average efficiency scores does not indicate that libraries included in the analysis are efficient. It is simply the result of adopting a particular model of DEA applied to a particular set of DMUs. Therefore, we cannot say that academic research libraries are more efficient than other organizations such as banks and hospitals that are evaluated in other studies.

From an analyst's point of view, the results seem quite disturbing because the analysis does not have enough discriminating power. There is very little to learn if most libraries are efficient, at the same time when we do know, for one reason or another, that there will be some inefficiencies among libraries studied.

To increase the resolution of the efficiency scores we can, in principle, do two things. First, the nonexistence of any constraints on weights allowed libraries to be assigned weights that have very little resemblance to reality; Table 7 illustrates

Table 7. Selected Weights for Libraries 38 (L38) and 87 (L87)

Library Code	ILLTOT	ILBTOT	LIBINST	REFTRANS	TOTCIRC
L87	0.09	0.08	0.13	0.10	0.03
L38	0.07	151.64	100.00	213.88	564.93

the point. The numbers in Table 7 represent the weights assigned to the output variables for two libraries: Library 87 (L87) and 38 (L38). Both libraries were evaluated efficient.

For Library 87, we can say that one unit of interlibrary loan transaction is worth as much as three units of circulation transaction. On the other hand, Library 38 took a radical approach in that it is assigned the weights that one unit of circulation is worth more than 8,000 times (= 564.93/0.07) as much as one unit of interlibrary loan transaction. While both libraries were evaluated efficient, they took wildly different paths to become efficient. Clearly, what happened to Library 38 cannot be justified. This leads us to the need for reasonable constraints on the weights, so that the results from the analysis become justifiable and applicable. The next section will deal with the selection of a specific form of constraints and derivation of the actual constraints.

Second, as Dyson et al. (1990) pointed out, the efficiency scores are sensitive to the number of variables included in the analysis. As the number of variables increases, so does the number of efficient units, because there is a wider chance for the units to become efficient by specializing in the new variable(s). So we should think about eliminating some of the variables from the model. We will attempt to do this in the sensitivity analysis section. The other way to increase the resolution of efficiency scores is to add more units in the analysis pool. Nunamaker (1985) suggests that the sample size should be at least three times larger than the number of variables included in a DEA model. This is equivalent to saying that by having a lot of competitors we can "raise the bar" in the competition. Unfortunately, this is not possible because we are dealing with a fixed population—all the academic research libraries that are members of the ARL.

Derivation of Constraints and Their Effects

In *The Constraints on Weights* section, we already laid out the basic approach to deriving reasonable constraints. The purpose of applying constraints, that is imposing a boundary on the weights, is to make the results more reasonable to the users of the analysis. But it will be impossible to arrive at the "correct" formulation of the relationships between variables that is applicable to every library in the analysis due to factors such as different management styles, geographic locations, and operating conditions. We have two goals in imposing constraints on the model. The primary goal is to avoid any nonsense due to mathematical optimiza-

Table 8. Cost of Services with Consulted Sources

Source	Description	Cost Reported	Year	Adjusted for 1997*
(1) Reference				
Cable (1980)	Average cost of search (excluding hidden costs)	$5.18	1980	$16.36
Spencer (1980)	Reference queries	$2.52	1980	$7.96
	Extended reference queries	$4.57	1980	$14.44
	Consultation, training, tours	$9.09	1980	$28.71
Kantor (1986) Cochrane	Query	$14.00	1982/3	$37.34
and Warmann (1989)	Full cost reference	$9.22	1989	$15.84
Robinson and				
Robinson (1994)	Average total cost per reference question handled	$6.84	1994	$8.38
				$18.43
				(Average)
(2) Interlibrary loans				
Roche (1993) [data	Borrowing	$18.62	1992	**$26.12**
from 1992]	Lending	$10.93	1992	**$15.33**
ARL/RLG average				
(3) Circulation				
Kantor (1986)	Per circulation cost (includes collection cost)	3.72	1982/3	**6.13**
(4) Group Presentation				
From ARL Statistics	Average hourly rate of			
(per participant)	professional staff (1996)	$34.96	1996	$37.41
	Assuming 2 hours and 14			
	attending per session	$4.99	1996	**$5.34**

Note: *Applied 7 percent annual increase except for circulation (3.5%).

tion. The secondary goal is to accommodate the differences among libraries by allowing the ratios to vary between the constraints rather than imposing a single, fixed set of weights. While the constraints inevitably introduce some arbitrariness to the analysis, in light of the fact that the goal of this study is to *evaluate* a tool (DEA) rather than to *prove* its usefulness, it seems desirable to apply the constraints and observe their effects on the results.

Cost of Services

The literature reports a wide range of cost figures for the same service category. There are several reasons for this. First, there are variations in incorporating indirect costs such as space and fringe benefits in calculating the total cost for a specific service. For the record, it should be noted that the current trend is to report both direct and indirect costs as a total price to reflect the true expen-

Table 9.   Ratios Between Weights Assigned to Services

			Fourfold Range		Twofold Range	
Service (A)	Service (B)	(A)/(B)	Lower (*1/4)	Upper (*4)	Lower (*1/2)	Upper (*2)
Reference	IL Borrowing	0.71	0.18	2.82	0.35	1.41
Reference	IL Lending	1.20	0.30	4.81	0.60	2.40
Reference	Circulation	3.01	0.75	12.04	1.50	6.02
Reference	Instruction	3.45	0.86	13.80	1.72	6.90
IL Borrowing	IL Lending	1.70	0.43	6.81	0.85	3.41
IL Borrowing	Circulation	4.26	1.07	17.05	2.13	8.53
IL Borrowing	Instruction	4.89	1.22	19.55	2.44	9.77
IL Lending	Circulation	2.50	0.63	10.01	1.25	5.00
IL Lending	Instruction	2.87	0.72	11.47	1.43	5.74
Circulation	Instruction	1.15	0.29	4.59	0.57	2.29

diture for services. Second, research libraries follow accounting policies and procedures of their parent organizations, so that aggregating various costs for a specific service becomes a difficult task involving a fair amount of guesswork and informed judgment.

With above caveats in mind, we have consulted the studies listed in Table 8 for guidelines in deriving service costs. (The "consensus" figure for each service is shown in the table in bold face.) Once again we explicitly state that the purpose of imposing constraints is to make the DEA results as realistic as possible. Our approach, is to use the cost of each service as the basis for its relative weight in comparison to other services. For instance, according to the recent study of inter-library loans sponsored by the ARL and RLG (Research Libraries Group), the average unit cost of borrowing in 1996 is $18.35 which seems to be almost equal to the 1992 figure of $18.62. At the same time, the average unit cost of lending has dropped from $10.93 in 1992 to $9.48 in 1996. This suggests that there have been improvements (perhaps communication technologies) in the ways that academic research libraries provide interlibrary services. One could argue at this point that the 1997 estimate of interlibrary loans based on a 7 percent annual inflation is well off track. But again, our concern is to constrain the relative weights of services, not to produce a precise calculation of service cost. Furthermore, setting ranges for the ratios of service costs certainly allows enough flexibility to accommodate such cost improvements. The fourfold range is quite generous; it is tightened in the twofold range.

Based on the unit cost of services derived above, we get the 10 ratios between five different outputs as displayed in Table 9. Table 9 shows that one reference transaction costs about 71 percent of one unit of interlibrary borrow-ing ($18.43/$26.12*100). We use this ratio as a surrogate or an indication of relative value of two outputs. The table also shows the two ranges of ratios in the factor of 4 and 2.

Table 10. Cost Information for Inputs

Year	Category	Units[*]	Total Cost[*]	Unit Cost
1995	Professional Staff	8,242	$332,752,579	$40,373
	Nonprofessional Staff	14,705	$313,687,653	$21,332
	Student Assistants	7,469	$74,137,023	$9,926
	Monograph Purchased	2,889,585	$173,567,824	$60
	Serial (Current)	2,762,558	$319,589,674	$116
1995	Professional Staff	8,349	$350,265,615	$41,953
	Nonprofessional Staff	14,702	$326,773,412	$22,226
	Student Assistants	7,667	$76,831,246	$10,021
	Monograph Purchased	2,815,990	$176,298,928	$63
	Serial (Current)	2,783,810	$346,120,125	$124

Note: [*]Total of 95 libraries.

Table 11. Ratios Between Weights Assigned to Inputs

Input (A)	Input (B)	(A)/(B)	Fourfold Range Lower (*1/4)	Upper (*4)	Twofold Range Lower (*1/2)	Upper (*2)
Professional Staff	Support Staff	1.89	0.47	7.56	0.95	3.78
Professional Staff	Student Staff	4.13	1.03	16.51	2.06	8.25
Professional Staff	Monograph	671.12	167.78	2684.48	335.56	1342.24
Professional Staff	Serial	343.20	85.80	1372.82	171.60	686.41
Support Staff	Student Staff	2.18	0.55	8.73	1.09	4.37
Support Staff	Monograph	355.08	88.77	1420.32	177.54	710.16
Support Staff	Serial	181.58	45.40	726.32	90.79	363.16
Student Staff	Monograph	162.66	40.66	650.63	81.33	325.31
Student Staff	Serial	83.20	20.80	332.80	41.60	166.40
Monograph	Serial	0.51	0.13	2.05	0.26	1.02

In the fourfold range, DEA takes the average ratio and could run it down to one-quarter (0.18) of the real value and all the way to four times (2.82) the real value. The twofold range allows the ratios to vary between one-half of the real value and the twice the real value.

Cost of Inputs

Similarly, the costs of inputs, and their ratios, were obtained directly from the ARL statistics. These are summarized in Table 10. Notice that the unit cost of a current serial is quite low, $116 in 1995 and $124 in 1996. This happened because we used the total number of serials instead of the number of paid serial subscriptions.

Because the unit costs have changed very little over the years, we used the average ratios instead of separate ratios for 1995 and 1996 as shown in Table 11. The

2   ***Table 12.***   Tested Constraints Sets

Constraints Set	Number of Ratios	Allowed Range
1	Only Input Ratios (10)	Fourfold (1/4-4) range
2	Only Output Ratios (10)	Fourfold (1/4-4) range
3	Both Input and Output Ratios (20)	Fourfold (1/4-4) range
4	Only Input Ratios (10)	Twofold (1/2-2) range
5	Only Output Ratios (10)	Twofold (1/2-2) range
6	Both Input and Output Ratios (20)	Twofold (1/2-2) range

Table 13.   Number of Libraries Evaluated Inefficient and Average Efficiency Score under Different Constraints

			Constraints					
		No	Four-fold Range (1/4-4)			Two-fold Range (1/2-2)		
Year	Group	Constraint	Input	Output	Both	Input	Output	Both
1995	Public	18	25	25	34	28	31	43
		(0.96)	(0.93)	(0.93)	(0.90)	(0.91)	(0.90)	(0.83)
	Private	3	4	5	7	6	5	11
		(0.98)	(0.96)	(0.96)	(0.94)	(0.95)	(0.96)	(0.91)
1996	Public	16	22	23	33	27	28	41
		(0.96)	(0.94)	(0.94)	(0.90)	(0.93)	(0.91)	(0.84)
	Private	1	5	2	7	6	4	12
		(0.99)	(0.95)	(0.98)	(0.94)	(0.94)	(0.96)	(0.89)

Notes: Public ($n = 65$), Private ($n = 30$). The numbers in the parentheses are the average efficiency scores.

corresponding ratios and ranges are shown in Table 11. Again we calculated the ratios in two ranges.

The Effect of Imposing Constraints

A total of 24 additional DEA analyses were performed after the constraints on the ratios are included. To observe the effect of adding more constraints and of restricting the boundaries, six conditions are imposed for each comparison group (public or private) and for each year (see Table 12).

We expected that tightening the range on the constraints and/or adding more constraints would increase the discriminating power of the analysis, and reveal more inefficient libraries. Some of the libraries might have seemed efficient only because there were no constraints and, thus, unrealistic weights make them look as good as possible. When this freedom is reduced, inefficiencies at these libraries are uncovered. Table 13 summarizes the number of inefficient libraries revealed in each constraint environment. The results from the previous, no constraint model are appended for easy comparison.

As we read the table from left to right, we notice a marked change both in the number of libraries evaluated inefficient (efficiency score $\theta < 1$) and the average efficiency scores. As the number of inefficient libraries goes up, the average efficiency score goes down. For instance, in 1995, without any constraints, about 28 percent (= 18/65*100) of the libraries in the public group were evaluated inefficient, whereas with the strictest constraint environment (twofold range, both input and output ratios), about two-thirds (= 43/65) of the libraries are evaluated inefficient. The average efficiency score fell from .96 to .83, respectively. In the private group, again in 1995, the number of inefficient libraries increased from 3 to 11, and the average efficiency score decreased from .98 to .91.

Another noticeable change is that, as we expected, adding both input and output ratios in the same ratio range reveal more inefficiency than does adding either input or output constraints on the ratios. Also, when the applied ratios are the same, the narrower range (twofold) will always find more inefficient libraries than the more generous range (fourfold). Thus, for instance, in 1996 for the public group, under output ratios, only a constraint environment imposing a fourfold range revealed 23 inefficient libraries while a twofold range revealed 28 of the libraries to be inefficient.

We believe that the twofold range using both input and output ratios seems to give us the reasonable discriminating capability that is required of an evaluation tool. Still, there are some differences in the two comparison groups. Under this particular constraint environment, in the public group, about two-thirds of the libraries seem to have some other libraries in the same group to learn from. On the other hand, in the private group, because two-thirds of the libraries are evaluated efficient, only about one-third of them will have peers to learn from. This difference should not be interpreted as an indication that academic libraries at the privately funded universities are better managed than their peers at the publicly funded institutions.

The difference might have been simply due to the relative number of units included in the analysis and the density of the observed data values. If the number of units in the analysis is large, then the competition among the units is more severe than with a smaller number of units. Also, if the observed data values are not concentrated, meaning that there is a greater variation of the size of the libraries, more libraries are likely to become somehow unique, and thus become efficient for no reason related to merit. Also, the libraries in the public group are more homogeneous in terms of their observed data values than the libraries in the private group.

Tables 14–17 show the distribution of efficiency scores under seven different evaluation environments during the two-year period. Notice that not only the number of (in)efficient libraries and the mean efficiency scores but also the distribution of the inefficient libraries are quite stable for both public and private groups over the two-year period. This suggests that the efficiency scores are stable from 1995 and 1996.

Table 14. Distribution of Efficiency Scores under
Different Constraints: Public Group, 1995 (n = 65)

Efficiency Score	No Ratio	Constraints					
		Fourfold Range (1/4-4)			Twofold Range (1/2-2)		
		Input	Output	Both	Input	Output	Both
1	47	40	40	31	37	34	22
.91-.99	5	6	7	9	5	8	9
.81-.90	9	7	8	8	8	7	7
.71-.80	3	10	7	10	11	8	13
.61-.70	0	1	2	6	2	5	5
< .60	1	1	1	1	2	3	9
Average	0.96	0.93	0.93	0.90	0.91	0.90	0.83
Number of libraries evaluated inefficient	18	25	25	34	28	31	43

Table 15. Distribution of Efficiency Scores under
Different Constraints: Public Group, 1996 (n = 65)

Efficiency Score	No Ratio	Constraints					
		Fourfold Range (1/4-4)			Twofold Range (1/2-2)		
		Input	Output	Both	Input	Output	Both
1	49	43	42	32	38	37	24
.91-.99	7	8	8	7	10	6	8
.81-.90	4	6	7	10	8	9	6
.71-.80	3	5	4	11	5	8	14
.61-.70	1	2	3	4	2	3	6
< .60	1	1	1	1	2	2	7
Average	0.96	0.94	0.94	0.90	0.93	0.91	0.84
Number of libraries evaluated inefficient	16	22	23	33	27	28	41

The consistency of the efficiency scores will be investigated in the next section.

We observe that the number of libraries that received less than a score of .60 increased quite substantially. For example, in the 1995 public group, there was only 1 library in the category when there were no constraints; but when the strictest constraints were imposed, the number went up to 9. Overall, the public group showed a larger decline in the average efficiency score than did their peers in the private group.

Table 16. Distribution of Efficiency Scores under
Different Constraints: Private Group, 1995 (*n* = 30

		Constraints					
		Fourfold Range (1/4-4)			Twofold Range (1/2-2)		
Efficiency Score	No Ratio	Input	Output	Both	Input	Output	Both
1	27	26	25	23	24	25	19
.91-.99	2	0	1	0	1	0	2
.81-.90	0	2	2	3	3	3	4
.71-.80	0	0	1	2	0	1	1
.61-.70	0	1	0	1	0	0	2
< .60	1	1	1	1	2	1	2
Average	0.98	0.96	0.96	0.94	0.95	0.96	0.91
No. of libraries evaluated inefficient	3	4	5	7	6	5	11

Table 17. Distribution of Efficiency Scores under
Different Constraints: Private Group, 1996 (*n* = 30)

		Constraints					
		Fourfold Range (1/4-4)			Twofold Range (1/2-2)		
Efficiency Score	No Ratio	Input	Output	Both	Input	Output	Both
1	29	25	28	23	24	26	18
.91-.99	0	1	1	3	1	1	2
.81-.90	0	1	0	0	1	1	4
.71-.80	0	1	0	1	1	0	2
.61-.70	1	0	0	1	1	0	0
< .60	0	2	1	2	2	2	4
Average	0.99	0.95	0.98	0.94	0.94	0.96	0.89
Number of libraries evaluated inefficient	1	5	2	7	6	4	12

Consistency of Efficiency Scores over a Two-year Period

A reliable evaluation system gives us stable results over a period of time. Thus, DEA should produce similar scores for the libraries unless there are significant changes in one of the following.

1. Observed data values (e.g., a big drop in the staff size or sharp increase in circulation due to a change in the loan policy).
2. Assigned weights. This is possible because DEA does not have information about the weights assigned to the libraries previously. The weights are

Table 18. Changes in the Observed Data Values over Two-year Period

Variables	Mean	Median	Range		
ILLTOT	3.92	0.44	−30.30	~	94.67
ILBTOT	8.18	5.21	−16.27	~	84.36
LIBINST	6.82	2.79	−95.38	~	129.00
REFTRANS	34.83	−0.52	−46.83	~	2820.87
TOTCIRC	2.08	−1.82	−29.47	~	133.85
VOLS	2.40	2.29	−4.75	~	9.64
VOLSADN	2.02	-3.74	−49.13	~	62.25
MONO	0.14	−1.83	−74.10	~	55.87
CURRSER	0.22	−0.38	−21.70	~	44.08
PRFSTF	0.74	0.00	−15.09	~	24.19
NPRFSTF	−0.56	0.00	−13.73	~	25.81
STUDAST	1.60	0.00	−25.00	~	44.44
TOTSTU	0.66	0.51	−17.62	~	24.35
GRADSTU	0.59	0.00	−41.53	~	64.80
FAC	−0.77	0.00	−46.64	~	19.41

Note: All numbers are in percentages (%).

recalculated every time there is a change in the observed data value or in the number of libraries in the analysis. It is possible that a library becomes efficient or inefficient without any changes in the observed data values, but simply by being assigned a different set of weights.

3. Configuration of the efficient frontier. Addition or removal of efficient unit(s) on the envelopment surface has an impact, sometimes quite dramatic, on the efficiency scores of other libraries.[16]

Table 18 shows the changes in the observed data values over a two-year period (1995–1996). It would be nice to have data for a more extended time period, but the current data would allow only a two-year comparison.[17] Not surprisingly, as we can see in the mean and the median values, the data are quite stable. The mean change of the reference transactions is quite high due to one library which reported a whopping 2,800 percent increase from the 1995 figure. In many cases, the median value might be a better indication of typical changes. Overall, the observed output data values show larger fluctuation than the observed input values.

Now with this fact in mind, we compare the efficiency scores from 1995 and 1996 for each comparison group. We only look at 3 evaluation environments:

1. when there are no constraints at all,
2. when the generous fourfold ranges on the constraints on the ratios between both input and output weights are present, and

Table 19.   Consistency of Efficiency Scores over
Two-year Period (1995–1996): Public Group

Changes in The Efficiency Scores	No Ratio	Fourfold Range Both Ratios	Twofold Range Both Ratios
Distribution			
No Change	44	25	16
0.01-0.05	8	22	36
0.06-0.10	8	10	4
0.11-0.15	2	4	0
0.16-0.20	2	1	4
0.21-0.25	1	2	2
0.26-0.30	0	0	2
> 0.30	0	1	1
Total	65	65	65
Average Change	0.03	0.04	0.06
Highest Change	0.25	0.36	0.52
Down Status	5	7	8
Up Status	3	6	6

Notes: Up Status means that a library was evaluated inefficient in 1995 but evaluated efficient in 1996. Down Status
means exactly the opposite. The direction of the changes are ignored. In tabulating the distribution, only the
magnitude of the changes are retained and analyzed.

3.   when the more restrictive twofold ranges on the constraints on the ratios
between both input and output weights are present.

Table 19 summarizes the results for the public group. When there is no constraint, the majority of libraries (44 out of 65) received the same efficiency scores
that they received in 1995. There are 5 libraries that were evaluated as efficient in
1995, but are evaluated as inefficient in the following year. There are fewer libraries who upgraded their efficiency status.

As we move from no constraint to the fourfold range constraint evaluation environment, and to an even stricter twofold range, the magnitude of changes in terms
of the average score change, the maximum change, and the changes in the efficiency status intensifies. Although there are considerably fewer libraries that
received the same efficiency scores during the two-year period, still the majority
of libraries posted a less than 5 percent change regardless of the evaluation environment.

There is one library (L89) which received a much higher efficiency score (>.30)
in 1996 than in 1995. In the twofold range, its efficiency score rose from a mere
.48 to a perfect 1.00 in 1996. Incidentally, the library reported a huge increase in
circulation transactions in 1996: it more than doubled the output of that particular
service. The same library was evaluated inefficient in 1995 in all 7 different eval-

Table 20.   Illustration of Changes in Benchmark
Comparison Sets over Two-year Period

Library Being Evaluated	Benchmark Set	
(focus library)	1995	1996
L07	L78 .65	L78 .59
	L20 .35	L20 .12
		L89 .29
L15	L01 .26	L01 .31
	L65 .20	L65 .20
	L78 .54	L78 .34
		L89 .15

Note: The values attached to a library indicate the relative weight that the library has in determining the projected point for the focus library being evaluated.

Table 21.   Consistency of Efficiency Scores over
Two-year Period (1995–1996): Private Group

Changes in the efficiency scores	No Ratio	Fourfold Range Both Ratios	Twofold Range Both Ratios
Distribution			
No Change	27	21	15
0.01-0.05	1	4	7
0.06-0.10	2	1	4
0.11-0.15	0	2	0
0.16-0.20	0	0	2
0.21-0.25	0	1	0
0.26-0.30	0	0	0
> 0.30	0	1	2
Total	30	30	30
Average Change	0.01	0.04	0.07
Highest Change	0.09	0.62	0.65
Down Status	1	2	3
Up Status	0	2	4

Note: Up Status means that a library was evaluated inefficient in 1995 but evaluated efficient in 1996. Down Status means exactly the opposite.

uation environments, even in the no constraint environment. This means that the library was not able to look efficient by simply varying the weights assigned to inputs or outputs. It became efficient only after a real change in the circulation transaction figure. At this point, we do not know what prompted the huge increase. But we can tell from this result that the efficiency score of libraries can respond to significant change even in a single variable.

When L89 was moved to the efficient frontier in the twofold evaluation environment in 1996, it affected the efficiency scores of two other libraries by being added to the benchmark comparison set of these libraries (see Table 20). In both cases, the library (L89) did not cause any existing efficient library to become inefficient. It simply altered the convex combination of the efficient frontier that the two inefficient libraries are compared against.

The results of the private group, shown in Table 21, give us a similar pattern of changes. Again there was one library that had a major change in the efficiency score and the efficiency status. This particular library was evaluated efficient in 1995 in all three evaluation environments. But in 1996, it has one missing variable: the total circulation transactions. This causes the efficiency score of the library to tumble from 1.00 to .38 in the fourfold range and to .35 in the twofold range. Interestingly, the library was evaluated efficient in 1996 when there was no constraint imposed on the weights. It was able to look efficient with one missing output by giving relatively big weights to its other output variables. When this freedom is removed, the effect of a missing value becomes quite evident.

Sensitivity and Noise Analysis

Up to this point, we have based our analyses on the initial list of 15 variables selected from the ARL statistics. Our intention was to cover various aspects of academic research libraries, in terms of their inputs and outputs, as much as we could. We learned in the *Efficiency Scores without Imposing Constraints* section that the number of variables as well as the size of the comparison group affects the efficiency scores. Because we have the fixed number of libraries in the comparison groups, we can vary the number of variables and observe the effect on the efficiency scores.

In doing the sensitivity analysis, we performed the following tests.

1. We dropped one variable at a time to observe the relative impact of each variable on the efficiency scores. Based on the observation of the results thus far, we would expect that the number of libraries evaluated efficient as well as the efficiency scores will go down as we take out variables from a base model where all 15 variables are utilized.
2. The results from the above runs will give us an indication of the possible candidates of variables for elimination. The best candidates are the ones that have little impact on the efficiency scores. We are also guided by common sense in arriving at a "minimum set of variables," because a variable can have a minimal effect on the efficiency scores but conceptually be critical to the model of library operation.
3. Apart from observing the effect of taking a variable or a set of variables from the base models, it seems useful to conduct what is called "noise anal-

Table 22. Effects of Dropping a Variable on the
Efficiency Scores: Output Variables (1995, public)

Changes in the Efficiency Scores	Interlibrary Lending	Interlibrary Borrowing	Library Instruction	Reference	Circulation
Distribution					
No Change	23	23	24	18	18
≤ 0.01-0.05	40	40	41	23	22
0.06-0.10	2	2	0	10	6
0.11-0.15	0	0	0	5	6
0.16-0.20	0	0	0	4	3
0.21-0.25	0	0	0	2	4
0.26-0.30	0	0	0	2	2
> 0.30	0	0	0	1	4
Total	65	65	65	65	65
Mean Efficiency Score	0.83	0.83	0.83	0.86	0.74
Average Change	0.01	0.01	0.00	0.06	0.09
Highest Change	0.11	0.07	0.01	0.36	0.63
Down Status	0	0	0	5	5
Up Status	0	2	0	6	0

Note: The mean efficiency score for the base model is .83.

ysis" where we enter either random dummy variable(s) or random noise in the actual data to observe the robustness of the analyses.

In all cases, the alternative evaluation environments are compared against their corresponding *base models*, the runs with the strictest constraints: *both input and output ratio constraints on the weights in the twofold range.*

We summarize the results in the following measures.

1. Changes in the average efficiency score. This will serve as a crude yardstick as to whether the treatment has a favorable or adversary effect on the efficiency scores.
2. Distribution of changes (in absolute terms) in the efficiency scores to observe the ranges of variation.
3. The biggest changes to find out what would have prompted them.
4. Number of libraries that changed their efficiency status. "Down Status" means that a library moved from a 100 percent efficient status to less than 100 percent efficiency and vice versa. Although a change of .01 and .70 are treated equally if the removal of a variable changed the status of a library, this measure will give us some indication of how much impact a treatment has on the familiar dichotomous characterization of efficiency status: "efficient" versus "not efficient."

The Effects of Dropping One Variable at a Time

Table 22 shows, for the 1995 public group, the results of employing alternative models when one output variable at a time is taken out of the base model. It shows, for example, that when the library instruction (measured by number of people who participated in it) variable is removed from the base model, hardly anything changes. More than one-third of the libraries (24 out of 65) are assigned the same efficiency scores as they were with the variable present in the base model. All the rest of the libraries (41 libraries) posted less than a .01 score change, which seems quite small. There was not a single library that switched its efficiency status, either from inefficient to efficient or vice versa. Therefore, the variable seems to be a good candidate if we need to cut down the number of variables. As a matter of fact, library instruction is neither a mature nor standardized output measure. It also depends on such factors as the size of facilities, institutional interest and support for this type of service, which seem to be less correlated with the kinds of inputs included in the analysis than the variables such as reference and circulation.

Removing either interlibrary lending or interlibrary borrowing also has very small impact on the efficiency scores. On the other hand, dropping either reference transactions or circulation seems to cause substantial changes. When we compare the base model with the model without reference transaction, contrary to what we expected, we see an improvement in the mean efficiency score: it rose from .83 to .86. More than one-third of the libraries (24 out of 65) experienced the score change of .05 or above.

The table shows that there was one library (L87) which lost .36 from its initial score when the reference variable is removed. Close examination of the raw data reveals that this library reported large reference activities. When this advantage disappears, it no longer becomes efficient and thus looks inferior to other libraries.

It is quite possible that those libraries that lost big scores when the reference variable was removed could have exerted such a dominance with their strong reference transaction activity, that a couple of libraries might have looked inferior just because of that. This explains why there are six libraries that become efficient (Up Status) when the model without reference transaction is tested. In fact, one library (L78) which lost .28 when the reference transactions are removed, was included in the benchmark comparison set of 6 libraries (L21, L22, L26, L38, L62, and L90) in the base model. All six libraries become efficient when the envelopment surface (efficient frontier) is pulled down, so to speak, with the disappearance of the reference transaction variable.

We can observe a similar pattern in the model when the circulation variable is taken out of the base model. In fact, we notice even bigger changes in the table: the average efficiency decreased by .09 and there is one library (L20) which lost .63 from its original efficiency score. Again, the libraries that lost efficiency scores in a big way are the ones that reported large circulation figures. But this

Table 23.   Effects of Dropping a Variable on the
Efficiency Scores: Output Variables (1996, public)

Changes in the Efficiency Scores	Interlibrary Lending	Interlibrary Borrowing	Library Instruction	Reference	Circulation
Distribution					
No Change	23	24	25	19	15
0.01-0.05	41	40	40	25	16
0.06-0.10	1	1	0	6	14
0.11-0.15	0	0	0	6	6
0.16-0.20	0	0	0	4	4
0.21-0.25	0	0	0	2	1
0.26-0.30	0	0	0	1	1
> 0.30	0	0	0	2	8
Total	65	65	65	65	65
Mean Efficiency Score	0.83	0.83	0.84	0.86	0.71
Average Change	0.01	0.01	0.00	0.06	0.13
Highest Change	0.10	0.07	0.03	0.36	0.70
Down Status	0	0	0	5	5
Up Status	0	2	0	6	0

Note: The mean efficiency score for the base model is .84.

time, their losses have not affected the efficiency scores of other libraries: none of the libraries upgraded their efficiency status. The same analyses, but now for the 1996 data shown in Table 23, display a strikingly similar pattern in the efficiency score changes where only reference and circulation transactions make noticeable differences when removed from the base models.

When we look at the results for the private group, in both 1995 and 1996 shown in Tables 24 and 25, once again the effects of reference and circulation truly stand out. In 1995, one library (L29) shows a huge change in the efficiency score when the interlibrary lending or circulation variable is eliminated from the base model. This library reported very large numbers in both categories of variables. When the interlibrary lending variable is missing from the base model, the efficiency score for this library decreases from 1.00 to .47. When the circulation variable is taken out, its score plunges to a mere .18 from a perfect 1.00. This happens because DEA assigned too large a weight to circulation for the library and when the variable is removed, it no longer can hold its efficiency score by adjusting the weights of other outputs. That is why there was such a sharp decrease.

We can conclude that, of the output variables, the reference and circulation variables have the biggest impact on the efficiency scores. These two variables are not only important as a matter of fact but are also treated as quite significant main outputs of academic research libraries. Does this mean that the other three variables are not worthy of inclusion in the DEA analysis? Probably not.

Table 24.   Effects of Dropping a Variable on the
Efficiency Scores: Output Variables (1995, private)

Changes in the Efficiency Scores	Interlibrary Lending	Interlibrary Borrowing	Library Instruction	Reference	Circulation
Distribution					
No Change	19	20	20	17	13
0.01-0.05	9	10	10	7	4
0.06-0.10	1	0	0	2	4
0.11-0.15	0	0	0	0	2
0.16-0.20	0	0	0	1	1
0.21-0.25	0	0	0	0	1
0.26-0.30	0	0	0	1	0
> 0.30	1	0	0	3	5
Total	30	30	30	31	30
Mean Efficiency Score	0.89	0.91	0.91	0.88	0.80
Average Change	0.02	0.00	0.00	0.05	0.12
Highest Change	0.53	0.03	0.01	0.45	0.82
Down Status	1	0	0	3	7
Up Status	0	0	0	2	0

Note: The mean efficiency score for the base model is .91.

Table 25.   Effects of Dropping a Variable on the
Efficiency Scores: Output Variables (1996, private)

Changes in the Efficiency Scores	Interlibrary Lending	Interlibrary Borrowing	Library Instruction	Reference	Circulation
Distribution					
No Change	17	18	18	16	10
0.01-0.05	11	10	12	3	6
0.06-0.10	1	2	0	3	1
0.11-0.15	0	0	0	4	5
0.16-0.20	0	0	0	2	2
0.21-0.25	1	0	0	0	0
0.26-0.30	0	0	0	1	1
> 0.30	0	0	0	1	5
Total	30	30	30	30	30
Mean Efficiency Score	0.88	0.89	0.89	0.89	0.75
Average Change	0.02	0.01	0.00	0.07	0.15
Highest Change	0.25	0.10	0.01	0.57	0.84
Down Status	1	0	0	2	8
Up Status	0	0	0	4	1

Note: The mean efficiency score for the base model is .89.

Table 26. Effects of Dropping a Variable on the Efficiency Scores: Input Variables (1995, public)

Changes in the Efficiency Scores	Total Students	Total Graduates	Faculty	Professional Staff	Support Staff	Student Staff	Volumes Held	Net Volumes Added	Monographs	Current Serials
Distribution										
No Change	60	51	59	25	25	25	52	27	23	23
0.01-0.05	4	8	5	37	31	40	9	22	32	35
0.06-0.10	0	2	1	2	7	0	4	6	2	5
0.11-0.15	1	1	0	1	2	0	0	3	7	1
0.16-0.20	0	2	0	0	0	0	0	3	1	1
0.21-0.25	0	1	0	0	0	0	0	2	0	0
0.26-0.30	0	0	0	0	0	0	0	1	0	0
> 0.30	0	0	0	0	0	0	0	1	0	0
Total	65	65	65	65	65	65	65	65	65	65
Mean Efficiency	0.83	0.82	0.83	0.82	0.84	0.83	0.83	0.79	0.81	0.84
Average Change	0.00	0.02	0.00	0.02	0.02	0.01	0.01	0.04	0.03	0.02
Highest Change	0.12	0.22	0.07	0.13	0.16	0.05	0.10	0.30	0.19	0.20
Down Status	1	5	0	0	0	0	4	7	2	2
Up Status	0	0	0	1	2	1	0	0	1	3

Note: The mean efficiency score for the base model is .83.

One thing we should consider is how closely related are the output variables and the input variables included in the analysis. For instance, it is clear that as the number of books or students increase, the number of books charged out by the users is likely to go up. Although the levels of library instruction and interlibrary lending activities will be larger at the libraries with bigger collections, there are some exogenous factors that seem to also affect the activity levels: outside demand or the library's participation in various library consortia in the case of interlibrary lending and the institutional support and facilities in the case of library instruction.

Now we do the same analysis for the 10 input variables. We use the same table format to report the results. The base models are the same as in the test of the output variables. We first look at the results of the public group in 1995 as shown in Table 26.

Among three variables that represent different groups of users, only the number of graduate students has some impact, although it seems minimal, on efficiency scores. Five of the libraries are downgraded to inefficient status. It should be noted that total students include both undergraduate and graduate students. Both total number of students and the size of faculty have almost negligible effect.

Among the staff variables, the professional staff and full-time support staff variables have more impact than does the student assistants variable. When the support staff variable is taken out of the base model, 9 libraries showed more than .05 efficiency score changes while without the student assistants variable, none of the libraries shows more than .05 change in efficiency scores.

The net volumes added variable seems to be more volatile when compared with other collection-related input variables. When the variable is removed from the base model, the mean efficiency score is decreased from .83 to .79. It is the biggest change among the input variables for the public group in 1995, but it falls short when compared to the changes produced by two output variables—reference and circulation.

When we look at the distribution of the net changes, without net volumes added (VOLSADN), one library (L23) lost by .30 points from its original score in the base model. This particular library does not have a big VOLSADN figure. But because it assigned much too big a weight to the variable, its efficiency score drops considerably when the variable is excluded from the base model. It was assigned a weight that is 91 percent of the total computed input weights, when on average at other libraries only 30 percent of the weights are assigned to that variable.

Figure 4 shows the scatter plot of the relative proportion of the weights assigned to the VOLSADN variable out of the total computed input weights[18] and the net score changes. It shows that significant changes in the efficiency score are always accompanied by a significant portion of its total input weight assigned to the variable. But it also shows that assigning a bigger weight to the variable is not the only condition for significant changes in the efficiency

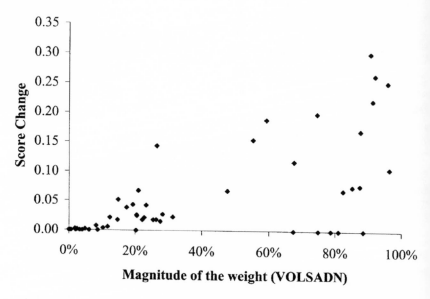

Figure 4. Scatter Plot of the Percentage of Total Input Weights Attached to the Net Volumes Added and the Net Efficiency Score Change When the Variable is Missing from the Base Model

scores. There are plenty of libraries that maintained their efficiency scores intact or with a minimum change even when a key variable, to which they assigned a large portion of the input weights, was removed from the model.

The fact that a library receives a particularly low or high efficiency score depending on how the weights are assigned, and not because the library has extreme observed data value in the inputs or outputs, raises a serious concern with the DEA approach. Unless people closely look at the weights, it is not easy to find out why there was a significant drop or increase in the efficiency. Furthermore, even if they found out what happened, there is little to say about why that happened. The extreme approach taken by DEA can often optimize on a single variable and when that particular variable is removed, the results might seem embarrassing.

The 1996 results for the same public group are not much different from the 1995 results. None of the variables caused more than a .03 change in the mean efficiency score. Overall, there are more libraries that lost their 100 percent efficiency status than libraries that climbed up to become 100 percent efficient (see Table 27).

The results for the private group in 1995 shown in Table 28 display a similar but slightly different effect. Here, removing the net volumes added (VOLSADN)

Table 27. Effects of Dropping a Variable on the Efficiency Scores: Input Variables (1996, public)

Changes in the Efficiency Scores	Total Students	Total Graduates	Faculty	Professional Staff	Support Staff	Student Staff	Volumes Held	Net Volumes Added	Monographs	Current Serials
Distribution										
No Change	62	48	58	25	24	25	55	37	22	25
0.01–0.05	2	10	7	30	35	40	8	18	33	26
0.06–0.10	0	3	0	10	5	0	0	6	7	13
0.11–0.15	0	1	0	0	1	0	1	4	2	0
0.16–0.20	0	1	0	0	0	0	1	0	1	1
0.21–0.25	1	0	0	0	0	0	0	0	0	0
0.26–0.30	0	1	0	0	0	0	0	0	0	0
> 0.30	0	0	0	0	0	0	0	0	0	0
Total	65	65	65	65	65	65	65	65	65	65
Mean Efficiency	0.83	0.82	0.84	0.82	0.85	0.84	0.83	0.82	0.83	0.83
Average Change	0.00	0.02	0.00	0.03	0.02	0.01	0.01	0.02	0.03	0.03
Highest Change	0.25	0.35	0.06	0.10	0.13	0.05	0.18	0.14	0.18	0.16
Down Status	1	5	0	0	0	0	4	7	2	2
Up Status	0	0	0	1	2	1	0	0	1	3

Note: The mean efficiency score for the base model is .84.

Table 28. Effects of Dropping a Variable on the Efficiency Scores: Input Variables (1995, private)

Changes in the Efficiency Scores	Total Students	Total Graduates	Faculty	Professional Staff	Support Staff	Student Staff	Volumes Held	Net Volumes Added	Monographs	Current Serials
Distribution										
No Change	25	27	26	19	19	19	24	28	19	19
0.01-0.05	3	2	3	6	8	11	4	2	6	6
0.06-0.10	0	0	0	3	3	0	0	0	1	4
0.11-0.15	1	0	0	0	0	0	1	0	3	1
0.16-0.20	0	0	0	2	0	0	0	0	0	0
0.21-0.25	0	1	0	0	0	0	0	0	1	0
0.26-0.30	0	0	0	0	0	0	0	0	0	0
> 0.30	0	0	1	0	0	0	1	0	0	0
Total	30	30	30	30	30	30	30	30	30	30
Mean Efficiency	0.89	0.90	0.89	0.89	0.92	0.90	0.88	0.91	0.89	0.93
Average Change	0.01	0.01	0.01	0.02	0.01	0.01	0.02	0.00	0.03	0.02
Highest Change	0.19	0.22	0.34	0.18	0.11	0.04	0.35	0.02	0.23	0.15
Down Status	1	2	1	0	0	0	3	1	0	0
Up Status	0	0	0	1	2	0	0	0	0	2

The mean efficiency score for the base model is .91.

Table 29. Effects of Dropping a Variable on the Efficiency Scores: Input Variables (1996, private)

Changes in the Efficiency Scores	Total Students	Total Graduates	Faculty	Professional Staff	Support Staff	Student Staff	Volumes Held	Net Volumes Added	Monographs	Current Serials
Distribution										
No Change	16	29	24	19	19	19	26	25	19	19
0.01-0.05	5	0	2	6	7	11	2	3	4	6
0.06-0.10	1	0	0	2	3	0	0	0	6	3
0.11-0.15	0	1	2	1	1	0	0	1	1	2
0.16-0.20	0	0	1	0	0	0	0	0	0	0
0.21-0.25	2	0	0	2	0	0	1	1	0	0
0.26-0.30	3	0	1	0	0	0	1	0	0	0
> 0.30	3	0	0	0	0	0	0	0	0	0
Total	30	30	30	30	30	30	30	30	30	30
Mean Efficiency	0.80	0.89	0.87	0.87	0.91	0.89	0.88	0.88	0.89	0.91
Average Change	0.09	0.01	0.03	0.03	0.02	0.01	0.02	0.01	0.03	0.02
Highest Change	0.60	0.18	0.30	0.21	0.11	0.04	0.28	0.21	0.16	0.14
Down Status	6	1	4	0	0	0	2	1	0	0
Up Status	0	0	0	0	1	0	0	0	0	0

Note: The mean efficiency score for the base model is .89.

Table 30. Changes in the Weights Assigned to the Total Students Variable

Libraries	1995 Base Model	1996 Base Model
L24	0.00	−374.43
L56	−9.02	−16.10
L86	−116.48	−308.56

variable has a quite negligible impact on the efficiency scores. The biggest change was only .02. This result is contrasted with the results in the public group where 7 of the 65 libraries were downgraded in efficiency status in both 1995 and 1996.

When the number of full-time support staff or current serials is removed, we see slightly better mean efficiency scores (.92 and .93 compared to .91) than in the base model. We now have a pretty good idea of what might have happened. In both cases, there are two libraries that are now added to the efficient frontier (Up Status) with the removal of either one of the variables.

We can spot the biggest surprise in the private group's 1996 results shown in Table 29. While the effects of all the other variables remain almost the same as in the results thus far, removing the total students variable from the base model caused the mean efficiency score to drop by .09, the biggest change among input variables in both public and private groups, and removed a net of six libraries from the efficient frontier.

Close examination of the weights attached to the observed data values of the libraries that lost significant portions of their efficiency scores reveals that big negative weights were assigned to the values of the total students variable. Because the variable is nondiscretionary, which is not subject to any proportional reduction even if a library is evaluated inefficient, a zero weight is usually assigned to it.

However, in some instances, DEA assigns a negative weight to a nondiscretionary variable because of the computations involving these variables. However, the weight itself is the absolute value of the calculated value. As a result, a library can look efficient with negative weights assigned to one or more nondiscretionary variable(s). When this almost invisible room for weight adjustment is taken away with the variable(s), the total students variable in our case, the library's inefficiency becomes evident.

Table 30 shows the weights assigned to the total students variable for those libraries that lost more than a score of .30 when the variable is removed in 1996. What is troubling is that the number of total students hardly changed from 1995 to 1996 for the three universities. Yet, DEA assigned completely different (negative) weights to the data in 1996.

To sum up, among input variables, the effects of dropping a variable is quite even across the variables with some isolated idiosyncrasies. There was no dominant variable that caused big changes in the mean efficiency scores. More often

Table 31. Effects of Dropping a Set of Variables
on the Efficiency Scores: 1995, Public Group

Changes in the Efficiency Scores	Interlibrary Lending and Library Instruction	Total Students and Faculty	Monographs and Current Serials	Combined
Distribution				
No Change	23	57	21	18
0.01-0.05	40	6	29	27
0.06-0.10	2	1	7	9
0.11-0.15	0	1	3	5
0.16-0.20	0	0	3	2
0.21-0.25	0	0	2	4
0.26-0.30	0	0	0	0
> 0.30	0	0	0	0
Total	65	65	65	65
Mean Efficiency Score	0.83	0.83	0.81	0.80
Average Change	0.01	0.00	0.04	0.05
Highest Change	0.11	0.12	0.25	0.25
Down Status	0	1	3	4
Up Status	0	0	1	1

Note: The mean efficiency score for the base model is .83.

with input variables than with output variables, big changes in the efficiency scores of individual libraries are accompanied by fluctuations in the weight assignment rather than changes in the observed data.

The Effects of Dropping Multiple Variables

Now that we know the relative impact of each variable on the efficiency scores when it is removed from the base model, we eliminate a set of variables to observe their combined effects. Among output variables, we keep reference (REFTRANS) and circulation transactions (TOTCIRC) variables because their impacts on the efficiency scores seem quite obvious. We also keep the interlibrary borrowing variable (ILBTOT) because among the variables left, it is most closely identified with user demand and user satisfaction. Among the user variables, we only keep the graduate students variable (GRADSTU) because it seemed to have the biggest impact. Also, graduate students often represent the most active group of users at academic research libraries.

Finally, we explore models without monographs purchased (MONO) and current serials (CURRSER) from the collection-related variables. The current serials variable does not seem to have its counterpart in output variables representing the

Table 32.   Effects of Dropping a Set of Variables
on the Efficiency Scores: 1995, Private Group

Changes in the Efficiency Scores	Interlibrary Lending and Library Instruction	Total Students and Faculty	Monographs and Current Serials	Combined
Distribution				
No Change	19	17	19	11
0.01-0.05	9	6	2	4
0.06-0.10	1	3	7	6
0.11-0.15	0	2	0	1
0.16-0.20	0	0	1	3
0.21-0.25	0	1	1	1
0.26-0.30	0	0	0	2
> 0.30	1	1	0	2
Total	30	30	30	30
Mean Efficiency Score	0.89	0.87	0.91	0.83
Average Change	0.02	0.04	0.04	0.10
Highest Change	0.52	0.34	0.24	0.52
Down Status	1	7	0	8
Up Status	0	0	3	2

Note: The mean efficiency score for the base model is .91.

level of their use. For the monographs variable, there seems to be some overlap with the net volumes added (VOLSADN). Therefore, we now have 3 output variables and 6 input variables from the initial total of 15 variables. Overall, the selection is somewhat biased to the results of the public group.

Tables 31–34 show the results when each set of variables is removed and when all six variables disappear from the base model. Table 31, for the public group in 1995, shows that taking out the two user variables has quite a small impact on the overall efficiency scores. The biggest change comes when we remove two collection variables. When all six variables are eliminated, the effect is even smaller than taking out the reference or circulation transactions. At the same time, the changes in the efficiency status are kept to a minimum. Therefore, if our goal is to cut down the number of variables while maintaining the efficiency scores at a similar level, the 9 variables included in the combined run might represent one ideal set.

For the private group, as shown in Table 32, there are more pronounced impacts compared to the results from the public group. When we dropped one variable at a time, there was not much difference in the results of two groups. But now when multiple variables are removed, we observe bigger changes in the efficiency scores in the private group than in the public counterpart.

Table 33. Effects of Dropping a Set of Variables
on the Efficiency Scores: 1996, Public Group

Changes in the Efficiency Scores	Interlibrary Loan and Library Instruction	Total Students and Faculty	Monographs and Current Serials	Combined
Distribution				
No Change	23	56	22	19
0.01-0.05	41	7	28	26
0.06-0.10	1	0	9	13
0.11-0.15	0	0	2	1
0.16-0.20	0	0	2	2
0.21-0.25	0	2	2	4
0.26-0.30	0	0	0	0
> 0.30	0	0	0	0
Total	65	65	65	65
Mean Efficiency Score	0.83	0.83	0.81	0.80
Average Change	0.01	0.01	0.04	0.05
Highest Change	0.10	0.25	0.21	0.25
Down Status	0	2	3	5
Up Status	1	0	1	1

Note: The mean efficiency score for the base model is .84.

When all six variables are taken out of the base model, a net of six libraries are eliminated from the existing efficient frontier. In the base model, there were 11 libraries that were evaluated inefficient. With a 9-variable set, there are 17 libraries of such status and the mean efficiency score is dropped to .83 from .91.

While we have achieved better discrimination among libraries using a smaller set of variables, we should be concerned about the implications of doing this. In the real world, the libraries that lose their efficient status will have good reasons to argue that the variables should not be removed.

Analyses with the 1996 data give results no different from those of 1995. The magnitude of change is about three times larger in the private group. This time, 12 libraries in the privately funded institutions are removed from the envelopment surface (efficient frontier) leaving only 7 libraries (out of 30) in the 100 percent efficient group.

The results thus far indicate that the same variables have a different impact on the efficiency scores depending on the comparison group, in our case public and private groups. Even within the same comparison group, the efficiency scores and the membership in the efficient frontier are significantly affected by how the weights are assigned to the data. The mean efficiency score and the size of the

Table 34.   Effects of Dropping a Set of Variables
on the Efficiency Scores: 1996, Private Group

Changes in the Efficiency Scores	Interlibrary Loan and Library Instruction	Total Students and Faculty	Monographs and Current Serials	Combined
Distribution				
No Change	17	9	19	6
0.01-0.05	11	7	6	6
0.06-0.10	1	2	2	5
0.11-0.15	0	1	1	0
0.16-0.20	0	2	1	3
0.21-0.25	1	2	1	2
0.26-0.30	0	2	0	4
> 0.30	0	5	0	5
Total	30	30	30	31
Mean Efficiency Score	0.88	0.76	0.90	0.75
Average Change	0.02	0.13	0.03	0.15
Highest Change	0.26	0.60	0.21	0.55
Down Status	1	12	0	12
Up Status	0	0	3	0

Note: The mean efficiency score for the base model is .89.

efficient frontier obtained from the minimum set of 9 variables give us a fair degree of discrimination.

Effects of Adding Dummy Variable(s)

There is some literature exploring effects of adding random input(s) or output(s) to a DEA analysis. Using the data from Charnes et al. (1981), Sexton et al. (1986) added one additional random input (from the interval of 1 to 99) to an existing model consisting of 3 outputs and 5 inputs. Unfortunately, they do not report either the average efficiency change or the range. But from a partial output, we can tell that not many DMUs were affected by the inclusion of a random input variable. One thing they report is that none of the DMUs lost their efficient status. This is consistent with what we have observed thus far: if we add more variables, we see more efficient units.

We test two types of noise in the data: one in the form of additional random input(s) and/or output(s) and the other in the form of random noise in the data themselves. If the results of these tests indicate that there is some level of change but not enough to alter the scores significantly, then we can say that our DEA model is robust to the inclusion of random noise.

Table 35.   Effects of Dummy Variable(s): 1995, Public Group

Changes in the Efficiency Scores	One Output	One Input	Two Outputs	Two Inputs	One Input, One Output (1)	One Input, One Output (2)
Distribution						
No Change	54	24	33	22	34	23
0.01-0.05	8	18	19	16	16	15
0.06-0.10	1	7	4	4	4	6
0.11-0.15	0	4	1	4	2	3
0.16-0.20	1	4	4	2	1	7
0.21-0.25	1	2	2	5	4	3
0.26-0.30	0	2	1	5	1	3
> 0.30	0	4	1	7	3	5
Total	65	65	65	65	65	65
Mean Efficiency Score	0.84	0.90	0.88	0.94	0.89	0.93
Average Change	0.01	0.07	0.04	0.10	0.06	0.09
Highest Change	0.23	0.42	0.48	0.45	0.47	0.48
Down Status	0	0	0	0	0	0
Up Status	1	10	8	19	11	17

Note: The mean efficiency score for the base model is .83.

Using Microsoft Excel's random number generator function,[19] we produced two sets of random variables (NOISE1, NOISE2) for 1995 and 1996. The possible range of values is from 0 to 100. We created 6 additional model specifications using two sets of random variables as shown in Table 35. Note that the same set of numbers was entered first as output and later as input to observe if there is any difference. We did not impose any constraints on the weights of the dummy variables.

Table 35 shows that a dummy variable produces quite different impacts depending on how it is treated, either as an input or output variable. When a noise variable (NOISE1) is treated as an output, more than 80 percent (54 out of 65) of the libraries kept their original efficiency score. The mean efficiency score improved only a little bit, by .01 point. It also shows that there was only one library which was moved from the inefficient group to the (efficient) frontier group.

But things change quite dramatically when the same variable entered the model as an input variable. Nearly two-thirds of the libraries (41 out of 65) are assigned different scores, 10 of them now moved to the efficient frontier. The mean efficiency score improved substantially, from .83 to .90. We observe a similar effect when two dummy variables are added to our base model. Overall, we can conclude that addition of variable(s) will most likely improve efficiency scores and the size of the efficient frontier. None of the libraries were removed from the envelopment surface.

Table 36. Effects of Dummy Variable(s): 1995, Private Group

Changes in the Efficiency Scores	One Output	One Input	Two Outputs	Two Inputs	One Input, One Output (1)	One Input, One Output (2)
Distribution						
No Change	22	24	19	21	21	22
0.01-0.05	2	4	3	4	3	2
0.06-0.10	3	2	3	4	3	2
0.11-0.15	0	0	0	0	0	3
0.16-0.20	2	0	2	1	2	0
0.21-0.25	0	0	0	0	0	0
0.26-0.30	1	0	1	0	1	1
> 0.30	0	0	2	0	0	2
Total	30	30	30	30	30	30
Mean Efficiency Score	0.94	0.92	0.96	0.93	0.94	0.95
Average Change	0.03	0.01	0.06	0.02	0.03	0.05
Highest Change	0.27	0.08	0.43	0.19	0.27	0.43
Down Status	0	0	0	0	0	0
Up Status	6	0	8	2	6	4

Note: The mean efficiency score for the base model is .91.

Table 37. Effects of Dummy Variable(s): 1996, Public Group

Changes in the Efficiency Scores	One Output	One Input	Two Outputs	Two Inputs	One Input, One Output (1)	One Input, One Output (2)
Distribution						
No Change	45	32	38	26	29	28
0.01-0.05	10	21	12	19	15	17
0.06-0.10	7	2	9	6	7	6
0.11-0.15	1	0	0	1	4	0
0.16-0.20	1	2	1	4	1	4
0.21-0.25	0	3	2	3	1	2
0.26-0.30	0	2	2	2	3	4
> 0.30	1	3	1	4	5	4
Total	65	65	65	65	65	65
Mean Efficiency Score	0.86	0.89	0.88	0.91	0.91	0.91
Average Change	0.02	0.05	0.04	0.07	0.07	0.07
Highest Change	0.33	0.47	0.36	0.47	0.45	0.47
Down Status	0	0	0	0	0	0
Up Status	1	12	9	16	12	18

Note: The mean efficiency score for the base model is .84.

Table 38. Effects of Dummy Variable(s): 1996, Private Group

Changes in the Efficiency Scores	One Output	One Input	Two Outputs	Two Inputs	One Input, One Output (1)	One Input, One Output (2)
Distribution						
No Change	19	25	19	19	18	23
0.01-0.05	7	1	4	3	4	2
0.06-0.10	2	2	3	4	3	2
0.11-0.15	0	0	0	0	1	0
0.16-0.20	2	0	2	2	3	0
0.21-0.25	0	2	0	1	0	1
0.26-0.30	0	0	0	0	0	0
> 0.30	0	0	2	1	1	2
Total	30	30	30	30	30	30
Mean Efficiency Score	0.92	0.92	0.95	0.95	0.95	0.94
Average Change	0.02	0.02	0.05	0.05	0.06	0.05
Highest Change	0.20	0.23	0.55	0.65	0.65	0.55
Down Status	0	0	0	0	0	0
Up Status	3	1	4	6	7	2

Note: The mean efficiency score for the base model is .89.

In the private group, as shown in Table 36, an output dummy variable has more impact on the efficiency score than does the input dummy variable. When the dummy variable was treated as an input, none of the libraries switched their efficiency status. However, when it is treated as an output, six libraries are now added to the efficient frontier. The results of the 1996 data, shown in Tables 37 and 38, repeat the same pattern displayed in the 1995 data.

What can we tell from the results? We can compare the results of our base model plus a maximum of two dummy variables in any combination with those of our first model without any constraints. We can say that the model with dummy variables still gives us a better resolution of inefficiency in terms of the mean efficiency scores and the proportion of inefficient libraries. While it is less likely that a DEA model has an input variable which is independent of the level of outputs or vice versa, the results reported here tell us that the addition of variable(s) can result in significant changes in the efficiency scores of libraries and the efficiency status of the libraries included in the analysis.

Effects of Random Noise in the Data

In addition to the analysis of the effects of adding random dummy variables to the base model, we added some noise in the data and observed the resulting changes in the efficiency scores and the efficiency status. We conducted four

Table 39.   Effects of Random Noise in the Data: Public Group

Changes in the Efficiency Scores	1995				1996			
	Run 1	Run 2	Run 3	Run 4	Run 1	Run 2	Run 3	Run 4
Distribution								
No Change	17	20	19	21	23	21	21	21
0.01-0.05	43	39	43	38	37	37	37	36
0.06-0.10	3	4	2	5	4	3	4	5
0.11-0.15	0	2	0	0	1	0	0	0
0.16-0.20	1	0	0	0	0	2	1	1
0.21-0.25	1	0	0	0	0	2	0	2
0.26-0.30	0	0	1	1	0	0	1	0
> 0.30	0	0	0	0	0	0	1	0
Total	65	65	65	65	65	65	65	65
Mean Efficiency Score	0.83	0.84	0.84	0.85	0.85	0.84	0.81	0.84
Average Change	0.02	0.02	0.02	0.02	0.02	0.03	0.03	0.02
Highest Change	0.25	0.13	0.29	0.29	0.15	0.26	0.44	0.23
Down Status	3	1	3	1	1	3	3	3
Up Status	3	3	3	6	6	4	1	4

Note: The mean efficiency score for the base model is .83 in 1995 and .84 in 1996.

Monte Carlo simulations of noise for each year. In each simulation, every bit of data was subject to a random distortion, causing it to vary uniformly according to a normal distribution whose mean is the original value and the standard deviation, 5 percent of its true value.[20]

Table 39 shows the results of the noise analysis for the public group. The mean efficiency score change was kept to a maximum of .03 point. The number of libraries that changed their efficiency status ranged from 4 to 7. The results for the private group, summarized in Table 40, show a slightly larger fluctuation in terms of the mean efficiency scores and also the proportion of libraries that switched their efficiency status.

Considering that the noise was added to every data element, the changes in the mean efficiency score indicate that the analysis is quite robust to some level of data error. But it does seem to cause sizable impact on the configuration of the efficient frontier. For individual libraries, the combined effects of potential data error can cause significant changes in the efficiency scores as evidenced by several extreme cases where the score changes by as much as .65.

Corroboration of DEA Efficiency Scores

While DEA produces a single measure of performance reducing a large amount of data, it is very important that the DEA efficiency results be validated or corroborated by available, more traditional measures such as cost efficiency ratios. For

Table 40. Effects of Random Noise in the Data: Private Group

Changes in the Efficiency Scores	1995				1996			
	Run 1	Run 2	Run 3	Run 4	Run 1	Run 2	Run 3	Run 4
Distribution								
No Change	17	18	16	19	17	14	16	14
0.01-0.05	8	7	8	10	9	12	6	13
0.06-0.10	3	4	3	1	2	2	4	0
0.11-0.15	0	1	1	0	0	0	1	0
0.16-0.20	1	0	0	0	1	0	0	1
0.21-0.25	0	0	0	0	0	2	2	2
0.26-0.30	0	0	0	0	0	0	1	0
> 0.30	1	0	2	0	1	0	0	0
Total	30	30	30	30	30	30	30	30
Mean Efficiency Score	0.90	0.91	0.87	0.90	0.93	0.88	0.87	0.87
Average Change	0.04	0.02	0.04	0.01	0.04	0.03	0.05	0.03
Highest Change	0.49	0.12	0.49	0.06	0.65	0.25	0.28	0.26
Down Status	2	1	3	0	1	4	2	4
Up Status	1	3	1	1	4	1	1	0

Note: The mean efficiency score for the base model is .91 in 1995 and .89 in 1996.

example, Byrnes and Valdmanis (1994), in their study measuring efficiencies of 123 community hospitals in California, found out that the hospitals evaluated as efficient in their DEA analysis have lower average cost (measured by cost per discharge) and higher average products (measured by discharge per beds).

This validation process is important for the users of DEA results, library directors in our case, who must be able to make relevant logical connections of this new measure to what they already know. However, this does not mean that DEA measures will only validate traditional measures. Both types of measures simply give us different kinds of information. Even when the DEA measures and other performance measures show conflicting results, that should not result in the rejection of either one of the measures.

We attempt to characterize DEA-efficient libraries using the following set of measures. First, we ask which variables included in the DEA analysis are better at predicting the efficiency scores. Second, we use cost figures and other ratios computed from the data to see if these measures can predict the DEA efficiency scores. Third, we use one library characteristic, the existence of a law and/or medical library, to see if it can explain the differences in the efficiency scores.

We use linear regression to explore connections between the DEA efficiency scores and the measures of library performance or the usual variables included in the study. We want to find out whether DEA provides some new information

Table 41. Correlation Among Variables Included in the DEA Analysis

CORR.	VOLS ADN	MONO	CURR SER	PRF STF	NPRF STF	STUD AST	TOT STU	GRAD STU	FAC	ILL TOT	ILB TOT	LIB INST	REF TRANS	TOT CIRC
VOLS	0.90***	0.47***	0.90***	0.88***	0.78***	0.78***	0.62***	0.81***	0.54***	0.49***	0.28*	0.54***	0.44***	0.76***
VOLS ADN	—	0.50***	0.83***	0.81***	0.75***	0.65***	0.56***	0.72***	0.50***	0.53***	0.23*	0.52***	0.41***	0.77***
MONO	—	—	0.52***	0.40***	0.33*	0.30*	0.24*	0.39***	0.20	0.14	0.27*	0.28*	0.30*	0.55***
CURR SER	—	—	—	0.78***	0.73***	0.74***	0.50***	0.74***	0.46***	0.47***	0.23*	0.44***	0.37***	0.69***
PRF STF	—	—	—	—	0.82***	0.79***	0.66***	0.80***	0.67***	0.48***	0.34**	0.68***	0.51***	0.78***
NPRF STF	—	—	—	—	—	0.59***	0.77***	0.77***	0.70***	0.39***	0.28*	0.63***	0.43***	0.79***
STUD AST	—	—	—	—	—	—	0.52***	0.66***	0.47***	0.54***	0.23*	0.52***	0.44***	0.55***
TOT STU	—	—	—	—	—	—	—	0.69***	0.78***	0.26*	0.23*	0.68***	0.46***	0.64***
GRAD STU	—	—	—	—	—	—	—	—	0.69***	0.48***	0.30**	0.53***	0.52***	0.72***
FAC	—	—	—	—	—	—	—	—	—	0.31**	0.21*	0.63***	0.38***	0.60***
ILL TOT	—	—	—	—	—	—	—	—	—	—	0.27*	0.26*	0.25*	0.38***
ILB TOT	—	—	—	—	—	—	—	—	—	—	—	0.28*	0.19	0.26*
LIB INST	—	—	—	—	—	—	—	—	—	—	—	—	0.48***	0.57***
REF	—	—	—	—	—	—	—	—	—	—	—	—	—	0.38***
TRANS	—	—	—	—	—	—	—	—	—	—	—	—	—	—

Notes: *p < .05; **p < .01; ***p < .001.

Table 42. Regressions Predicting the Efficiency
Scores from Data Variables: No Constraint

	Public				Private			
	95		96		95		96	
Predictor	β	t	β	t	β	t	β	t
VOLS	0.114	0.30	0.121	0.31	1.338	1.67	1.548	2.34[*]
VOLSADN	−0.372	−1.42	−0.452	−1.92	−0.539	−1.33	−0.672	−2.07
MONO	−0.645	−4.53[***]	−0.443	−3.31[**]	−0.559	−2.57[*]	−0.666	−3.35[**]
CURRSER	0.378	1.40	−0.027	−0.10	1.520	2.09	0.709	1.21
PRFSTF	−0.433	−1.40	−0.508	−1.71	0.002	0.00	−0.729	−1.42
NPRFSTF	−0.363	−1.50[*]	0.039	0.16	−2.097	−2.77[*]	−0.833	−1.37
STUDAST	−0.174	−0.87	0.090	0.47	−0.888	−2.36[*]	−0.793	−2.43[*]
TOTSTU	−0.045	−0.22	−0.289	−1.37	−0.174	−0.58	−0.222	−0.74
GRADSTU	−0.013	−0.06	0.385	1.44	−0.013	−0.04	0.065	0.23
FAC	−0.486	−2.61[*]	−0.621	−2.91[**]	−0.248	−1.04	−0.272	−1.17
ILLTOT	0.027	0.20	0.092	0.73	0.042	0.17	−0.126	−0.68
ILBTOT	0.291	2.59[*]	0.111	0.99	0.260	0.97	0.335	1.63
PRESPTCP	0.398	2.50[*]	0.462	2.66[*]	0.228	0.81	0.160	0.62
REFTRANS	0.350	2.78[**]	0.125	0.88	0.297	1.29	0.441	1.77
TOTCIRC	0.955	4.62[***]	0.917	4.60[***]	0.434	1.39	0.611	2.22[*]

Notes: Public 1995: Total $R^2 = .525$, $F(15,49) = 3.614$, $p < 0.001$.
Public 1996: Total $R^2 = .513$, $F(15,49) = 3.436$, $p < 0.01$.
Private 1995: Total $R^2 = .756$, $F(15,14) = 2.889$, $p < 0.05$.
Private 1996: Total $R^2 = .827$, $F(15,14) = 4.458$, $p < 0.01$.
[*]$p < .05$; [**]$p < .01$; [***]$p < .001$.

about the libraries, or whether the existing measures are just as effective as this complex technique in identifying inefficiencies.

Regressions Using Variables Included in the Analysis

Before comparing the DEA results with other library measures, we ran regression analyses to determine whether the DEA efficiency scores can be predicted from the variables included in the analysis. This may seem obvious because the efficiency scores are calculated from these variables. What we have to find out is if the variables that have the most impact on the efficiency scores are the ones that library managers regard as most important.

Table 41 shows the correlation among variables included in our DEA analysis. It shows that many variables are highly correlated with each other; thus, there is a potential problem of multicollinearity. Furthermore, the efficiency score is not normally distributed due to the fact that a fair number of libraries received the highest score of 1.

Among output variables, the total circulation variable is very highly correlated with most of the other variables regardless of variable type. The least correlated

Table 43. Regressions Predicting the Efficiency
Scores from Data Variables: Twofold Range

Predictor	Public				Private			
	95		96		95		96	
	β	t	β	t	β	t	β	t
VOLS	0.326	1.25	0.312	1.05	−0.164	−0.23	−0.359	−0.45
VOLSADN	−0.869	−4.82***	−0.528	−2.95**	−0.716	−1.96	−0.047	−0.12
MONO	−0.164	−1.67	−0.106	−1.04	−0.218	−1.12	0.030	0.12
CURRSER	−0.133	−0.72	−0.235	−1.14	1.102	1.69	−0.098	−0.14
PRFSTF	−0.725	−3.40**	−0.904	−4.00***	0.828	1.63	0.011	0.02
NPRFSTF	−0.108	−0.65	−0.005	−0.03	−0.998	−1.47	−0.208	−0.28
STUDAST	−0.060	−0.43	0.029	0.19	−0.976	−2.88*	−0.474	−1.19
TOTSTU	−0.002	−0.02	−0.084	−0.52	0.097	0.36	0.122	0.33
GRADSTU	−0.247	−1.65	−0.214	−1.05	−0.432	−1.46	−0.288	−0.82
FAC	−0.145	−1.13	−0.164	−1.01	−0.358	−1.67	−0.149	−0.53
ILLTOT	0.169	1.83	0.058	0.61	−0.201	−0.90	0.019	0.08
ILBTOT	0.134	1.73	0.064	0.75	0.457	1.90	0.083	0.33
PRESPTCP	0.188	1.72	0.168	1.28	−0.291	−1.16	−0.498	−1.57
REFTRANS	0.528	6.11***	0.459	4.27***	0.523	2.52*	0.460	1.51
TOTCIRC	0.979	6.88***	1.053	6.95***	0.908	3.23**	1.266	3.77**

Notes: Public 1995: Total R^2 = .775, $F(15,49)$ = 11.274, p < 0.001.
Public 1996: Total R^2 = .718, $F(15,49)$ = 8.318, p < 0.001.
Private 1995: Total R^2 = .803, $F(15,14)$ = 3.807, p < 0.01.
Private 1996: Total R^2 = .743, $F(15,14)$ = 2.698, p < 0.05.
*p < .05; **p < .01; ***p < .001.

variable is the interlibrary borrowing variable which depends more on the resources of other libraries. Table 42 shows the regression results when there were no constraints at all. It shows, for example for the public group in 1995, that more than 50 percent of the variation in the efficiency scores is accounted for by the predicting model. The beta coefficients generally agree with the model in that output measures have positive weights and most input measures have negative weights.[21]

Among the input variables, the monographs purchased (MONO), the full-time support staff (NPRFSTF), and the faculty (FAC) variables are the statistically significant predictors. Among the output variables, with the exception of the interlibrary lending variable, all variables turned out to be statistically significant predictors. In the private group, while the proportion of variance accounted for by the models is high, the number of statistically significant predictors decreased, especially among the output variables.

If we remember that the majority of the libraries were evaluated efficient without imposing any constraints, we should not assign too much meaning to the regression results reported here. Furthermore, the results may have been influenced by the fact that we have a large number of highly correlated predictors.

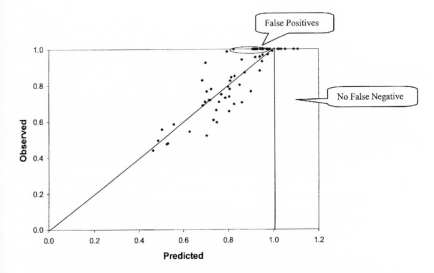

Figure 5. Scatter Plot of the Predicted Efficiency Scores
Derived from the Regression Equations and the Observed
DEA Efficiency Scores Using 1995 Data.

Table 43 shows the results of the regression predicting the efficiency scores when the most strict (twofold range) constraints were imposed. We observe that in all four cases, the R^2 values are quite high, ranging from 72 percent to 80 percent. However, we should read the results with caution because the data seem to have violated several assumptions regarding the test.

The results for the public group seem to yield a noticeable pattern in terms of the direction and the magnitude of the beta coefficients, and of the statistically significant predictors. In both 1995 and 1996, the net volumes added (VOL-SADN), the number of professional staff (PRFSTF), the reference transaction (REFTRANS), and the total circulation (TOTCIRC) variables were all found to be statistically significant predictors.

Using the coefficients calculated in the regression equations, for each library we can plug in the data to get the scores predicted by the regression model. We can plot the observed DEA efficiency scores against the predicted scores from the regression equations as shown in Figure 5. It shows the scatter plot for the public group using 1995 data.

We notice that the data points are placed closely along the line. This tells the degree of agreement between the observed and predicted scores. Imagining that the observed inefficiency is a "disease," two kinds of diagnostic (prediction) errors can occur: false positive and false negative.

Table 44. Regression Predicting the Efficiency
Scores with Minimum Set of Variables: Public Group

	1995		1996	
Predictors	β	t	β	t
VOLSADN	−.805	−5.890***	−.476	−3.281**
PRFSTF	−.669	−4.544***	−.905	−6.160***
REFTRAN S	.493	5.736***	.434	4.801***
TOTCIRC	.787	6.151***	.847	6.772***

Notes: 1995: Total $R^2 = .671$, $F(4,60) = 30.563$***; 1996: Total $R^2 = .627$,
$F(4,60) = 25.215$***; **$p < .01$; ***$p < .001$.

Table 45. Regression Predicting the Efficiency Scores
with Minimum Set of Variables: Private Group

Predictors	β	t	β	t
STUDAST	−.792	−4.272***	−.922	−4.792***
REFTRANS	.181	1.111 n.s.	.388	2.412*
TOTCIRC	.576	3.377**	.746	4.433***

Notes: 1995: Total $R^2 = .442$, $F(3,26) = 6.875$**; 1996: Total $R^2 = .514$,
$F(3,26) = 9.182$***, n.s. = not significant; *$p < .05$; **$p < .01$; ***$p < .001$.

False positive occurs when the regression predicts inefficiency while the DEA detects no inefficiency. The figure shows a fair number of false positive cases. False negative occurs when the regression predicts efficiency while the DEA results show inefficiency. There are no false negatives in the figure. We can tell that using regression models to predict the efficiency score can be quite elusive, due to the inherent problems associated with the model itself and also due to the risk of misjudgment of efficiency status.

We ran two additional regression analyses for the public group with the statistically significant predictors only. The results are summarized in Table 44. Compared with the regression model having all 15 predictors, this reduced set model retains a significant portion of the R^2 value. All four variables represent the most important aspects of the inputs and outputs included in the analysis. This seems to provide a partial validation of the DEA results in the sense that a large portion of the efficiency scores can be explained by those variables that bear more significance to library managers.

For the private group, it would be difficult to form a similar minimum set of predictors (see Table 45). We took three predictors that were statistically significant in 1995 results, and ran two additional regressions. While the model is statistically significant in both years, it lost a substantial portion of the R^2 value compared to the model using all 15 variables. The inclusion of the full-time equivalence of student assistants variable in the model makes the model less appealing. Close exam-

Table 46. Regression Predicting the
Efficiency Scores with a Subset of Variables

	Public		Private	
Model	R^2	F	R^2	F
All Inputs	.373	3.207[**]	.490	1.826 n.s
Collection	.336	7.587[***]	.224	1.808 n.s.
Staff	.212	5.457[**]	.198	2.141 n.s.
User	.156	3.752[*]	.323	4.128[*]
All Outputs	.122	1.645 n.s.	.150	.846 n.s.

Notes: The results are for the 1995 data. n.s. = not significant. [*]$p < .05$; [**]$p < .01$; [***]$p < .001$.

ination of the residual plots indicate that the assumption of linearity was largely compromised.

We ran a further regression analysis to find out if the efficiency scores can be predicted using only a subset of the variables. As Table 46 shows, that was not the case. The R^2 measure deteriorates substantially as we reduce the whole set of variables to subsets such as input variables, output variables, collection variables, user variables, or staff variables.

Predicting DEA Scores Using Cost and Ratio Figures

We would like to compare the DEA efficiency scores with some available performance measures. Unfortunately, such measures are really difficult to get. This may be due to the fact that we are not evaluating a particular service function. But even if we were, there simply is not a measure that we can use across the sample included in the study. One exception to this is the recent study of the cost of interlibrary transactions in 113 university and college libraries by Jackson (1998). However, the published report has only the aggregate numbers. Acquisition of the data for the individual libraries would require a written consent from the libraries that participated in the study. Therefore, what follows should not be regarded as something validating the DEA scores but rather as attempts to characterize the efficient libraries using available measures.

We ran a series of regressions using the following sets of predictors:

1. Library Expenses,
2. Measures of User Activities, and
3. Measures of Library Resource Utilization.

Library Expenses. We have not included library expenses in the DEA analysis for the following reasons. First, in theory, all the input can be collapsed into one variable—library budget—of which the bulk is spent on staff salary. If we used the library budget as the input, we are ignoring the regional, institutional differ-

Table 47. Summary Statistics of Library Expenses (1995)

	Public		Private	
Predictors	Mean	SD	Mean	SD
Library Budget	$15,041,921	$6,294,961	$18,999,941	$12,200,242
Per Student Expense	$695	$200	$1,763	$1,054
Per Faculty Expense	$10,907	$3,706	$16,508	$8,333

Note: The summary statistics are for the 1995 data.

Table 48. Regression Using the Library Expenses (1995)

	Public		Private	
Predictors	β	T	β	t
Library Budget	−.40	−2.96**	−.47	−2.03 n.s.
Per Student Expense	−.18	−1.05 n.s.	−.19	.41 n.s.
Per Faculty Expense	.05	.29 n.s.	.51	1.81 n.s.

Notes: Public: Total R^2 = .24, $F(3,61)$ = 6.57**; Private: Total R^2 = .22, $F(3,26)$ = 2.485 n.s.; n.s. = not significant; **$p < .01$.

ences due to the differences in the cost of living and compensation practices. Second, using library budget does not reveal potential inefficiencies in the inputs which can be valuable information for management purposes.

We have three predictors in the model: library budget (total expenditure) per student and per faculty expenditure. Table 47 shows the summary statistics for the predictors. Overall, libraries at privately funded universities are spending more money per user than their counterparts at publicly funded universities. What we want to know is whether the DEA scores favored the small spenders, or libraries with smaller budget size or those spending less per library user.

The regression results summarized in Table 48 show that while the models were statistically significant, the portion of variance explained by the model (R^2) is quite low. In the public group, library budget was the significant predictor. In the private group, there was no significant predictor. Therefore, we can say that for the public group, there is partial evidence that the smaller the budget is, the higher the efficiency score will be.

Measures of Per User Activities.   We calculated four output ratios per student from the ARL statistics.[22] We provide summary statistics for the ratios in Table 49. The table shows that while the average ratios at the private group is larger, there is a larger variability in the private group than in their peers in the public group. What we want to find out is if there is any association between these output ratios and the DEA efficiency scores. Unfortunately, the regression results in Table 50 show that the model is not statistically significant.

Table 49. Summary Statistics of the Measures of Per User Activities (1995)

	Public		Private	
Predictors	Mean	SD	Mean	SD
Interlibrary Borrowing	1.78	1.40	2.46	1.89
Library Instruction	.54	.28	.53	.37
Reference Transaction	10.08	9.99	10.93	7.51
Circulation Transaction	32.63	15.18	50.29	38.01

Note: The summary statistics are for the 1995 data and per student (TOTSTU).

Table 50. Regression Using the Measures of Per User Activities (1995)

	Public		Private	
Predictors	β	T	β	t
Interlibrary Borrowing	−.14	−1.04 n.s.	.02	.10 n.s.
Library Instruction	−.03	−.21 n.s	−.03	−.14 n.s.
Reference Transaction	.24	1.86 n.s	.18	.93 n.s.
Circulation Transaction	−.09	−.67 n.s	.32	1.60 n.s.

Notes: Public: Total $R^2 = .08$, $F_{(4,60)} = 1.23$ n.s.; Private: Total $R^2 = .13$, $F_{(4,25)} = .92$ n.s.; n.s. = not significant.

Table 51. Summary Statistics of the Measures of Resource Utilization (1995)

	Public		Private	
Predictors	Mean	SD	Mean	SD
Library Instruction Participants[a]	153.30	74.75	78.17	76.46
Reference Transactions[a]	2,762.96	2,117.63	1,383.20	818.23
Circulation to Total Volume	.23	.09	.15	.07

Notes: The summary statistics are for the 1995 data.
[a] Per professional staff.

Resource Utilization. Finally, we derived three measures of library resource utilization as summarized in Table 51. The first two measures have to do with the production of outputs directly related with professional staff. Because individual libraries will have their own way of providing services, the measures are only an approximation of productivity of professional staff. The third measure, total circulated items[23] out of total volumes held, provides us some indication of what portion of the collection is being used actively. The table also clearly shows why the two groups have to be analyzed separately.

The regression results in Table 52 show that the models are statistically significant with relatively low R^2 values. In the public group, the number of reference transactions per professional staff was a significant predictor. In the private group, it was total circulated items over total volumes held.

Table 52.   Regression Using the Measures of Resource Utilization (1995)

	Public		Private	
Predictors	β	T	β	T
Library Instruction Participants [a]	.09	.71 n.s.	−.38	−1.84 n.s.
Reference Transactions [a]	.35	2.93**	.21	1.09 n.s.
Circulation to Total Volume	.22	1.81 n.s	.55	2.95**

Notes: [a]Per professional staff.
Public: Total R^2 = .18, $F(3,61)$ = 4.44**; Private: Total R^2 = .27, $F(3,26)$ = 3.25*; n.s. = not significant, *$p < .05$, **$p < .01$.

Table 53.   Summary Statistics of 4 Library Types

Category (Have law and/ or medical library?)	Public (n = 65)			Private (n = 30)		
	Count	Mean	SD	Count	Mean	SD
Neither	18	.87	.13	5	1.00	.00
Only Law	15	.83	.21	3	.88	.07
Only Medical	6	.91	.16	3	1.00	.00
Both	26	.79	.18	19	.87	.19

Note: The reported statistics the 1995 data.

Explaining DEA Scores Using Library Characteristics

The ARL statistics provide information about the presence of a law and/or medical library in the reporting university library. It is believed that having either of these special libraries may mean a bigger burden on the library in terms of resource requirements such as collection and personnel. Table 53 shows the number of libraries in four possible categories along with the mean efficiency scores for each group.

We can see that the proportion of libraries with both law and medical libraries is higher in the private group (19 out of 30) than it is in the public group (26 out of 65). In both groups, libraries with only a medical library or without both are the ones with the highest mean efficiencies. Libraries with both law and medical libraries represent the lowest mean efficiency. What is surprising is that research libraries having a medical library got the same or higher mean efficiency score than the libraries with neither of them.

Table 54 shows the results of the one-way ANOVA on the DEA efficiency scores by four types of libraries. Apparently the existence of a special library does not influence the DEA efficiency scores. Unequal sample size bars any further conclusions.

Table 54. ANOVA Summary Table for Mean Differences by Library Type

	Public				Private			
Source	df	SS	MS	F	df	SS	MS	F
Between Groups	3	.11	.037	1.27 n.s	3	.09	.032	1.28 n.s.
Within Groups	61	1.80	.029		26	.64	.025	
Total	64	1.91			29	.73		

Note: n.s. = not significant.

Characterization of Libraries Using Optimal Weights

DEA determines the efficiency scores by the judicious assignment of weights. We now consider a possibility of using weights to characterize the libraries included in the analysis. To do that we need to answer two crucial questions.

1. Do weights mean something?
2. Are they consistent enough to be used as tools of describing the libraries?

We attempt to answer above questions in the following sections.

Do Weights Make Sense?

While the weights can be regarded simply as mathematical conduits for calculating the efficiency scores, they implicitly represent a relative value system that allows each library to achieve its best efficiency rating. Two kinds of enhancements of the data were performed to regulate the assignment of weights. First, because the weights are inversely proportional to the values of the variables (Ali 1994), we scaled the data into similar ranges to offset this artificial effect. Second, we also imposed a set of constraints on the ratios of the weights, so that the weights can better reflect the reality, the relative cost of providing different services and of procuring resources. We derived the ratios from the published studies of cost of services and from the data itself.

The first thing we noticed about the weights is that, because they are optimized for individual libraries (DMUs) instead of taken from a fixed range of values, we cannot use them as they appear in the calculations. They need some processing to be suitable for further analysis. Table 55 shows the ranges of weights from one of the DEA runs (1995 public group with the most strict set of constraints) and should demonstrate why some form of transformation is needed for further analysis. For every variable, the maximum value is at least several thousand times as much as the minimum value.

For each library, we calculated the relative proportion of the weights assigned to the inputs and to the outputs. This is to say that one library assigned 50 percent

Table 55. The Ranges of Raw Weight Values

Category	Variable	Low	High
Output	Interlibrary Loan	.20	1709.75
	Interlibrary Borrowing	.11	977.00
	Participants in Library Instruction	.02	100.00
	Reference Transactions	.83	5129.25
	Total Circulation Transactions	1.11	6839.00
Input	Total Volumes Held[a]	.00	88.81
	Net Volumes Added	.01	15178.03
	Monographs Purchased	.03	9360.74
	Current Serials	.03	11558.82
	Professional Staff	.06	19844.32
	Nonprofessional Staff	.04	16798.71
	Student Assistants (FTE)	.01	2607.80
	Total Full-time Students[a]	.00	5.28
	Total Graduate Student [a]	.00	1946.20
	Full-time Faculty[a]	.00	295.97

Notes: [a]Nondiscretionary variables. The weights for these variables are normally zero. The real values appear as negative numbers in DEA calculations due to model algebra. The weights were assigned to scaled variable values.

Table 56. Descriptive Statistics of Weights (%): Public 1995

Category	Variable	Mean	SD	Min.	Max.	Skewness	Kurtosis
Output	ILLTOT	10.21	3.21	5.45	15.63	−0.18	−1.19
	ILBTOT	5.75	1.79	3.19	9.22	−0.21	−1.17
	LIBINS	1.32	0.32	0.60	1.88	−0.86	0.33
	REFTRAN S	41.29	10.39	34.53	67.91	1.75	1.79
	TOTCIRC	41.44	9.90	20.73	51.01	−1.04	−0.59
Input	VOLSADN	30.20	33.76	0.00	96.42	0.87	−0.85
	MONO	14.05	8.91	0.64	31.52	0.14	−1.04
	CURRSER	11.71	7.53	0.63	29.86	0.45	−0.52
	PRFSTF	24.83	13.23	1.08	47.91	−0.18	−1.04
	NPRFSTF	16.01	9.36	0.91	36.73	0.17	−0.47
	STUDAST	3.20	1.95	0.27	7.45	0.28	−0.73

Note: The nondiscretionary variables were excluded in the calculations because they are normally assigned a zero weight.

of its total output weights to the reference service while another library assigned only 10 percent of the weights to that particular service. Table 56 shows the descriptive statistics of the computed proportional weights for the 1995 public group.

The table shows, among the outputs, that the reference (REFTRANS) and total circulation (TOTCIRC) variables combined received more than 80 per-

Table 57. Descriptive Statistics of Weights (%): Private 1995

Category	Variable	Mean	SD	Min.	Max.	Skewness	Kurtosis
Output	ILLTOT	7.43	3.26	4.59	15.17	1.13	−0.26
	ILBTOT	4.50	1.93	2.61	9.16	0.81	−0.68
	LIBINS	0.96	0.38	0.54	1.89	0.68	−0.63
	REFTRANS	51.81	12.89	34.53	67.91	−0.16	−1.69
	TOTCIRC	35.30	10.54	21.72	51.01	0.18	−1.47
Input	VOLSADN	15.58	29.14	0.00	91.56	1.86	2.14
	MONO	18.07	9.73	1.17	31.64	0.00	−1.11
	CURRSER	12.04	4.35	1.14	17.00	−1.44	1.31
	PRFSTF	29.28	12.95	3.91	47.85	−0.29	−0.56
	NPRFSTF	20.71	9.62	1.66	40.09	−0.09	0.07
	STUDAST	4.33	2.24	0.57	8.49	0.28	−0.87

Note: The nondiscretionary variables were excluded in the calculations because they are normally assigned a zero weight.

cent of the output weights. On the other hand, the library instruction (LIBINS) variable was almost ignored in the weight assignment because on average it received only 1 percent of the total output weights. As for the two interlibrary transactions, lending service received about the twice as much weight as did its borrowing counterpart. The ranges of the output weights tell us that while there is enough room for variation, the maximum value is no bigger than three times the minimum value.

Among the inputs, the net volumes added (VOLSADN) and the professional staff (PRFSTF) variables combined account for more than 50 percent of the total weights assigned to the inputs. Notice that the standard deviation of the net volumes added (VOLSADN), which includes bound serials, is bigger than the mean. This may be due to the fact that VOLSADN is the only variable that was not constrained by the ratios on the weights. The ranges of the values clearly indicate that input weight assignment is highly variable even when the constraints were imposed.

Table 57 shows the descriptive statistics for the 1995 private group. The statistics exhibit basically the same pattern that we saw in the public group. Again, the reference and circulation variables combined dominated among the output variables. Two staff variables, professional staff (PRFSTF) and nonprofessional staff (NPRFSTF), take up about one-half of the total input weights. The other one-half is more or less evenly split among three collection variables.

To summarize, the results thus far indicate that the weights roughly reflect reality, in terms of the relative costs of services and resources. In particular, output weights may as well be used to characterize individual libraries when the raw weight values are converted into the relative proportions of the total output weights. However, we should also point out that this way of character-

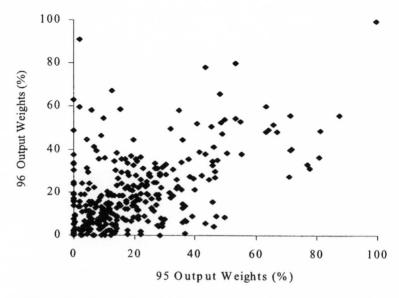

Figure 6.   Scatter Plot of 1995 Output Weights (measured by the percentage of total output weights) by 1996 Output Weights (%) *No Constraints* Were Imposed (public group)

ization is purely based on mathematical optimization. It does not necessarily correspond to the value system held at the libraries. However, at least we can present data derived from this type of analysis to the library administrators for their consideration.

Consistency of Weights Over a Two-year Period

We now turn to the issue of consistency of weights. If the weights fluctuate too much over a period of time, we would not be able to use them to describe the libraries included in the DEA analysis. Furthermore, inconsistency presents a serious threat to the reliability as well as to the validity of a DEA analysis because, in reality, ARL major data elements change rather slowly.

Figures 6 to 8 illustrate that, for the output weights, the presence of the constraints quite effectively regulates the weight assignment over the two-year period. This is also validated in the regression results summarized in Table 58. As we move from the no constraints environment to the generous fourfold range constraints and to the more strict twofold range, both the beta coefficients and the R^2 measure increase. In the twofold range constraints, more than

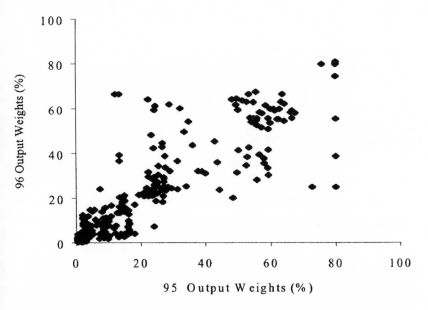

Figure 7. Scatter Plot of 1995 Output Weights (measured by the percentage of total output weights) by 1996 Output Weights (%) when *Fourfold Range* of Constraints Were Imposed (public group)

Table 58. Regression 1995 Output Weights (%) on 1996 Output Weights (%): Public Group

Environment	β	t	R^2	F
No Constraints	.52	10.94[***]	.27	119.73[***]
Fourfold Constraints	.87	32.36[***]	.76	1047.44[***]
Twofold Constraints	.96	58.21[***]	.91	3388.12[***]

Note: [***]$p < .001$.

90 percent of the variation in the 1996 weights can be explained by the previous year's weights.

For the input weights, we cannot make the same conclusions. Quite the contrary, as Table 59 shows, the R^2 value goes down with the addition of constraints. Figure 9 indicates that there are quite a number of outliers along the x and y axes.

Tables 59 and 60 show the regression results for the private group. The results are almost the same that we saw in the results of the public group. For the input weights, in the twofold range constraints environment, the R^2 values

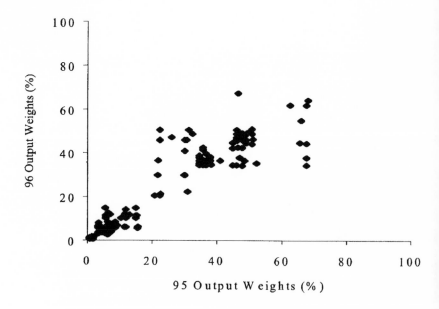

Figure 8. Scatter Plot of 1995 Output Weights (measured by the percentage of total output weights) by 1996 Output Weights (%) when *Twofold Range* of Constraints Were Imposed (public group)

Table 59. Regression 1995 Output Weights (%) on 1996 Output Weights (%): Private Group

Environment	β	t	R^2	F
No Constraints	.24	3.00**	.06	8.97**
Fourfold Constraints	.86	20.40***	.74	415.99***
Twofold Constraints	.94	33.66***	.88	1133.08***

Note: *p < .01; ***p < .001.

Table 60. Regression 1995 Input Weights (%) on 1996 Input Weights (%): Private Group

Environment	β	t	R^2	F
No Constraints	.65	11.30***	.42	127.58***
Fourfold Constraints	.52	8.21***	.28	67.41***
Twofold Constraints	.17	2.28*	.03	5.19*

Note: *p < .05; ***p < .001.

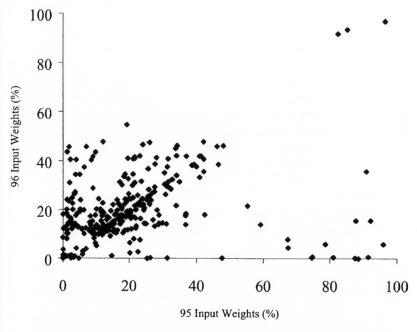

Figure 9. Scatter Plot of 1995 Input Weights (measured by the percentage of total input weights) by 1996 Input Weights (%) when *Twofold Range* of Constraints Were Imposed (public group)

drop down to a mere 3 percent. Again, we see a lot of outliers along the two axes in Figure 10.

Summary

In this section, we summarize the results to our research questions.

1. Can DEA be applied for evaluating library efficiency?

People have developed two broad measures to evaluate libraries. One is called effectiveness, which has to do with how much good the library does for its users. In this study effectiveness is operationalized by how much service the library provides. The other is called efficiency, which has to do with the relationship between the amount of service provided and the amount of resources consumed. We can put those two concepts in a single graph.

The basic measure of effectiveness will be some aggregation of all the services provided, which is the height (a) in Figure 11. The basic measure of efficiency (a/b) is calculated by comparing the aggregated services provided to some aggregation of

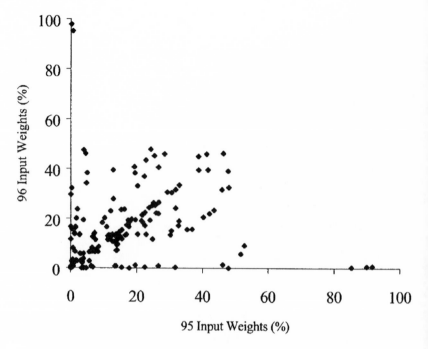

Figure 10.   Scatter Plot of 1995 Input Weights (measured by the
percentage of total input weights) by 1996 Input Weights (%) when
Twofold Range of Constraints Were Imposed (private group)

the resources utilized, which is the base of the triangle (b). The efficiency scores in
this study are actually relative efficiency scores, calculated by dividing the efficiency
of one library by the efficiency of some "best" library. We call a library 100 percent
efficient either if it consumes less inputs than other libraries producing the same
amount of outputs or if it produces more outputs than others, while maintaining the
same level of inputs.

We used a complex analytical technique called the data envelopment analysis
(DEA) to compute this relative efficiency score in the presence of multiple inputs
(resources) and multiple outputs (services) through rigorous assignment of
weights to the inputs and outputs. Each library was given the best chance to look
as good as possible in its mix of inputs and outputs.

This study used the annual statistics from the Association of Research Libraries
(ARL) for the population of 95 academic research libraries in the United States.
For the purpose of valid peer comparison, the libraries are grouped by the main
funding source of the parent institutions (publicly funded vs. privately funded).

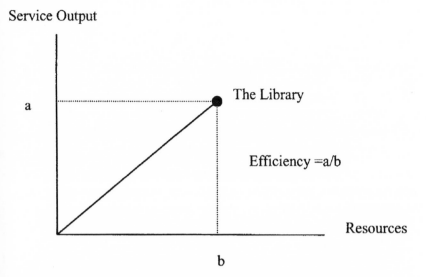

Service Output

Figure 11. Relationship Between the Effectiveness and Efficiency

We used a total of five output variables, encompassing all the service measures reported in the statistics: interlibrary loans, interlibrary borrowings, reference transactions, total circulation, and library instruction. On the input side, we include two types of variables, discretionary and nondiscretionary. "Discretionary" variables include two main resources libraries use to provide services: materials (4 variables) and staff (3 variables). "Nondiscretionary" variables, which are beyond the control of the library administrator, include measures of the number of library users in several categories. They are treated as input variables because they help to determine how much service the library can provide. In this study, we focused on inefficiencies in inputs: the DEA recommendations are represented as in the calculated input reduction for libraries deemed inefficient.

We used a specialized DEA program called IDEAS and we provided the detailed procedures and samples of the reports in the Appendix. The results of the initial DEA model gave us a low resolution of inefficiency: most libraries were deemed to be efficient (see Table 6). We then applied several sets of constraints in the form of limits on the ratios of assigned weights. The constraints not only improved the resolution but also the interpretation of weights.

Through a series of sensitivity analyses, we explored the relative impacts of the variables included in the study on the efficiency scores. Among output variables, removal of reference transactions and circulation variables made the biggest changes on the efficiency scores. All input variables seemed to affect the effi-

Table 61.   Mean Efficiency Scores in Different Weight Constraints

Year	Group	No Ratios	Fourfold Ratios	Twofold Ratios
1995	Public	.96 (28%)	.90 (52%)	.83 (66%)
	Private	.98 (10%)	.94 (23%)	.91 (37%)
1996	Public	.96 (25%)	.90 (51%)	.84 (63%)
	Private	.99 (3%)	.94 (23%)	.89 (40%)

Notes: Public ($n = 65$), Private ($n = 30$). The numbers in the parentheses are percentage of libraries evaluated inefficient.

ciency scores to more or less the same degree. However, taking out a variable sometimes can have a huge effect on individual libraries either decreasing the efficiency scores substantially or changing their efficiency status, from efficient to inefficient. The selection of variables is not purely a technical issue. For practical, wide applications of DEA, we recommend that the full set of variables be retained in the analysis.

In addition to sensitivity analysis, we added random noise in the data and observed the resulting changes in the efficiency scores and the efficiency status. We conducted four simulations of noise for each year. In each simulation, every observed data element was subject to a random distortion, causing it to vary according to a normal distribution whose mean is the original value and the standard deviation, 5 percent of its true value. The results are remarkably consistent in terms of changes in the mean scores (.02–.03 for public, .01–.05 for private). The number of libraries that changed their efficiency status was from 4 to 7 in the public group and from 1 to 5 in the private group. Furthermore, the technique is fairly robust despite the presence of random dummy variables.

We conclude that the DEA technique can be successfully implemented to research libraries in the United States. This study provides a baseline approach as well as results that can be further extended to studies using similar techniques to investigate the problem of assessing library efficiency.

2.   What are the relevant criteria in determining constraints on weights?

The basic DEA model assumes that all inputs and outputs are equally important. One of the key improvements on this basic model is to constrain the weights assigned to inputs and outputs, so that the results reflect the reality in which the libraries operate.

For the output variables, the constraints ideally should tell us about the relative values or contribution to the goals and objectives of parent organizations. However, this kind of information is not easily available. Instead, we looked at various studies of costs of library services to find out the average costs of providing services. On the input side, the constraints should provide the relative costs of

Table 62. Consistency of Efficiency Scores Over Two-year Period

	Public (n = 65)	*Private (n = 30)*
Mean efficiency score change	.06	.07
Libraries with less than .05 change	52	22
Efficiency status change	14	7

acquiring various resources. From the ARL data, we were able to derive the average costs of these inputs.

In applying these derived average costs of services and inputs, we were guided by the techniques already developed (assurance region by Thompson et al. 1990) and the DEA application software capability. The average ratios among outputs and inputs were first calculated. Instead of imposing a fixed single ratio on the weights, we provided a range over which the weights can vary. This would permit that the evaluation account for the differences in individual libraries.

Because we do not know the extent of such differences in performance and the exact effect of imposing constraints, we applied two kinds of ranges: the fourfold and twofold ranges. In the fourfold range, which is more generous, the ratios can vary from one-quarter of the computed average to four times the real value. The twofold range is more realistic because the ratios should fall between one-half of the true value and two times the true value. The results, as summarized in Table 61, show that the imposition of constraints has a significant impact on the mean efficiency scores and the proportion of libraries deemed inefficient.

In the public group in 1995, the mean efficiency score dropped by .13 points when a twofold range of constraints on the weights was imposed. The proportion of libraries evaluated as inefficient rose from 28 percent to 66 percent, about two-thirds of the libraries.

Clearly the constraints improved the technique's analytical power by uncovering more inefficiencies. Furthermore, the fact that the constraints were derived empirically from past studies of the costs of library services and from the actual data improves the validity of the DEA results reported here. However, we should also remember at the same time that there is no "correct" way of imposing constraints. The two ranges used in this study are only guidelines.

3. Are the efficiency scores stable over a period of time?

Library statistics are extremely stable. The biggest median change of all 15 variables over the two-year (1995–1996) period was 5 percent. All the input variables on average changed by less than 3 percent during the same period, most of them less than 1 percent. Therefore, it would be logical to expect that the efficiency scores will stay more or less the same. If there was too much fluctuation, it would be a big threat to the technique's reliability and validity. Table 62 shows the consistency of efficiency scores and the efficiency status over the two-year period.

The mean efficiency score was changed on average by 6 percent for the public group and by 7 percent for the private group. For the majority of libraries, there was either no change or a less than 5 percent change. However, the composition of the efficient frontier, measured by the number of libraries that change their efficiency status, shows a moderate change.

Close examination of the results show that significant changes accompanied changes in the observed data values of a similar magnitude. These results suggest that the DEA technique produces quite stable results and can be used to track efficiency over an extended period of time.

4.   Can we tell, with given results, what distinguishes (or determines) technically efficient libraries from inefficient ones as determined by DEA?

We looked for the variables or library characteristics that are closely associated with libraries with high efficiency scores. For the public group, libraries with large net volumes added and professional staff tend to have lower efficiency scores. On the other hand, libraries producing more reference transactions and circulation are more likely to be assigned higher efficiency scores. For the private group, the total circulation was the only statistically significant predictor of efficiency scores over the two-year period.

When all 15 variables included in this study were used in the regression analyses to predict efficiency scores, a substantial portion of variation in the scores (in both groups) were accounted for by the model with R^2 values ranging between .72 and .80. However, when only a subset of the variables is used, such as input variables, output variables, staff variables, collection variables, or user variables, the R^2 measures deteriorate quite rapidly.

The amount of library expenditure per student and per faculty were not a significant predictor of efficiency scores. But, in the public group, the size of library budget was a significant predictor meaning that libraries with a smaller budget are more likely to be assigned a higher efficiency rating. This was not the case in the private group. Interestingly, none of the per user activities, measured by the number of various services outputs per student, was a significant predictor of the efficiency scores in both comparison groups.

Among the measures of library resource utilization, for the public group, the number of reference transactions handled per professional staff was a significant predictor. For the private group, libraries with a larger proportion of total volumes actively circulated tend to have higher efficiency scores.

Finally, as expected, university libraries that have both law and medical libraries tend to have lower mean efficiency scores (.79 for public, .87 for private) than libraries with neither of them (.87 and 1.00, respectively) due to increased resource requirements. However, the differences were not statistically significant.

5. Are the optimal weights characteristics of the library?

We want to know if the extent to which computed weights for the inputs and outputs, especially under a constrained environment, can be used to characterize the libraries included in the analysis. Because the observed weight values vary too much within the same DEA set of runs, we calculated the relative proportions of weights out of total input weights and total output weights. In general, the relative proportions of output weights show less variability than those of input weights.

Among the output weights, the reference transactions and circulation variables combined were assigned a substantial portion of the total output weights. Among the staff input variables, the professional staff variable was always assigned the largest share. Among collection variables, the two groups show different results. In the public group, the net volumes added variable received twice as much the weight as the monographs purchased and the current serials variables. In the private group, the weights are more or less evenly split among three variables.

The distribution of relative proportion of weights seem to roughly reflect "reality" in the sense that the outputs were usually regarded as more important and the more expensive inputs received bigger weights. However, we must note that this characterization is based on mathematical computations with no study of the relative value systems held at libraries.

As for the consistency of weight assignments, only output weights measured by the relative proportions show a satisfactory level of consistency over a two-year period. It is interesting to observe that while, for the output weights, tightening constraints substantially improved the R^2 values, for the input weights, it was exactly the opposite.

We conclude that there is a potential that the weights can be used to characterize libraries. The results of this study provide baseline information about the overall distribution of weights and the consistency of such distribution.

DISCUSSIONS AND CONCLUSIONS

The proposed research applied a complex analytical tool, Data Envelopment Analysis (DEA), to determine whether it can provide better understanding of the relative efficiencies of academic research libraries. Instead of telling us performance relative to the average performance among libraries examined, this method, with a proper model of library inputs and outputs, is proposed as a means of identifying the best practices in the peer groups and provides an efficiency score for each library with specific recommendation for efficiency improvement. Although our focus was more toward applying this tool to the study sample and making sense out of the results than to refining underlying techniques, several notes about the DEA technique itself seem to be in order.

Table 63.   DEA Results for a Hypothetical Library

Variable	Data (a)	Projected (b)	Inefficiency = 1 − (b/a)	Proportional Reduction	Slack	Total Reduction
VOLSADN	100	80	0.20	6.25	13.75	20.00
MONO	80	75	0.06	5.00	0.00	5.00
CURRSER	50	45	0.10	3.13	1.87	5.00
PRFSTF	25	20	0.20	1.56	3.44	5.00
NPRFSTF	20	10	0.50	1.25	8.75	10.00
STUDAST	5	4	0.20	0.31	0.69	1.00

The Definition of Efficiency and of Efficiency Score

We have mentioned already that DEA analysis provides an array of information such as efficiency scores, excessive inputs or outputs (which are called "slack"), optimal weights (the mu's and the nu's) assigned to variables for individual DMUs, the benchmark comparison set (through lambda's) and so on. But we have found that many published studies of DEA applications focus on only one kind information that DEA has to offer: efficiency scores.

Now let us take a closer look at how efficiency scores are computed. In an input-oriented DEA evaluation, the theta (θ) values stand for the efficiency score for the DMUs included in the analysis. Suppose we have the following DEA results for one hypothetical library as shown in Table 63.

The table shows the observed values of 6 discretionary variables (in the second column) along with the computed projected values (in the third column) that can move this imaginary library to the efficient frontier. For each variable, we calculate the inefficiency that is the share of the reduced input out of the observed value. We can say that this library could produce the same amount of output as does the virtual (efficient) library but, for instance, using 20 percent less of net volumes added (VOLSADN). The technical problem here is that there are multiple inputs with varying degrees of inefficiency.

In deciding the efficiency score for this library, which is 1 minus the proportional input reduction required, the DEA formulation took a conservative approach. Rather than picking up the biggest inefficiency, 50 percent for the non-professional staff (NPRFSTF), it chose the lowest inefficiency, 6 percent for the monographs purchased (MONO), as the basis for calculating the efficiency score. The efficiency score for the library is calculated as .94 (= 1 − .06).

In fact, this way of calculating the efficiency score makes sense computationally as well as logically. What if DEA selected the biggest inefficiency in the inputs in determining the overall efficiency score? In this case, we would have excessive reduction of inputs in 5 out of 6 input variables. This will create some difficulties in interpreting the results.

What about the residuals (shown under "slack") after the 6 percent across the board reduction? In DEA they are called the slack—excess inputs even after the proportional reduction. Nonetheless, by forcing inefficiency scores of individual variables into a single, overall efficiency measure (θ), DEA introduces several potential problems. The problems arise not because it has done something wrong, but because of how the results are presented and because of the tendency for the users to look at the efficiency scores alone.

It is quite possible then, that one library gets an efficiency score of .90 but with a huge slack while another library gets a .70 efficiency score with virtually no excess input. Aside from the inherent efficiency in two organizations, the results will make people at the library with a score of .90 happier than people at the library with .70 if these two libraries were in the same evaluation sample. DEA has been put forward as a method that gives a single measure of efficiency in the presence of multiple inputs and outputs. But that comes with a price, as we have shown. Of course, decision makers are advised to consider several other things, besides the efficiency score, when it comes to interpret the results. But this advice might as well be unheeded because the efficiency score usually looms large in people's minds. The bottom line is that we should not rely only on the efficiency scores produced by DEA to estimate the efficiency of libraries.

Another point about the DEA efficiency score comes from our analysis of the results. By definition, again in the input-oriented evaluation, a DEA-efficient library wastes no inputs compared to other DMUs at a similar output level. But what about inefficient libraries? Does a library become inefficient if there is a waste in at least one input? Or do the inefficient libraries have inefficiencies in all of the included inputs? Close examination of the results show that it is an "all or nothing" situation. The libraries evaluated as efficient have neither waste—represented as proportional reduction—nor slack in any of the inputs. On the other hand, the libraries evaluated as inefficient have waste not in some inputs but in all inputs.

This result should not come as a surprise, because it can be deduced from the discussion of how the efficiency score is determined. If the inefficiency in at least one input variable is zero, then the library is an efficient one due to the definition of efficiency score. But a question arises as to the applicability of DEA formulation's "all or nothing" approach to measuring efficiency to the real world. In fact, many organizations are called inefficient because some of their operations are not efficient, not because all of them are not efficient. It will be inappropriate to say that a library fails in everything it does if it is not on the efficient frontier.

Interpretation of Weights

The weights represent, at least implicitly, a relative value system that allows each library included in the analysis to achieve the best possible efficiency rating. The assumption here is that the same value system is also applicable to all the other libraries in the analysis. As Dyson et al. (1990) aptly put it, "the choice of weights is both a weakness and strength of this approach." It becomes a weakness because even if a library is evaluated as efficient, the calculated weights might be totally unrelated with the real values of the library. It is a strength because it is a strong statement for those libraries evaluated as inefficient even when the most favorable weights have been applied to get the best score.

In the basic DEA formulation, it is quite common that the assigned weight values for a library can differ by several thousand times. It is quite unlikely that a unit of circulation can be a thousand times more important than one unit of a typical reference transaction or vice versa.

Thus, we introduced the constraints on the weights to prevent libraries being assigned outrageous weights. The imposition of weights seemed to control effectively the variation of possible weights. However, when we compare the weights of a library over a two-year period, we found that in some instances the assigned weights have changed dramatically. This abrupt shift of values requires explanation. If one is interested in comparing the efficiency scores of a comparison group for an extended period of time, a technique might be developed for the DMUs to retain their own stable value systems. One other issue regarding adding constraints is that the efficiency scores are in fact influenced by how and what kinds of constraints are imposed.

For a small group of comparison samples, it might be possible to fine tune the constraints to get more refined weight values. Another approach, proposed by Halme et al. (1999), is to get the decision maker's preferences and incorporate them directly into DEA analysis. In our study, this kind of information was not available because each library is an independent entity responsible directly to its own parent organization.

We have shown that the DEA technique can be operationally applied to the problem of assessing the relative efficiencies of American research libraries. However, this does not mean that the results are directly transformed into actionable recommendations in the real world. On the contrary, there are a host of issues that need to be considered.

From the perspective of library managers, there are several practical issues regarding the technique. First and foremost, although the DEA technique has some intuitive appeal, it is difficult to understand its formulations and some subtleties related to interpretation of key measures produced. This is the same problem that other applications of operations research techniques have suffered. McDonald and Micikas (1994) noted that the complexity of the models, arbitrary, unverified assumptions, and lack of adequate definitions that such research involves are the main stumbling blocks that hinder widespread use of tools of operations research.

Cost is another issue. Although small-scale analysis can be performed with readily available software packages such as Microsoft Excel or SAS, this also requires a fair amount of knowledge of the inner workings of the DEA technique.

Specialized DEA software packages, such as IDEAS used in this study, are now available but with rather high price tags (usually in the range of several hundreds if not thousands of dollars). We hope that the popularity of the technique in many other sectors will eventually bring the cost down and make it more accessible.

In terms of applicability of the results, we note the following issues. First, we conducted the analysis without revealing the identity of the libraries. But to find out whether libraries can learn something from the best practices, the identities of the libraries in the benchmark comparison set should be available to libraries labelled as inefficient by DEA. Then those libraries can visit and study the ways in which their peers achieve the efficiency that they do.

In DEA, efficiency improvement is possible by rearranging the inputs or outputs. But without knowledge about how various inputs are combined to produce different levels of outputs, it is difficult to fine-tune or tweak the arrangement. On the other hand, if the managers at the library think that outputs can be increased only by adding more inputs, the DEA results may provide a different perspective and thus lead to other possible solutions.

It is quite possible that the libraries regarded as efficient by DEA have strength in only one service output. But DEA does not tell us whether that strength exists at the cost of other outputs. The interaction in the production process is a thorny issue that is not resolved through DEA.

Also, we assumed in this study that discretionary variables are under the control of library administrators. But in reality, although they may have some discretion, it is questionable how much control the administrators have on the levels of library inputs. What if the institution has a tenure system for librarians? Even when the institution does not adopt a tenure system for librarians, retaining and/or increasing the number of librarians may be mistaken for proof of the capability of library directors, limiting their willingness to reduce staff.

It is more complicated with the outputs. While we believe that the inclusion of library users in the analysis would certainly improve the validity of the model, there are other important factors, such as user demand and that capability of both users and the library, that have not been incorporated into the model.

One problem encountered during the course of this study is that the present data do not capture the level of serials' use. In light of the fact that libraries are increasingly spending a significant portion of their materials budget to keep up with expensive journals,[24] it is unfortunate that we do not have a single measure that tells something about the level of serials' use. Another issue is that while the data capture the traditional research library activities, they are lacking the increasing presence in research libraries of nontraditional services such as the document and data access in the networked environment and the services provided by so-called data librarians.

For library practitioners, this study provides a way to identify the best practices for the purpose of benchmarking. DEA represents a solid, quantitative approach for benchmarking, not relying on intuition or common sense but based on actual data provided by the libraries.

For validation of the study, it will be necessary to carry out some case studies to see if the libraries can benefit from the DEA analysis. That is, will they learn something useful by looking into the processes at their benchmarking peers identified through DEA, and will what they learn enable them to improve their efficiency scores?

Finally, the results of this DEA analysis are intended to assist decision making at the libraries examined. But it is quite likely that the efficiency score will be regarded as a total measure of accomplishment of the library. As we have illustrated, the results should be treated only tentatively due to the limitations of the technique and the study. Furthermore, the results should be viewed in totality: not the efficiency score alone, but also various other measures such as the weights assigned and the composition of the benchmark peer group.

For this study we chose to apply DEA to research libraries because of their magnitude in terms of the size of their operations and the impacts that they have on scholarly communication. We believe that the DEA technique can be applied to other types of libraries, especially to public and school libraries where performance measurement is increasingly being mandated.

To the field of efficiency measurement, the work reported here represents a novel application of the DEA technique. Specifically, the derivation of constraints might be of some relevance to other studies facing the same issue. Also, the fact that we included users as a special kind of input might have an implication for future application of DEA.

In conclusion, DEA seems to have flexibility and expandability that other traditional measures lack. It provides a technical means to identify the best practices that inefficient libraries should look into and can improve performance. The approach is to look at other libraries, not the ones that are simply big or conventionally "good," but the ones that function efficiently and from which better ways of doing things can be learned. Furthermore, while it will take some years for the academic library community to come up with measures that capture user activities in the networked, digital environment, this study has provided a baseline approach that can be continued in the new era.

APPENDIX

Running DEA Analysis Using IDEAS

The IDEAS Program

We analyzed data using the commercial program called IDEAS (v5.1; available from Software 1 consulting Inc., P.O. Box 2453, Amherst, MA 01004-2453). The following section describes how the IDEAS program works.

Data Preparation

First of all, we create a dBase type file structure in IDEAS. Then a data file which is in ASCII format is imported into the structured file. Users can browse the data file and can also manually edit it.

```
95US200.DBF
                65
                 5
                10
                 1
    ILLTOT      OUTPUT-D        7       1.00        0.00
    ILBTOT      OUTPUT-D        8       1.00        0.00
    PRESPTCP    OUTPUT-D        9       1.00        0.00
    REFTRANS    OUTPUT-D       10       1.00        0.00
    TOTCIRC     OUTPUT-D       11       1.00        0.00
    VOLS        INPUT--D        3       1.00        0.00
    VOLSADN     INPUT--D        4       1.00        0.00
    MONO        INPUT--D        5       1.00        0.00
    CURRSER     INPUT--D        6       1.00        0.00
    PRFSTF      INPUT--D       12       1.00        0.00
    NPRFSTF     INPUT--D       13       1.00        0.00
    STUDAST     INPUT--D       14       1.00        0.00
    TOTSTU      INPUT--N       15       1.00        0.00
    GRADSTU     INPUT--N       16       1.00        0.00
    FAC         INPUT--N       17       1.00        0.00
    (TYPE =  1)
    (TYPE =  1)
    VRS
    Invariant
    Input
    X
                20              0
    95US200.ASC     STD.RTO
```

Note: The line reading

VOLS	INPUT—D	3	1.00	0.00

means that the data in the 3rd column (3) of input will have the label "VOLS." It is an input variable (INPUT) which is subject to control by the management (D). It is not to be rescaled (1), and no logarithmic transformation is to be made (0). Some INPUT variables are considered to have an effect on the library economics, but to not be under the control of the decision makers at the library. The total number of students at a university (TOTSTU) is an example of such a variable, and is flagged "N" in the third column of the parameter file.

Exhibit 1. Sample Envelope File

Setting up the Parameters

Once the data are ready, users should create an "envelope" (.env) file which stores all the parameter information needed to perform a DEA analysis. Exhibit 1 is an example of an envelope file used in our analysis. It specifies the data file name (95US200.DBF), the number of DMUs included for the analysis

PRFSTF	NPRFSTF	0.5906	2.3626
PRFSTF	STUDAST	3.4391	13.7565
PRFSTF	MONO	0.8389	3.3556
PRFSTF	CURRSER	0.8580	3.4321
NPRFSTF	STUDAST	2.9114	11.6456
NPRFSTF	MONO	0.7102	2.8406
NPRFSTF	CURRSER	0.7263	2.9053
STUDAST	MONO	0.1220	0.4880
STUDAST	CURRSER	0.1248	0.4992
MONO	CURRSER	0.5114	2.0455
REFTRANS	ILBTOT	5.2500	21.1500
REFTRANS	ILLTOT	3.0000	12.0000
REFTRANS	TOTCIRC	0.7500	3.0100
REFTRANS	LIBINS	25.8000	103.5000
ILBTOT	ILLTOT	0.2833	1.1367
ILBTOT	TOTCIRC	0.0710	0.2843
ILBTOT	LIBINS	2.4400	9.7700
ILLTOT	TOTCIRC	0.1250	0.5000
ILLTOT	LIBINS	4.2900	17.2200
TOTCIRC	LIBINS	17.1000	68.7000

Exhibit 2. Sample Ratio File

(65), the number of output (5) and input (10) variables, the names and nature of the variables, the DEA model selected (Variable Returns to Scale, Input Oriented Invariant), the number of ratios constrained (20), the name of the file containing the constraints (STD.RTO), and so on. The envelope file can be modified and used over and over again.

Program Run and Report Generation

When the data file and the envelope file are ready, one can perform the analysis. IDEAS creates various output tables in separate files. An individual report that summarizes all the results for a DMU can also be requested. Exhibit 3 is an example of an individual DMU report.

Automation of the IDEAS Program

When the notions of DEA were first thought of, the computation, which amounts to solving a separate linear programming problem (Hillier and Lieberman 1986) for every DMU, required custom programming to do the calculations. If this is to be used for exploration of several hypotheses, it represents an enormous amount of work. Today, linear programming, while it remains algebraically rather abstract, has become a built-in oper-

```
DEA REPORT

 DEA:
 NAME: B                        MODEL: VRS/I/INV/2nd
 Unit:    2                     Number of Units in Analysis:    3
 -------------------------------------------------------------------
 ----------         DATA     PROJECTED INEFFICIENCY         PRICE
 Outputs...
 REFER    (D)      20.00         24.00         4.00        .05000
 CIRC     (D)      35.00         35.00          .00        .02857
 Inputs....
 BOOKS    (D)      25.00         16.00        -9.00        .04000
 STAFF    (D)      13.00          9.00        -4.00        .33286
 -------------------------------------------------------------------


 Analysis of Projection------------
               Proportional  Residual..
 REFER              .000       4.000
 CIRC               .000        .000
 BOOKS             7.692       1.308
 STAFF             4.000        .000
 ----------------------------------------

 Iota:                   .64495 Theta:                     .69231
 Delta:                  1.891 Sigma:                       .252
 V-input:                5.327 V-output:                   2.000
 Omega:                 1.43571
 Comparison Set:
 A          .66667           C            .33333
```

Exhibit 3.   Sample IDEAS Report

```
 KEYSTACK ! "I" ! "M" ! "U" ! "STD" 13 "G" 13 "Q" ! 13
 "P" /w36 0 "STD" 0 13 /w36 0 "Q" 0 "Q" 0 "Q" /w36   0
 "P" 0 "STD" 0 13 /w36  0 13 0 "E"
 IDEAS
```

Note: This file holds all the necessary keystrokes after KEYSTACK command and feeds them to IDEAS
program. The letter(s) enclosed in double quotations are the actual user keyboard inputs. "!"s and
"0"s clear the keyboard buffer and the number 13 is an ASCII code for Enter keystroke. /w(ait)
option delays the next keystroke in the keystack buffer by a specified number of clock "ticks."

Exhibit 4.   Batch File Automating IDEAS Runs

ation in state-of-the-art spreadsheets. For example, the "Solver" procedure in Excel v5.0 or above is a general optimizer, which solves, as a
special case, linear programming problems.

The IDEAS program makes it simple to perform very complicated DEA calculations, and will do each of the several linear programming problems. However, it is limited in the sense that the user may run only one analysis at a time. That is, we can create a number of envelope and ratios files, representing different sets of libraries or of constraints, but we had to pass their names into the IDEAS program interactively. To automate this procedure, we turned to the 4DOS shell program for MS-DOS,[25] which enabled us to pre-load hundreds of keystrokes into a batch file and thus perform multiple DEA runs without further interaction. In this way, we are able to run several dozens of complicated DEA analyses in a matter of 10 to 20 minutes. Without this automation process, running that many analyses would take many hours and be prone to a variety of human errors. Exhibit 4 shows a sample batch program that we used in the analysis.

NOTES

1. A program summary is available at http://www.nacubo.org/website/members/bomag/1297/benchmarking.html

2. These ratios are reported in the ARL's web site at http://www.arl.org/stats/arlstat/INDICATO.HTML

3. There are studies that did not rely on linear models, notably Chressanthis (1995) and Kantor (1981b).

4. An updated version of the bibliography is available at http://www.warwick.ac.uk/~bsrlu (Warwick Business School at University of Warwick).

5. There can be two extreme cases. In one extreme, we can think of a library whose service depends wholly on external sources through interlibrary loans. In the other extreme, a library uses its internal collection exclusively, not borrowing from other libraries at all. Certainly we do not see either of these extreme cases in academic libraries.

6. Chapter 5 of Charnes et al. (1994) provides a review of available software packages.

7. Here we use the input orientation model for the purpose of illustration. An analogous formulation is possible for the output orientation model.

8. μ_1 is the weight for the reference output. μ_2 is for the circulation. In the same way, v_1 and v_2 refer to the weights for the books and staff, respectively.

9. λ_A, λ_B, λ_C refer to the weights of the libraries A, B, and C.

10. http://www.arl.org/stat. The human readable, interactive version is also available at http://fisher.lib.virginia.edu/newarl/

11. Detailed definitions of the variables are available on the ARL web site at ftp://www.arl.org/stat/machine/95-96/doc96.txt

12. We explored the issue of constraints on weights in Shim and Kantor (1998a) and the preliminary results are reported in Shim and Kantor (1998a, 1998b).

13. See, for example, Saracevic and Kantor (1997a), and references cited therein.

14. 1 Consulting (P.O. Box 2453, Amherst, MA 01004-2453; Tel. 413-256-1211).

15. This is partly due to the commitment made in Shim and Kantor (1998a) which started the investigation of applying DEA to research libraries.

16. This kind of change is what Sexton et al. (1986) referred to as interactive change because its impact is not limited to one DMU but can be widespread. The other type of change is called isolated

change. It happens when an inefficient unit is assigned a different efficiency score while remaining inefficient. It does not alter the efficiency score of other units.

17. Most of the output measures entered the data set only after 1995.

18. The nondiscretionary variables were excluded in the calculation because they are normally assigned the zero weights.

19. The exact function is = RAND()*100.

20. The actual MS Excel function was $Y_i = X_i * (1 + .05*NORMINV(RAND(),0,1,))$ where X_i stands for original observed value and Y_i the new value with noise. RAND() generates a random number between 0 and 1. NORMINV (probability, mean, s.d.) function calculates the standard score (z score) for the corresponding probability from the normal distribution with the given mean and standard deviation.

21. In interpreting regression results we pay close attention to the beta coefficients (β). They are standardized regression coefficients. They tell us about the direction and the relative magnitude of the predictors. If the coefficient has a plus sign, then the corresponding predictor has a positive correlation with the dependent variable. The relative importance of a predictor is reflected by the magnitude of the coefficient. The *t*-statistic tells us whether the coefficients are significantly different from zero.

22. The 30 performance indicators published by the ARL provides only one output ratio: items borrowed by user.

23. Note that the same item may well be charged out more than several times in a given period.

24. The proportion of serials expense out of total materials expense rose from 45 percent in 1976 to 63 percent in 1996. The serials expense accounted for 14 percent of the total budget in 1976, 23 percent in 1996.

25. JP Software Inc., P.O. Box 1470, East Arlington, MA 02174.

REFERENCES

Ahn, T.S., A. Charnes and W.W. Cooper. 1988. "Some Statistical and DEA Evaluations or Relative Efficiencies of Public and Private Institutions of Higher Learning." *Socio-Economic Planning Sciences* 22(6): 259-269.

Ali, A.I. 1994. "Computational Aspects of DEA." Pp. 63-88 in *Data Envelopment Analysis: Theory, Methodology, and Application*, edited by A. Charnes, W.W. Cooper, A.Y. Lewin and L.M. Seiford. Norwell, MA: Kluwer.

ARL. 1994. *Membership in the Association of Research Libraries* [on line]. Available: http://www.arl.org/stats/qualcov.html.

Banker, R.D., A. Charnes and W.W. Cooper. 1984. "Some Models for Estimating Technical and Scale Inefficiencies in Data Envelopment Analysis." *Management Science* 30(9): 1078-1092.

Banker, R.D. and A. Maindiratta. 1988. "Nonparametric Analysis of Technical and Allocative Efficiencies in Production." *Econometrica* 56(6): 1315-1332.

Barr, R.S., L.M. Seiford and T.F. Siems. 1993. "An Envelopment-Analysis Approach to Measuring the Managerial Quality of Banks." *Annals of Operations Research* 45: 1-19.

Baumol, W.J. and M. Marcus. 1973. *Economics of Academic Libraries*. Washington, DC: American Council on Education.

Berry, W.D. and S. Feldman. 1985. *Multiple Regression in Practice*. Newbury Park, CA: Sage.

Bessent, A.M., E.W. Bessent, J. Kennington and B. Regan. 1982. "An Application of Mathematical Programming to Assess Productivity in the Houston Independent School District." *Management Science* 28(12): 1355-1367.

Boxwell, R.J. 1994. *Benchmarking for Competitive Advantage*. New York: McGraw-Hill.

Byrnes, P. and V. Valdmanis. 1994. "Analyzing Technical and Allocative Efficiency of Hospitals." Pp. 129-144 in *Data Envelopment Analysis: Theory, Methodology, and Application*, edited by A. Charnes, W.W. Cooper, A.Y. Lewin and L.M. Seiford. Norwell, MA: Kluwer.

Buckland, M.K. 1975. *Book Availability and the Library User.* New York: Pergamon.

Cable, L.G. 1980. "Cost Analysis of Reference Service to Outside Users." *Bulletin of the Medical Library Association* 68(2): 247-248.

Charnes, A. and W.W. Cooper. 1962. "Programming with Linear Fractional Functionals." *Naval Research Logistics Quarterly* 9(3/4): 181-185.

Charnes, A., W.W. Cooper, A.Y. Lewin and L.M. Seiford, eds. 1994. *Data Envelopment Analysis: Theory, Methodology, and Application.* Norwell, MA: Kluwer.

Charnes, A., W.W. Cooper and S. Li. 1989. "Using DEA to Evaluate the Efficiency of Economic Performance by Chinese Cities." *Socio-Economic Planning Sciences* 23: 325-344.

Charnes, A., W.W. Cooper and E. Rhodes. 1978. "Measuring the Efficiency of Decision Making Units." *European Journal of Operations Research* 2: 429-444.

_____. 1981. "Evaluating Program and Managerial Efficiency: An Application of Data Envelopment Analysis to Program Follow Through." *Management Science* 27(6): 668-697.

Chaudhry, A.S. and S. Ashoor. 1994. "Comprehensive Materials Availability Studies in Academic Libraries." *Journal of Academic Librarianship* 20(5/6): 300-305.

Chressanthis, G.A. 1995. "The Cost Structure and Benefit Impact of Academic Libraries at American Research Libraries." Pp. 308-330 in *Communications Colloque International E'conomomie de l'information.* Lyon-Villeurbanne, France: Center des Etudes et de recherches en science de l'information, May 18-20.

Chilingerian, J.A. 1994. "Exploring Why Some Physicians' Hospital Practices Are More Efficient: Taking DEA Inside the Hospital." Pp. 167-193 in *Data Envelopment Analysis: Theory, Methodology, and Application*, edited by A. Charnes, W.W. Cooper, A.Y. Lewin and L.M. Seiford. Norwell, MA: Kluwer.

Ciliberti, A.S., M.F. Casserly, J.L. Hegg and E.S. Mitchell. 1987. "Material Availability: A Study of Academic Library Performance." *College & Research Libraries* 48(6): 513-527.

Cochrane, L.S. and C. Warmann. 1989. "Building on the First Century." Pp. 55-62 in *Proceedings of the fifth national conference of the association of college and research libraries*, edited by J.C. Fennell. Chicago, IL: Association of College and Research Libraries.

Cook, W.D., A. Kazakov and Y. Roll. 1994. "On the Measurement and Monitoring of Relative Efficiency of Highway Maintenace Patrols." Pp. 195-210 in *Data Envelopment Analysis: Theory, Methodology, and Application*, edited by A. Charnes, W.W. Cooper, A.Y. Lewin and L.M. Seiford. Norwell, MA: Kluwer.

Cooper, M.D. 1983. "Economies of Scale in Academic Libraries." *Library and Information Science Research* 5: 207-219.

_____. 1984. "Economies of Scale in Large Academic Libraries." *Library and Information Science Research* 6: 321-333.

Cooper, W.W., R.G. Thompson and R.M. Thrall. 1996. "Introduction: Extensions and New Developments in DEA." *Annals of Operations Research* 66: 3-45.

Council for Aid to Education. 1997. *Breaking the Social Contract: The Fiscal Crisis in Higher Education* [on-line]. Available: http://www.rand.org/publications/CAE/CAE100/index.html

De Prospo, E.R., E. Altman and K.E. Beasley. 1973. *Performance Measures for Public Libraries.* Chicago, IL: Public Library Association (ALA).

Dittman, D.A., R. Capettini and R.C. Morey. 1991. "Measuring Efficiency in Acute Care Hospitals: An Application of Data Envelopment Analysis." *Journal of Health and Human Resources Administration* 14(1): 89-108.

Dyson, R.G. and E. Thanassoulis. 1988. "Reducing Weight Flexibility in Data Envelopment Analysis." *Journal of the Operational Research Society* 39(6): 563-576.

Dyson, R.G., E. Thanassoulis and A. Boussofiane. 1990. *A DEA (Data Envelopment Analysis) Tutorial* [on-line]. Available: http://www.warwick.ac.uk/~bsrlu/

Easun, M.S. 1992. "Identifying Efficiencies in Resource Management: An Application of Data Envelopment Analysis to Selected School Libraries in California." Ph.D. dissertation, University of California, Berkeley.

Farrell, M.J. 1957. "The Measurement of Productive Efficiency." *Journal of Royal Statistical Society, Series A* 120: 253-281.

Ferguson, A.W. and K. Kehoe. 1993. "Access vs. Ownership: What Is Most Cost-effective in the Sciences?" *Journal of Library Administration* 19(2): 89-99.

Ferrier, G.D. and C.A.N. Lovell. 1990. "Measuring Cost Efficiency in Banking: Econometrics and Linear Programming Evidence." *Journal of Econometrics* 46(1/2): 229-245.

Forsund, R.R. and E. Hemaes. 1994. "A Comparative Analysis of Ferry Transport in Norway." Pp. 285-312 in *Data Envelopment Analysis: Theory, Methodology, and Application*, edited by A. Charnes, W.W. Cooper, A.Y. Lewin and L.M. Seiford. Norwell, MA: Kluwer.

Frei, F.X. and P.T. Harker. 1996. *Projections onto Efficient Frontiers: Theoretical and Computational Extensions to DEA*. Philadelphia: Financial Institutions Center at the Wharton School, University of Pennsylvania.

Golany, B. and Y. Roll. 1989. "Application Procedure for DEA." *Omega* 17(3): 237-250.

Gossen, E. and S. Kaczor. 1997. "Variation in Interlibrary Loan Use by University at Albany Science Department." *Library Resources & Technical Services* 41(1): 17-28.

Griffiths, J. and D.W. King. 1993. *Special Libraries: Increasing the Information Edge*. Washington, DC: Special Libraries Association.

Halme, M., T. Joro, P. Korhonen, S. Salo and J. Wallenius. 1999. "A Value Efficiency Approach to Incorporating Preference Information in Data Envelopment Analysis." *Management Science* 45(1): 103-115.

Hamburg, M., L.E. Ramist and M.R.W. Bommer. 1972. "Library Objectives and Performance Measures and Their Use in Decision Making." *Library Quarterly* 42: 107-128.

Hayes, R.M., A.M. Pollack and S. Nordhaus. 1983. "The Application of the Cobb-Douglas Model to the Association of Research Libraries." *Library and Information Science Research* 5(3): 291-325.

Hillier, F.S. and G.J. Lieberman. 1986. *Introduction to Operations Research*, 4th ed. Oakland, CA: Holden-Day.

Jackson, M.E. 1998. *Measuring the Performance of Interlibrary Loan Operations in North American Research and College Libraries*. Washington, DC: Association of Research Libraries.

Jacobs, N.A. and R.C. Young. 1995. "Measuring Book Availability in an Academic Library: A Methodological Comparison." *Journal of Documentation* 51(3): 281-290.

Johnes, G. and Johnes, J. 1992. "Apples and Oranges: The Aggregation Problem in Publication Analysis." *Scientometrics* 25(2): 353-365.

Kantor, P.B. 1976. "Availability Analysis." *Journal of the American Society for Information Science* 27(6): 311-319.

_____. 1981a. "Levels of Output Related to Cost of Operation of Scientific and Technical Libraries: Part I. Techniques and Cumulative Statistics." *Library Research* 3(1): 1-28.

_____. 1981b. "Levels of Output Related to Cost of Operation of Scientific and Technical Libraries: Part II. A Capacity Model of the Average Cost Formula." *Library Research* 3(1): 141-154.

_____. 1984. *Objective Performance Measures for Academic and Research Libraries*. Washington, DC: Association of Research Libraries.

_____. 1986. "Three Studies of the Economics of Academic Libraries." Pp. 221-286 in *Advances in Library Administration and Organization*, Vol. 5, edited by G.B. McCabe and B. Kreissman. Greenwich, CT: JAI Press.

Kyrillidou, M. 1998. "An Overview of Performance Measure in Higher Education and Libraries." *ARL* 197(April): 3-7.

Leibenstein, H. and S. Maital. 1992. "Empirical Estimation and Partitioning of X-inefficiency: A Date-Envelopment Approach." *American Economic Review* 82(2): 428-433.

Lubans, J., Jr. and S. Anspaugh. 1990. "The Private Academic Library and its Political Environment." Pp. 154-163 in *Politics and the Support of Libraries*, edited by E.J. Josey and K.D. Shearer. New York: Neal-Schuman.

Mazur, M. 1994."Evaluating the Relative Efficiency of Baseball Players?" Pp. 369-391 in *Data Envelopment Analysis: Theory, Methodology, and Application*, edited by A. Charnes, W.W. Cooper, A.Y. Lewin and L.M. Seiford. Norwell, MA: Kluwer.

McDonald, J.A. and L.B. Micikas. 1994. *Academic Libraries: The Dimensions of Their Effectiveness.* Westport, CT: Greenwood Press.

Michalko, J. 1993. "Higher Education, the Production Function, and the Library." *Journal of Library Administration* 19(3/4): 11-22.

Mitchell, B.J., N.E. Tanis and J. Jaffe. 1978. *Cost Analysis of Library Functions: A Total System Approach.* Greenwich, CT: JAI Press.

Mitchell, E.S., M.L. Radford and J.L. Hegg. 1994. "Book Availability: Academic Library Assessment." *College & Research Libraries* 55(1): 47-55.

Norton, R. 1994. "Which Offices or Stores Really Perform Best? A New Tool Tells." *Fortune*, October 31, p. 38.

Nunamaker, T.R. 1983. "Measuring Routine Nursing Service Efficiency: A Comparison of Cost per Patient Day and Data Envelopment Analysis Models." *Health Services Research* 18(2, Part 1): 183-205.

Nunamaker, R. 1995. "Using Data Envelopment Analysis to Measure the Efficiency of Non-profit Organizations: A Critical Evaluation." *Managerial and Decision Economics* 6(1): 50-58.

Palmour, V.E., E.C. Bryant, N.W. Caldwell and L.M. Gray. 1972. *A Study of the Characteristics, Costs, and Magnitude of Interlibrary Loans in Academic Libraries.* Westport, CT: Greenwood Press.

Rashid, H.F. 1990. "Book Availability as a Performance Measure of a Library: An Analysis of the Effectiveness of a Health Sciences Library." *Journal of the American Society for Information Science* 41(7): 501-507.

Rehman, S.U. 1993. "Comparative Measurement of Book Availability in Academic Libraries." *International Information and Library Review* 25(3): 183-193.

Revill, D.H. 1987. "'Availability' as a Performance Measure for Academic Libraries." *Journal of Librarianship* 19(1): 14-30.

Robinson, B.M. and S. Robinson. 1994. "Strategic Planning and Program Budgeting for Libraries." *Library Trends* 42: 420-447.

Roche, M.M. 1993. *ARL/RLG Interlibrary Loan Cost Study.* Washington, DC: Association of Research Libraries.

Saracevic, T. and P.B. Kantor. 1997a. "Studying the Value of Library and Information Services. Part I. Establishing a Theoretical Framework." *Journal of the American Society for Information Science* 48(6): 527-542.

_____. 1997b. "Studying the Value of Library and Information Services. Part II. Methodology and Taxonomy." *Journal of the American Society for Information Science* 48(6): 543-563.

Seiford, L.M. 1994. "A DEA Bibliography (1978-1992)." Pp. 437-469 in *Data Envelopment Analysis: Theory, Methodology, and Application*, edited by A. Charnes, W.W. Cooper, A.Y. Lewin and L.M. Seiford. Norwell, MA: Kluwer.

Seiford, L.M. and R.M. Thrall. 1990. "Recent Developments in DEA: The Mathematical Programming Approach to Frontier Analysis." *Journal of Econometrics* 46: 7-38.

Sengupta, J.K. 1987. "Production Frontier Estimation to Measure Efficiency: A Critical Evaluation in Light of Data Envelopment Analysis." *Managerial and Decision Economics* 8(2): 93-99.

Sexton, T.R. 1986. "The Methodology of Data Envelopment Analysis." Pp. 7-29 in *Measuring Efficiency: An Assessment of Data Envelopment Analysis*, edited by R.H. Silkman. San Francisco, CA: Jossey-Bass.

Sexton, T.R., R.H. Silkman and A.J. Hogan. 1986. "Data Envelopment Analysis: Critique and Extensions." Pp. 73-105 in *Measuring Efficiency: An Assessment of Data Envelopment Analysis*, edited by R. H. Silkman. San Francisco, CA: Jossey-Bass.

Shim, W. and P.B. Kantor. 1998a. *A Novel Approach to the Evaluation of Libraries.* Final report to the Council on Library and Information Resources (CLIR). New Brunswick, NJ: SCILS, Rutgers University.

_____. 1998b. "A Novel Economic Approach to the Evaluation of Academic Research Libraries." Pp. 400-410 in *Proceedings of the Annual Meeting of the American Society for Information Science 35.*

Spencer, C.C. 1980. "Random Time Sampling with Self-observation for Library Cost Studies." *Bulletin of the Medical Library Association* 68(1): 53-57.

Stubbs, K.L. 1996. *ARL Statistics, 1992-1995: A Guide to the Machine-readable Version of the Arl Statistics* [on-line]. Available: http://arl.cni.org/stat/machine/94-95/doc95.txt

Thompson. R.G., L.M. Langemeier, C.-T. Lee, E. Lee and R.M. Thrall. 1990. "The Role of Multiplier Bounds in Efficiency Analysis with Application to Kansas Farming." *Journal of Econometrics* 46: 93-108.

Van House, N., B.T. Weil and C.R. McClure. 1990. *Measuring Academic Library Performance: A Practical Approach* Chicago, IL: American Library Association.

Zairi, M. 1996. *Effective Benchmarking: Learning from the Best.* London: Chapman & Hall.

ABOUT THE CONTRIBUTORS

David P. Bunnell has been the Associate Director for Public Services at Mercer University's Main Library since 1997. He holds an M.S.L.S. from the University of Kentucky, an M.A.T.S. from United Theological Seminary (Dayton, Ohio), and a B.A. from Urbana University (Urbana, Ohio). He has been a member of the GALILEO Assessment Committee for two years.

Catharine Cebrowski is Library Director at the University of Monterrey, Mexico. Previously, she held the position of Business Information Service Librarian in the International Business Information Center at Thunderbird. Catharine received her M.L.I.S degree from Louisiana State University and holds a B.A. in Latin American Studies from the University of Virginia.

Kim Dority is Director, Jones International University library. Previously, she was Visiting Associate Director of the University of Denver Library and Information Sciences program. The author of several books, Ms. Dority received her M.L.S. from Duke University in 1982 and is now adjunct faculty and on the board of the Duke University M.L.S. program.

Wes Edens is Electronic Resources Librarian at Thunderbird. He was previously on the staff of the Chester Fritz Library at the University of North Dakota. He holds an M.L.S. and a B.S. in Business Administration from the University of Arizona.

Martin Garnar, M.L.I.S. 2000 from the Library and Information Services Department of the University of Denver, is a reference librarian at Dayton Memorial Library of Regis University (Denver, CO), which has been a leader in distance education since the 1980s.

Carol Hammond is the Director of the International Business Information Center at Thunderbird, The American Graduate School of International Management.

She has held previous positions in the libraries at UCLA, Gonzaga University, and Arizona State University West. In addition to an M.S.L.S. from the University of Illinois, she has a B.A. in History from Colorado State University and a M.A. in History from Gonzaga University.

Carol Ritzen Kem is Sociology Collection Bibliographer at the University of Florida in Gainesville. She received a B.A. in history from Drury College in Springfield, Missouri, an M.A. in history from the University of Illinois at Urbana-Champaign, an M.L.S. from the University of North Carolina at Chapel Hill, and a Ph.D. in Education (Higher Education Administration/leadership) from the University of Florida. She is active in professional associations and as a consultant on work behavior type.

W. Bede Mitchell is University Librarian at Georgia Southern University. He earned his M.L.S. at the University of Michigan and his Ed.D. at Montana State University. Prior to his appointment at Georgia Southern University he served as Associate University Librarian at Appalachian State University.

Isadore Newman is one of six Distinguished Professors at The University of Akron, having served on the faculty of the College of Education since 1971 where he specializes in research design and statistical analysis. He holds a B.A. from the University of Miami, an M.A. from the New School of Social Research, and a Ph.D. from Southern Illinois University. Newman has published 9 books, 82 articles and book chapters, and 56 ERIC documents, and has given more than 200 presentations at local, state, national and international conferences.

Jon P. O'Donnell is currently an Associate Professor of Computer Information Science at Clarion University of Pennsylvania. He received his B.S. in Business Information Systems from San Diego State University, an M.S. in Computer Information Science from Cleveland State University, and an Ed.D. in Higher Education Administration from The University of Akron.

John C. Painter, Ed.D., is Library Director at the Stephen J. Betze Library, Delaware Technical & Community College, Georgetown, Delaware. Painter received his Library Science degree from Drexel University and his research interests in library advisory committees occurred during his doctoral studies at Wilmington College.

Mary Lynn Rice-Lively is Assistant Dean and Coordinator of Information Technology at the Graduate School of Library & Information Science at The University of Texas at Austin. She has has a Ph.D. from The University of Texas at Austin and an M.L.S. from the University of North Texas. Research and publishing interests include social sensemaking and qualitative research in networked or computing environments.

Wonsik Shim is an assistant professor at the Florida State University's School of Information Studies. Shim holds a Ph.D. in library and information science from Rutgers University. His research interests center on the identification of best practices among libraries and the effective use of that information for the decision-making process.

Ann Tolzman is the Instructional Programs Librarian at Thunderbird. She previously held a position with The University of Advancing Computer Technology in Phoenix, Arizona. With an undergraduate degree in English/Pre-Law from Marquette University and an M.L.I.S. from the University of Wisconsin, she spends her time bringing the library into the classroom with specially designed courses that teach students how to use available information resources.

INDEX